D1194010

NARRATIVE INTERLUDES: MUSICAL TABLEAUX IN EIGHTEENTH-CENTURY FRENCH TEXTS

TILI BOON CUILLÉ

Narrative Interludes

Musical Tableaux in Eighteenth-Century French Texts

UNIVERSITY OF TORONTO PRESS
Toronto Buffalo London

© University of Toronto Press Incorporated 2006
Toronto Buffalo London
Printed in Canada

ISBN-13: 978-0-8020-3842-5
ISBN-10: 0-8020-3842-5

Printed on acid-free paper

University of Toronto Romance Series

Library and Archives Canada Cataloguing in Publication

Cuillé, Tili Boon
    Narrative interludes : musical tableaux in eighteenth-century
French texts / Tili Boon Cuillé.

    Includes bibliographical references and index.
    ISBN-13: 978-0-8020-3842-5
    ISBN-10: 0-8020-3842-5

    1. Art and literature – France – History – 18th century.
    2. Aesthetics, French – 18th century.   3. French literature – 18th century –
History and criticism.   4. Opera – France – History and criticism.

    ML1727.3.C966 2005   842'.5   C2005-904229-X

University of Toronto Press acknowledges the financial assistance to
its publishing program of the Canada Council for the Arts and the
Ontario Arts Council.

To my family

Contents

Illustrations

Preface

Si l'on pouvait se figurer les impressions dont notre âme serait susceptible, avant qu'elle connût la parole, on concevrait mieux l'effet de la peinture et de la musique.

[If we were able to imagine the impressions to which our soul was susceptible before coming to language, we would better understand the effect of painting and music.]

Staël, *De l'Allemagne*

In the eighteenth century, opera was still considered a subset of belles-lettres, or what we now refer to as literature. A combination of text and music, sound and spectacle, it brought the musical and the visual arts together under the aegis of poetry. While today opera has, by and large, become the domain of the musicologist and is linked to music via the score, in the eighteenth century it remained the domain of the philosopher and was linked to literature via the text. As Rousseau observed, echoing Plato: 'C'est au Poëte à faire de la Poësie, et au Musicien à faire de la Musique; mais il n'appartient qu'au Philosophe de bien parler de l'une et de l'autre' (It is for the Poet to write Poetry, and the Musician to compose Music: but it belongs only to the Philosopher to speak finely of them both).[1] Epic poetry and tragedy preceded the novel as literary arts par excellence and opera was widely understood to be poetry or tragedy set to music. Yet with the rise of the novel and of instrumental music in the course of the eighteenth century, the 'fields' of literary and musical studies became increasingly distinct. Since the eighteenth century, therefore, the philosophes and authors who participated in the contemporary opera debates have become the subject of a different discipline from the topic of their discussion. This book is an effort to bridge a gap that has widened since the period in question in order to examine the impact of eighteenth-century musical discourse on literary texts.

Nowhere in Europe was this discourse so polemical as in eighteenth-century France. My study is situated in the heyday of aesthetic debate, between 1750 and 1810 to be exact. During this period, two battles were waged between the proponents of French and Italian opera, painters witnessed an upsurge against the rococo, theoreticians of the *drame* cast the traditional genres of tragedy and comedy into question, and the sentimental novel was born. These small-scale aesthetic revolutions, some of which were fresh outbreaks of skirmishes that dated back to earlier in the century, the century before, or even as far back as Plato's *Republic* and Aristotle's *Poetics*, took the form of public debates about the sung and spoken theatre, fostered the genres of music, art, and literary criticism, and brought about a gradual change in the affective response of the reading and theatre-going public. This book is part of a growing body of critical works on music and literature, which were linked in eighteenth-century discourse via the French intellectual interest in opera. A number of insightful analyses of the battles waged between Rousseau, Rameau, and the philosophes have been published in the past fifteen years. I take these analyses a step further by examining the repercussions of these debates on eighteenth-century French fiction. Taking the mid-century opera quarrels as my point of departure, I bring the eighteenth-century cultural discourse on music and musicians to bear on the works of Diderot, Cazotte, Beaumarchais, Charrière, Cottin, Krüdener, and Staël. By reading these authors' literary works in light of their treatises on art and society, I seek to convey the significance of their musical tableaux, the subject of my study and a term I will define.

One of the common denominators of the eighteenth-century aesthetic debates was a pervasive concern with the efficacy of human expression. In his 1719 treatise *Réflexions critiques sur la poësie et sur la peinture* Jean-Baptiste Dubos made a definitive and extremely influential break with the past by claiming that painting was more powerful than poetry. The basis for his claim was, on the one hand, that painting provides a more direct and exact imitation of nature than does poetry and, on the other, that painting appeals to the beholder via the conduit of the eye rather than the ear. Dubos explains the superiority of the eye over the ear in the following passage:

La Peinture se sert de l'œil pour nous émouvoir ... La vue a plus d'empire
sur l'ame que les autres sens ... Ainsi les bruits & même les sons naturels
ne nous affectent pas à proportion des objets visibles. Par exemple, les cris
d'un homme blessé que nous ne voyons point, ne nous affectent pas, bien
que nous ayons connoissance du sujet qui lui fait jetter les cris que nous
entendons, comme nous affecteroit la vuë de son sang & de sa blessure.
On peut dire, métaphoriquement parlant, que l'œil est plus près de l'ame
que l'oreille.

[Painting uses the eye to move us ... Sight has greater ascendancy over the
soul than the other senses ... Thus noises and even natural sounds do not
affect us to the same extent as visible objects. For example, the cries of a
wounded man whom we do not see do not affect us, even if we are aware
of the subject that occasions the cries that we hear, as much as would the
sight of his blood and his wound. Metaphorically speaking, we can say
that the eye is closer to the soul than the ear.][2]

In this passage Dubos contrasts the sight of an accident to its sound. To
his mind, the immediacy of the accident's visual impact makes a stronger appeal to the onlooker's imagination and to his or her ability to
empathize with the victim than the abstraction of his cries. He tempers
this valorization of the eye over the ear, however, by specifying that the
effect of music added to spectacle is stronger still:

Les accens funébres de la symphonie que Lulli a placé dans la Scène de
l'Opera d'Amadis ... font autant d'impression sur notre oreille que le
spectacle ... en [fait] sur nos yeux. Notre imagination attaquée en même
tems par l'organe de la vue & par l'organe de l'ouïe, est beaucoup plus
émue ... que si nos yeux seuls étoient séduits.

[The funerary accents of the symphony that Lully placed in the scene from
the opera *Amadis* ... make as great an impression on our ear as the spectacle ... does on our eyes. Our imagination, simultaneously assailed by the
organ of seeing and by the organ of hearing, is far more moved ... than if
our eyes alone were seduced.][3]

In questioning poetry's precedence over other art forms, Dubos cast
doubt upon the efficacy of language as a means of artistic expression.

Though poetry no longer occupied the pinnacle of the aesthetic hierarchy, by mid-century there was still some disagreement as to which art

form should be her rightful successor. As James Johnson has demonstrated, most listeners at mid-century harboured a mimetic understanding of music, believing that certain musical passages could be identified as representing natural phenomena (bird song, a fresh spring morning, a beautiful sunrise, an oncoming storm) or emotional states (ecstasy, alarm, fury, despair).[4] Accordingly, the emotions the listeners sustained were thought to resemble those they would normally feel in the presence of nature or the human condition. An occasional slippage in contemporary aesthetic treatises indicates, however, that certain eighteenth-century thinkers suspected music of occasioning emotions that did not fall neatly into mimetic categories. Charles Batteux dedicated his 1747 treatise *Les Beaux-Arts réduits à un même principe* to proving that all arts conform to the principle of mimesis, yet risked undermining his thesis entirely by expressing doubt as to whether music conforms as nicely. While he agreed with Dubos that poetry should be set apart from the visual arts because it speaks to the soul via the ear instead of the eye, he drew a further distinction between poetry and music, stating that the medium of poetry is the spoken word and that of music is the voice, or sound. Because the meaning of pure sound is less readily deciphered than that of words, he claimed, music appeals to the emotions rather than the intellect. Batteux thus distinguished music from poetry based on its heightened appeal to the emotions, much as Dubos had distinguished painting from poetry based on its direct appeal to the soul.

For Batteux, however, music possessed an additional, disquieting feature, namely, that the object of its imitation, or indeed the emotion it occasioned, could not be readily identified: 'Il y a des passions qu'on reconnoît dans le chant musical, par exemple, l'amour, la joie, la tristesse: mais pour quelques expressions marquées, il y a mille autres, dont on ne sçauroit dire l'objet' (There are passions that we recognize in musical song, for example, love, joy, and sadness, but for each of these expressions there are a thousand others whose subject we cannot determine). He suggests that if unable to identify the specific passion the music evokes, the listener should not try: 'Il suffit qu'on le sente, il n'est pas nécessaire de le nommer' (It suffices to feel it; it is not necessary to name it).[5] Batteux's intimation that the object of music's imitation may not be recognizable left the door open for his readers to question whether music was an imitative art at all. His suggestion that music was capable of inducing an affective response that the listener could not identify and therefore could not control rendered it morally suspect.

Later in the century, Rousseau went still farther by proclaiming unequivocally that music has a more powerful effect on the listener's emotions than either poetry or painting. While he concedes in his *Essai sur l'origine des langues* that 'l'on parle aux yeux bien mieux qu'aux oreilles' (one speaks to the eyes much more effectively than to the ears), he qualifies his statement by stipulating that 'lorsqu'il est question d'émouvoir le cœur et d'enflammer les passions, c'est toute autre chose' (when it is a question of moving the heart and enflaming the passions, it is an altogether different matter). Using an example that directly counters the passage from Dubos's treatise cited above, Rousseau claims that witnesses of an accident are much more vividly affected by the oral account of the victim's suffering than by the sight of his wounds. The sound of the voice, which signifies successively rather than simultaneously, strikes the listener 'à coups redoublés' (with repeated blows) and is consequently more powerful than a split-second image.[6] While Rousseau attributed the power to move the listener to language and music alike, he continued to associate the greatest energy of expression with voice and the unconstrained melodic line, in which the two were united.

From mid-century on, therefore, painting and music began to displace poetry as the art that appealed most forcefully to the beholder, yet which of the two was more powerful (or pernicious) remained a subject of debate. Without venturing to determine which art form ultimately exercised the greatest hold over the spectator, I submit (with Dubos) that the *combination* of the musical and the visual arts in the musical tableau, or musical performance staged for a beholder inscribed within the text, enhances the appeal to the beholder's emotions via the ear *and* the eye, via successive *and* simultaneous signification, rendering it a particularly powerful persuasive device. In *The Surprising Effects of Sympathy*, David Marshall makes invaluable connections between eighteenth-century art and society, between spectatorship and sympathy, between imitation and identification. Yet music is conspicuously absent from his analysis. While Marshall takes Dubos's revision of the aesthetic hierarchy in favour of painting as his point of departure, I focus on the somewhat later development in which philosophers began to entertain the possibility that music was more powerful still. If Marshall's work sheds light upon the relationship between the novel and theatre, mine is intended to shed light upon the relationship between the novel and opera, or sung theatre, which arguably unseated spoken theatre as an object of aesthetic concern in the course of the eighteenth century.

Diderot and Rousseau were among the eighteenth century's most vocal critics of language's limitations. Though engaged in an active intellectual exchange, they differed in their choice of alternate sign system, for Diderot displayed a predilection for the visual and Rousseau for the musical arts. As Alexandra Wettlaufer demonstrates in her recent study *In the Mind's Eye*, Diderot sustained Dubos's line of inquiry by investigating the expressive potential of gesture and pantomime in his writings on painting and the theatre of the 1750s and 1760s.[7] It was in this context that Diderot explored the relationship between tableau and beholder and made his famous call for tableaux over coups de théâtre that has given rise to a body of criticism that one might call tableau theory. In my introduction I return to Diderot's art and theatre criticism in order to grasp the meaning of the term 'tableau' as he defined it. I then trace the relationship of tableau and beholder from their original context in painting and the theatre to narrative in order to rectify our modern understanding of the tableau in the text. Finally, I demonstrate how eighteenth-century authors enhanced the expressive power of the narrative tableau by drawing not only on contemporary theories of the visual arts but on contemporary theories of music.

While Diderot and Rousseau both questioned the adequacy of language and actively experimented with alternate sign systems, Rousseau was by far the more controversial of the two. His statements about the arts and artists raised the ire of his contemporaries and readers, particularly of those who felt directly implicated by his claims. Despite the scope and influence of his contributions to literature, philosophy, and the social sciences, Rousseau considered himself to be first and foremost a musician and wrote more prolifically on the subject of music than any other author of his time. The distinctions he made between the capacity of the different nations and sexes to access, convey, or respond to musical expression fanned the flames of contemporary debate. My book consists of two parts, which take as their point of departure two of Rousseau's more incendiary remarks. In his *Lettre sur la musique française* of 1753 Rousseau asserted that Italian was a more musical language than French. This claim did not sit well with the French, whose national spirit was fundamentally linked to their language, and had implications not only for French poets and composers, who together strove to strike the ideal balance between text and music, but also for French authors, whose primary means of artistic expression was thereby called into question. Rousseau circulated his letter in the midst of the *Querelle des Bouffons*, the debate that raged in the Parisian journals between partisans of French and Italian opera in the years 1752–4. The distinction between the *Querelle des Bouffons* and the *Querelle des Anciens et des Modernes* of the preceding century suggests why the French went on the defensive in the course of the opera debates. While the French compared themselves to their classical predecessors during the literary-historical controversy, the point of comparison during the opera debates was their Italian contemporaries. The arguments, in the two instances, were similar. In the earlier quarrel, French literary decadence was negatively compared to the simplicity and purity of the Ancients. In the later quarrel, French musical artifice was negatively compared to the simplicity and purity of Italian song. Although the Moderns could claim that their literature was the most perfect reincarnation of the classical model, even the proponents of French opera were obliged to concede that Italian opera, not French, was the direct descendant of their classical forebears. In the earlier quarrel, then, the French had reason to believe that the rest of Europe would strive to emulate them, while in the later quarrel they found themselves reduced to emulating the Italians. If the *Querelle des Anciens et des Modernes* contributed to the triumph of the French language the *Querelle des Bouffons* constituted nothing less than a crisis of the same. Yet to question the adequacy of the French language was to question France's right to its cultural hegemony over Europe. Aesthetic inquiry was therefore considered to have serious political implications.

Previous studies of Rousseau's writings on music have read them in the context of his debate with Rameau, in the context of the eighteenth-century opera quarrels, or in the broader philosophical context of his *Essai sur l'origine des langues*. I have chosen instead to investigate the response of French authors who participated in the opera quarrels to Rousseau's attack on their language. These authors include the intriguing, highly influential figures of Diderot, Cazotte, and Beaumarchais, who single-mindedly resisted Rousseau's claim that the French language was unmusical. In Part One, entitled 'Music and Language: *La Querelle des Bouffons*,' I reveal the national overtones of their opposition to Rousseau's assertions in their early aesthetic treatises. I then examine the repercussions of their stance on the musical tableaux in their literary works. Well-versed in contemporary aesthetics themselves, Diderot, Cazotte, and Beaumarchais experimented with the analogy Rousseau established between music and language and the relationship Diderot established between the tableau and the beholder.[8] In so doing they enriched the language and literature that were thought to be deficient by infusing them with the music French was purportedly unable to convey.

Rousseau's infamous letter was by no means his only controversial legacy. In his writings on education and the theatre of the 1750s and 1760s, he suggested that women are less capable of excelling in the arts or of governing their artistic sensibility than are men. This claim struck a chord with the French public, who harboured grave doubts about the compatibility of musicality and morality, and had implications for aspiring women authors, composers, and musicians. The growing conviction, around mid-century, that music somehow escaped the rules of mimesis, that what it evoked was therefore difficult to determine and the response it occasioned impossible to control, contributed to the notion that musical sensibility in a female performer or beholder was a sign that she could be led astray. The connection between music and its moral implications for women can be seen in Mlle de l'Espinasse's contemporary treatise on education:

> Quant à la musique, je la regarde comme le véhicule de toutes les passions. Les sons entrent dans l'âme mieux que les paroles, et je pense que la sagesse d'une femme a de la peine à chanter un air tendre sans en sentir l'effet et sans en faire l'application à un objet particulier, lorsqu'il se rencontre.

> [As for music, I consider it to be the vehicle of all the passions. Sounds enter the soul more easily than words and I think that a woman's modesty is hard put to sing a tender air without feeling its effect and applying it to a particular object, once encountered.][9]

The role that late eighteenth-century women writers accorded their musically inclined heroines has been partially obscured by the larger question of the gifted woman's place in society. Previous studies of Rousseau's writings on women have called attention to the aspersion Rousseau cast upon female genius in his *Lettre à d'Alembert* and his *Emile*, most notably in the following notorious passage:

> Toutes ces femmes à grands talents n'en imposent jamais qu'aux sots. On sait toujours quel est l'artiste ou l'ami qui tient la plume ou le pinceau quand elles travaillent; on sait quel est le discret homme de lettres qui leur dicte en secret leurs oracles. Toute cette charlatanerie est indigne d'une honnête femme. Quand elle aurait de vrais talents, sa prétention les avili-

rait. Sa dignité est d'être ignorée, sa gloire est dans l'estime de son mari, ses plaisirs sont dans le bonheur de sa famille.

[All these women of superior talent only impress the foolish. One always knows who the artist or friend is who holds the pen or the brush when they work. One knows who the discreet man of letters is who dictates their oracles to them in secret. All this charlatanry is unworthy of an honest woman. If she has real talents, her pretension will reduce their value. Her dignity lies in being ignored, her glory in her husband's esteem, her pleasure in her family's happiness.][10]

In Part Two, entitled 'Music and Morality: *La Querelle des Femmes*,' I call attention instead to passages in which Rousseau and his contemporaries addressed the morality of women's musical pursuits. I then examine the responses of Rousseau's readers to his writings on women in what can only be described as feminist treatises *avant la lettre*. These readers, including Charrière, Cottin, Krüdener, and Staël, subsequently became popular and influential authors in their own right. As in Part One, I investigate the repercussions of their resistance to Rousseau on the musical tableaux in their literary works. Drawing upon the aesthetics their predecessors had explored, they designed tableaux that served to dissociate musicality and immorality in the public imaginary, reducing the obstacle that stood in the way of women's musical pursuits.

The central concern of Part Two is, in a sense, a corollary of Part One, for curiosity as to how music and language signified gave rise to speculation as to the nature of their effect on the listener. Inquiry into the aesthetics of the sung and spoken theatre, and the musical and visual arts of which they were comprised, were thus closely linked to considerations of their moral implications. While Rousseau's writings were, to a large extent, emblematic of their time, he brought matters to a head by engaging in a certain amount of gate keeping; distinguishing between those who did and did not have access to the enhanced expression music was thought to afford – French or Italians, men or women – and provoking a response from those who felt their nation or sex had been excluded. My book thus turns from sign systems to their moral repercussions, from aesthetic innovation to social resistance, from the role of the nation in Europe to the role of women in the nation, in accordance with the century's shifting preoccupations. The authors whose works I examine are exceptional in that they were directly involved in the eighteenth-century opera quarrels, aspired to write text and music themselves, or kept abreast of the contemporary aesthetic debates. Consequently, the form and function of the musical passages in their texts differ dramatically from the stock musical scenes characteristic of the French literary tradition. Rather than introducing music primarily as theme, symbol, or metaphor, these authors drew upon contemporary innovations in the aesthetics of the musical, visual, and performing arts to forge a powerful textual device in the form of the musical tableau. In so doing, they discovered an apt vehicle for their political convictions. Each of the following chapters opens with an analysis of the manifestos, in the form of letters or prefaces, some serious, others farcical, in which these authors voiced their responses to Rousseau and culminates in an analysis of the musical tableaux in their literary works.

Thus far the authors in my study – with the possible exception of Diderot – have tended to remain in Rousseau's shadow. By the end of my study I hope to have liberated them from it entirely. While Rousseau undeniably generated, or aggravated, the questions with which his contemporaries and readers were forced to contend, his contemporaries and readers came up with the means of representing, resisting, or resolving these issues in their texts. Diderot, Cazotte, and Beaumarchais were troubled by Rousseau's statements concerning music and language and their implications for the French. Charrière, Cottin, Krüdener, and Staël were troubled by Rousseau's statements concerning music and morality and their implications for women. Each of them, after his or her own fashion, contributed to the creation of a new discursive device, the musical tableau, which they placed at the service of their aesthetic or social concerns. In so doing, they rendered the conventional musical scene virtually obsolete, enhanced the national and gender politics with which such scenes were invested, and considerably expanded the possibilities for portraying music textually. The aesthetic issues that these authors explored, the moral quandaries that they addressed, and the memory of the unusually fraught eighteenth-century French musical milieu that they preserved furnished the basis for the arresting scenes of music in literature, the revolutionary aesthetics of the theatre, the emerging theories of music and nationalism, and the transcendent musical heroines of the nineteenth century. While the Romantics occasionally surpassed their predecessors in literary reputation, they readily acknowledged their literary debt.

In a recent dialogue addressing the place of music in cultural studies, Charles Dill observed that while musical and visual culture were of increasing importance in the eighteenth century they were understood primarily in literary terms and were therefore engaged in the struggle to develop their own language. Now that the tables have turned, so to speak, I seek to straddle the divide that remains in current criticism between discussions of musical and visual culture and analyses of literary works. In the same dialogue Downing Thomas warned that cultural studies risks privileging the political over the aesthetic, disregarding the integrity of literature-as-artwork. I have endeavoured to avoid this pitfall.[11] The arenas in which text and music staged their encounter in the early modern period included, quite logically, songs, opera, theatre, and the novel. The musical tableau is situated at the nexus of literary, musical, and visual aesthetics, or – to emphasize the parallel with opera – of words, music, and spectacle. The ensuing discussion consists of a substratum that explores the social and aesthetic context of musical discourse in eighteenth-century French society and an overarching narrative that tells a chronological tale of the development of the musical tableau in eighteenth-century French literature. I leave it to my readers to determine which is more fundamental to my argument, the harmonic colour or the melodic line.

A Note on Translations and Spelling

For ease of cross-referencing in both languages, I have used recent translations of Rousseau's *œuvre* as well as of the major literary works I analyse when available. All other translations are mine unless otherwise indicated. I have respected the spelling of the editions I have cited throughout.

Acknowledgments

For their insights, encouragement, and faith in the final product, I am deeply indebted to the following people: to Jean-Marie Roulin for striking the ideal balance between scholarly independence and guidance as he directed my dissertation; to Gary Tomlinson for countless hours of inspiring conversation; to Lynn Hunt for her unwavering support and her watershed questions. Together they formed a committee that allowed me to think beyond the confines of a single discipline. To Liliane Weissberg and Jerry Singerman, who have always been of excellent counsel, and to Gerald Prince, who provided the structures upon which I would subsequently play. To Pierre Frantz, who discussed his work with me in Paris, and to Jacqueline Letzer and Robert Adelson, who allowed me a sneak preview of *Women Writing Opera*. Last but not least, to my grad school cronies, who never let me get away with anything.

Since those days, I have benefited from several invaluable scholarly exchanges. My enduring thanks go to Downing Thomas and Roberta Marvin, who directed the summer research seminar at the Obermann Center for Advanced Studies, University of Iowa, entitled 'Opera in Context: Interdisciplinary Approaches to Creation, Performance, and Reception,' and to Carolyn Abbate, who directed the NEH summer seminar 'Opera: Interpretation Between Disciplines' at Princeton University. To the members of these groups, along with those of the Eighteenth-Century Interdisciplinary Salon at Washington University, which has provided me with an intellectual haven for the past five years, I extend my very warmest thanks. I am particularly grateful to my friends and colleagues in St. Louis, who have been extremely supportive of my research endeavours, especially to Pascal Boyer, Michael Sherberg, and Harriet Stone, who painstakingly read my entire manuscript.

I would like to thank my editor, Jill McConkey, and her colleagues, who transformed an otherwise daunting process into a very positive experience, as well as my anonymous readers for their invaluable suggestions. I would also like to thank the editors of *Studies in Eighteenth-Century Culture, Women in French Studies, Operatic Migrations: Transforming Works and Crossing Boundaries*, and *Phrase and Subject: Studies in Music and Literature*, for their careful reading of my work and for permission to draw upon materials included in my previous publications.

Finally, my project would be incomplete were I not to acknowledge the source of the various strands of thought that wend their way through it. My heartfelt thanks to my father, James, who sowed the seeds of my interests in literature, opera, and film, my mother, Olivian, who has always been intrigued by questions of language and alternate sign systems, and my sister, Jessica, who has become my partner in scholarly endeavours. To my husband, Lionel, for sharing my fascination for peculiar texts, for encouraging me when my faith in my abilities flagged, and for enabling me to pursue my passions on both sides of the Atlantic, I remain forever grateful. For Elena, who arrived on the fateful 17th of November, whose presence graced the final revisions of this text, and who is soon to discover the children's books that live on in its pages, I offer special thanks.

NARRATIVE INTERLUDES

Interlude (in·ter·lude), *n.*

1. a relatively short period of time between two longer periods, during which something happens that is different from what has happened before and what follows.
2. a short play, piece of music, or other entertainment performed during a break in the performance of a long work.

C'est un des grands avantages du musicien de pouvoir peindre les choses qu'on ne sauroit entendre, tandis qu'il est impossible au Peintre de réprésenter celles qu'on ne sauroit voir, et le plus grand prodige d'un art qui n'agit que par le mouvement est d'en pouvoir former jusqu'à l'image du repos. Le sommeil, le calme de la nuit, la solitude, et le silence même entrent dans les tableaux de la musique ... Que toute la nature soit endormie, celui qui la contemple ne dort pas, et l'art du musicien consiste à substitüer à l'image insensible de l'objet celle des mouvemens que sa présence excite dans le cœur du contemplateur.

[One of the great advantages of the musician is to be able to paint things that we cannot hear, whereas it is impossible for the painter to represent what we cannot see. The most prodigious feat of an art that acts primarily through movement is to be able to create the impression of rest. Sleep, the calm of night, solitude, and even silence enter into the tableaux of music ... Even if all of nature is asleep, he who contemplates it is not. The art of the musician consists in substituting for the insensitive object the movements that its presence excites in the heart of the beholder.]

Jean-Jacques Rousseau, *L'Essai sur l'origine des langues*

Introduction: Tableau Theory

Jacques, en déshabillant son maître, lui dit :
'Monsieur, aimez-vous les tableaux?
LE MAÎTRE. – Oui, mais en récit ...

[Jacques, while undressing his master, said:
'Master, do you like tableaux?'
THE MASTER. – Yes, but in stories ...]

Diderot, *Jacques le fataliste*

The literature of the eighteenth century is redolent with musical scenes. I use the word 'scenes' intentionally, for I distinguish between conventional literary depictions of music in novels and the 'tableaux' that eventually upstaged them. Musical scenes representative of the French literary tradition occur in such texts as Riccoboni's *Le Marquis de Cressy*, in which the young heroine recounts how her music teacher sought to take advantage of her during her harpsichord lessons, using the music itself, as well as the unusual intimacy the lessons afforded, to persuade her of his undying affection. Once the heroine receives incontrovertible proof of his fervour, her tutor goes off to administer to the needs of other pupils awaiting his instruction. Diderot parodies such scenes in *La Religieuse* when Sophie wonders aloud at the effect her music has on the mother superior, who sighs audibly as she runs her hands over the bare shoulders and breast of her talented young protégée, seemingly transported by her harpsichord playing. Laclos, too, makes reference to this tradition when he casts Danceny as Cécile's music teacher in *Les Liaisons dangereuses*, having him tuck his first love letter between the strings of her harp.

Jean-Jacques Rousseau took a decisive step away from these conventional depictions of music as sex symbol, demonstrating how the tradition could be both respected and vastly enriched. In part I, letter XLVIII of his epistolary novel *Julie, ou la Nouvelle Héloïse*, Rousseau has Saint-Preux recount his conversion from French to Italian music. Though identical to the scenes evoked above in terms of plot (Saint-Preux is Julie's music teacher), this letter contains a wealth of information concerning the contemporary perception of music and musicians. Asking that Julie burn her French music, Saint-Preux neatly recaps the arguments of those (Rousseau foremost among them) who found French music to be stilted and artificial and who were pained by the contortions French singers had to go through in order to render their art. He then describes, with increasing passion, the extraordinary impression he sustained while listening to an Italian castrato:

> Je me mis à écouter cette musique enchanteresse, et je sentis bientôt, aux émotions qu'elle me causait, que cet art avait un pouvoir supérieur à celui que j'avais imaginé. Je ne sais quelle sensation voluptueuse me gagnait insensiblement. Ce n'était plus une vaine suite de sons comme dans nos récits. A chaque phrase, quelque image entrait dans mon cerveau ou quelque sentiment dans mon cœur; le plaisir ne s'arrêtait point à l'oreille, il pénétrait jusqu'à l'âme.

> [I began to listen to that enchanting music, and I soon sensed from the emotions it provoked in me that this art had a power greater than I had imagined. Some unknown voluptuous sensation imperceptibly came over me. It was no longer an empty sequence of sounds, as in our *récits*. At each phrase some image entered my brain or some sentiment my heart; the pleasure did not stop at the ear, but entered the soul.]

Losing his awareness of the performance as such, Saint-Preux is suddenly persuaded that he hears not the music but the emotion it expresses and sees not the castrato but the characters whose sentiment the music evokes: 'Je perdais à chaque instant l'idée de musique, de chant, d'imitation; je croyais entendre la voix de la douleur, de l'emportement, du désespoir; je croyais voir des mères éplorées, des amants trahis, des tyrans furieux' (I lost at every moment the notion of music, song, imitation; I thought I was hearing the voice of grief, rage, despair; in my mind's eye I saw mothers in tears, lovers betrayed, furious Tyrants). Finally – and this is the crux of the matter – Saint-Preux foresees a time when Julie will become so well versed in the Italian style that she will join him in a duet, presumably in the hopes that she, and not the castrato, will be the one to transport him to another sensorial realm:

> Je n'avais qu'un regret, mais il ne me quittait point; c'était qu'un autre que toi formât des sons dont j'étais si touché, et de voir sortir de la bouche d'un vil *castrato* les plus tendres expressions de l'amour ... Ah! que le cœur prêtera d'énergie à l'art si jamais nous chantons ensemble un de ces duos charmants qui font couler des larmes si délicieuses!

> [I had only one regret; but I was never free from it; it was that someone other than you should produce sounds I was so moved by, and to see the most tender expressions of love coming from the mouth of a vile *castrato* ... Ah what energy the heart will lend to art, if ever we sing together one of those enchanting duets that draw such delicious tears!][1]

Yet the moment that Saint-Preux envisions is never realized. Rousseau stops short of creating the musical tableau that the reader can practically see. Decorum, indeed, may have demanded that he refrain from writing it, for its effect would certainly have rendered Saint-Preux less capable of obeying Julie's request that he depart, and Julie less capable of sticking to her moral resolutions.

Rousseau was thus on the verge of creating a musical tableau in a literary text. A tableau, as opposed to a scene. If we pause a moment to consider what his tableau might have entailed, the difference between the two will become more apparent. A musical scene – a generic category – might involve any evocation or reminder of music, such as the words of a song or the presence of an instrument or performer. The instrument may or may not be played, the song may or may not be accompanied, and the performance may be described in more or less detail. The only distinction between the scenes of music in the texts of Riccoboni, Diderot, and Laclos that I mentioned above and run-of-the-mill seduction scenes, for instance, is the presence of a harp or a harpsichord. Largely thematic, the musical scene is part and parcel of the plot and does little to transform the narrative on an emotional level. A listener may be present, but does not give the impression of being affected by the sound of the music. Simply put, a musical scene is made up of the props associated with a musical performance, yet the reader gleans little to no sense either of the music or of its effect. A musical tableau – or musical performance staged for a beholder inscribed within the text – is structured in accordance with the aesthetics of sight and sound and brings an extra dimension into play by foregrounding the catalytic role of music in the narrative and the emotional dynamic that the performance sets in motion between performer and beholder. Prior to his conversion experience, Saint-Preux believed that music's effect on the listener was 'purement mécanique et physique' (purely mechanical and physical), having little to do with either the sentiments or the soul. His initial convictions were therefore ideally suited to the creation of a conventional musical scene, in which the instrument's presence would be purely symbolic, the accompaniment to the song relatively insignificant, and the performer an object of desire. Once the castrato initiates him into the subtleties of the art, however, the situation changes. Revealing 'le lien puissant et secret des passions avec les sons' (the powerful and secret connection of the passions with the sounds), the castrato leads Saint-Preux to the following vital insight: 'l'imitation des tons divers dont les sentiments animent la voix parlante donne à son tour à la voix chantante le pouvoir d'agiter les cœurs et ... l'énergique *tableau* des mouvements de l'âme de celui qui se fait entendre est ce qui fait le vrai charme de ceux qui l'écoutent' (the imitation of the various registers by which sentiments animate the speaking voice confers in turn on the singing voice the power to stir hearts, and ... the performer's energetic *tableau* of the movements of his soul is what constitutes the true charm of the listeners).[2] In the course of the scene, therefore, Saint-Preux becomes sufficiently aware of the power of music over the sentiments and the soul to become fully engaged, both emotionally and imaginatively, in a musical performance.

Rousseau thus sets the stage for the creation of a musical tableau. Yet Saint-Preux's account of his conversion experience remains far too discursive to be considered a tableau in and of itself. He recounts (tells) his experience, he does not represent (show) it. We learn of his conversion; we do not witness it. Rousseau nevertheless appeals to the reader's imagination when he has Saint-Preux anticipate the day that he and Julie will join hearts and voices in a musical duet. Giving free reign to fancy, we can envision the elements that would have comprised the resulting musical tableau had Julie chosen to fulfil Saint-Preux's wishes. The tableau that Rousseau did *not* write might have unfolded as follows. The forward-moving progression of the narrative, in which Saint-Preux recounts his experiences, activities, convictions, and concerns, would momentarily be suspended, giving way to a detailed description of the sight and sound of Julie's performance, as seen through Saint-

Preux's eyes. Time would momentarily come to a halt as Saint-Preux takes in every detail of Julie's appearance and expression, conjuring up her image in the mind's eye of the reader. Gradually ceasing his own activity and forgetting his concerns, Saint-Preux would become absorbed in his contemplation of the singer and her song. Intoxicated by the timbre of her voice, which betrays Julie's own emotional involvement, Saint-Preux would soon find himself unable to distinguish between the music's powerful hold on his senses and the nature of his sentiment for the singer. In keeping with Rousseau's conviction that a duet should consist of the alternation rather than the union of two voices, the couple would then reverse their roles, Saint-Preux assuming the position of the performer and Julie that of the beholder. At a given moment during the performance, the accord between the emotion the music conveyed and its resonance in the heart of the listener would suddenly collapse the distance between the lovers, conveying a sense of the sound and its intensified emotional effect to the reader via the silent textual medium. Though Rousseau did not realize this musical tableau, he provided his contemporaries and readers with the raw materials from which they could construct their own, as well as the necessary aesthetic preconditioning to sustain their full affective impact. He generated the impulse to create such tableaux, moreover, not by setting a literary example, but by expressing views that tended to exacerbate the controversy surrounding musical aesthetics and their political implications.

Rousseau first revealed his taste for polemics, as opposed to diplomacy, in the course of the *Querelle des Bouffons*, the opera quarrel that divided Parisian public opinion into the proponents of French and Italian music in the early 1750s. For the next half century he remained a fervently admired yet intensely controversial figure. His role in eighteenth-century French society can, perhaps, be most accurately described as that of a 'grain de levain' (grain of yeast), the metaphor that Diderot used to characterize Rameau's nephew. Though Rousseau was not nearly as eccentric as the walk of life to which Rameau's nephew belongs, Diderot's description of those individuals who 'rompent cette fastidieuse uniformité que notre education, nos conventions de société, nos bienseances d'usage ont introduite' (breaks that tedious uniformity which our education, our social conventions, and our customary good manners have brought about) perfectly conveys the effect that Rousseau's writings had on his contemporaries.[3] Rousseau demonstrated particular concern in his writings for the aesthetic compatibility of music and language and for the moral compatibility of the arts and society.[4] Certain of Rousseau's statements posed a problem for contemporary authors, however, most notably those statements that appeared to cast into question their capacity to write. Two of his contentions struck a particularly dissonant chord, one that Rousseau's contemporaries and readers felt obliged to resolve. In his *Lettre sur la musique française*, Rousseau declared that the French language was unmusical, an allegation that directly affected those authors who used the French language as their primary means of expression. In his writings on education and the theatre, Rousseau maintained that women had no capacity for artistic genius and raised concerns about the morality of their musical pursuits, assertions that posed a problem for women authors who were musically inclined. I contend that those authors who felt implicated by Rousseau's remarks harnessed the power of his aesthetics in order to contest his claims. They did so within the space of what I have chosen to call the musical tableau.

The definition of the tableau started to evolve in the latter half of the eighteenth century in ways that scholars have only recently come to appreciate.[5] Diderot was the first to use the word 'tableau' in the modern sense of the term.[6] In his *Entretiens sur le Fils naturel* of 1757 Diderot alludes to the difficulty in defining the concept, for when faced with the challenge his main character, Dorval, finds himself at a loss. Expressing his preference for the tableau over the coup de théâtre, Dorval can but provide an example of each, relying upon the Moi character to gloss his examples and furnish the following working definition of the term:

> J'entends. Un incident imprévu qui se passe en action, et qui change subitement l'état des personnages, est un coup de théâtre. Une disposition de ces personnages sur la scène si naturelle et si vraie, que, rendue fidèlement par un peintre, elle me plairait sur la toile, est un tableau.

> [I understand. An unforseen incident that transpires in the action and that suddenly changes the situation of the characters is a coup de théâtre. A disposition of these characters on the stage so natural and true that, if faithfully rendered by a painter, it would please me on the canvas, is a tableau.][7]

A coup de théâtre, or sudden, sensational turn of events, is thus a disruptive intrusion from without that immediately affects the action of the play. A tableau, on the other hand, arises naturally from within, affecting the disposition of the characters on stage, which is considered 'true' or convincing. Diderot's cursory definition of the tableau left quite a bit of leeway for scholars who wished to clarify or expand upon the concept. Rather than remaining a subject of literary or art criticism, therefore, the tableau has become a subject of critical theory. Michael Fried and Pierre Frantz have admirably elaborated Diderot's theory of the relationship between the tableau and the beholder in the domains of painting and the theatre.[8] The epigraph to this introduction suggests, however, that Diderot also had a notion of a tableau 'en récit,' one that he treats rather humorously in *Jacques le fataliste et son maître*.[9] While Jay Caplan and David Denby have proposed insightful analyses of the tableau in narrative, certain aspects of its definition stand in need of clarification. In the following pages I will return to Diderot's notion of the tableau in painting and the theatre, as defined by Fried and Frantz, in an effort to retain the full force of Diderot's original conception as I identify its equivalent within narrative. Only then will I undertake to define the subject of my study: the musical tableau or, otherwise stated, the tableau of a musical performance staged within a text.

According to Pierre Frantz, Diderot's original motivation for proposing that plays be held to a painterly standard was to enhance the verisimilitude of stage performances.[10] The following passage from Diderot's *Entretiens sur le Fils naturel*, in which Dorval elaborates upon his notion of the tableau, supports this interpretation:

Il faut que l'action théâtrale soit bien imparfaite encore, puisqu'on ne voit sur la scène presque aucune situation dont on pût faire une composition supportable en peinture. Quoi donc! la vérité y est-elle moins essentielle que sur la toile? Serait-ce une règle qu'il faut s'éloigner de la chose à mesure que l'art en est plus voisin, et mettre moins de vraisemblance dans une scène vivante, où les hommes mêmes agissent, que dans une scène colorée, où l'on ne voit, pour ainsi dire, que leurs ombres?

[Theatrical action must still be quite imperfect since we almost never see a situation on stage of which we could make a tolerable composition in painting. What! Is truth less essential there than on canvas? Is it a rule that the closer art is to its subject the further we must stray from it, investing a live scene, in which men themselves act, with less verisimilitude than a coloured scene in which we see, so to speak, but their shadows?][11]

The call for tableaux in the theatre was thus a call for verisimilitude, or credibility, on stage. Dorval's preference for tableaux over coups de théâtre coincided with a general movement in favour of stage naturalism which entailed an effort to define the domains of the actors and the spectators more clearly.[12] At mid-century, the common practice in French theatres was to allow spectators of distinction to be seated on stage.[13] No clear line of demarcation existed, therefore, between the stage and the audience, between the realm of action and reaction. Actors maintained the practice, moreover, of facing front, declaiming their lines to the audience, and thus calling attention to the performance as such. Only if the spectators were banned from the stage and if their presence ceased to be acknowledged by the actors could playwrights hope to sustain the illusion that the events unfolding before the spectators' eyes were real. Dorval's plea for a natural disposition of actors on stage was thus, in effect, a plea that the actors turn away from the audience and towards one another, grouping themselves around the purported focus of their concern and giving the impression that they were truly engaged in the task at hand. It was a plea for a fourth wall, an invisible wall that purportedly separated the actors from the spectators, allowing them to maintain the fiction of the spectators' absence, and enabling the spectators in turn to believe in the fiction before them.[14]

An exact correlation can be drawn between Diderot's notion of the tableau in the theatre and the new conception of painting that he developed in the 1760s, which Michael Fried first brought to critical attention.[15] Diderot's stated preference for genre over history painting suggests a similar desire to shift the locus of the drama from action to reaction. He preferred that artists portray subjects in a painting, like characters on the stage, grouped naturally around a central event, absorbed in the task at hand and seemingly oblivious to the onlooker's presence, rather than facing forward and, in effect, acknowledging that they are posing.[16] By having the characters turn their backs on the beholder, the artist effectively 'seals off the space or the world of the painting,' once again erecting a sort of fourth wall.[17] In denying the beholder's presence, both painted and staged tableaux implicitly deny their own fictional status, thereby enhancing the credibility, or persuasive power, of the depicted event. Fried's most significant insight – which opened the floodgates to what we might call tableau theory – was to identify the central paradox that Diderot's writings on the theatre and art criticism seem to suggest, namely that the tableau must deny the beholder's presence *in order* to sustain his attention.

Given that Diderot's narratives are still widely read, whereas his plays are no longer staged, Caplan has proposed that the tableau ultimately proved more effective as a literary than as a stage device. Claiming that Diderot's tableaux appeal to the theatre of the imagination, he defines the tableau in narrative as 'the dialogic relationship between a certain kind of spectacular narration and its reader, or rather, its "beholder."'[18] He thus establishes a natural equivalence between the beholder of a painting, the spectator of a play, and the reader of a text. Caplan conceives of the relationship between tableau and beholder as even more mutually binding than does Fried, stipulating that it is not enough for the tableau merely to sustain the beholder's attention. Instead 'the beholder is required to *participate* in the tableau while also (paradoxically) being excluded from it.'[19] The nature of this participation is by no means purely intellectual. Taking his cue from Diderot's call for tableaux to be used in the *drame bourgeois* and Fried's association of genre painting with scenes of domesticity, Caplan notes that tableaux frequently depict tragic loss within a family. Invoking the aesthetics of sacrifice, he explains that the tableau, as a depiction of loss, appeals to the beholder's sympathies, inducing him to project himself emotionally into the tableau and thereby compensating for the family's lack and becoming part of the tableau's structure. The beholder is thus – by extension – part and parcel of the tableau itself. Though Caplan's description of the tableau as a scene of loss may not be universally applicable, it is valuable in that he manages to break down the hermetic seal which, in Fried's analysis, seems to separate the world of the tableau from that of the beholder. He thereby renders the emotional exchange across the transgressed boundary more fluid. Yet – and this is my chief complaint – because Caplan defines the tableau in terms of an ongoing dialogical relationship, the boundaries of his narrative tableaux remain somewhat open-ended and are therefore difficult to compare structurally with Diderot's notion of the tableau in the theatre and painting.

Denby helps clarify the contours of the narrative tableau in his theory of sentimental fiction. His first care is to distinguish between the narrative tableau and the print (or illustration), which most closely approximates what we are inclined to think of as a tableau in a text. Unlike the print, Denby states, the tableau does not literally interrupt the narrative line. It nevertheless constitutes a break in the narrative's linear progression and functions 'in a spatial rather than a temporal dimension.'[20] The narrative tableau thus retains the simultaneity of effect that was associated with the visual arts in eighteenth-century

France and was one of the primary means of distinguishing them from poetry and music, which signified sequentially.[21] Implicitly then, the tableau momentarily disrupts the linear progression of the text and signifies on a perpendicular plane leading from author to reader as the author constructs, the characters embody, and the reader imaginatively and emotionally participates in the tableau. Modern narratological definitions of the tableau classify it as a subset of description as opposed to narration, confirming the notion that the linear progression of the narration is interrupted.[22] This classification accurately reflects Diderot's predilection for simultaneity over sequentiality (as opposed to Rousseau's preference for the reverse) and points to an inner tension in the musical tableau, which – as a combination of music and image – necessarily combines the two.

While Diderot's use of a term borrowed from painting within the context of the theatre suggests a certain number of parallels, or analogies, between the two artistic mediums, it also raises a fundamental question. In applying a term taken from an art form that is, by definition, static to an art form that is, by definition, mobile, Diderot created a certain amount of confusion, or ambiguity, as to which mode was ultimately to be given the upper hand. Consequently, a fairly pervasive association exists between Diderot's theory and the tradition of tableaux vivants. Angelica Goodden, for instance, illustrates the notion of tableaux in the theatre by providing examples from a number of eighteenth-century plays in which contemporary paintings were literally recreated on stage, characterizing Diderot's aim as a 'desire to create a type of drama that would furnish painters with a gallery of pictorial images.'[23] This analogy between a play and a picture gallery tends to invest stage performances with a certain iterative stasis. The danger of incorporating tableaux into the theatre, Goodden warns, lay in 'too close an identification of stage picture and artist's canvas, for drama presupposes a degree of movement in its unfolding which is necessarily absent from a painting.'[24] Critical analyses that characterize the tableau as a 'fetishistic snapshot' or a 'freeze frame' have clearly succumbed to such a danger.[25] Yet the threat of stasis is fundamentally at odds with Diderot's own characterization of the tableau.[26] Dorval's call for tableaux over coups de théâtre locates the drama not in the action unfolding before the spectators' eyes but in the characters' (and, by extension, the spectators') *reaction* to a central event. This interpretation is born out by Dorval's description of the tableau of motherly love:

Quoi donc, pourrait-il y avoir rien de trop véhément dans l'action d'une mère dont on immole la fille? Qu'elle coure sur la scène comme une femme furieuse ou troublée; qu'elle remplisse de cris son palais; que le désordre ait passé jusque dans ses vêtements, ces choses conviennent à son désespoir ... La véritable dignité, celle qui me frappe, qui me renverse, c'est le tableau de l'amour maternel dans toute sa vérité.

[What! Could there be anything too vehement in the action of a mother whose daughter is to be immolated? Let her race across the stage like an enraged or troubled woman, let her fill the palace with her cries, let her disarray be visible in her clothing, these things suit her despair ... True dignity, that which strikes me, which bowls me over, is to be found in the tableau of maternal love in all its truth.][27]

When confronted with the tableau described above, we as beholders witness not the act of immolation but the mother's reaction to the loss of her child. The spectacle of her despair as she tears across the stage, rending the air with her cries, is far from static, and Dorval in turn is overwhelmed by the vehemence of her response. Diderot thus clearly conceived of the tableau as emotionally charged and it was, in all likelihood, its emotional plenitude, rather than any 'ideal fixity,' that rendered the tableau worthy of the painter's brush.

Fried observes that Diderot's writings on the theatre of the 1750s gave rise to a 'new *explicitly dramatic* conception of painting' in his *Salons* of the 1760s. This remark suggests a certain reciprocity between Diderot's desire to introduce tableaux into the theatre and drama into painting and invites us to look more closely at Fried's discussion of the paintings Diderot preferred in order to get a better sense of the effect he wished contemporary playwrights to achieve.[28] While the absorptive activities of the figures depicted in the tableaux that Diderot found appealing are restful or contemplative, they are by no means immobile. Instead, the figures are engaged in drawing, painting, recitation, dictation, reading aloud, proclaiming to an assembly, playing games of cards or knucklebones, and restraining ungrateful sons, squirming cupids, or small yapping dogs. According to Fried, the absorptive state arises from the 'suspension of activity and fixing of attention.'[29] Yet the suspended activity does not entirely cease. On the contrary, the depicted figures are either absorbed *in* the activity at hand, which they pause to consider, or their attention is arrested *despite* the activity at hand, which carries on without them. Thus the painting, though static, conveys movement. Fried lays emphasis on the tableau's mobility, stating that 'for Diderot ... a painting had to do more than demonstrate a central dramatic idea: it had to set that idea in motion ... right before his eyes.'[30] He describes the resulting composition as 'emotionally charged, highly moralized, and dramatically unified.'[31] Emotional dynamism, morality and dramatic unity were, moreover, the very qualities with which Diderot wished to invest his staged tableaux in the context of the *drame bourgeois*, a genre that was patterned after daily life and on which the spectators were meant to model their behaviour.

A similar tension between stasis and movement is apparent in Denby's definition of the tableau in narrative. Denby states that the tableau's function is 'to freeze narrative, to suspend temporal progression so that the set of forces which the narrative has brought together in a particular moment may be allowed to discharge their full affective power.'[32] He thus simultaneously invokes the immobility suggested by the verbs 'to freeze' and 'to suspend' and the relative mobility of the verb 'to discharge.' Here, however, the tension resides not between two possible interpretations of the tableau itself, but between the tableau and the surrounding text. Whereas tableaux are often described as interrupting the forward-moving action of the narrative (or the development of the plot), in Denby's definition the verbs of stasis apply to the narrative and the verb of movement to the tableau. This inversion of our expectations is justified, however, for while the narrative itself can be said to unfold or progress, its forward-moving action frequently forestalls the expression of emotion. By suspending the narrative action and focusing the attention of characters and readers alike on the spectacle before them, the tableau gives the emotions time to accrue and releases their pent-up energy. Thus, though the tableau interrupts the narrative progression, it remains internally, emotionally dynamic. The narrative is momentarily suspended, or frozen, not the tableau.

In a definition of the narrative tableau that is admirable for its brevity, Michel Delon asserts that 'il s'agit ... de *donner à voir* par l'écriture' (it's a question of *making visible* through writing).[33] While this definition closely resembles the notion of hypotyposis that both Goodden and Frantz have identified as the tableau's rhetorical predecessor, it draws our attention to another of the tableau's essential features.[34] As Denby states, 'the constitution of a particular description as a tableau is dependent upon an explicit or implied relation of looking, on the setting up of a distance between observer and observed.'[35] Yet this specification leaves us wondering 'who sees?'[36] Is making something visible (*donner à voir*) dependent upon the presence of a viewer? Denby seems to suggest that the looker, like the act of looking, can be either explicit or implicit, present or absent. Caplan emphasizes the beholder's absence, yet his insistence that 'the absence of the beholder is so crucial to the structure of Diderot's written tableaux that we must speak of the beholder as a character in it' leads us to wonder why narrative tableaux might not also be identified by the presence of an *inscribed* beholder.[37] If we think back to Fried's original characterization of the relationship between tableau and beholder, we recall that his final example of *Belisarius Begging for Alms* (*Bélisaire demandant l'aumône*) involves a beholder inscribed *within* the tableau (figure 1).

The subject of *Belisarius Begging for Alms*, though unique, is exemplary, for Fried traces it through its renderings by several of Diderot's contemporaries, including two versions by Jacques-Louis David. What Fried finds intriguing in Diderot's description of the original tableau by Luciano Borzone (initially attributed to Van Dyke) is his fascination not with the figure of the blind Belisarius receiving alms but with the soldier who is transfixed at the sight of him, having recognized the blind man as his former commander. Whereas the paintings that Diderot, and later Fried, have analysed to this point all contained a single spectacle of absorption, this painting, in effect, contains two. The blind man, who according to Fried constitutes the spectacle of absorption par excellence, is essentially self-absorbed.[38] The soldier is in turn absorbed by the spectacle of Belisarius's blindness. According to Diderot's description, it is the soldier's absorption and dismay that appeals to our emotions. By identifying with the role of the beholder in the tableau, the beholder outside the tableau is granted a more intimate means of access to the scene before him.[39] The underlying paradox of the relationship between tableau and beholder which structures the tableau device is, moreover, once again at work, for the presence of a beholder inside the tableau all the more effectively denies the presence of a beholder outside the tableau, and thus the fiction of the beholder's absence is maintained.[40] Once we have noted the example in which Fried declares the presence of the inscribed beholder, it becomes apparent that his previous examples are, in fact, littered with the same. Except for those tableaux in which a single figure absorbed in his or her own reflections is depicted, practically all of the tableaux involve inscribed beholders. It is their reaction that directs our attention to the object of their absorption, admiration, or concern. The key distinction that Diderot draws between '[c]elui qui agit et celui qui regarde' (the one who acts and the one who watches) serves not only to differentiate the figures within the tableau from those outside the tableau but also to differentiate the figures within the tableau from one another.[41] The despairing families, attentive assemblies, engaged listeners, sympathetic onlookers, and artists in the tableaux Fried describes are, along with the beholder outside the tableau, all examples of 'ceux qui regardent' or, in other words, of inscribed beholders.

The tableaux that attracted first Diderot's and later Fried's attention, can thus be divided into three categories. The first consists of figures absorbed in their own thoughts or activities. These are, essentially, tableaux of introspection. The subject of the figure's reverie (a soap bubble, a dead bird, a crucifix) is not necessarily the object of his gaze. The figure is thus an example of 'celui qui agit' and we are the ones engaged in the act of looking. In the second category, the figure in the tableau is engaged in the act of looking, yet casts his gaze upon an inanimate object, such as a painting or a sculpture, which he strives to reproduce on his canvas. The figure is thus an example of 'celui qui regarde' and we look both at and beyond the figure to the object of his gaze. The third category consists of tableaux that depict both a primary figure involved in her own thoughts or activities (crying over broken eggs) and secondary figures whose attention is arrested by the spectacle before them (her despair). In this instance the tableau is comprised both of 'celui qui agit' and 'celui qui regarde,' the gaze of the latter directs our own attention towards the former, and we are aware both of the central figure's emotions and of the reaction of those around her. Narrative tableaux can also take these three forms. The reader's attention can be directed towards a character absorbed in his or her own thoughts or activity, with no mediating level; the reader can be asked to share the perspective of a character who is riveted before, say, the tableau of nature; or the reader's attention can be directed over the shoulder (or focalized through the eyes) of one character, the beholder, towards another character, the performer. It is this last variety that will retain my attention, for it is the structure that naturally emerges when a musical performance is staged within a text.

The suggestion that the tableau can take the form of a performance within the text raises the question of the tableau's relationship to the *mise en abyme*.[42] In his detailed study of the evolution of the *mise en abyme* since André Gide, Lucien Dällenbach stipulates that the term, as Gide originally conceived it, was meant to refer to a contained work (whether painting or text) that was the *exact replica* of the work that contained it.[43] Gide's later work, however, indicates not only that he was equally intrigued by *in*exact replicas of the text within the text but also that he was interested less in the reflection of the text itself than in the reflected relationship between the narrator and the text. Dällenbach ultimately rejects the phrase 'l'œuvre dans l'œuvre' (the text within the text) in favour of 'le récit spéculaire' (the mirror within the text) as a more accurate description of the *mise en abyme*, for two reasons.[44] First, the mirror retains the notion of reflection, yet it is a reflection with a difference, such as that implied by a mirror-image, which is a reversal as opposed to a copy of the original. Second, the mirror leaves room for the possibility that the contained item not be a text at all but rather another art form entirely, such as a painting, a play, or a musical passage. Such generic shifts are generative, Dällenbach claims, in that they multiply the means of representing the text within the text, which would otherwise be quite limited, and call attention to the differential relationship between producer, artwork, and receiver that Gide found so intriguing.[45]

Dällenbach identifies two additional features of the *mise en abyme* that are of interest to us here. The first is its intra- or metadiegetic quality.[46] This stipulation implies that the reader must take into account two levels of the text, the level being imitated (diegetic) and the level of the imitation (intra- or metadiegetic). The second is its anachronic form.[47] The *mise en abyme* constitutes a fundamental disruption of the narrative's temporality. Dällenbach describes this disruption as a pause, or a suspension of narrative time.[48] He specifies, moreover, that the *mise en abyme*, as a concise version of the text, condenses narrative time accordingly: 'convertit le temps en espace, transforme la successivité en contemporanéité' (converts time into space, transforms successiveness into contemporaneousness).[49] The tableau resembles the *mise en abyme* in both respects. It functions on two narrative levels, that of the performer and that of the beholder, and it disrupts the sequential progression of the narrative, emphasizing instead the simultaneity of the accrued sensory effect. Yet the tableau reflects neither the text as a whole nor the relationship between narrator and text (which so fascinated Gide) but rather the relationship between text and reader. While narrative tableaux need not include an inscribed beholder, those that do constitute, in effect, *mises en abyme* of the relationship between text and reader.[50]

The type of tableau I will be discussing is also structurally related to the play within the play, the subject of Georges Forestier's meticulous analysis of seventeenth-century French theatre. Like the tableau featuring an inscribed beholder, 'il y a théâtre dans le théâtre à partir du moment oú un au moins des acteurs de la pièce-cadre se transforme en spectateur' (there is a play within the play as soon as at least one of the actors in the frame play becomes a spectator), or what Forestier refers to as a 'spectateur intérieur' (internal spectator).[51] The play within the play is thus defined by the 'rapport regardant-regardé' (seeing-seen relationship).[52] Forestier insists, moreover, on the metadiegetic, or split-level, structure of the play within the play, observing that while the internal spectacle interrupts the progress of the external action, the gaze of the internal spectator provides a certain continuity between levels. Acknowledging its relationship to the *mise en abyme*, he emphasizes the fact that the play within the play is defined by a 'dédoublement structurel' (structural doubling) rather than a 'dédoublement thématique' (thematic doubling).[53] Interestingly, the mad scenes and dream sequences that we have come to associate with opera and Hollywood musicals frequently conform to this structure.[54] While the 'œuvres-cadres' (frameworks) in Forestier's study are plays rather than narrative, the 'spectacle intérieur,'or play within the play, may take the form of a ballet or *chanson* (song).[55] My discussion thus rejoins his in my chapter on Beaumarchais, whose Figaro plays were modelled, in part, on Molière's *comédies-ballets*. The play within the text that can be found in Staël's *Corinne, ou l'Italie*, however, is not the subject of my analysis, which is dedicated to the musical tableau.

The salient features of the tableau are, therefore, as follows. Whether in painting, on stage, or in a literary text the tableau favours simultaneity over sequentiality and reaction over action. Though it momentarily suspends (or emblematizes) the progression of the narrative, the tableau itself is internally dynamic. This feature is so crucial to my understanding of the tableau that when this dynamic is not set in motion I will consider the tableau to have failed. This emotional dynamism is frequently conveyed via an inscribed beholder to the reader of the text, in which case the tableau serves as a *mise en abyme* of the relationship between text and reader. The tableau thus functions on more than one level. Accordingly, I will occasionally distinguish between the levels of performer and beholder or between the story and the discourse. While Denby has associated the tableau with the structure of the sentimental text, the 'explicit or implied relation of looking' that he identifies as a defining feature of the tableau is also a recognizable trait of libertine fiction.[56] A certain tension between virtue and eroticism is thus implicit in the tableau's structure.[57] Fried's characterization of absorption in Chardin's paintings carries overtones of faith, trust, simplicity, truth, and tranquility. Absorption loses its innocence, however, when Fried reminds us that Diderot was aroused by the sight of suggestively torn garments in Greuze's paintings of children. Peter Szondi identifies the tableau as the propagator of bourgeois morality and Denby calls it the focal point of a sentimental community.[58] Caplan puts a twist on the matter, however, stating that the tableau 'is ethically, and *therefore* erotically moving, a perversity that is too frequently overlooked.'[59] The beholder, called by another name, is essentially a voyeur, as is, by extension, the reader. This dual nature on which the tableau plays enhances its power as a persuasive device, as not only the characters but also the reader are likely to prove susceptible to the seductions of the text.

Bearing in mind the form and function of the narrative tableau, we can now consider what transpires when music is added to the mix. Narrative tableaux, as we have seen, occur when the action is momentarily suspended and the characters direct their attention towards a central event. Accordingly, the attention of the beholder shifts from what the characters are doing to what they are perceiving (seeing, hearing). Fried's examples indicate that the central event that retains the attention of a figure in a tableau can be (1) his or her own thoughts, (2) an artwork (a painting or a sculpture), or (3) the actions of another figure. In theory, though, the event that retains the figure's attention could also be a play or a musical performance. As we saw previously, paintings, though static, convey movement. Similarly, though 'essentially silent,' they convey sound.[60] If we take a closer look at the paintings that retained Diderot's attention, we note that several of the activities in the paintings Fried analyses are vocalized (recitation, dictation, reading aloud, proclaiming to an assembly). Moreover, Fried includes playing the violin in his list of absorptive activities.[61] The surrounding figures are thus engaged, alternately, in absorptive reflection, looking, and listening. A musical performance constitutes an equally absorptive activity, or central event, capable of sustaining the rapt attention of performer and beholder alike (figure 2). In François Boucher's *La Leçon de musique* (The Music Lesson), for instance, the attention of the young woman is fully focused on the pages of the song before her, concentrating, presumably on the correspondence between text and music as the young man, whose gaze she studiously avoids, provides the musical accompaniment. Narrative tableaux of musical performances tend to be of the third variety I identified, containing a performer and an

inscribed beholder, both of whom are absorbed in the music that cata-
lyzes their emotional response. Varying degrees of emphasis can be laid
on the level of the performer or the level of the beholder, however, so
that they approach the limiting cases of category one (absent beholder)
or category two (inanimate performer). The drama can thus centre
around either the spectacle that the characters are perceiving or the
spectacle of the characters perceiving. In late eighteenth-century France,
undoubtedly in response to treatises detailing the effect of the visual
and performing arts upon the emotions, authors demonstrated a marked
preference for the latter. The presence of an inscribed beholder is essential to the structure of the musical tableau, for without the beholder's
mediation, it is extremely difficult for the reader to grasp (let alone
sustain) the effect of the musical performance across the silent textual
medium. Encouraged to look over the character's shoulder, as it were,
we as readers perceive what the inscribed beholder perceives, and
strive to hear what he or she hears, sharing in his or her perspective,
enhanced emotion, and resulting strength of conviction.[62]

In eighteenth-century France, musical tableaux became a privileged
site for aesthetic innovation and social resistance. The authors whose
texts I examine created musical tableaux in which they experimented
with the implications of Rousseau's aesthetic insights and strategically
opposed his views. They thus transformed the role of music in literary
texts from a simple accompaniment to scenes of seduction into the
vehicle of their own ideological convictions: a powerful persuasive
device placed at the service of literary, musical, and social reform. The
twentieth century is indebted to the authors in my study for certain
concepts and theatrical effects that still retain their appeal for viewers of
modern-day cinema. The musical tableaux of the eighteenth century
are, I would argue, the ancestors of a modern variety, yet one that is
somewhat different from that which Roland Barthes has identified.
Barthes associates Diderot's tableaux with Brecht's 'epic scenes' and
Eisenstein's 'shots,' yet this is precisely the association that I find misleading when music is added to the mix.[63] In order to make this distinction clear I would like momentarily to overstep another boundary, this
time between prose fiction and film, and consider Laura Mulvey's
article 'Visual Pleasure and Narrative Cinema' in which she associates
the two. Mulvey addresses the split-level structure of classical film
narrative, investigating the allure that the characters hold for one another as well as that which they hold for the spectators. Calling our
attention to the potentially erotic or voyeuristic conditions of viewing,
Mulvey describes the imaginative participation of the beholder

(gendered male), noting that his inability to participate in the event that unfolds before him obliges the beholder to project his repressed desire onto the performer (gendered female). The gaze, or vector of desire, can either be complicit (channeled through a character as inscribed beholder), triangulated (putting the cinematographer in cahoots with the audience), or boomerang (exposing the voyeurism of the spectator as such). The structure of viewing that Mulvey identifies has benefited from the insights of the eighteenth-century French philosophes. She clearly refers to a Diderotian 'hermetically sealed' world in which actors are 'indifferent to the presence of the audience.'[64] Her evocation of the contrast between the darkness of the auditorium and the stage lights, which separates the spectators from the actors and from one another, is reminiscent, moreover, of Rousseau's *Lettre à d'Alembert*.[65] Yet Rousseau suggested that music manages to bridge these gaps, transmitting emotion from stage to audience and uniting the spectators in a communal response. Mulvey, like Marshall, confines her discussion to the relationship between spectacle and narrative. In a parenthetical aside she notes, however, that 'the musical song-and-dance numbers interrupt the flow of the diegesis.'[66] Even more vividly than in narrative we are struck by the fact that song-and-dance numbers, while they interrupt, suspend, or freeze narrative progression, are internally dynamic and frequently enable the narrative to make an incremental leap in emotional terms. The cinematographic equivalent of the musical tableaux I propose to analyse is therefore not Eisenstein's shot (of the unmediated, though by no means static variety) but rather the song-and-dance number. Though Diderot originally called for tableaux within the spoken theatre, his *drames*, along with those of his contemporaries Beaumarchais and Sedaine, furnished the libretti for a new vein of *opéra-comique* that proved to be quite popular in Vienna. The lineage of the musical tableau can thus be traced not only through the spoken theatre to experimental film but through the sung theatre and operetta to the modern musical. Its aesthetic structure and affective power can also be observed in films that involve song-and-dance numbers without qualifying as musicals per se. The reader who recalls the sudden release of Tom Ewell's imagination when he hears a passage of Rachmaninoff (or Chopsticks) in *The Seven Year Itch*, the off-beat, bittersweet rapport between Irene Dunne as performer and Cary Grant as beholder in *The Awful Truth*, or the unexpected tear Cher sheds during her night at the opera in *Moonstruck*, will form a more accurate mental image of the subject of my discussion.

PART ONE

Music and Language
La Querelle des Bouffons

1 Diderot and Musical Mimesis

Avant Uremifasolasiututut, personne n'avait distingué les nuances délicates qui séparent le tendre du voluptueux, le voluptueux du passionné, le passionné du lascif: quelques partisans de ce dernier prétendent même que si le dialogue d'Utmiutsol est supérieur au sien, c'est moins à l'inégalité de leurs talents qu'il faut s'en prendre qu'à la différence des poètes qu'ils ont employés ... 'Lisez, lisez, s'écrient-ils, la scène de *Dardanus*, et vous serez convaincu que si l'on donne de bonnes paroles à Uremifasolasiututut, les scènes charmantes d'Utmiutsol renaîtront.'

[Before Uremifasolasiututut, nobody had distinguished the delicate nuances that separate the tender from the voluptuous, the voluptuous from the passionate, the passionate from the lascivious. Some partisans of the latter have even gone so far as to suggest that if the dialogue of Utmiutsol is superior to his, it is less the fault of the inequality of their talents than of the difference between the poets they employed. 'Read, read, they cry, the scene from *Dardanus*, and you will be convinced that if one were to give good words to Uremifasolasiututut, the charming scenes of Utmiutsol would be reborn.']

Diderot, *Les Bijoux indiscrets*

Critical analyses of the *Querelle des Bouffons* tend to lump Denis Diderot somewhat unceremoniously with the proponents of Italian music, based in part upon the side of the opera house on which he chose to sit.[1] Though Diderot sat with his fellow philosophes in the *coin de la reine* – the side of the Parisian Opéra associated with the proponents of Italian music and the foreign queen – his early aesthetic writings indicate that he did not unilaterally endorse the criticism of the French language that

Rousseau levied in his *Lettre sur la musique française*. In a youthful sally taken from *Les Bijoux indiscrets*, Diderot derisively compares the music of the increasingly popular Rameau (Uremifasolasiututut) to that of Lully (Utmiutsol), the pride of France. With the words 'Lisez, lisez ... la scène de *Dardanus*, et vous serez convaincu que si l'on donne de bonnes paroles à Uremifasolasiututut, les scènes charmantes d'Utmiutsol re-naîtront,' he betrays his conviction that the quality of an operatic com-position is determined not by the character of the language but by the quality of the poet.[2] While profoundly aware of the obstacles to artistic expression, Diderot nevertheless managed to preserve his conviction that, given the right artist, such obstacles could be overcome. His faith in the regenerative potential of sign systems set him apart from Rous-seau, who attributed the shortcomings of French music to the French language and deemed the French incapable of improving either. Unlike Rousseau, Diderot was persuaded that the expressive power of sign systems would be enhanced rather than restricted by virtue of their combination. From his early aesthetic treatises through the climactic musical tableau in his posthumously published *Neveu de Rameau*, Dide-rot reiterated his conviction that France would one day give birth to the long-awaited poetic genius and persisted in his experimentation with various means of overcoming the linguistic obstacles that Rousseau identified in his incendiary letter. Diderot's preoccupation with the visual arts and the aesthetics of the theatre, which I explored in the introduction, was thus gradually infused with a curiosity about music, an art that seemed to evade and threatened to overturn the otherwise neatly stacked aesthetic hierarchy. Over the years, Diderot expanded his notion of the relationship between tableau and beholder to accommodate the most elusive of the sister arts by playing upon the mimetic structure of music and superimposing sign systems in his texts.

Diderot began his musings on the interrelation of language and music shortly before the onset of the *Querelle des Bouffons*, responding to Batteux's influential 1747 treatise *Les Beaux-Arts réduits à un même prin-cipe* with a treatise of his own. A close examination of Diderot's 1751 *Lettre sur les sourds et muets* reveals certain key differences between his insights about language and music and those that Rousseau was to espouse not long afterwards. Because he wrote his letter before Rous-seau published his influential texts of the early 1750s, it is relatively free of the cross-pollination of ideas that was to become apparent as the two young friends started to allude to one another's work.[3] In his letter

Diderot reexamines the question of inversions in the French language, a subject that Batteux, Condillac, and the Académie had treated previously. Batteux argued that French is a language of inversions, whereas Latin maintains the natural order of ideas. Accusing Batteux of over-simplification, Diderot considers two different scenarios in order to put Batteux's hypothesis to the test. First, he compares French syntactic order to the order in which the senses naturally receive sensory impressions. Were someone to attempt to identify an object, Diderot observes, his senses would first be struck by the size, shape, and colour of the object. Only then, based upon this information, would he be able to identify what he sees. Accordingly, the description of the object, rendered by adjectives, naturally precedes its identification, represented by a noun. Yet French places the adjective after the noun, and is therefore inverted with respect to the natural order of ideas ('l'ordre naturel').[4] Thus far, Diderot's experiment seems to confirm Batteux's hypothesis. He goes on, however, to imagine what would transpire should the same individual attempt to describe the object in question to someone else, thereby having recourse to language. The quickest means of orienting the listener, he points out, would be to identify the object before describing it, placing the noun before the adjective as occurs in French. Diderot thus concludes that while French is inverted with respect to the natural order of ideas, it conforms perfectly to conversational logic ('l'ordre d'institution').

Diderot's counterargument suggests that the role of language is to mediate not between the object of perception and the beholder but between the beholder and the listener to whom the beholder attempts to describe the object of perception ('la communication de la pensée étant l'objet principal du langage' [the communication of thought being the primary goal of language]).[5] Conversational logic, not original perception, Diderot seems to imply, is the more appropriate frame of reference when gauging a language's efficacy. The French, he concludes, convey their ideas with utmost clarity. Yet Diderot attenuates the force of his conclusion by acknowledging that clarity has come at a price, for French lacks the power of original perception: 'Nous avons gagné à n'avoir point d'inversions, de la netteté, de la clarté, de la précision, qualités essentielles au discours; et ... nous y avons perdu de la chaleur, de l'éloquence et de l'énergie' (By having no inversions we have gained sharpness, clarity, and precision, qualities essential to discourse, but ... we have lost warmth, eloquence, and energy).[6] As the language of common sense and pure reason, French is well suited to science and philosophy, but not to literature and the stage.[7] Diderot notes this loss of energy primarily in written French, for which he holds French authors responsible. French authors had gone too far, he claims, in their progressive refinement of the language, consistently giving preference to a noble over an impassioned figure of speech. Whereas poets, orators, and musicians are still very much attuned to the wealth of linguistic possibilities, modern prose writers have become so disdainful of certain 'lowly' phraseologies that Diderot foresees a time when French, like Chinese, will have separate spoken and written forms.[8]

While Diderot's words carry a strong sense of a crisis of the French language, he did not – and herein lies the fundamental distinction between Diderot's and Rousseau's letters – consider it to be unsalvageable. Instead, he was persuaded that each language could be as expressive as the talent of the writer would allow: 'Entre les mains d'un homme ordinaire, le grec, le latin, l'anglais, l'italien ne produiront que des choses communes; le français produira des miracles sous la plume d'un homme de génie' (In the hands of an ordinary man, Greek, Latin, English, and Italian will only produce commonplaces. French will produce miracles from the pen of a man of genius).[9] While Diderot's account of the loss of energy in written French appears at first glance to anticipate the negative teleology that would become apparent in Rousseau's writings, a positive teleology is in fact at work in the *Lettre sur les sourds et muets*. Unlike Rousseau, Diderot harboured little nostalgia for language's origins. Rather than idealizing initial utterances as the purest expression of human sentiment, he referred to them disparagingly as 'la *balbutie* des premiers âges' (the *babble* of the first ages), consisting of 'un mélange confus de cris et de gestes, mélange qu'on pourrait appeler du nom de langage animal' (a confusing mixture of cries and gestures, a mixture that one might call by the name of animal language). The three stages of linguistic development that he identifies reveal his positive teleological perspective, 'l'état de *naissance*, celui de *formation*, et l'état de *perfection*' (the state of *birth*, that of *education*, and that of *perfection*). This linguistic evolution culminated, he claimed, in French, which bears the fewest traces of the growing pains that tend to accompany early linguistic development.[10] The loss of energy in written French thus results not from the degradation of the language but from its progressive and, indeed, excessive refinement. Like French bread, its ingredients have been purified to such an extent that some of the flavour has been lost. Though French writers had in a sense overshot their mark, their language nevertheless remained at the apex of an evolutionary chain and, according to Diderot, it was not too late to revitalize it.

Diderot's analyses of poetic lines in his letter enhance our sense that despite his dissatisfaction with the current state of written French, he had not lost faith in its expressive potential. In vivid contrast to Rousseau's subsequent claim that the French language lacked lyricism, Diderot provides several examples of how perfectly the meaning of certain words is conveyed through their sonority. Citing a passage from Voltaire's *La Henrïade*, he claims he is able to infer the meaning of one of the words from the sound of its final syllable, saying: 'L'effroi des mers est montré à tout lecteur dans *épouvantées*; mais la prononciation emphatique de sa troisième syllabe me découvre encore leur vaste étendue' (every reader is shown the terror of the seas in *horrified*, but the emphatic pronunciation of the third syllable goes on to reveal their vast expanse). Quoting a line from Boileau's *Le Lutrin*, he savours the presence of onomatopoeia in the language: 'Combien il est heureux pour un poète qui a le *soupir* à peindre, d'avoir dans sa langue un mot dont la première syllabe est sourde, la seconde tenue, et la dernière muette' (How fortunate it is for a poet who must depict a *sigh* to have in his language a word whose first syllable is muted, the second sustained, and the last silent). This appreciation of isolated words (*épouvantées*, *soupir*) extends easily to the scansion of the poetic line, as we can see in the following gloss of the same text:

On lit *étend les bras* ... ces bras étendus retombent si doucement avec le premier hémistiche du vers, que presque personne ne s'en aperçoit, non plus que du mouvement subit de la paupière dans *ferme l'œil*, et du passage imperceptible de la veille au sommeil dans la chute du second hémistiche *ferme l'œil et s'endort*.

[We read *extends his arms* ... These extended arms fall back so gently at the first hemistiche of the verse that almost no one notices. No more than the sudden movement of the eyelid in *closes his eyes* and the imperceptible passage from waking to sleep in the fall of the second hemistiche *closes his eyes and falls asleep.*][11]

Diderot's valorization of French pronunciation and emphasis, his recognition of the poetic value of pronounced and silent syllables alike, and his awareness of the subtle undulations of the poetic line and of its figurative potential, set him apart from his Genevan friend who, shortly thereafter, would attribute the shortcomings of French music to the language's deplorable lack of figures and accentuation.[12]

At this early stage in the development of his aesthetic convictions, Diderot's musical analyses, like his scansion of poetic lines, are strikingly un-Rousseauian. Rather than accuse language of placing an undue constraint upon musical expression, he suggests each art form works within similar constraints, for poetry is allowed to depart from the logic of syntax only for the sake of harmony of style just as music is allowed to depart from the rules of harmony only for the sake of logic of expression.[13] His comparison suggests that a certain reciprocity is possible between the text and the music. Diderot blamed neither language in general nor the French language in particular for the shortcomings of French music. He was rather inclined to attribute the deficiencies of each medium to the sorry lack of contemporary artists to display poetic genius.[14]

Though he remarked that he had begun his musical education just two days prior to writing his *Lettre sur les sourds et muets*, Diderot attempted to go beyond the conventional understanding of the music of his day.[15] The following passage from his letter reveals that he harboured a certain ambivalence towards the mimetic understanding of music which, as James Johnson has argued, was characteristic of mid-century audiences. Simply put, the mimetic understanding of music was a conviction that music imitated nature or the passions. The sentiment produced in the listener was thought to be akin to that which he or she would sustain in the presence of the natural phenomena or the human condition that the music evoked.[16] In his response to Mlle de la Chaux, who wrote asking him to clarify certain passages of his letter, Diderot remarks that the contemporary understanding of how music signifies strikes him as somewhat restrictive:

> La peinture montre l'objet même, la poésie le décrit, la musique en excite à peine une idée. Elle n'a de ressource que dans les intervalles et la durée des sons; et quelle analogie y a-t-il entre cette espèce de crayons, et le printemps, les ténèbres, la solitude, etc. et la plupart des objets? Comment se fait-il donc que des trois arts imitateurs de la nature, celui dont l'expression est la plus arbitraire et la moins précise, parle le plus fortement à l'âme? Serait-ce que montrant moins les objets, il laisse plus de carrière à notre imagination; ou qu'ayant besoin de secousses pour être émus, la musique est plus propre que la peinture et la poésie à produire en nous cet effet tumultueux?

[Painting shows the object itself, poetry describes it, music barely evokes the notion. Its only resources are the intervals and the duration of sounds, and what analogy is there between this sort of pencil and the spring, the dusk, solitude, etc., and most objects? How is it then that of the three arts that imitate nature, the one whose expression is the most arbitrary and the least precise speaks the most forcefully to the soul? Is it that by showing the objects less it gives more leeway to our imagination or that needing to be shaken in order to be moved, music is better suited than painting or poetry to produce this tumultuous effect in us?][17]

Diderot suspects music of disobeying the mimetic rules of painterly reproduction and poetic description, and asks what the length of silences and sounds has to do with the representation of objects. Despite the fact that there is no correlation between the two, or, as he suggests, *because* there is no correlation, music is the most arbitrary and (therefore) the most powerful of the arts.[18] Diderot thus denies that the aesthetic hierarchy should be stacked in favour of mimesis despite (or because of) his inability to account for music's ineffable effect on the listener.

The year after Diderot wrote his *Lettre sur les sourds et muets* the second of the century's three major opera debates erupted.[19] The *Querelle des Bouffons* stands apart from the others by virtue of the central importance the participants accorded to the French language. It ostensibly began when Friedrich Melchior Grimm published his *Lettre sur Omphale* in 1752.[20] Grimm admonished the French for not being able to distinguish between good and bad music and exhorted them to cultivate their national taste. His plea gave rise to a fairly civil exchange concerning the relative merits of French and Italian music but was hardly provocative enough to explain the proportions the debate eventually assumed. The arrival of an Italian troupe that performed Pergolesi's one-act opera buffa entitled *La Serva padrona* during the intermission of Lully's five-act *tragédie en musique, Acis et Galathée,* later that year further defined the terms of the debate by enabling the French to make a direct comparison of the two musical styles.[21] At that point, participants in the debate started to congregate on opposite sides of the opera house – the French sympathizers on the side of the French king and the Italian sympathizers on the side of the foreign queen – thus symbolically enhancing the political overtones of the controversy.[22] The tenor of the exchange nevertheless remained courteous and the arguments even-handed.

Diderot entered the *Querelle des Bouffons* shortly thereafter and was promptly associated with the Italian sympathizers, partially on the strength of his sitting with his fellow philosophes in the *coin de la reine* and partially because he offered a point-by-point rebuttal of an early challenge from the *coin du roi* in his *Arrêt rendu à l'amphithéâtre de l'Opéra*. Soon, however, he became the self-proclaimed arbiter of the quarrels. In his letter addressed *Au petit prophète de Boehmischbroda* of February 1753 he chastized partisans on both sides of the quarrel for their antagonism and their insufficient knowledge of their subject. Proposing to render the terms of the debate more precise, he encouraged the participants to compare a passage from Lully's *Armide* to a similar passage from Tarradellas' *Sésostris* to determine which was more pleasing.[23] He then aptly summed up the salient arguments of the two camps by predicting that they would come to the following conclusion: 'le Musicien de la France doit tout à son Poëte; qu'au contraire le Poëte de l'Italie doit tout à son Musicien' (the French musician owes everything to his poet while the Italian poet owes everything to his musician). Diderot cautioned, however, that he was advocating a comparison of the composers and their music, not of the librettists or their poems. Emphasizing that the French language was not on trial, he intimated that for the French participants in the quarrel to suggest as much would be disloyal to their language and (implicitly) their nation: 'N'allez pas dire que la Musique d'*Armide* est la meilleure qu'on puisse composer sur des paroles Françoises. Loin de défendre notre mélodie ... ce seroit abandonner notre langue' (Do not say that the music of *Armide* is the best that can be composed for French words. Far from defending our melody, [to assume this stance] would be to abandon our language).[24] Diderot wished to impress upon his fellow countrymen that, while they might profitably critique the poetry and music that had been composed to date, they could not pass judgment on the poetry and music that had yet to be written. He thus believed linguistic and musical reform to be both necessary and possible. Diderot's protective stance towards the French language, his refusal to allow it to become a casualty of the quarrel, and his faith in the French capacity for reform set him apart from the critique that Rousseau would soon levy.

Diderot's third contribution to the quarrel reveals that, despite his preference for the *coin de la reine* and his plea of neutrality, he was quite ready to laud a pleasing example of French music if such were to be found. In his parodic *Les Trois chapitres*, written just after the successful debut of Rousseau's *Devin du village* in March of 1753, Diderot essentially refutes the pro-Italian stance that Grimm had expressed in his farcical tale *Le Petit prophète de Boehmischbroda*. In Grimm's tale, the *petit prophète* became so enamoured of Italian music that he could no longer compose French minuets. In Diderot's tale, on the contrary, the *petit prophète* returns to the opera to hear Rousseau's *Devin du village*. Far from finding the work to his distaste, the *petit prophète* wishes he could join the orchestra so as to do the work justice. Diderot derides not the opera but its execution, stating that the Italian singers are better trained than the French and that the talent of the performers, not the music or language, determines the success of the work.[25] He distinguishes between Rousseau's work and the French music that had disappointed the *petit prophète* in Grimm's text: 'Il n'en était pas cette fois comme la pre-mière ... le récitatif était autre chose que les airs; il distingua très bien l'un de l'autre, parce que le musicien les avait distingués, et il en fut tout surpris' (This time was not like the first ... the recitatif differed from the airs, he could easily distinguish the one from the other, for the musician had distinguished between them, and he was quite surprised).[26] The *petit prophète* is impressed by the complementarity of the vocal and musical lines and 'jugea que le musicien devait être content du poète et que le poète devait être content du musicien' (deemed that the musician must be satisfied with the poet and the poet must be satisfied with the musician), calling attention to the unusual fact that poet and composer were, in fact, one and the same.[27] Diderot would later adopt this combination as his ideal for the lyric stage. The *petit prophète*'s admira-tion of Rousseau's opera was neither innocent nor unusual in the context of the *Querelle des Bouffons*, for both the king and the *orchestre de l'Opéra* understood Rousseau's *Devin du village* to be a contribution to the French side of the quarrel, an interpretation they rapidly revoked once he circulated his *Lettre sur la musique française*.[28] Diderot's *Trois chapitres* suggests that he continued to hold out hopes for the future of French music, expressing appreciation of Rousseau's opera before Rousseau showed his true colours.

The innovative final scene of *Les Trois chapitres* indicates that Diderot was already starting to use his writings to experiment with aesthetic recombinations that would enable him to overcome the language/ music divide that Rousseau found so aggravating. Without announcing a return to questions of music and language, Diderot has his narrator witness a pantomime set to music. Only with difficulty does the reader recognize the scene as a pantomime, for the characters appear to be conversing. Yet the narrator reveals in unexpected asides that not the characters but the violins are doing the talking: 'Ils s'écrièrent avec surprise (ou plutôt les violons pour eux, car ils ne faisaient tous que des signes, et c'étaient les violons qui parlaient)' (They protested with surprise [or rather the violins did for them, for they did nothing but make signs and the violins did the talking]). Though at times it seems that the 'conversation' between the violins is simply a metaphor for the musical question-response that characterizes the minuet, at others the violins appear to be capable of imparting information to the listeners, particularly when the narrator implies that they can corroborate his story: 'Et cela est vrai, car les violons me le dirent' (And that's the truth, for the violins told me so).[29] Diderot plays upon the fact that the orchestra is meant to convey and, indeed, enhance the characters' emotions: 'Et Colette pleura sur ses bonnes amies, et ses bonnes amies pleuraient sur elle, et les violons pleurèrent aussi' (And Colette cried over her good friends, and her good friends cried over her, and the violins cried too), once again alluding to the capacity of instruments to imitate human or natural sounds and making it impossible to determine whether the violins are on stage or in the pit.[30] Parodic though his vision may be, by the end of it Diderot seems to suggest that the combination of music and pantomime may be as or even more effective than 'la pantomime réunie au discours' (pantomime united with speech), which he would subsequently propose as a means of rendering the French language more expressive.

The *Querelle des Bouffons* would, in all likelihood, have died down not long after Diderot's attempts to mediate the dispute, had it not been for Rousseau's sudden decision to publish his *Lettre sur la musique française*. Diderot's efforts to divert the focus of the opera quarrels from language to music were effectively countermanded when Rousseau staged his direct assault on the French language itself. Rousseau's argument was, in short, that national music takes its character from the national language, that the French language is not propitious to a musical setting, and that the French can therefore have no music. Among the shortcomings he attributed to the language were the abundance of consonants and mute or nasal sounds, the paucity of open vowels, and the irregularity of syllables. This combination of elements, he argued, rendered it impossible for the French to produce either melody or rhythm.[31] Rousseau attributed the capacity to produce melody and rhythm to the Italians, who possessed, he claimed, the most musical of the European tongues. If one considers the three volumes of collected letters from the quarrel, the disproportionate response that Rousseau's missive elicited is astonishing. Though he released his *Lettre sur la musique française* in the final year of the quarrel (purportedly to lighten his briefcase), a full two-thirds of the letters were written to rebut his claims.[32] The tone of the letters changed, furthermore, from one of gentle irony to a virulence that matched his own. According to Rousseau's *Confessions*, it was at this point that the controversy reached the level of a national crisis, a claim that, according to Servando Sacaluga, was scarcely exaggerated.[33] The king revoked the offer of a pension he had tendered after the first performance of Rousseau's *Devin du village* and very nearly replaced it with a *lettre de cachet*. The *orchestre de l'Opéra* stopped rehearsing the work and elected to burn it instead. Various explanations have been offered for the proportions that the *Querelle* eventually assumed. Sacaluga attributes the sudden conflagration to the efforts of the king and his mistress to divert attention from parliamentary discord, Johnson to the fear of an ultramontane conspiracy that threatened church and state alike, and Robert Wokler to the apprehension that the debates would have revolutionary consequences.[34] The weight of the evidence suggests, however, that the participants in the debates were particularly sensitive to the content of Rousseau's letter itself.

The *Querelle des Bouffons* was and is considered to be a debate about French and Italian music. Had Rousseau confined his statements to music alone, however, the repercussions would have been limited and the resistance slight, for many of those who wrote in opposition to Rousseau's letter conceded that French music stood in need of reform. Instead, Rousseau attributed the shortcomings of national music to the national language, stating that 'toute Musique Nationnale tire son principal caractére de la langue qui lui est propre' (every national music derives its principal character from its own language).[35] The French immediately grasped the implications of his argument, for if Rousseau's claims were founded and the French language were lacking, then not only French music, but French theatre, French literature, and France's cultural hegemony over Europe stood to suffer. One of the participants in the debate summed up the general perception of Rousseau's letter by mistakenly – though accurately – referring to it as his 'Lettre contre la Langue & la Musique Françoise' (Letter against the French Language and Music).[36] Another predicted that his letter would have an alarming series of repercussions, stating with irony: 'Mon Discoureur éternel se borne, par une modération sans éxemple, & bien digne de la Philosophie, à vouloir anéantir seulement le goût, la Musique, l'Opera, la Poësie, & la Langue Française, pour faire la place nette au triomphe d'Italie' (My eternal discursor restricts himself, with exemplary moderation that is worthy of philosophy, to wanting to annihilate taste, music, opera, poetry, and the French language, to make way for the triumph of Italy).[37] Aware that the implications were especially grave insofar as their authors were concerned, the French asked: 'Si la langue Françoise n'avoit ni douceur, ni harmonie, où en seroient nos Poëtes? Comment viendroient-ils à bout de faire des Vers? Notre Censeur voudroit-il nous rendre encore la versification impossible?' (If the French language were neither sweet nor harmonious where would our poets be? How would they manage to write verses? Does our censor wish to go so far as to render versification impossible?).[38] While the participants were ready to concede that French music could stand some improvement, all but a few of them dismissed Rousseau's critique of the French language out of hand. Willing to grant Italy the laurels for possessing a music of international appeal, the French refused to relinquish the distinction they themselves had acquired for possessing the international language.

Feeling that they had been disgraced as a nation, the partisans of French music united against the foreign threat which, as the wording of their ripostes makes plain, was perceived to be not Italy but Rousseau.[39] The unilateral nature of the Parisian reaction was a response not only to the parallel Rousseau drew between music and language, but also to his association of music and language with the concept of nation. That language was one of the defining features of a nation was fairly well established. It appears in the definition of nation provided by the dictionary of the Académie Française in the 1694, 1740, and 1762 editions: 'constituée par tous les habitants d'un même Etat, d'un même pays, qui vivent sous les mêmes lois et usent du même langage' (constituted by all the inhabitants of the same nation, of the same country, who live under the same laws and use the same language).[40] The association between language and nation would be reaffirmed shortly thereafter in the *Encyclopédie*'s definition of 'langue' as the '[t]otalité des usages propres à une nation pour exprimer ses pensées par la voix' (totality of usages that belong to a nation to express its thoughts with the voice).[41] The idea that *music* might be a defining feature of a nation, however, was just starting to emerge and is more rightly associated with the birth of the German and Italian nations in the nineteenth century.

By making the musical debate a matter of national pride, Rousseau catalyzed what can only be described as a united national stance. His letter was denounced as libellous and his correspondents remarked, gravely, that 'les Nations n'aiment pas à se voir ainsi dégrader' [sic] (nations do not like to see themselves thus degraded).[42] Calling Rousseau the 'Quixote of Geneva,' the French wondered aloud *when*, precisely, the Parisians had begun to hail Lake Geneva as the source of good taste.[43] Less cattily but more vituperatively, one participant asked, 'Comment ose-t-il ... s'associer à notre Nation pour l'insulter? Il dit, partout, *notre Nation, notre Musique, notre Langue*. Depuis quand se croit-il naturalisé parmi nous, & à quel titre auroit-il mérité de l'être?' (How dare he ... associate himself with our nation in order to insult it. He keeps saying our nation, our music, our language. Since when does he consider himself to be naturalized and by what right does he deserve to be?).[44] Rousseau thus infused what started out as an aesthetic controversy with a particular brand of national spirit.[45] Though France's position in Europe would not be seriously threatened until the next century, it was nonetheless briefly challenged in the context of the *Querelle*.[46] The French, who would claim Rousseau as the father of their nation in the thick of the Revolution, collectively disowned him in 1753, attributing the perceived problems with the pronunciation of their language to the fact that one of its critics was German and the other Swiss.[47] As one participant put it, speaking on behalf of his fellow countrymen:

Si M. R. n'en vouloit même qu'à la Musique, encore pourroit-on de sa petite humeur un peu chagrine se faire un rehaut de plaisir & de satisfaction ... Mais il en veut tout de bon, & très-sérieusement à la Musique Françoise, comme Françoise; & en fait de querelle de Nation, il ne doit pas être surpris de voir que tout Citoyen, tout sujet est Soldat.

[If Mr R. had something against music alone we might derive some pleasure and satisfaction from his bad mood ... But he has, quite seriously, something against French music as French and in matters of national disputes, he should not be surprised to see that every citizen, every subject, is a soldier.][48]

Diderot neither responded directly to Rousseau's letter, nor did he take further part in the *Querelle des Bouffons*. It is clear that he read Rousseau's letter, however, for he borrowed its terminology when writing his *Entretiens sur le Fils naturel* some five years later. Reiterating the complaint that written French had lost its energy, which he had previously voiced in his *Lettre sur les sourds et muets*, Diderot has Dorval wonder aloud when this gradual restriction of the written language will end: 'Le théâtre français attendra-t-il ... que son dictionnaire soit aussi borné que le dictionnaire du théâtre lyrique, et que le nombre des expressions honnêtes soit égal à celui des expressions musicales?' (Will the French theatre wait for its dictionary to be as limited as that of the lyric theatre and for the number of honest expressions to equal the musical expressions?).[49] Here, Diderot's allusion to the passage from Rousseau's letter in which he makes reference to the 'très-petit nombre de mots sonores que notre langue peut fournir' (the very small number of sonorous words that our language can furnish), is unmistakable.[50] Yet the obstacle to the successful composition of French opera, as Diderot perceived it, lay not in the range of vocabulary available to librettists, but in the limited range of vocabulary that librettists typically chose. Lully may have been capable of greater things, Dorval ventures, had he not been held back by Quinault's choice of subject: 'Il n'a manqué à [Lulli] que des poèmes d'un autre genre' (The only thing that [Lully] lacked was poems of another genre).[51] Diderot takes issue, moreover, with the common choice of subject for French operas, expressing astonishment that anyone could expect the lyric theatre to live up to its potential if the plots are based on fables alone. Tragedies, with the range of expression used by a Racine, not a Quinault, are required. The range of vocabulary and the power of individual words would thus dramatically increase. Citing a passage from *Iphégenie*, Dorval triumphantly proclaims:

> Voici un ... morceau ... où il n'y a ni *lance*, ni *victoire*, ni *tonnerre*, ni *vol*, ni *gloire*, ni aucune de ces expressions qui feront le tourment d'un poète tant qu'elles seront l'unique et pauvre ressource du musicien ...
>
> *Non, je ne l'aurai point amenée au supplice ... Non ... ni crainte, ni respect ne peut m'en détacher... Non ... barbare époux ... impitoyable père ... venez la ravir à sa mère ... venez, si vous l'osez ...* Voilà les idées principales qui occupaient l'âme de Clytemnestre, et qui occuperont le génie du musicien.

> [Here is a ... piece ... in which there was neither *cast* nor *victory* nor *thunder* nor *flight* nor *glory*, nor any of the expressions that will continue to torment the poet as long as they are the unique and poor resource of the musician ...
>
> *No, I would not have subjected her to torture ... No ... neither fear nor respect can separate me from her ... No ... barbarous husband ... pitiless father ... come steal her from her mother ... come, if you dare ...* Here are the main ideas that occupied Clytemnestra's soul and that will occupy the genius of the musician.][52]

Diderot's perusal of Rousseau's letter had thus by no means convinced him that French music was either nonexistent or an oxymoron. As Dorval remarks, 'Si le genre lyrique est mauvais, c'est le plus mauvais de tous les genres. S'il est bon, c'est le meilleur' (If the lyric genre is bad it is the worst of all the genres. If it is good, it is the best). Diderot recognized the hazards of composing opera, yet believed they could be overcome. His criticism was reserved for the actual rather than the potential state of the lyric theatre. Because opera requires a synthesis of several art forms – each an apposite imitation of nature in its own right – its successful composition requires particular skill. Instead of despairing of finding an artist capable of achieving such a synthesis Dorval becomes downright messianic in his phraseology:

> Un sage était autrefois un philosophe, un poète, un musicien. Ces talents ont dégénéré en se séparant ... Un grand musicien et un grand poète lyrique répareraient tout le mal.
>
> Voilà donc encore une carrière à remplir. Qu'il se montre, cet homme de génie qui doit placer la véritable tragédie, la véritable comédie sur le théâtre lyrique. Qu'il s'écrie, comme le prophète du peuple hébreu dans son enthousiasme: *Adducite mihi psaltem*, 'qu'on m'amène un musicien', et il le fera naître.

> [Formerly, the wise man was a philosopher, a poet, a musician. These talents degenerated once separated ... A great musician and a great lyric poet would make up for it.
>
> Here, then, is another prospective career. Let him make his presence known, this genius who will place true tragedy, true comedy, on the stage of the lyric theatre. Let him exclaim, like the prophet of the Hebrew people in his enthusiasm, *Adducite mihi psaltem*, 'Bring me a musician,' and he will be brought to life.][53]

Prior to the circulation of the *Lettre sur la musique française*, the *petit prophète* was persuaded that Rousseau himself was such an artist. Five years later, however, Dorval intimated that such an artist was yet to come. Though Diderot's characters can by no means be considered his *porte-paroles*, the underlying suggestion remains that in the wake of Rousseau's attack Diderot maintained his faith in reform but lost his faith in the reformer.

Diderot had started to work on his own program of reform for the lyric theatre as early as his *Lettre sur les sourds et muets* by envisioning various ways of synthesizing language and music. The mid-century tendency to compare music to language stemmed in part from the fact that both sign systems signified sequentially rather than simultaneously. Rousseau was convinced that therein lay their chief virtue.[54] Diderot, on the contrary, harboured an ideal of simultaneity towards which artists who used language and music as their primary means of expression were meant to strive.[55] Three models of his ideal of simultaneity are apparent in his *Lettre sur les sourds et muets* alone: the 'clavecin oculaire,' the 'hiéroglyphe,' and the 'tableau.' Language, Diderot claimed, would benefit from being modelled more closely on a contemporary invention known as the 'clavecin oculaire' (harpsichord for the eyes). The harpsichord, whose existence Père Castel postulated in his *Optique des couleurs* of 1740, allowed the 'musician' to play a concert in colour rather than sound. Unable to grasp the true purpose of the instrument, the 'sourd de naissance' (born-deaf) to whom Diderot imagines showing the instrument at first presumes that each colour represents a letter of the alphabet, allowing the musician to compose sentences. Struck by this notion, Diderot speculates what it would be like if the instrument could render language simultaneous by giving voice to several concepts at once: 'chaque bouche disant son mot, toutes les idées ... seraient rendues à la fois' (each mouth having its word to say, all ideas ... would be rendered at once), and proposes this model as a linguistic ideal, stating that '[a]ucune langue n'approcherait de la rapidité de celle-ci' (no language would approach the rapidity of this one).[56] He is even more impressed, however, by the second analogy that occurs to his friend. Upon seeing the harpsichord reproduce visually what he cannot hear, the 'sourd de naissance' believes he has finally grasped the nature of music.[57] While Diderot concedes that his friend's understanding of music as an alternate system of communication is a far cry from reality, he nonetheless recognizes that his friend has hit upon a sort of musical ideal, akin to his own ideal of language: 'S'il ne rencontra pas exactement ce que c'était [que notre musique], il rencontra presque ce que ce devrait être' (If he did not fully understand what [our music] was, he almost grasped what it should be).[58] Père Castel's vision of simultaneity of colour thus gives rise to the possibility of a linguistic or musical equivalent in Diderot's text.

Diderot's second model of linguistic simultaneity, the hieroglyph, hearkens back to, yet outstrips, the rhetorical notion of hypotyposis, which Angelica Goodden defines as 'a description rendered in language so vivid that the speaker seems to paint, and the listener to see, the scene described.'[59] The hieroglyph is defined as that which transforms everyday conversation into poetic expression. The poet's muse renders him capable of both speech and representation; of addressing the mind, the soul, and the imagination of the listener at once. In such moments, Diderot claims, sequentiality is replaced with simultaneity and poetry becomes emblematic.[60] The hieroglyph is also defined as that which defies translation.[61] It consists of the resonances (or overtones) that are audible only to a native speaker, and one of remarkable taste and sensitivity at that, for all is lost on the 'ordinary reader.'[62] Reversing our common understanding of the hieroglyph as a pictograph that requires not one but a series of words to convey its meaning, Diderot uses the term to refer to a series of words (or musical notes) that call an image to mind. This ideal of simultaneity applies not to language alone, however, but to music, painting, and pantomime, '[t]out art d'imitation ayant ses hiéroglyphes particuliers' (every art of imitation having its own hieroglyphs).[63] Challenging Batteux to distinguish between the hieroglyphs employed by language, music, and painting, Diderot proceeds to compare them himself, concluding from his experiment: 'C'est la chose même que le peintre montre; les expressions du musicien et du poète n'en sont que des hiéroglyphes' (The painter shows the thing itself of which the expressions of the musician and the poet are but hieroglyphs).[64] Even the hieroglyph, then, remains at a somewhat unsatisfactory remove from the ideal simultaneity of the tableau itself.

The tableau stands apart from Diderot's other metaphorical models, for it is used not to approximate but rather to incarnate his ideal. In the following oft-cited passage from the *Lettre sur les sourds et muets*, Diderot explains that the mimetic arts are meant to recreate, insofar as possible, the simultaneity of the artist's original vision:

Notre âme est un tableau mouvant d'après lequel nous peignons sans cesse: nous employons bien du temps à le rendre avec fidélité; mais il existe en entier et tout à la fois: l'esprit ne va pas à pas comptés comme l'expression. Le pinceau n'exécute qu'à la longue ce que l'œil du peintre embrasse tout d'un coup. La formation des langues exigeait la décomposition; mais *voir* un objet, le *juger* beau, *éprouver* une sensation agréable, *désirer* la possession, c'est l'état de l'âme dans un même instant.

[Our soul is a moving tableau which we constantly strive to reproduce. We consecrate a great deal of time to its faithful rendering, but it exists entirely and of a piece; the mind does not go step by step as does expression. The brush takes time to execute that which the painter's eye takes in at a glance. The creation of language required decomposition, but *to see* an object, *to judge* it beautiful, *to feel* an agreeable sensation, and *to desire its possession*, is the state of the soul in a single instant.][65]

Diderot thus chooses to liken the simultaneity of the artist's original vision neither to the 'clavecin oculaire' nor to the hieroglyph but to the tableau – a tableau 'mouvant,' it should be noted, and not the static version to which critics frequently allude.[66] The 'clavecin oculaire' and the hieroglyph thus merely emulate the ideal that the tableau embodies. Diderot sustained the hope of finding a medium of expression that would enable artists to reconstitute the unity of their original vision throughout his subsequent writings. As we have seen, he attempted the union of music and pantomime in the conclusion to his *Trois chapitres* of 1753. He expressed faith in the notion of 'la pantomime réunie au discours' (pantomime united with discourse) in his *Entretiens sur le Fils naturel* of 1758.[67] Later that year, in *De la poésie dramatique*, he suggested a certain equivalence between his notion of pantomime and the artist's vision: 'La pantomime est le tableau qui existait dans l'imagination du poète, lorsqu'il écrivait' (Pantomime is the tableau that existed in the poet's imagination as he wrote).[68] Ultimately, Diderot would attempt to realize his ideal of simultaneity by uniting music, language, and gesture in 'la pantomime de l'homme-orchestre' (the pantomime of the one-man-band) of *Le Neveu de Rameau*, his posthumous masterpiece to which I now turn.

Le Neveu de Rameau is without a doubt the work in which Diderot's musings on aesthetic theory had the greatest impact on textual form.[69] The pantomime of music is one of the most singular and perhaps the most counterintuitive of Diderot's aesthetic innovations. Why, one might ask, would he choose to convey a primarily sonorous medium via a primarily silent one? And yet the notion of conveying music via the text is already paradoxical, and requires, in some sense, a paradoxical solution.[70] Though Diderot seems to accord equal importance to music and gesture in this unlikely combination, each has previously been underrated in critical studies. John Neubauer makes the startling assertion that Rameau's nephew 'creates no genuine music and his performance often sinks to the level of pantomime.'[71] He thus radically underestimates the importance of pantomime in Diderot's aesthetics, overlooking such recommendations as that drawn from *Les Entretiens sur le Fils naturel*, in which Dorval states: 'Il faut s'occuper fortement de la pantomime; laisser là ces coups de théâtre dont l'effet est momentané, et trouver des tableaux' (We must preoccupy ourselves with pantomime, abandon coups de théâtre, whose effect is but short-lived, and find tableaux).[72] Such passages attest to Diderot's conviction that pantomime would help restore some of the lost vigour of expression to written French and that the tableau and pantomime alike would bring us closer to his ideal of simultaneity and immediacy of expression. In the introduction to his highly accredited edition of Le Neveu de Rameau, Jean Fabre offhandedly dismisses the musical passages in the text: 'Il existe dans l'œuvre des zones anciennes, conservées telles quelles, et d'où la vie s'est retirée. La plus grande partie des développements sur la musique, par exemple, ou du moins sur l'opéra' (Some dated, lifeless passages can be found in the work, conserved in their original state. Most of the excurses on music, for instance, or at least on opera). He further insists that 'tout ne représente guère que la liquidation de ce que Diderot avait à dire, lors de la Querelle des Bouffons où, au fond, il n'avait pas grand'chose à dire' (it is but the liquidation of what Diderot had to say during the Querelle des Bouffons, when he basically did not have much to say).[73] I have argued that Diderot's contributions to the Querelle constituted a significant point of departure from and source of resistance to Rousseau's attack on the French language. In the following pages I will demonstrate not only that the life has by no means ebbed from the musical passages in Diderot's text but that these passages were designed to restore life to the French language. My argument is in keeping with a large body of astute analyses of the music and pantomime in the Neveu de Rameau. Others have long since drawn attention to the musical passages in Diderot's philosophical dialogue, tracking down the sources of the musical references that the Nephew seamlessly weaves together and deducing from the multiplicity of nationalities and genres he intersperses that Diderot's musical ideal lay in their combination. Yet breaking the Nephew's most extended musical pantomime and the monologue it accompanies down into its successive stages reveals a gradual progression in the Nephew's discourse on music and language and a gradual transformation in the object of his imitation. Remaining attuned to the affective response of the beholder I will pinpoint *when*, precisely, Diderot (or the Nephew) manages to penetrate the layers of mediation that separate the object of mimesis, the performer, and the beholder so as to express music via the text.

Before addressing Diderot's extended 'pantomime de l'homme-orchestre' we must examine (by way of contrast) two earlier examples of musical pantomime in the text. The two examples occur in rapid succession. In the first the Nephew takes up an imaginary violin and in the second, seats himself at an invisible harpsichord, rendering music that is almost recognizable, so perfectly do his limbs adopt the musician's positions and his facial expressions convey the successive emotions that the pieces inspire. Far from being penetrated with the performer's emotion, however, in the first example Moi is filled with a vivid sense of the pain that the violinist's exertions occasion in him. The Philosopher perceives, but does not feel, the emotions that the music is meant to inspire, and is soon distracted by a peculiarity of the Nephew's playing. The Nephew occasionally interrupts his performance on the violin in order to tune it: 'S'il fait un ton faux, il s'arrete; il remonte ou baisse la corde; il la pince de l'ongle pour s'assurer qu'elle est juste; il reprend le morceau la où il l'a laissé' (If he plays out of tune he stops and adjusts the peg, tries the string with his thumb and takes up the piece where he left off). Similarly, once the Nephew is seated before the harpsichord, the Philosopher remarks that 'ce qu'il y avoit de bizarre; c'est que de tems en tems, il tatonnoit; se reprenoit, comme s'il eut manqué et se depitoit de n'avoir plus la piece dans les doigts' (what was strangest was that every so often he would stumble and grope around, as if making a mistake and being annoyed at his fingers' forgetfulness).[74] The Nephew's imperfect rendering of the score is, in exchange, a perfect rendering of a typical performance, and thus gives him away. Rather than pantomiming music per se the Nephew pantomimes a musical performance, beset with the difficulties and errors to which such performances are prone. Whereas a pantomime of music might be expected to move the beholder, a pantomime of a musical performance would do nothing of the kind for the bodily contortions of singers and musicians were a subject of mockery in the eighteenth century, and this is no exception. Sure enough, the Nephew's antics do not disrupt the conversation. Though Lui is sweating profusely, he maintains the utmost presence of mind. His mental state, indeed, resembles that of the gifted actor, as Diderot describes it in his *Paradoxe sur le comédien*: 'Moi, je lui veux beaucoup de jugement; il me faut dans cet homme un spectateur froid et tranquille; j'en exige, par conséquent, de la pénétration et nulle sensibilité, l'art de tout imiter, ou, ce qui revient au même, une égale aptitude à toutes sortes de caractères et de rôles' (Personally, I want him to have good judgment, I want this man to be a cold and tranquil spectator. I require, therefore, discernment without sensitivity, a gift for imitation or, what amounts to the same thing, an equal aptitude for all kinds of characters and roles).[75] The Nephew's complete control, and the emotional distance he maintains from the characters he assumes, allows him to play a hundred different roles in rapid succession, never for a moment becoming personally affected by one of the states that he imitates to perfection. The Philosopher remains equally unperturbed, expressing neither excessive admiration nor excessive dismay. Though these pantomimes of the musician interrupt the dialogue, obliging us to watch the Nephew's antics through the Philosopher's eyes, they do little more than stimulate our intellectual appreciation of the Nephew's versatility. By imitating a flawed performance, the Nephew forestalls the Philosopher's emotional investment in the spectacle before him, thereby ensuring the tableau's failure.

For a successful tableau we are obliged to await the 'pantomime de l'homme-orchestre,' as it has come to be called, yet this pantomime surges forth from an extended discourse on music that must be broken down before it can be followed. Contrary to Fabre's dismissal of the passage as uniform and outdated, the Nephew's discourse can be subdivided into the different stages of eighteenth-century debate starting from the *Querelle des Bouffons* but moving in the direction of an idealized future that the Nephew can only postulate. The Nephew's views run the gamut, in the course of his monologue, from conventional to revolutionary. His point of departure is, indeed, the musical discourse of the early 1750s, for he furnishes a definition of musical mimesis that he claims is equally applicable to the other arts:

> Le chant est une imitation, par les sons d'une echelle inventée par l'art ou inspirée par la nature, comme il vous plaira, ou par la voix ou par l'instrument, des bruits physiques ou des accents de la passion; et vous voyez qu'en changeant la dedans, les choses à changer, la définition conviendroit exactement a la peinture, a l'éloquence, a la sculpture, et a la poesie.

> [A melody is a vocal or instrumental imitation using the sounds of a scale invented by art – or inspired by nature, as you prefer; it imitates either physical noises or the accents of passion. You can see that by changing a few words in this definition it would exactly fit painting, eloquence, sculpture or poetry.][76]

The Nephew's assertion that mimetic representation is the underlying principle of all art forms is more reminiscent of Batteux than Diderot, who casts doubt upon this conviction as early as his *Lettre à Mlle de la*

Chaux, yet his reminder of the definition of imitation is of capital importance for what ensues. The Nephew's observation that 'Quand on entend, *Je suis un pauvre diable*, on croit reconnoitre la plainte d'un avare' (When one hears 'I am but a poor wretch' one recognizes the complaint of a miser) and 'vous me direz ... quelle difference il y a, entre les vraies voyes d'un moribond et le tour de ce chant' (tell me what difference exists between the form of this air and the ways of the dying) is thus perfectly in keeping with Johnson's description of mid-eighteenth-century audiences' mimetic understanding of music.[77] He goes on, moreover, to recap both sides of the opera debate. First he defends the Italian side: 'Il n'y a rien de plus evident que le passage suivant que j'ai lu quelque part ... L'accent est la pepiniere de la melodie' (Nothing is more self-evident than the maxim I read somewhere ... accent is the source of melody). Where would he have read such a thing, we might ask, if not in Rousseau's *Lettre sur la musique française*? Then he defends the French side: 'Ma foi, ces maudits bouffons, avec leur *Servante maitresse*, leur *Tracollo*, nous en ont donné rudement dans le cu' (Yes, these confounded bouffons with their *Serva padrona* and their *Tracollo* have given us a stout kick in the butt).[78]

Thus far the Nephew has done little more than recapitulate the prevalent positions on music of the previous ten years. He soon launches into the political repercussions of the nation's position, however, going somewhat beyond the statements Diderot was prepared to make at the time of the quarrels.[79] Confessing to the Philosopher that, truth be told, the French are secretly disenchanted with their music ('Baillez donc, messieurs; baillez' [Go ahead, gentlemen, yawn away]), he attests to a nationwide shift in taste. Scoffing at the notion that once the French had developed a taste for Italian music they could be expected to make do with their accustomed fare, he foretells the consequences of consorting with foreigners: 'Le dieu etranger se place humblement a coté de l'idole du pais; peu a peu, il s'y affermit; un beau jour il pousse du coude son camarade; et patatras, voila l'idole en bas ... cette methode politique qui marche a son but, sans bruit, sans effusion de sang, sans martyr, sans un toupet de cheveux arraché, me semble la meilleure' (The foreign god takes his place humbly next to the native idol, little by little asserts itself, and one fine day elbows out his fellow – before you can say Jack Robinson, there's the idol on its back ... the political method that aims quietly and directly at the goal, without bloodshed, martyrdom, or so much as a queue of hair cut off, is obviously the best).[80] Though the Nephew does not condemn this subtle form of political subversion, his words nevertheless suggest that Diderot had thought through the political implications of the French preference for Italian music. By blending French with Italian lyrics, and vocal with instrumental music each time he breaks into song, the Nephew implies that Europeans must learn to transcend such factionalism before they can hope to be musically innovative.[81]

The Nephew goes on to predict that the Italians will leave their indelible mark on French music. His analysis of the accentuation of the Italian language, his explanation of the word 'chant,' and his account of music's ability to render silence can, moreover, be traced directly to Rousseau's writings.[82] Yet his predictions concerning the future of the French language are not in the least Rousseauian. Echoing Dorval, Rameau's Nephew is inclined to speak on Lully's behalf: 'Qu'on fasse mieux la scene, *Ah! j'attendrai* sans changer les paroles; j'en defie' (Let anyone try a better setting of the scene 'I await the dawn' without changing the words: it can't be done). He thus reiterates the common view that Lully had done the best he could given the poems Quinault had provided. His implicit contention is that the poetic line must evolve before the musical line can do so. The Nephew then becomes messianic in turn:

Il ne faut pas mepriser quelques endroits de Campra, les airs de violon de mon oncle, ses gavotes; ses entrées de soldats, de pretres, de sacrificateurs ... Mais avant peu, serviteur a l'Assomption; le careme et les Roix sont passés. Ils ne scavent pas encore ce qu'il faut mettre en musique, ni par consequent ce qui convient au musicien. La poesie lyrique est encore a naitre. Mais ils y viendront.

[Nor must you despise certain pieces by Campra, or my uncle's works for violin, his gavottes, his military and religious processions ... But, before long, good-by to *L'Assomption*, *Le Carême* and *Les Rois*. They don't as yet know what to choose for setting to music, that is, what will suit a composer. True lyric poetry has yet to be born. But they'll catch on.][83]

Fabre suggests that the words 'serviteur a l'Assomption; le careme et les Roix sont passés' should be interpreted to mean 'la musique française a fait son temps, qu'elle est bien morte' (French music has had its day, it is dead and gone).[84] Yet the Nephew refers not to French music as a whole, but to the French tradition of heralding saviours and kings. He thus predicts that the pomp of religious and regal themes will soon be outdated, making way for the domestic scenes that Dorval describes in the *Entretiens*, which were beginning to constitute the new aesthetic of the French *opéra-comique*. Rameau's Nephew says neither that French music is dead, nor, for that matter, that French poetry cannot be improved, nor that either one of them should cede the laurels for lyricism to the Italians. Instead, he insists that while it may be harder for the French to come up with a viable lyric line, given the intransigence of the language, they can do so if they keep their phrases short, suspend their meaning, and grant the musician the poetic license to omit, repeat, add, or contort any word that he chooses.[85] The Nephew expresses surprise that the French did not discover for themselves that the simpler and more passionate the vocal line, the closer it will resemble declamation:

> Quiconque avoit ecouté ... une Passion, n'importe laquelle, pourvu que par son energie, elle meritât de servir de modele au musicien, auroit du s'apercevoir de deux choses: l'une que les sillabes, longues ou breves, n'ont aucune durée fixe, pas meme de rapport determiné entre leurs durées; que la passion dispose de la prosodie, presque comme il lui plait.

> [All you had to do was to listen to ... any Passion whatever, provided it is energetic enough to supply the musician with a pattern. You would then have noticed two things: one, that long and short syllables have no fixed values, not even a fixed relation between them; and two, that passion rules over prosody almost at will.][86]

Here the Nephew directly counters Rousseau's contention that the French cannot have any music because the syllables in the French language are of indeterminate length. On the contrary, passion naturally distorts the length of the syllables, the Nephew claims. Consequently, each language should serve as an equally viable vehicle of emotion. There is therefore no indication throughout Diderot's fictional dialogue that he had altered his original conviction, in light of Rousseau's argument to the contrary, that the French language, and therefore French music, were salvageable.[87]

In the midst of his exposition on French language and music the Nephew breaks into the 'pantomime de l'homme-orchestre.' The critical tendency is to treat this pantomime, like the discourse that it accompanies, as an entity, and yet by breaking it down into stages we can more fully appreciate Diderot's technique of playing upon the structure of mimesis and superimposing sign systems.[88] At this point the stage is set for the creation of a musical tableau, for the Philosopher is watching and describing the Nephew's performance, which momentarily suspends the forward-moving momentum of their dialogue. This time, however, the tableau is dynamic, revealing both an internal progression and an emotional breakthrough. Diderot makes the reader aware of the resistance, the near-impenetrability, of the layers of mediation (music, the instrument, the instrumentalist, the ear) that separate the beholder from the object of imitation by creating an intermittent tableau that first approaches, then backs away from, but ultimately attains its goal. At first glance, the 'pantomime de l'homme-orchestre' resembles the pantomimes of musical performance described above. As the Nephew impersonates the characters on stage and their vocal inflections – 'il est pretre, il est roi, il est tyran, il menace, il commande, il s'emporte; il est esclave, il obeit. Il s'apaise, il se desole, il se plaint, il rit; jamais hors de ton, de mesure, du sens des paroles et du caractere de l'air' (he is a priest, a king, a tyrant; he threatens, commands, rages. Now he is a slave, he obeys, calms down, is heartbroken, complains, laughs; never overstepping the proper tone, speech, or manner called for by the part) – he provokes raucous laughter among the onlookers. Once he starts to weave together the musical and lyric lines of the *Lamentations* of Jomelli, however, two things occur that bring us closer to the creation of a musical tableau. First, the Philosopher remarks that the Nephew is losing his critical detachment: 'Lui n'apercevoit rien; il continuoit, saisi d'une alienation d'esprit, d'un enthousiasme si voisin de la folie, qu'il est incertain qu'il en revienne' (He noticed nothing, he kept on, in the grip of mental possession, an enthusiasm so close to madness that it seemed doubtful whether he would recover). The Nephew is no longer the aloof actor, whose mind coolly dictates his actions, dissociating them from his emotions. Then, as the Nephew sings the passage from the *Lamentations*, the Philosopher observes that 'il l'arrosa d'un torrent de larmes qui en arracherent a tous les yeux' (he drenched [it] in tears which drew their like from every onlooker).[89] So beautiful is the Nephew's rendition of the music, so moving the spectacle of his emotion, that he manages to bypass the Philosopher's senses and move him to tears. The Philosopher, indeed, goes so far as to suggest that the Nephew has taken possession of the onlookers' souls, 's'emparant de nos ames, et les tenant suspendues dans la situtation la plus singuliere que j'aie jamais eprouvée' (gripping our souls and keeping them suspended in the most singular state of being that I have ever experienced). Yet the sensation that accompanies the Philosopher's reaction remains that of the 'spectateur dédoublé' (doubled spectator) who simultaneously empathizes with and criticizes the characters' plight on stage, as the following exclamation reveals: 'Admirois-je? Oui, j'admirois! etois-je touché de pitié? j'etois touché de pitié; mais une teinte de ridicule etoit fondue dans ces sentiments, et les denaturoit' (Did I admire? Yes, I did admire. Was I moved to pity? I was moved. But a streak of derision was interwoven with these feelings and denatured them).[90] Thus, while the critical detachment that separates the Philosopher from the Nephew has started to slip, it has not yet entirely dissipated.

As rapidly as we have telescoped in we are obliged to telescope out, for as the pantomime proceeds, the Philosopher rapidly regains his critical distance and the Nephew demonstrates that his powers of imitation are in no way diminished. The Nephew reverts to imitating the orchestra (the instruments and instrumentalists) or, at best, of embodying it by giving voice to its sound, as the designation 'la pantomime de l'homme-orchestre' would suggest:

> Mais vous vous seriez echappé en eclats de rire, a la maniere dont il contrefaisoit les differents instruments. Avec les joues renflées et boufies, et un son rauque et sombre, il rendoit les cors et les bassons; il prenoit un son eclatant et nazillard pour les hautbois; precipitant sa voix avec une rapidité incroyable, pour les instruments a cordes dont il cherchoit les sons les plus approchés; il siffloit les petites flûtes, il recouloit les traversieres, criant, chantant, se demenant comme une forcené; faisant lui seul, les danseurs, les danseuses, les chanteurs, les chanteuses, tout un orchestre, tout un theatre lyrique ...

> [Yes, you too would have burst out laughing at the way in which he aped the different instruments. With swollen cheeks and a somber throaty sound, he would give us the horns and bassoons. For the oboes he assumed a shill yet nasal voice, then speeded up the emission of sound to an incredible degree for the strings, for whose tones he found close analogues. He whistled piccolos and warbled traverse flutes, singing, shouting, waving about like a madman, being in himself dancer and ballerina, singer and prima donna, all of them together and the whole orchestra, the whole theater ...][91]

Out of breath and perspiring profusely, the Nephew again shows himself capable of impersonating everyone on stage and in the pit in rapid succession, occasioning, as the Philosopher anticipates, the beholder's amusement. His antics no longer move us to tears, but to laughter. At this point, however, the Nephew takes another plunge, giving rise to the following, truly singular description:

> Que ne lui vis je pas faire? Il pleuroit, il rioit, il soupiroit; il regardoit, ou attendri, ou tranquille, ou furieux; c'etoit une femme qui se pame de douleur; c'etoit un malheureux livré a tout son desespoir; un temple qui s'eleve; des oiseaux qui se taisent au soleil couchant; des eaux qui murment [*sic*] dans un lieu solitaire et frais, ou qui descendent en torrents du haut des montagnes; un orage, une tempete, la plainte de ceux qui vont perir, melée au sifflement des vents, au fracas du tonnerre; c'etoit la nuit, avec ses tenebres; c'etoit l'ombre et le silence; car le silence meme se peint par des sons. Sa tete etoit tout a fait perdue.

> [What did he not attempt to show me? He wept, laughed, sighed, looked placid or melting or enraged. He was a woman in a spasm of grief, a wretched man sunk in despair, a temple being erected, birds growing silent at sunset, waters murmuring through cool and solitary places or else cascading from a mountaintop, a storm, a hurricane, the anguish of those about to die, mingled with the whistling of the wind and the noise of thunder. He was night and its gloom, shade and silence – for silence itself can be depicted in sound. He had completely lost his senses.][92]

In this passage the Nephew neither imitates the orchestra, nor gives voice to its sounds. Instead, he imitates the objects of music's imitation, namely the passions ('c'etoit une femme qui se pame de douleur; c'etoit un malheureux livré a tout son desespoir') and nature itself ('des oiseaux qui se taisent au soleil couchant; des eaux qui murment [*sic*] dans un lieu solitaire et frais, ou qui descendent en torrents du haut des montagnes; un orage, une tempete'). In his *Dictionnaire de musique* Rousseau had postulated, moreover, that music alone, of all the arts, can imitate silence ('c'etoit la nuit, avec ses tenebres; c'etoit l'ombre et le silence; car le silence meme se peint par des sons').[93] By imitating the objects of music's imitation, the Nephew, in effect, *becomes* music. He neither imitates a musical performance, nor gives a musical performance, but attains the same mimetic remove from nature as music itself.[94] The repetition of 'c'étoit' in the passage above collapses the distance between nature and passion, their evocation by the performer, and their perception by the beholder, elliding the distinction between the original image in the mind's eye of the artist and its recreation in the soul of the beholder. The Nephew, who was previously 'voisin de la folie,' now loses his head entirely as the critical distance that separated him from the beholder disappears altogether.

Walter Rex responds to the question 'Quelle est la fonction de la musique dans *Le Neveu de Rameau*?' (What is the function of the music in *Rameau's Nephew*?) by asserting that the musical pantomimes, like the other pantomimes in the text, reveal that imitation is the common denominator of ethics and aesthetics alike.[95] By this token, not only is music's presence in the pantomime purely incidental, but music is mimetic and the Nephew the perfect *comédien*. As we have seen, however, both music and the Nephew escape the confines of these definitions, for music 'est la plus arbitraire et la moins précise' of the imitative arts, and the Nephew ultimately loses the *sangfroid* by which the actor is defined.[96] Jane Rush takes the opposite tack in an attempt to account for the Nephew's momentary loss of control, explaining that 'le Neveu, en tant que comédien *sensible*, est voué à l'échec' (as a *sensitive* actor, the Nephew is destined to fail).[97] Though the Nephew may indeed be doomed to failure, Rush's characterization of him as a sensitive actor fails to account for his ability to switch roles with speed and accuracy without being remotely affected by the characters and situations he portrays, a skill that Diderot attributes to the actor's *in*sensitivity. My analysis raises a third possibility, namely, that during the 'pantomime de l'homme-orchestre' we witness the artist at the moment of conception, of inspiration, rather than in the process of execution. In this phase even the actor reveals himself to be a sensitive soul: 'Et pourquoi l'acteur différerait-il du poète, du peintre, de l'orateur, du musicien? Ce n'est pas dans la fureur du premier jet que les traits caractéristiques se présentent, c'est dans les moments tranquilles et froids, dans des moments tout à fait inattendus' (And why would the actor differ from the poet, from the painter, from the orator, from the musician? It is not in the fury of the first draft that the characteristic traits are visible but in the cold and tranquil moments, in moments that are completely unexpected).[98] We observe the Nephew (and by no means impassively), not during the 'moments tranquilles et froids,' but 'dans la fureur du premier jet;' a stage common to the arts of the actor, the orator, and the musician alike. In the course of the 'pantomime de l'homme-orchestre,' Diderot thus gradually elides not only the distance that separates performer and beholder but the distance that separates the Nephew's power of expression from the power of original perception.

The moment at which music and the Nephew alike manage to evade their respective definitions as art and artist constitutes the apex of Diderot's aesthetic innovation. It is his response to the question, 'Comment dire la musique?' (How does one express music verbally?). As Béatrice Didier notes, 'la solution la plus originale chez Diderot [est de] faire mimer le langage musical par un personnage pour le faire entendre à travers le texte' (Diderot's most original solution [is to] have a character mime musical language in order to make it heard across the text).[99] Her words suggest that the language of the text, like the language in the text, constitutes an obstacle to expression. Yet *when*, precisely, Diderot manages to penetrate the linguistic obstacle on the levels of the story and the discourse has continued to defy analysis. The crucial realization when reading 'la pantomime de l'homme-orchestre' is twofold. First, the discourse interspersed with the pantomime is not uniform but follows a progression that reveals a continued faith on Diderot's part in the powers of French musical and linguistic expression to equal and potentially merge with that of their Italian contemporaries, eliminating the need to hierarchize or perhaps even to distinguish between national traditions. Second, the pantomime itself consists of several layers of mediation that separate the object of imitation (nature, passion, silence) from the performer and the beholder. These the Nephew gradually penetrates or sheds. The designation 'l'homme-orchestre' is thus somewhat misleading, for it seems to place the Nephew either at the level of the pantomime of an orchestra or of the orchestra itself, which executes rather than imitates. Yet the breakthrough occurs not when the Nephew imitates the musicians and their instruments (the orchestra), nor yet when he becomes the orchestra, emitting music, but when he imitates the object of music's imitation. Only when he is at the same mimetic remove from nature, passion, and silence as music itself does he penetrate the last layer of mediation. This moment, in which the Nephew loses all awareness of his surroundings, is the only one in which the reader can, however fleetingly, believe in the sincerity of the Nephew's performance and of the Philosopher's admiration. At this instant we would indeed be hard put to determine which is the greater sign of genius, the actor's perfect control, or the musician's loss thereof.

In his *Lettre sur la musique française*, Rousseau argued that the French language placed undue constraints on musical expression. Ideally, then, music should be conveyed via a medium that can overcome linguistic obstacles, whether in song, speech, or writing. To Diderot's mind, pantomime was the logical, and arguably the only means of portraying music textually. Diderot's experiment in the theatre, where he plugged his ears in order to sustain the emotional impact of the actors' gestures more fully, implies that he considered gesture to convey emotion more readily than speech.[100] The Nephew's pantomimes of the violinist and the harpsichord player indicate, moreover, that Diderot was acutely aware of the aspects of performance (errors, contortions) that prevent a listener from sustaining the full effect of the music itself. By having the Nephew mime music, Diderot eliminates both the linguistic obstacles and the hazards of performance that might compromise music's ability to affect the beholder inscribed within the text. Diderot's response to the accusations levied against the French language and his own dissatisfaction with the written medium was to interpolate pantomime between music and the inscribed beholder, obviating the linguistic obstacle on the level of the story. Replacing the sequentiality of the listening experience with the simultaneity of the viewing experience and availing himself of the conduit of the eye rather than the ear, which was still widely considered to be the most immediate route to the soul, Diderot renders the beholder's impression all the more vivid. He thus came as close as possible to recreating the simultaneity of the artist's original perception in the soul of the beholder and of rendering the music as audible as its effect is palpable across the text.

Resisting Rousseau's negative assessment of the French language to the bitter end, Diderot played upon the degrees of removal that separate the stages of perception, transmission, and reception, which characterize both the structure of mimesis and the structure of the tableau. By superimposing sign systems within the framework of the tableau, in which the reader looks over the beholder's shoulder – aware of the immediacy of his perception and guided by his emotional response – he ensured that the reader would in turn be affected by the collapse of the intervening layers of mediation. He thereby managed to convey the immediacy of the emotional exchange between performer and beholder and the simultaneity of their perception to the reader while continuing to use French on the level of the discourse. So persuasive is the Nephew's musical pantomime that the Philosopher remarks, 'Il est sûr que les accords résonnaient dans ses oreilles et dans les miennes,' leaving a certain ambiguity as to whether the conviction that the chords resonate in both their ears is that of the performer (he is certain) or the beholder (it is certain). So as to ensure that the reader in turn can fully participate in the tableau, Diderot places us just out of ear-shot, the position that he himself liked to occupy when listening to music so as to fill in the interstices with his imagination, free from the cognitive constraints of composition and performance. The moment of clairvoyance is exceedingly brief, yet were the progression through sequential discourse and the shedding of mimetic layers less gradual we would be inclined to underestimate the difficulty of attaining this degree of immediacy within the aesthetic of imitation and society of masks by which the Nephew and his author were bound.

2 Cazotte and Reader Re-creation

Lully n'est plus à l'Opéra
Le favori de Polymnie
Bientôt Rameau s'éclipsera
Malgré sa savante harmonie.
Jéliotte n'a rien de surprenant,
Vive les bouffons d'Italie!
Aujourd'hui tout Français galant
Ne se montre qu'en fredonnant
Et trin, trin, trin, et sou et giou
C'est à qui sera le plus fou.

[Lully is no longer at the Opera
The favourite of Polyhymnia
Soon Rameau will be overshadowed
Despite his savvy harmony.
Jéliotte is not surprising,
Long live the 'bouffos' of Italy!
Today, every galant Frenchman
Always steps out humming
And tra, la, la and hi-de-ho
It's enough to drive you mad.]

Cazotte, 'Il nous vient ici tous les ans'

Jacques Cazotte's sympathies lay, unequivocally, with the *coin du roi*, the side of the Paris Opéra associated with the proponents of French opera and the French king. He was resolutely opposed to Rousseau's statements about French music and the French language alike, and stated as much in one of the most prompt and convincing rebuttals of Rousseau's *Lettre sur la musique française* written in the course of the *Querelle des Bouffons*. The earliest records of Jacques Cazotte's artistic expression are his songs and romances, for which he composed both words and music. 'Il nous vient ici tous les ans,' a song that he wrote in the course of the opera debates, makes a specific allusion to the controversy. Though the line 'Vive les bouffons d'Italie!' initially appears to endorse the growing popularity of Italian music, Cazotte's opposition of the term 'bouffons' – referring to singers in short Italian comedies – to the famous names of Lully and Rameau makes it difficult for anyone hearing the song to take the Italian threat seriously. Instead, it suggests that the devotees of the latest musical trends are making themselves ridiculous by trying to emulate Italian vocal ornamentation. This note of incredulity at the idea that Italian opera might seriously risk unseating the French sets the tone for the two letters Cazotte contributed to the opera quarrels. Though Cazotte, who was suspected of being anti-Enlightenment and anti-philosophe, is not typically paired with Diderot, the Enlightenment philosophe par excellence, the two of them crossed party lines, so to speak, during the *Querelle des Bouffons*, joining forces in their defence of the French language against Rousseau. The two are also linked historically by virtue of their shared fascination for Rameau's nephew, Diderot as author of the work that immortalized him, and Cazotte as his room-mate and lifelong friend.[1] Cazotte's personal devotion to such an unconventional figure helps counterbalance other biographical details that attest to his political conservatism and tend to colour critical readings of his texts. Lauded as the precursor of fantastic fiction, Cazotte's writings are often read through the lens of the mystical leanings he displayed towards the end of his life and of his opposition to the Revolution, which he ultimately did not survive. He is rarely credited with the ingenuity for which Diderot and Beaumarchais are touted, yet he shared their fascination for the protean multiplication of aesthetic possibilities in generically indeterminate literary texts. The humour and insouciance of his style is apparent in the song lyrics cited above, which were only the beginning of a prolonged fascination for the association of text and music. In the following pages I will attempt to rescue Cazotte from the stigma that accompanied his death, bringing his first-hand knowledge of the French operatic tradition and the surrounding controversy to bear on his literary texts, revealing the theoretical sophistication of his musical tableaux, and reading him alongside those authors to whom he should rightfully be compared.

Unlike Diderot, who saw beyond the listening habits of mid-eighteenth-century audiences, Cazotte's writings indicate that he was perfectly in step with the times. Johnson, indeed, cites Cazotte's contributions to the *Querelle des Bouffons* to illustrate the phenomenon of mimetic listening that was characteristic of mid-century audiences. Mimetic listening, once again, stems from the conviction that music, which was thought to represent nature or the passions, has the power to conjure up in the listener the image or sensation that he or she naturally sustains when in the presence of nature or the human condition.[2] When listening to a sublime passage from Mondonville's *Titon et Aurore*, for instance, Cazotte exclaims: 'On croit en même tems voir épanouir les fleurs, tomber la rosée, entendre les gazouillemens des oiseaux, sentir le tressaillement de la nature aux approches du jour' (At the same time we think we see the flowers open and the dew fall, hear the twittering of the birds, and feel nature shiver at the approach of day).[3] This understanding of how music signifies, which is limited to its capacity to imitate nature, is somewhat conservative in comparison to Diderot's inclination to question such a literal understanding and Rousseau's emphasis on music's capacity to express human sentiment. Cazotte indicates that he, too, sees beyond the limitations of his statement, however, when he employs a preposterously negative image to characterize a musical passage that he disliked: 'Il semble que le Musicien ait cherché à peindre le pénible & inutile effort que fait un octogénaire mourant pour arracher un phlegme de sa poitrine' (It seems that the musician sought to depict the painful and useless effort that a dying octogenarian makes to dislodge the phlegm from his chest).[4] Cazotte's ability to carry mimetic listening to the point of parody indicates that he was aware of the musical convention as such and was inclined to place such an awareness at the service of his own satirical ends.

The title of Cazotte's first contribution to the opera debate, *La Guerre de l'opéra: Lettre à une dame de Province* of February 1753, reveals that Cazotte, like Diderot and Rousseau, viewed the debate as a struggle between nations. Yet the bark of his letter is worse than its bite, for it remains, by and large, an objective analysis of the two sides of the quarrel in which he presents the strengths and weaknesses of the French and Italian traditions. The French, he states, are especially gifted at declamation and dance, but their music is entirely dependent on the quality of the lyric line.[5] The Italians, on the other hand, excel in ornamentation and instrumentation, but it is impossible to sing their songs if unaccompanied.[6] Nostalgically, Cazotte acknowledges that Italy was the wellspring of European musicality. He stipulates, however, that the French tradition ultimately distinguished itself from the Italian in response to a specific national sensibility.[7] The pacific nature of Cazotte's observations contrasts strongly with his characterization of the opera debate not as a quarrel but as a war, announcing that 'La Musique Italienne ... est aux prises avec la Musique Françoise. Imaginez tous les desordres d'une guerre en même tems étrangere et civile' (Italian and French music ... are at loggerheads. Imagine all the disorder of a war both civil and foreign).[8] While he claims not to take sides, moreover, he ultimately concludes that victory has gone to the French. Though he soft-pedals his stance, Cazotte's first contribution to the quarrels thus already indicates where his true sympathies lie.

Its martial metaphors notwithstanding, the conciliatory tone of Cazotte's first letter does not remotely prepare us for the second. The radical difference between the two is indicative of the impact that Rousseau's missive had upon its readers. Cazotte wrote his *Observations sur la lettre de J.J. Rousseau sur la musique française* in November of 1753 in direct response to Rousseau's *Lettre sur la musique française*.[9] The analogies that he used for effect in his first letter give way in his second to an overtly national stance. Abandoning all pretence of neutrality, it soon becomes clear that, were war to be declared, his arms belong to his country. Georges Décote, Cazotte's biographer and the editor of his correspondence, regrets that Cazotte let his emotions get the better of him in his second contribution to the opera quarrels, sacrificing his tone of agreeable banter for one of caustic indignation. He reproaches Cazotte for attempting to defend the French opera on the grounds of 'sensibilité' instead of logic. Admonishing him for having attempted to follow Rousseau into territory that he did not fully understand, Décote states that Cazotte 's'est engagé ... avec tant de vigueur, dans une querelle musicale vers laquelle ne semblaient pas particulièrement le porter ses compétences techniques en la matière' (took part ... with such vigour in a musical quarrel for which his technical ability in the subject did not particularly seem to have prepared him).[10] Décote's suggestion that music should be judged according to logic rather than personal taste is, however, by no means a given.[11] Furthermore, while he intimates that Cazotte was insufficiently versed in music theory to refute Rousseau's critique, Décote also cites those who argue that Rousseau was unqualified to level such a critique in the first place.[12] If Rousseau's attribution of the shortcomings of French music to the French language is unfounded, how can Cazotte be considered unfit to refute him, regardless of the extent of his musical training?

Cazotte's second contribution to the opera quarrels invites us to consider whether his rebuttal can be considered extravagant given the radical nature of Rousseau's claims. Cazotte defends French opera on the grounds that it affords him the 'plaisir de convention' (pleasure of convention) that accompanies an audience's ability to recognize and respond to the familiar effect of their own national music.[13] Whereas Italian music might be superior, he argues, it does not respond to a certain cultural conditioning the French have received that leads them to prefer their own sung theatre. Cazotte thus concedes the accuracy of Rousseau's central claim: 'Je lui accorderai que notre langue est moins propre à la Poësie lyrique que l'Italienne. Je lui accorderai, s'il veut, que les Italiens plus passionnés que nous pour la Musique l'ont en général plus perfectionnée' (I will grant him that our language is less suited to lyric poetry than Italian. I will grant him, if he wishes, that the Italians, who are more passionate about music than we are, have in general perfected it to a greater extent). He contests the logic of Rousseau's conclusions, however, stating with irony: 'Donc il faut brûler les Poëmes de Quinault, donc il a été ou il est impossible qu'on fasse en Musique rien de bon sur ces Poëmes, ni sur aucun autre' (Therefore we should burn Quinault's poems. Therefore it was or is impossible that we compose any good music to accompany these poems or any others).[14] Implicitly then, the fact that the Italians remain, thus far, unsurpassed in the musical arts does not mean that the French should discard all past and future compositions. The weakest link in Rousseau's logic – and the suggestion that got Cazotte's goat – was not the notion that the French musical tradition was inferior to the Italian but rather the suggestion that the French 'n'ont point de Musique et n'en peuvent avoir' (do not at all have a Music and cannot have any).[15] Realizing that a single positive example, albeit hypothetical, was enough to undermine Rousseau's carefully constructed argument, Cazotte suggested that his opponent's reasoning was little better than a house of cards:

> Je me résume & je dis: Il peut exister un Opéra François bien fait pour la Scêne, dont les airs soient chantans & touchans pour nous, dont les Ballets pleins de caractère soient à la fois agréables et variés, & dans lequel les Chœurs tantôt entrent dans la marche générale de l'action, tantôt servent à augmenter l'impression du plaisir. Peut-être aucun de nos Opéras ne

réunit-il toutes ces perfections. Mais il suffit que ma supposition soit dans l'ordre des choses possibles, pour que presque tout l'ouvrage de M. Rousseau porte sur rien.

[To summarize, I say: We can conceive of a French opera that is well suited to the stage, whose arias strike us as lyrical and touching, whose ballets are full of character and are both agreeable and varied, and in which the choruses at times take part in the action and at others serve to enhance our impression of pleasure. Perhaps none of our operas unite all of these perfections. But it is enough that my supposition be possible, for almost the entirety of Mr Rousseau's work to come to nothing.][16]

While Cazotte's stance is decidedly pro-French, his argument is nationalist *avant la lettre* only in the sense that he wishes to accord to each nation its own music. He ridicules the suggestion that France abjure her opera for the sake of a foreign musical tradition, yet finds the notion that other nations should sacrifice their traditions to the French to be equally absurd:

Notre Opéra est en proportion pour nous, ce qu'est pour les Anglois leur Théâtre Dramatique; c'est un Spectacle Nationnal. L'une et l'autre Nation auroit tort de vouloir le rendre universel. Mais l'une & l'autre Nation entendant bien ses intérêts, auroit grand tort de détruire son Théâtre pour en élever sur ses ruines un étranger, quel qu'il fût.

[Our opera is for us what their dramatic theatre is for the English: it is a national spectacle. Either nation would be wrong to try to render it universal. But each nation understands its own interests and would be wrong to destroy its theatre in order to erect a foreign one, regardless of which one, on its ruins.]

To drive his point home Cazotte pretends to reason in Rousseau's vein, suggesting that Rousseau petition the English to admit France's superiority in spoken theatre and to replace their productions of Shakespeare with Molière. The English, Cazotte predicts, 'nous le renverroi[ent] corrigé' (will send him back to us chastised).[17]

Though one might assume, in Rousseau's defence, that he exaggerated his claims for the sake of argument, it is difficult to question Cazotte's rebuttal, for his strategy consists in poking holes in the logic of his opponent. While I do not mean to suggest that Rousseau was wrong, therefore, I do wish to point out that neither was Cazotte. His lack of formal training detracts neither from the soundness of his reasoning nor from his powers of observation as a regular opera-goer and musical dilettante. The political implications of the musical issues being discussed enhanced their apparent urgency. Décote elaborates upon the threat that the opera quarrels posed to a man of Cazotte's political convictions:

> Toujours sensibilisé par son conservatisme et son nationalisme, il n'a pas manqué de considérer cette querelle musicale comme une tentative de subversion, de révolution dans les moeurs. Et il l'a dénoncée en termes d'autant plus vifs qu'il y voyait sans doute l'expression indirecte et comme le prélude d'une attaque contre la société elle-même, sinon contre l'ordre politique établi.

> [Always sensitized by his conservatism and nationalism, he did not fail to consider this musical quarrel as an attempt to subvert, to revolutionize custom. And he denounced it in terms that were all the more vivid for having seen, undoubtedly, the indirect expression or prelude of an attack on society itself if not on the established political order.][18]

Décote's reading of Cazotte's apprehensions concurs with Wokler's thesis that the *Querelle des Bouffons* led to a democratization and social levelling that certain Enlightenment thinkers strove to promote and that others viewed with dismay.[19] Though I contest the notion that Cazotte was 'toujours sensibilisé par son conservatisme et son nationalisme,' his contributions to the opera quarrels nonetheless suggest that he understood their potential political repercussions and that he considered Rousseau's missive to pose a serious threat to France. Cazotte's subsequent writings reveal, moreover, that he was also interested in the aesthetic aspect of the controversy. Contrary to Décote's assertion that Cazotte 'ne devait plus jamais aborder [le] sujet [de la musique française]' (would never broach the subject [of French music] again), the textual evidence suggests that Cazotte continued to gravitate towards questions of language, music, and national identity over the course of the next two decades.[20]

In 1762, ten years after the opera quarrels erupted, Cazotte published his first lengthy work in the form of a twelve-canto poem in the chivalric vein entitled *Ollivier*. Two of Cazotte's early romances have been identified as the predecessors of the poem, yet the origin of the musical themes in the fourth canto has not yet attracted critical attention.[21] In the preface to his poem, Cazotte announces his intent to write a narrative that brings together a wide variety of genres after the fashion of Ariosto's *Orlando Furioso*.[22] Set at the time of the crusades, when the Christian armies sought to wrest Palestine from the Muslims, Cazotte's poem tells the tale of a young man named Ollivier who dared to love above his station and fathered the child of the heroine, Agnès, incurring the wrath of her father, the Count of Tours. Each canto recounts an adventure that befalls Ollivier, Agnès, their confidantes Enguerrand and Fleur-de-Mirte, or their persecutors as the Count of Tours seeks to avenge his daughter. While certain of the cantos are confined to the adventures characteristic of chivalric romance, others involve whimsical borrowings from the tradition of oriental tales and still others are allegorical, containing allusions to the Olympian gods. Yet the fourth canto stands out against this background of eclectic genres as belonging to the traditions of neither myth, nor folk tale, nor romance. Instead, it is a parody of Rousseau's *Lettre sur la musique française* that has not previously been recognized as such.

Cazotte's fourth canto constitutes a departure from the poem's main story line. In it, the heroine's handmaid, Fleur-de-Mirte, goes in search of her lover Enguerrand when he does not return from his quest to find his master Ollivier. Assuming her lover has joined the crusades, Fleur-de-Mirte boards a ship for the Holy Land, but soon finds herself shipwrecked and stranded on an island. In mock tribute to the tradition of incorporating a utopia into a larger narrative framework, Cazotte takes advantage of Fleur-de-Mirte's sojourn on the island of the Mélologues to return to the questions of the ideal form of expression that was widely debated during the *Querelle des Bouffons*.[23] The intervening years evidently enabled him to resume the tone of banter so characteristic of his writing yet absent from his second contribution to the quarrel. Treating his adversary's ideas with gentle satire, Cazotte fancifully considers what would come to pass were the analogies that Rousseau had drawn between music and language taken literally.[24]

The island on which Fleur-de-Mirte finds herself stranded is inhabited by the Mélologues who, as their name suggests, use music to communicate.[25] Several details in Cazotte's canto point to Rousseau and his *Lettre sur la musique française* as the subject of his parody. Zerbin, a musician and language teacher who, by virtue of his dual expertise, has managed to crack the Mélologues' code, explains to Fleur-de-Mirte that a fairy's curse has deprived the islanders of their ability to speak.

He refers to the Mélologue who thought of replacing language with music as a *philosophe*, a denomination that is singularly out of place amidst the exotic names and outlandish events of the poem and that clearly refers to Cazotte's historical context rather than Zerbin's. Though Rousseau's rupture with the *philosophes* dates from the successful performance of his *opéra-comique, Le Devin du village*, in 1752, Cazotte continued to refer to him as such (with a tone of mock deference) in his *Observations sur la lettre de J.J. Rousseau sur la musique française*.[26] The *philosophe* in question, Zerbin goes on to explain, 'observant le goût que sa nation avoit pour la musique, les facilités, les connoissances qu'elle avoit dans ce genre, imagina qu'il en pouvoit tirer parti pour suppléer au défaut de la parole' (observing his nation's taste for music and the aptitude and knowledge it had in this genre, thought he could take advantage of it to compensate for the lack of speech).[27] Though Rousseau does not envision a loss of capacity for human speech in his letter, he does provide the history of the parallel development of music and language, explaining that speech, or declamation, gave rise to song, which in turn gave rise to instrumental music. As instrumental music gradually diverged from vocal music it ceased to be unduly constrained by language, but conserved its essential features.[28] This analogy is behind the Mélologues' decision to adopt music as an alternate means of communication and furnishes the basis of Cazotte's parody.

In his *Lettre sur la musique française*, Rousseau focuses first on the structural similarities between music and language, comparing metre to syntax: 'La mesure est à peu près à la mélodie ce que la Syntaxe est au discours: c'est elle qui fait l'enchaînement des mots, qui distingue les phrases et qui donne un sens, une liaison au tout' (Meter is approximately to melody as Syntax is to discourse: it is what constitutes the link among the words, what distinguishes phrases, and what gives a meaning, a connection to the whole).[29] He then turned his attention from form to content, claiming that music is not only structured like a language but is equally capable of conveying ideas. When attempting to convey a complex concept, Rousseau recommends that the composer 'sépare[ ] tout à fait le chant de l'accompagnement ... destinant uniquement ce dernier à rendre l'idée accessoire' (completely ... separate the song from the accompaniment ... devoting the latter uniquely to rendering the accessory idea), thereby implying that music itself is capable of conveying thought.[30] Indeed, music's meaning is at times so clear that the listener can actually discern a contradiction between the lyrics and the accompaniment. To support this statement, Rousseau provides the example of a passage from Lully's *Armide* in which the words read '*Achevons; je frémis. Vengeons-nous; Je soupire*' (End it; I tremble. Avenge myself; I sigh) whereas the music, by virtue of staying on the same chord, says in effect '*Achevons; achevons. Vengeons-nous; vengeons-nous*' (End it; end it. Avenge myself; avenge myself).[31] Implicitly, then, music is as apt at conveying meaning as speech itself. As Zerbin remarks, the philosophe's proposal that the Mélologues adopt music as an alternate form of communication did not go uncontested, but rather led to 'quelques disputes élevées entre les virtuoses' (some disputes raised among the virtuosos). These disputes constitute a fairly transparent reference to the *Querelle des Bouffons*, in the course of which those who preferred 'le discours le plus sensé' (the most sensible speech) were pitted against those who maintained that the only discourse that is pleasing to the ear is 'astreint à une mesure, formant une mélodie, ayant un caractère' (subject to a metre, forming a melody, having a character).[32] Cazotte thus echoes the very terms of Rousseau's letter, in which he describes French as a logical language, well-suited to philosophy yet ill-suited to song, for it has 'ni mesure, ni caractère, ni mélodie' (neither metre, nor character, nor melody).[33]

Rousseau's analogy between music and language provided Cazotte with a blueprint for his tale. He designed the fourth canto of his poem as a practical experiment in what would ensue if Rousseau's analogy were extended and a group of individuals actually chose to communicate through music instead of speech. When Fleur-de-Mirte regains consciousness after being rescued by the islanders, she finds herself surrounded by mute, instrument-bearing natives all playing at once. Their playing does not in the least resemble the polite, harmonious interchange that constitutes the king's council, which will later afford her the pleasure of an evening of chamber music. Instead, each Mélologue simply reacts upon his instrument, with no attempt at coordinating the different musical lines. The result is a deafening noise.[34] Rousseau describes the effect of such poor coordination of musical lines in his letter, predicting a similar result: 'De faire chanter à part des Violons d'un côté, de l'autre des Flutes, de l'autre des Bassons, chacun sur un dessein particulier, et presque sans rapport entre eux, et d'appeller tout ce cahos, de la Musique, c'est insulter également l'oreille et le jugement des Auditeurs' (To make the Violins play by themselves on one side, the Flutes on the other, the Bassoons on another, each with a particular design and almost without any relationship among them and to call all this chaos Music, is to insult equally the ear and the Judgment of the listeners).[35] He observes, moreover, that 'plus on entasse des chants mal à propos, et moins la Musique est agréable et chantante, parce qu'il est impossible à l'oreille de se prêter au même instant à plusieurs mélodies, et que l'une effaçant l'impression de l'autre, il ne résulte du tout que de la confusion et du bruit' (the more the songs are heaped up inappropriately, the less the Music is pleasant and tuneful, because it is impossible for the ear to lend itself to several melodies at the same time, and because – since the one effaces the impression of the other – the result is merely confusion and noise).[36] Though Cazotte was certainly sufficiently familiar with the sounds of an orchestra preparing to play to have come up with this description on his own, Rousseau's letter may well have reinforced his decision to begin his tale on a discordant note.

From the noisy protest that accompanies her every attempt to speak, Fleur-de-Mirte soon deduces that she is meant to hold her tongue and starts to observe her surroundings in silence. As she passes from the countryside to the town and from there to the palace, a hierarchy of musical instruments gradually becomes apparent. The shepherds play Breton bagpipes, the children play Jews harps, the pages play recorders, the members of the king's council play the strings, the chief secretary plays the harpsichord, the princess a mandolin, and the king the instrument of his choice. Once the tour of the island is complete Zerbin, the interpreter, finally breaks the silence long enough to recount the history of the island and to explain the rules that govern the Mélologues' system of communication. Just as someone might change linguistic register, tone, form of address, or use of vocabulary according to the social venue, the Mélologues modify how they play to suit the occasion. Like speech, their playing is coded, and if their tone or register is somewhat off it is considered a musical *faux pas*. 'Quelquefois par distraction,' Zerbin explains, 'on tombe dans de singulieres équivoques. On joue un air haut avec son égal, on reçoit un galant homme du ton dont on recevroit un laquais, & on se sert d'un air bas devant un homme de fortune dont on veut faire sa dupe' (Sometimes, if not paying attention, one falls into singular ambiguities. One takes a high tone with one's equal, one receives a gentleman with the tone one would use with a servant, and one uses a condescending tone with a wealthy man whom one would like to outsmart). Much as linguistic registers are modified according to class and profession, one's instrument, like one's tone, is indicative of social station. As Zerbin remarks: 'Il ne conviendroit pas qu'un senateur jouât du fifre ou de la musette organisée' (It would be inappropriate for a senator to play the fife or the bagpipes).[37] Though the Mélologues are described as Saracens, their social hierarchy and pretensions bear a strong resemblance to the French society of the Ancien Régime. This resemblance suggests that Cazotte's island is not a depiction of the ideal, which is meant to cast aspersion on the real, but is rather a farcical depiction of French society itself.

The kind of instruments the Mélologues play and how they play them also portrays character and sentiment. Character, as we saw above, is one of the three components, along with melody and metre, that Rousseau considered essential to good music; a subject that he discusses at some length, frequently associating character with an accompanying emotion. Metre contributes to the character the music conveys, yet Rousseau distinguishes between the character of French music, which is slavishly governed by metre ('elle est forcément triste sur une mesure lente, furieuse ou gaye sur un mouvement vif, grave sur un mouvement modéré' [it is inevitably sad on a slow meter, furious or gay on a lively movement, grave on a moderate movement]) and that of Italian music, which varies irrespective of metre ('Elle est, quand il plaît au Musicien, triste sur un mouvement vif, gaye sur un mouvement lent' ([it is, if it so pleases the Musician, sad on a lively movement, gay on a slow movement]).[38] Here, Rousseau uses the term 'character' to refer to the words in the text that the music accompanies, or the sentiment they are meant to convey. Later, however, he uses the word in the sense of characteristic, or trait, stating that the flexibility of the Italian language, which permits inversions, unlike French: 'laisse au goût du Musicien la liberté ... de donner à chaque Acteur un tour de chant particulier, de même que chaque homme à son geste et son ton qui lui sont propres, et qui le distinguent d'un autre homme' (leaves to the Musician's taste the freedom ... of giving to each Actor a particular melodic contour, so that each man has the mannerism and the tone that belong to him and that distinguish him from another man).[39] This is the sense of the word 'character' that Cazotte ultimately adopts. As Zerbin explains, 'Il est des instrumens d'état; il en est aussi de caractère' (There are instruments of rank; there are others of character). A lover may therefore choose to rely on the limpid tones of a flute whereas a gossip may prefer a violin's range and rapidity.[40] A special turn of phrase known as the 'la turlutaine du cour' (courtly refrain) allows certain worldly individuals (including courtiers, hypocrites, and the nouveau riche) to express a range of emotions that match the situation at hand, effectively masking their true nature. Cazotte thus creates not only an extended system of musical and linguistic equivalences but an amusing social commentary that – far from defending the status quo – exposes the artificiality of appearances and of social convention.

Once he has recounted the history of the island and the rules governing the Mélologues' system of communication, Zerbin offers to instruct Fleur-de-Mirte in the art of playing an instrument so that she might converse with the king. For her first lesson, Zerbin explains that a 'si' means yes and a 'sol' means no, but that Fleur-de-Mirte can nuance her statements by adding a sharp or flat.[41] Cazotte's explanation of the effect of sharps and flats on the listener hearkens back to Rousseau's account of having read one of Rameau's works. Rousseau credits Rameau with the observation that each interval has a different effect on the soul and that 'les tierces & les sixtes mineures doivent produire des affections différentes de celles que produisent les tierces & les sixtes majeures' (the minor thirds and the sixths ought to produce affects different from those which the major thirds and sixths produce).[42] Since the shift between major and minor is usually achieved by raising or lowering the third a half-step – in other words, by adding a sharp or a flat – this description may well have provided the inspiration for how to nuance the meaning of a 'si' or a 'sol,' which, notably, are a third apart. Once again, Rousseau's letter is not the only possible source of such a basic musical observation, which Cazotte could easily have gleaned from his own dabbling in the art. The presence of the detail in Rousseau's letter nevertheless helps confirm that, regardless of the source of Cazotte's musical knowledge, the letter itself is the subject of his parody.

Another of Rousseau's salient points in all likelihood incited Cazotte to stage a musical conversation in his text. Rousseau was quite adamant in his criticism of the convention of the musical duet, for the notion of two people singing at once with no attempt at mutual understanding violated his fundamental conviction that music is capable of conveying both meaning and affect. If a duet is to abide by the laws of nature and verisimilitude, Rousseau claimed, it should resemble a musical dialogue:

> Les Duo sont hors de la Nature; car rien n'est moins naturel que de voir deux personnes se parler à la fois durant un certain tems, soit pour dire la même chose, soit pour se contredire, sans jamais s'écouter ni se répondre ... Or le meilleur moyen de sauver cette absurdité, c'est de traiter le plus qu'il est possible le Duo en Dialogue, & ce premier soin regarde le Poëte;

ce qui regarde le Musicien, c'est de trouver un chant convenable au sujet, & distribué de telle sorte, que chacun des Interlocuteurs parlant alternativement, toute la suite du Dialogue ne forme qu'une mélodie.

[Duos are beyond Nature; for nothing is less natural than to see two persons speaking together all at once for some time, either to say the same thing or to contradict one another, without ever listening or responding to one another ... Now, the best way of avoiding this absurdity is to handle the Duo as much as is possible in Dialogue, and this first concern regards the Poet; what regards the Musician is to find a song suited to the subject and distributed in such a fashion that, each of the Interlocutors speaking alternately, the whole series of the Dialogue forms only one melody.][43]

In this passage Rousseau passes from the descriptive to the prescriptive mode, going beyond his observation that music is structured like a language to recommend that music be composed according to conversational logic in order to lend a certain plausibility to dramatic scenarios. In an ingenious reversal of Rousseau's logic, Cazotte chooses to stage not a duet based upon a conversation but a conversation based upon a duet, taking care to abide by Rousseau's stipulation that each party speak or play in turn.

Now that Cazotte has conditioned the reader (if not the heroine) to comprehend the islanders' idiom, the stage is set for a parodic tour de force. From the very beginning of her music lesson it has been patently evident that Fleur-de-Mirte is walking into a trap, for Zerbin has taught her the sort of equivocal speech that tends to get women into compromising situations, showing her how to play 'un *oui* qui ne signifie rien, et un *non* qui ne veut pas dire non' (a *yes* that means nothing and a *no* that does not mean no).[44] Pleased with his pupil's progress, Zerbin enthusiastically informs the king of 'sa docilité à prendre des leçons, et des facilités naturelles et acquises qu'elle avait pour devenir dans peu une excellente écolière' (her willingness to take lessons and her natural and acquired ability to become an excellent pupil in little time).[45] The king's interest in Fleur-de-Mirte is visibly enhanced by Zerbin's account of her willingness to learn, a comment fraught with sexual implications. The implications are rendered even more explicit by the comedy that ensues. King Macore, a man of many instruments, arrives for the interview bearing a flute, the choice that Zerbin had previously attributed to the lover. His performance, moreover, bears an exact resemblance to Rousseau's explanation as to how a musician should convey passion:

'C'est par [la hardiesse des *modulations*] que le Musicien ... fait exprimer les réticences, les interruptions, les discours *entre-coupés* qui sont le language des passions impétueuses' (It is by [the boldness of the *modulations*] that the Musician ... can express the reticences, the interruptions, the *faltering* speeches which are the language of impetuous passions).[46] Cazotte draws his description of Macore's performance almost verbatim from Rousseau's text: 'Alors, Macore changea de *modulation*, et ne s'expliqua presque plus que par quelques sons *entre-coupés*, bas et tremblans' (Then Macore changed *modulation*, and expressed himself almost entirely through *faltering*, low, and timorous sounds). Unfortunately, the king is not a gifted musician: 'Le bon monarque manquoit d'haleine, n'avoit ni doigts ni embouchure; son jeu n'étoit point détaché, point net; de sorte que son compliment, qui n'étoit d'ailleurs qu'un tissu de lieux communs, pouvoit passer, quant au fond & à la forme, pour un très insipide morceau de symphonie' (The good king lacked breath, had neither fingering nor embouchure, his playing was neither articulate nor clear, so that the form and content of his compliment, which was nothing but a web of commonplaces, might have been mistaken for a rather insipid symphonic passage).[47] His performance thus resembles the 'ennuyeuse suite de sons modulée au hazard' (tiresome series of sounds, modulated by chance) that Rousseau associates with the French rather than the Italian tradition.[48] Undaunted, King Macore perseveres, and his efforts are soon rewarded. Having persuaded Fleur-de-Mirte that the best return for the king's hospitality would be to demonstrate that she has mastered the rudiments of his language, Zerbin advises her to respond to Macore's questions with the notes Zerbin tells her to play. Throughout her conversation with the king, therefore, Fleur-de-Mirte obediently plays 'sol's and 'si's in accordance with Zerbin's signals, thereby indicating whether she approves or disapproves the king's speech without having any idea what he is saying. Her suspicions are finally aroused when the king throws himself at her feet, kisses her hands in rapture, pays off Zerbin, and parades out playing a fanfare; but by that time they are engaged. Cazotte thus parodies not only the notion that music is structured like a language but also the prevalent association in contemporary French literature of music with sensuality, invoking the French literary trope in which a music lesson inevitably leads to the seduction of the female pupil. By creating a scenario in which the wronged heroine, once wise to the situation, demands immediate reparation and safe escort off the island, however, Cazotte manages to draw attention to the prevalence of such scenes without becoming complicit.

While the tone Cazotte uses to treat the various aspects of Rousseau's argument in the fourth canto of his poem is less acerbic than the one he employed in the course of the opera quarrels, the upshot of his tale is essentially the same. Zerbin expresses dissatisfaction with the outcome of the debates in which music was preferred to spoken language, saying, 'Je suis bien éloigné de croire que l'idiome soit à son point de perfection' (I am far from believing that the idiom has attained perfection). He regrets the ultimate triumph of pleasurable over logical expression, much as Cazotte regretted the valorization of Italian lyricism over the more familiar conventions of the French operatic tradition. His observation that measure and melody – the characteristics that Rousseau identified as the earmarks of good music – eventually prevailed over common sense calls the pragmatic value of Rousseau's musical analyses into question. '[E]n conséquence de cette décision, qui a prévalu,' Zerbin ruefully remarks, 'les cerveaux se sont bien fatigués, et le bon sens a extrémement souffert' (As a result of this decision, which prevailed, brains wore themselves out and common sense suffered greatly). In this passage we sense Cazotte's frustration, shared by many participants in the debate, that the discussions had gone on for so long and to so little avail. Cazotte thus echoes his own point of ten years before – when he urged Rousseau to leave the choice of what they preferred to listen to up to the French – by stating that the only ones who really manage to say what they mean are not the philosophes, with their refined linguistic (or musical) sensibility, but the people: 'Le peuple, qui n'a pas le temps de s'occuper d'idées aussi vaines, écorche les oreilles, va plus de tête que de mesure, & cependant touche plus droit au but; car il rend nettement ce qu'il veut dire' (The people, who do not have time to preoccupy themselves with such vain ideas, scorch our ears, stubbornly ignore the beat, and yet get straight to the point for they express more clearly what they wish to say).[49] With these words, Cazotte suggests that popular sentiment, not the aesthetic convictions of the intellectual elite, should be the measure of a nation's taste. Cazotte's familiar stance in favour of an indigenous (or national) music thus acquires distinctly democratic overtones, with an antiintellectual, anti-artistocratic ring to them. Though Cazotte's political convictions are, admittedly, not to be confused with those of his fictional character, the import of his tale flatly contradicts critical readings that characterize his fiction as misogynist and pro-establishment.

In 1772, two full decades after the onset of the quarrels, Cazotte again took up the question of music and language in the only literary work for which he has been duly lauded. *Le Diable amoureux* has received far more critical attention than the rest of Cazotte's œuvre and yet little note has been taken of the operatic allusions in the work. Critical studies of Cazotte's novella fall primarily into two categories: those that attempt to identify its possible sources and those that consider it to be the source of the genre of fantastic fiction. Both approaches spring from a central paradox in the text that critics have found baffling ever since Fréron dubbed it Cazotte's greatest achievement: his integration of the 'merveilleux' (marvellous) into his novella in such a way as to give 'un air de vraisemblance à tout ce qui s'écarte le plus de la nature' (an air of verisimilitude to all that is farthest from nature).[50] Yet attempts to identify the origin of the marvellous elements in the text do not account for how Cazotte came to weave them into a logically and psychologically consistent narrative, the feat that led Pierre-Georges Castex and Tzvetan Todorov to herald *Le Diable amoureux* as the predecessor of fantastic fiction.[51] Another art form existed in Cazotte's day, however, that was expressly designed to render the marvellous *vraisemblable*, namely the French opera. While it is unlikely that any single opera could be identified as having the same plot line or marshalling the same components as Cazotte's *Diable amoureux*, contemporary theories of the *tragédie en musique* nonetheless furnished a vital conceptual foundation for Cazotte's literary creation, contributing to his ability to reconcile the *merveilleux* with the *vraisemblable* and enabling him to transform his work from a text that arose from prior trends into one that gave rise to a new genre.[52]

Critics who scour *Le Diable amoureux* for some indication of the origin of Cazotte's text frequently cite the references to the opera in his opening pages, yet at no point do they concede that these allusions may also be signs of his source.[53] Cazotte's previous musical experience should be enough to alert us to this possibility, however. As we have seen, the metaphors he employed to describe the effect of musical passages were not only characteristic of eighteenth-century audiences but revealed that he was aware of mimetic listening as trope and was able to push it to the point of parody. Having drawn the inspiration for his poem *Ollivier* from two of his own romances as well as from Rousseau's *Lettre sur la musique française*, Cazotte was experienced in shifting between lyrical and narrative modes.[54] The 'plaisir de convention' that he derived from listening to French opera and doggedly defended during the *Querelle des Bouffons* clearly stemmed from a sense of what French operatic convention was. Cazotte was so confident that he had mastered opera's generic requirements, indeed, that when his brother encouraged him to try his hand at an *opéra-comique*, he vowed to take as his subject the next word that came to his brother's mind. As good as his boast, he submitted 'Les Sabots' (The Wooden Shoes), a one-act opera written in a single night in collaboration with Rameau's nephew, to the Comédie-Italienne where the performance met with some success.[55]

Décote finds the description of French opera that Cazotte provides in his contributions to the *Querelle des Bouffons* to be somewhat contradictory. Yet the contradiction he identifies bears a close enough resemblance to the central paradox of *Le Diable amoureux* to warrant closer scrutiny. In *La Guerre de l'opéra*, Cazotte declares: 'Nous n'envions point aux étrangers le plaisir qui résulte pour eux de la violation des regles & des bienséances; c'est à elles que nous devons des chefs-d'œuvres dans tous les genres' (We do not envy foreigners the pleasure that they derive from the violation of rules and propriety; it is to these that we owe our masterpieces in every genre).[56] Décote is puzzled by the fact that Cazotte subsequently seems to reject this defence of classicism in his *Observations sur la lettre de J.J. Rousseau*, where he states triumphantly: 'Asservis dans nos Tragédies ordinaires aux unités, aux vraisemblances, aux régles les plus exactes, nous avons abandonné nos Opéras aux prestiges de l'imagination' (Subjected in our ordinary tragedies to the unities, to verisimilitude, to the most exact rules, we have abandoned our operas to the powers of the imagination).[57] Cazotte's evident appreciation of opera's creative possibilities leads Décote to conclude that, torn between his loyalty to classicism and his delight in the powers of the imagination, Cazotte simply gave preference to whichever elements struck his fancy, with little concern for consistency.[58] I propose, to the contrary, that Cazotte does not confront this apparent contradiction in his own writing because, according to the operatic theories circulating at the time, his simultaneous appreciation of the realm of classicism (the *vraisemblable*) and the realm of the imagination (the *merveilleux*) was quite consistent.

The French operatic stage was one of the sole remaining strongholds of the marvellous in the eighteenth century. Whereas numerous critical studies attest to its prevalence, Catherine Kintzler's *Poétique de l'opéra français de Corneille à Rousseau* constitutes the most thorough treatment of the subject to date.[59] Kintzler derives the rules that came to govern the French *tragédie en musique* in the years 1740–60 from a combination of late seventeenth and early eighteenth-century operas and theoretical treatises, citing the abbé de Mably as evidence that the rules, though unwritten, were nevertheless common knowledge.[60] On the one hand, the opera, which evolved in counter distinction to the spoken theatre, was the designated realm of the *merveilleux*. On the other hand, the opera, like the spoken theatre, was subject to the classical strictures of *vraisemblance* that were enforced by audience expectations. The rules that came to govern the operatic stage combined these two limiting factors in a single code, which Kintzler dubs 'la vraisemblance du merveilleux.'[61] This code bears an uncanny resemblance to the contradiction Décote identifies at the heart of Cazotte's contributions to the *Querelle des Bouffons* and to the paradox that critics have identified at the heart of Cazotte's novella. Cazotte wrote *Le Diable amoureux* some twenty years after the *Querelle des Bouffons* had subsided and after the grand era of the *tragédie en musique* that Kintzler describes. Yet the century's third opera debate was brewing at the time and Gluck's reform opera, which preserved his predecessors' penchant for marvellous subjects and conserved a certain respect for French operatic tradition, was all the rage. Though Cazotte did not participate directly in the *Querelle des Gluckistes et des Piccinnistes*, which I will discuss at greater length in the following chapter, he revised his manuscript as the proponents of French and Italian music carried on their pamphlet war. A perusal of this manuscript indicates that Cazotte remained very much committed, despite the intervening decades, to the aesthetic he had so vigorously defended during the *Querelle des Bouffons*. It suggests, moreover, that Cazotte's awareness of the unwritten code that governed French operatic convention contributed to his ability to reconcile its seemingly incompatible elements in another artistic domain.

Let us now turn our attention to a comparison of the aesthetics that governed the eighteenth-century operatic stage with those that are at work in Cazotte's text. According to Kintzler, because historical subjects, unity of place, and logical explanations were characteristic of the theatre, marvellous subjects, frequent and sudden changes of locale, and supernatural explanations were relegated to the opera.[62] A first (or zero) degree of the marvellous thus arose from the very nature of the event, for eighteenth-century audiences went to the opera anticipating that marvellous events would occur on stage.[63] Once the marvellous was indelibly associated with the operatic world, composers were free to introduce other elements that were, by and large, unknown on the stage of the spoken theatre without disrupting the logic of the presentation: music, for instance, might quite appropriately accompany the appearance of a god; dancing might convey the fact that demons move differently than mortals; machinery might show where demons and deities come from; and changes of locale might depict the various realms they inhabit or magical transformations they undergo.[64] An example from *Le Diable amoureux* serves to illustrate how such inversions might have an impact on the form of a text written with the French opera in mind. When Alvare, the hero of Cazotte's novella, wishes to impress his friends the necromancers by having the devil do his bidding, Cazotte invokes the language of the stage, calling Béelzébuth's transformation of the vault in the ruins of Portici into a banquet hall a 'changement de la scène' (change of scene) executed 'plus promptement qu'une décoration ne s'élève à l'Opéra' (more swiftly than the scenery is erected at the Opera).[65] On stage a change of scenery usually indicates a change in locale. In Cazotte's text, accordingly, each change in locale takes place with the same rapidity as the original change of scenery. Falling asleep in his carriage in Naples, Alvare awakens to find himself in Venice.[66] Bent on arriving in Brenta before nightfall, he makes the journey in the space of a paragraph.[67] While such rapid progress in no way departs from the story-logic, and tends to call to mind the folk tale tradition of the seven-league boots, Cazotte himself suggests the analogy to a change of scenery on the operatic stage.[68]

Ultimately, the domain of the sung theatre was definitively distinguished from that of the spoken. An exacting public still required that the two types of theatre adhere to similar standards of *nécessité* and *vraisemblance*, however.[69] A librettist could not, for example, stray too far from a tale with which the spectators were already familiar or introduce effects that were not motivated by the story.[70] Nor was the librettist permitted to tamper with the public's conception of the marvellous. The hierarchy of supernatural powers had to be observed, as did their habitat: a greater god had power over a lesser; each could only exert those powers they were known to possess; and gods had to descend from above, whereas demons were obliged to ascend from below.[71] Composers and librettists were therefore careful to avoid disrupting the narrative logic. Kintzler provides a telling example of how 'le merveilleux faible' (the weak marvellous) could be enhanced while remaining within the bounds of the audience's expectations: '[I]l sera normal et bienséant,' she writes, 'qu'un demi-dieu, amoureux d'une mortelle, emploie ses dispositions particulières à des fins de séduction: il donnera quelque divertissement enchanté ... il se livrera à quelques métamorphoses destinées à éblouir l'objet de son amour' (It would be normal and proper for a demigod, in love with a mortal, to dedicate his special powers to the ends of seduction. He will give an enchanted entertainment ... he will give himself over to some metamorphoses destined to impress the object of his affection).[72] A comparison of *Le Diable amoureux* with this example reveals that Cazotte, in many respects, followed a similar schema. Given this line of reasoning, for instance, nothing is more natural than that Béelzébuth appear to Alvare first as a horrific camel to test his fortitude, then as a spaniel to show submission, and finally as a divinely beautiful woman thinly disguised as a page boy in order to seduce him. The page boy's willingness to transform the vault in which Alvare stands into a banquet hall and then, after a quick costume change, entertain Alvare's guests is also perfectly in keeping with the rules that governed the operatic stage.

Occasionally, operatic plots necessitated a second degree of the marvellous in order to enhance the impact of a climactic event, an effect that Kintzler dubs 'le merveilleux fort' (the strong marvelous).[73] Yet composers and librettists were obliged to prepare the audience for such moments before taking things to the next level. Humans were expected to exhaust their own resources before having recourse to superior powers; magicians and demigods were meant to proceed from the ordinary to the supernatural or violent and not the reverse.[74] Cazotte observes this recommended order in the opening sequence of *Le Diable amoureux*. Soberano, the necromancer whom Alvare has asked to initiate him into the secrets of his science, initially proceeds with caution. After savouring Alvare's astonishment when his invisible servant Calderon fills his pipe, Soberano sends Alvare away to regain his composure before revealing anything further. The two meet repeatedly in the course of the next several days, Soberano carefully choosing which of Alvare's questions to answer and which to avoid. His patience worn thin, Alvare finally expresses his overwhelming desire to communicate with the spirits and boasts that he will pull the devil's ears. At this, Soberano protests: 'Vous n'avez pas subi votre temps d'épreuve; vous n'avez rempli aucune des conditions sous lesquelles on peut aborder sans crainte cette sublime catégorie' (You haven't yet undergone your trial period; you have fulfilled none of the conditions that enable one to approach this sublime realm without fear) insisting that another two years is the usual term of apprenticeship.[75] Though Alvare proceeds with far less caution, he agrees, at least initially, to rely on Soberano's help, and to learn the fundamentals of his art before seeking direct commerce with the spirit world. The entire preamble to Béelzébuth's appearance, which consists of a series of delaying tactics, thus conforms to the conventional means of preparing an audience for the intensification of the marvellous on the operatic stage.

Once the stage is set for the enhancement of the marvellous, librettists and composers could gradually build towards the 'moment merveilleux fort.' Kintzler provides an example of how this was done from an opera by Lully whose works Cazotte was, in effect, defending when he took the side of the French opera in the *Querelle des Bouffons*. The example she provides is strikingly similar to the subsequent development of *Le Diable amoureux*:

> Par exemple, Cybèle, qui aime Atys, commence par flatter son orgueil; puis elle le terrorise et fait pression sur lui par l'intermédiaire des songes; enfin, ce n'est qu'après l'échec de ce second moyen, déjà extraordinaire en lui-même, qu'elle passe véritablement à l'action: On entre ici dans le merveilleux tragique, le plus fort de tous. A la violence Cybèle joint l'appel à des forces surnaturelles ... Mais ce moyen se révèle peu efficace: alors, et alors seulement, elle se tourne vers des forces plus puissantes; c'est l'invocation d'Alecton qui sort des Enfers. ... Suivent, en série, toutes les scènes d'horreur que l'on voudra.

> [For example, Cybèle, who loves Atys, begins by flattering his pride; then she terrorizes and puts pressure on him through the mediation of dreams. It is not until the failure of this second means, already extraordinary in and of itself, that she goes into action. Here we enter into the tragic marvellous, the strongest of all. To violence, Cybèle adds a call for help from supernatural forces ... but this means proves to be relatively ineffective. Then, and only then, she takes recourse to more powerful forces: the invocation of Alecton who emerges from hell.][76]

Though it is unclear whether the antagonist in *Le Diable amoureux* is one (devil) or several (camel, spaniel, sylph), the novella roughly follows the sequence of gradual intensification that Kintzler outlines. Soberano attempts to stave off Alvare's impatience by flattering his pupil ('[il] commence par flatter son orgueil'), telling him that as he is uninformed, he is apt for instruction. This strategy backfires, however, for the notion of his aptitude quickly goes to Alvare's head and leads imperceptibly to his boast that he will pull the devil's ears. Once Alvare invokes the devil, Béelzébuth makes an initial attempt to subdue Alvare by appearing in the form of a camel ('[il] le terrorise'). When this method fails,

Béelzébuth takes the form of Biondetta, in love with Alvare. While in Biondetta's company, Alvare falls into an artificially deep sleep en route to Venice and later dreams of Biondetta and his mother acting at cross purposes ('et fait pression sur lui par l'intermédiaire des songes'). Biondetta eventually explains that she is a sylph, a supernatural being, though not of the most powerful kind ('à la violence [elle] joint l'appel à des forces surnaturelles'). Unable to win Alvare's complete submission in her present form, however, Biondetta resumes the form of the camel and confesses herself to be 'le grand diable d'enfers' ('c'est l'invocation d'Alecton qui sort des Enfers'). Thus the chief means of subjugating Alvare occur in the order outlined above: flattery, terror, dreams, recourse to supernatural forces, and invocation of the devil. Whereas in Cazotte's definitive version it remains unclear whether Alvare merely dreams of the devil or the devil actually tempts Alvare via a dream, in an earlier version the first part (outlined above) was followed by a second in which Alvare, possessed, did indeed undergo 'toutes les scènes de l'horreur que l'on voudra.'[77]

If the finished operatic work is to appear *vraisemblable*, it is, of course, of the utmost importance that the transitions between instances of the marvellous be as smooth as possible. The various means of passing from the 'merveilleux faible' to the 'merveilleux fort' are governed, Kintzler posits, by two laws: the law of increasing dramatic progression and the law of contrasts, which she explains as follows:

> La loi de la progression croissante désigne la nécessité de ne pas faire survenir trop tôt les moments forts et de les préparer par une logique dramatique ... Celle du contraste porte plutôt sur le mode de surgissement ponctuel des moments forts: ayant été préparés de telle sorte que le spectateur s'y attend en général, ils surviennent cependant à un moment précis où il ne s'y attend pas en particulier.

> [The law of increasing [dramatic] progression states the necessity of not allowing the strong moments to arise too soon and to prepare their occurrence through dramatic logic ... That of contrast determines how to bring on these strong moments: having been prepared so that the spectator expects them in general they nevertheless arise when he does not particularly expect them.][78]

These laws can be combined in various proportions to create two different effects. The law of increasing dramatic progression can predominate and thus 'laisser la tragédie assez longtemps dans une ambiance faible et indécise, et repousser le moment fort assez loin' (let the tragedy linger in a feeble and indecisive ambiance and postpone the climax for a while), a tactic that Lully frequently employed. Alternatively, the law of contrasts can predominate and 'amener assez rapidement un moment fort, qui échoue ou ne débouche sur rien de décisif, en amener un autre plus puissant, et ainsi de suite jusqu'au moment culminant, qui aboutit enfin en provoquant le dénouement' (bring about a climax fairly rapidly, which fails or does not lead to anything decisive, then bring about another, stronger one, and so on, until the culminating moment, which finally arrives and provokes the denouement).[79] As should be clear from the previous discussion, this is the pattern that governs the order of events in *Le Diable amoureux*. The camel's original appearance, for instance, occurs very early on but has little to no immediate consequences, whereas its later appearance shatters Alvare's nerve completely and promptly brings matters to a head. Interestingly, Kintzler stipulates that such a pattern is often reserved for scenes from hell and characterizes the operas of Rameau, who had started to upstage Lully in Cazotte's day. It was therefore in vogue at the moment Cazotte was writing on behalf of the French opera and would have been brought to mind whenever his friend Jean-François Rameau intoned one of his uncle's harmonic passages.

In order to ensure that the transition between natural and supernatural would be imperceptible, librettists often had recourse to various forms of mediation. The three that Kintzler claims were most common prove to be the same three that Cazotte employs. They include natural phenomena, magic formulas and invocations, and demigods such as nymphs, 'petits démons' (little demons), and 'êtres hybrides' (hybrid beings).[80] Natural phenomena, and particularly storms, were one of the most common objects of eighteenth-century musical mimesis. Rameau, who wished to gratify his audience by providing orchestral sound effects whose natural counterpart they could easily identify, wrote several very recognizable storm sequences. Cazotte's tale includes a crucial storm scene on the road to Estramadure. His description suggests, however, that sprites rather than storm heads may have been responsible for the tumult:

L'orage, après s'être annoncé de loin, approche et *mugit* d'une manière épouvantable. Le ciel paraissait un brasier agité par les vents en mille sens contraires; les coups de tonnerre, *répétés* par les antres des montagnes voisines, retentissaient horriblement autour de nous. Ils ne se succédaient pas, ils semblaient *s'entre-heurter*. Le vent, la grêle, la pluie, *se disputaient entre eux* à qui ajouterait le plus à l'horreur de l'effroyable tableau dont nos sens étaient affligés.

[The storm, after announcing its arrival from afar, began to draw near with a terrible *roar*. The sky looked like a live fire stirred in a thousand different directions by the wind: the thunderclaps *echoing* in the caverns of the nearby mountains, resounded frightfully around us. They did not follow one upon the other, but seemed rather to *collide*. The wind, hail and rain *quarreled amongst themselves* for the right to add the most horror to the frightening tableau assailing our senses.][81]

The storm resembles a sporting match between supernatural beings. Cazotte thus leaves it up to his reader to choose which intermediaries are at work in this scene, nature or spirits. The remainder of the tale is veritably littered with creatures of indeterminate supernatural rank. Alvare inadvertently invoked Biondetta, a sylph, when attempting to conjure up the devil. Biondetta admits that it was she who transformed the vault in the 'ruines de Portici' (ruins of Portici) with the aid of 'les Sylphes, les Salamandres, les Gnomes, [et] les Ondins' (the Sylphs, Salamanders, Gnomes, and Undines).[82] Towards the end of their travels she introduces Alvare to characters who bear a strong resemblance to devils and witches.[83] Kintzler's list of possible intermediaries thus suggests an operatic origin for Cazotte's frequent allusions to the arts of divination, allusions that critics are inclined to attribute to Cazotte's subsequent flirtation with mystic sects.[84]

Eighteenth-century French audiences were inclined to accept the presence of marvellous agents and events because they were seated in the sung rather than the spoken theatre. As Kintzler aptly puts it, however: 'N'importe qui ne peut pas faire n'importe quoi' (No matter who cannot do no matter what).[85] The restrictions to which Cazotte subjects the marvellous agents and events in his narrative, leaving his readers uncertain as to whether to explain what happens according to the laws of nature or to the laws of the supernatural, resemble those that governed the contemporary operatic stage. This unwritten code tacitly determined who was allowed to do what, when, and how so as to produce the most dramatic effect possible while forestalling the spectators' incredulity. The order of events, the intervention of supernatural agents, and the obstacles that the hero encounters in Cazotte's novella also correspond to functions that Vladimir Propp identifies as essential to the basic structure of the folk tale. Kintzler herself notes, moreover, that the agents that appeared on the operatic stage are 'bien connu[s] des théoriciens du conte' (well known to the theoreticians of the folk tale) and were 'fortement exploité[s] par la littérature fabuleuse' (widely exploited by fabulous literature).[86] The mere presence of such agents and events in *contes de fée* and the *merveilleux oriental* is not enough to account for Cazotte's unprecedented accomplishment, however, which subsumes all supernatural elements into a narrative that respects the laws of the natural world.[87] Furthermore, while the agents in folk tales frequently take the form of animals, sorcerers, and sprites, at no point do they assume the guise of an opera singer, which is precisely what Biondetta does in Cazotte's narrative when she takes the form of 'la signora Fiorentina,' *improvisatrice*, who performs a 'récitatif *obligé* et une ariette pathétique qui terminaient le troisième acte de l'opéra dans lequel elle devait débuter' (obligatto recitative and pathetic arietta, which concluded the third act of the opera in which she was to perform).[88] The explicit allusions to the opera in Cazotte's novella may thus indeed be considered signs of the source, if not of the agents and events in his narrative, then of the aesthetic that enabled him to reconcile the *merveilleux* and the *vraisemblable* in his work.

In addition to revealing the conceptual foundation of Cazotte's novella, the textual allusions to the opera provide the raw material for two riveting musical tableaux that constitute the most aesthetically sophisticated moments in *Le Diable amoureux*. Once Biondetta transforms the vault in the ruins of Portici into a banquet hall 'plus promptement qu'une décoration ne s'élève à l'Opéra,' the allusions start to multiply.[89] Assuming the guise of a page boy at Alvare's request, Biondetto, as he is now called, serves a delightful repast to Alvare's guests, then exits and, after a quick costume change, reappears, harp in hand, as 'la signora Fiorentina.' Mildly surprised, Alvare requests that the signora perform for them, giving rise to the first musical tableau. Alvare and the necromancers watch and listen as the signora, seated before them, performs her recitatif and aria, accompanying herself on the harp. All eyes are upon the signora, and the spectators are 'saisis par la vérité de la scène au point de se frotter les yeux' (rub their eyes, so struck are they by the reality of the scene). So persuasive is the performance that Alvare and the necromancers momentarily forget that they themselves have conjured up the spectacle: 'nous croyions être au plus délicieux concert' (we ... believed ourselves to be at the most delightful of concerts).[90]

Alvare is particularly captivated by the singer and her song, focusing his attention on her hands, her fingers, the curve of her nails, her penetrating glance, and the elegance of her waistline. His pleasure in looking is troubled, yet enhanced, when he recognizes the page boy's silhouette across the signora's clothing. The page, who was already disarmingly attractive, becomes even more so by virtue of having cross-dressed: 'Je jette l'œil sur lui à la dérobée: figurez-vous l'Amour en trousse de page; mes compagnons d'aventure le lorgnait de leur côté d'un air où se peignait la surprise, le plaisir, et l'inquiétude' (Stealing a furtive glance at him, I see an image of Cupid in a page's costume. My companions make eyes at him in turn, with an air that betrays surprise, delight and uneasiness).[91] Alvare's uncertainty as to whether Fiorentina is a cross-dressed boy or a cross-cross-dressed woman leaves him both aroused and perplexed. His uncertainty as to whether the creature before him is human or devil creates a further source of discomfort which is increased when, hours later, the memory of the music still haunts him. 'Ce chant mélodieux ... ce son de voix ravissant, ce parler qui semblait venir du cœur, retentissaient encore dans le mien, et y excitaient un frémissement singulier' (The melodious sound ... that ravishing tone of voice, that manner of speaking which seemed to come straight from the heart, still resounded in my own and there aroused a most curious flutter).[92] So seductive is the memory of la Fiorentina's song that Alvare suddenly realizes he may soon be bound to Béelzébuth by ties not of gratitude but of affection.[93] Alvare's description of the tableau of Fiorentina's performance indicates that he is aware of its illusory nature, and yet he has difficulty maintaining his incredulity, for it is both aurally and visually persuasive.

Though the humanity and sexual identity of the creature who performs this musical tableau are equally uncertain, all evidence points to the singer, or her song, being Italian. The numbers that she performs are taken from the opera in which she is to appear in Venice. The contrast between the sex of the singer and the gender of his/her clothing also calls to mind the deceptive physique of the Italian castrati whose voice and effeminacy was still prized in Italy but not in France. The description of the sound that the signora Fiorentina produces and of its effect on Alvare, moreover, closely resembles Rousseau's characterization of Italian music: 'La dame chante. On n'a pas, avec plus de gosier, plus d'âme, plus d'expression: on ne saurait rendre plus, en chargeant moins. J'étais ému jusqu'au fond du cœur' (Then the lady sang. None with greater voice could ever have more soul or expression;

nor impart more with less effort. I was touched to the bottom of my heart).[94] Rousseau held soul, expression, absence of superfluous ornamentation, and the ability to touch the heart of the listener to be attributes of the Italian style. While Cazotte's decision to include a performance of Italian as opposed to French music in his novella may seem surprising in view of his position during the opera quarrels, his characterization of Italian opera in Rousseauian terms is by no means untrue to his former stance. For one thing, he never contested Rousseau's argument that Italian music was more expressive and poignant than French music. He simply defended the right of the French to listen to their own opera and denied that the superiority of Italian opera was suffcient reason to banish French opera from the stage. What is more, in *La Guerre de l'opéra*, Cazotte characterized Italians as excessive: 'La nature est différente chez nous de ce qu'elle est chez les Italiens: chez eux l'amour est lascif, la gayeté minaudiere, & la colere convulsive' (Our nature is different than that of the Italians. For them, love is lascivious, gaity is affected, and anger convulsive).[95] Such a viewpoint suggests that Cazotte chose Italy as the setting for *Le Diable amoureux* in part because he considered it to be the land of temptation, a notion supported by his choice to send Alvare on a Venetian gaming spree, losing his money in the casinos and compromising his Spanish virtue in the Italian bordellos. This possibility is reinforced by the fact that he designates Italian as the language of the camel, the most immediate and certain incarnation of the devil in the story, who twice addresses Alvare with the deafening question *'Che vuoi?'* (What do you want?).[96] By having Alvare fall prey to the haunting beauty of foreign music, Cazotte evokes the political overtones of the opera debates, in which he came quite close to suggesting that Rousseau was a negative and unwanted foreign influence and that the French who supported his views were guilty of treason. Cazotte thus draws attention to the power of Italian song to speak to the soul and to seduce the senses, a dual power that can be particularly nefarious if the singer is the devil in drag.[97] He highlights the subversive nature of Biondetta's diabolical role by having her sing the songs of a people who, though not yet a nation unto themselves, nevertheless posed a serious challenge to France's sense of self.

The second musical tableau in *Le Diable amoureux* arguably merits the name still more than the first, for it so perfectly fulfil the requirements for a tableau that Clément-Pierre Marillier selected it as the subject of one of his drawings. The narrative is suspended, quite literally, by the insertion of the engraving by Jean-Michel Moreau based on Marillier's drawing between the lines of the text (figure 3).[98] The print depicts the moment when Alvare watches through the keyhole as Biondetta accompanies her song on a harpsichord that she has painstakingly reassembled.[99] Biondetta's back is to the door and she is seemingly unaware of the beholder's presence. In his note on the illustrations Cazotte lauds the artist for the stroke of genius that inspired him to accentuate the demarcation between the inside world of the performance and the outside world of the inscribed beholder by illuminating the room in which Biondetta is seated and darkening the corridor in which Alvare crouches.[100] The illustration thus emphasizes the distinction between the roles of performer and beholder, evoking stage lights on the one side and an audience cloaked in darkness on the other. It also lends an aura of forbidden knowledge to the blatantly voyeuristic tableau.

Seated at her harpsichord, Biondetta performs two pieces of music in close succession. The first is an improvisation in prose. Prose improvisation closely resembles declamation, which Rousseau considered to be the form of vocal expression that best represented the original conjunction of music and language.[101] Its free form permits a more direct expression of passion than would a set piece and thus helps communicate Biondetta's emotion to Alvare. Biondetta enhances the effect of her music by modelling the empathy Alvare is meant to feel, wiping her eyes as though moved by her own performance or the emotions to which she gives voice. Then, as though beginning in earnest, Biondetta places a book on her harpsichord bench that enables her to reach the keys and see her music. The second piece she performs is more formal than the first, for Alvare recognizes the air she plays. He describes the tune as a barcarole, an unmistakably Italian form, and claims it was quite popular in Venice. Cazotte provides the song that Biondetta sings, written out in full within the text, a common novelistic practice. Less conventionally, however, he also provides a full-page illustration featuring the piece of music that is presumably propped up on Biondetta's harpsichord (figure 4). This additional illustration enhances the musical tableau's effect as a *mise en abyme* of the relationship between text and reader. Alvare, on the one hand, is driven wild by the sensuality of the experience, exclaiming, 'Le son de la voix, le chant, le sens des vers, leur tournure, me jett[aient] dans un désordre que je ne puis exprimer' (The tone of her voice, her manner of singing, the sense of the verses, their turn of phrase, throw me into a state of confusion that I cannot put into words) before racing madly across Venice in an effort to escape the memory of the singer's charms, still unsure of whether she is devil or woman.[102] The page of sheet music invites the reader to share more fully in Alvare's experience, not by vicariously participating in his sensory upheaval but by recreating the performance and sustaining the effect of the music. By making it possible for the reader to hear the music first-hand, Cazotte creates a tableau in which the music quite literally breaks through the surface of the text. The two illustrations thus implicitly extend the scope of the performer's power from Alvare (the inscribed beholder) to the reader. In the first, the reader watches Alvare watch Biondetta, and is thus affected not only by Biondetta's tears but by Alvare's rapt attention. In the second, the reader is privy not only to the visual but to the sonorous power of the tableau as Cazotte invites us to assume the position of either the performer or the beholder and to experience music's power to touch the heartstrings directly.

Through the music of Biondetta's songs is purportedly Italian, Cazotte renders it impossible to determine the language of the story. There is no telling whether the camel, the little white dog, the page boy, and Biondetta are devil, sylph, or mortal. There is also no telling what language they speak. The '*improvisatrice* romaine' presumably sings in the native Italian her name suggests, but does she continue to speak Italian when she resumes the guise of a page? If Biondetta is the devil, she may well change language with her physical form. If she is a sylph, she may have had to choose a nationality when she chose her sex. The other characters are of Spanish, Flemish, and Neapolitan origin. Though they may be willing to listen to Italian opera, in what language do they converse? Because language and music were so closely associated in eighteenth-century aesthetics, the language of the story, or its obfuscation, necessarily affects our interpretation of the musical tableaux. Cazotte writes the lyrics of the second musical tableau, both in the text and in the score, in French. Presumably, however, he provides the lyrics in French to accommodate the reader, maintaining a distinction between the language that the characters are speaking and the language in which the narrative is written. Since the words of Biondetta's song are of her own invention (for she sets her original lyric line to a popular tune, in keeping with the musical tradition of the *vaudeville*) they could be in any of the languages that Alvare understands.

If Biondetta does indeed set French lyrics to an Italian tune, as the page of music suggests, we are confronted with one of those composites of French words and Italian airs that Rousseau was accused of having written and that Cazotte claimed truly merited the name 'bouffonerie,' affording the reader a bit of comic relief from the seductions of Biondetta's song.[103] The possibility that Biondetta may be singing in Italian, and that the lyrics, along with the rest of the text, are provided in French for the reader's sake alone, has its own implications, however, for it suggests that the effect of Italian music is essentially the same regardless of the language it accompanies. If we are to assume, that is, that the reader can recreate Alvare's experience by listening to a performance of the page of music in the text, then the fact that Alvare hears the words in Italian whereas the reader hears them in French must not significantly alter the emotional impact of the music, suggesting that there is a suitable French equivalent for each Italian expression. In effect, Cazotte reiterates his argument of two decades previous, to wit: 'le Dictionnaire [n'est] pas si étroit que M. Rousseau se l'imagine' (the dictionary is not as limited as Mr. Rousseau thinks).[104]

Thus, even unto the song she sings, Biondetta – female or male, human or supernatural, devil or sylph – remains a being of unknown or composite origin. There is something truly unsettling in the fact that Cazotte deliberately avoids pinning down Biondetta's primary language as well as that used at any one moment by the characters in the story. In so doing he prevents Biondetta from being fully associated with the camel, whose language is Italian and whose character is diabolical, leaving us uncertain as to her identity. Franc Schuerewegen argues that *Le Diable amoureux* should indeed be considered the first example of fantastic fiction, for the reader experiences the same thrill of uncertainty as to Biondetta's nature and affiliations throughout the story that Alvare experiences for only the first half of the tale.[105] The musical tableaux contribute to the fantastical nature of the narrative, for they are particularly effective in communicating Alvare's combined arousal and apprehension to the reader. They appear, moreover, to be part and parcel of Biondetta's plot. Though Alvare commands her to appear as the signora Fiorentina, he does not anticipate being captivated by the performance, which Biondetta uses for her own ends. The pains she takes to reconstruct the harpsichord suggests, moreover, that the instrument forms a critical part of her strategy. Her sung soliloquy is, in all likelihood, staged and is part of her plan to gain possession either of Alvare's body (if she is a sylph) or of his soul (if she is the devil). Playing on the notion that music was thought to speak not only to the senses and the emotions but ultimately to the soul, Cazotte places the soul of the reader equally at risk by enabling us to recreate and therefore sustain the effect of Biondetta's song.

Todorov defines the fantastic as a hesitation on the part of the main character or the reader as to whether to interpret the course of events according to the laws of nature or the laws of the supernatural.[106] Cazotte's musical tableaux clearly contribute to Alvare's uncertainty. In the first tableau, when absorbed in the performance by the signora Fiorentina, Alvare is unable to determine the identity or the sex of the creature before him, and cannot tell whether the provenance of her voice is demonic or divine. Cazotte ensures that the reader shares Alvare's uncertainty by continually shifting the personal pronouns (il/ elle) and the declension of the creature's name (Biondetto/Biondetta) in the text. Alvare would have managed to walk away from the scene with relative impunity, had he not been haunted by Biondetta's image and the memory of her song. The reader is thus unable to use the text as authority and is forced to rely on Alvare's eyes and ears. The second tableau enhances the tension between virtue and eroticism already present in the first tableau. While Biondetta's words do little more than claim victim status and proclaim the sincerity of her love, Alvare finds her performance so arousing that he can no longer deny the sensual nature of his response and is obliged to flee. The reader is thus unsure whether to give greater credence to the (virtuous) words of the song or to their (erotic) effect on the beholder. By having Alvare observe Biondetta's performance through the keyhole, Cazotte plays, moreover, on the fine line that divides the tropes of sentimental literature from those of libertine fiction. Less certain still is the effect Biondetta's song would have on the reader should the reader choose to recreate her performance and essentially take Alvare's place. Confronted with the interpolated sheet of music, the reader cannot help but wonder whether the devil must do the singing or the devil is in the song. We would have to share Alvare's temerity before ceding to the temptation that the sheet music affords. Cazotte thus leaves us with the distinct impression that just as Alvare risks losing his soul if he consents to sleep with the devil, we may risk lose ours if we consent to listen or play.

Cazotte never relented in his campaign against Rousseau's musical convictions, from his overt rebuttal of them in the *Querelle des Bouffons*, to his parody of them in the fourth canto of *Ollivier*, to his exposure of their subversive effect in *Le Diable amoureux*. The deliberate stereotyping coupled with a refusal to pin down nationalities and languages in *Le Diable amoureux* suggests that Cazotte was disenchanted with the petty quarrels as to which language was superior, an attitude that Zerbin expressed when he remarked that the debates had gone on too long and to no avail. By associating Italian music with the devil's seductions, Cazotte preserved its negative connotations. By intimating that the translation of the lyric line does not alter music's ability to move the listener, Cazotte threw a wrench in Rousseau's argument that the strengths and weaknesses of a national music should be attributed to the national tongue. Cazotte's first-hand acquaintance with the rules that governed French opera helped foster a unique blend of *vraisemblance* and *merveilleux* that gave rise to a new literary genre. His creative response to the question of whether music could be expressed via the French language to which Rousseau had attracted such widespread attention gave rise to a musical tableau in which the music in the text penetrates the levels of both story and discourse, subjecting the reader to its uncanny allure. Writing, as it were, from opposite sides of the opera house, Diderot and Cazotte helped fan the flames of resistance not to Rousseau's recognition that the French opera was in need of reform but to his prediction that reform was doomed to failure.

3 Beaumarchais's Staged Songs

Or, Messieurs, la co-omédie
Que l'on juge en cè-et instant,
Sauf erreur, nous pein-eint la vie
Du bon peuple qui l'entend.
Qu'on l'opprime, il peste, il crie,
Il s'agite en cent fa-açons;
Tout finit-it par des chansons ...

[And so our comic course is rer-run.
You ask if there is sense behind the fun?
I believe it paints the hope and fear
Of all who are forgathered here.
When good people are oppressed too long
They kick and shout, for they are ser-strong.
But all will end not in tears but ser-song.]

Beaumarchais, *Le Mariage de Figaro*

Pierre-Augustin Caron de Beaumarchais was too young to have participated directly in the *Querelle des Bouffons*, yet he grew up in its shadow, so to speak. Raised in a milieu that fostered his interest in the performing arts, he was trained in music from an early age, and his first position at court was that of music teacher to the daughters of Louis XV.[1] In the decades that followed the publication of the *Lettre sur la musique française* it became clear that Rousseau's critique of French music and the French language was to have generative consequences, for its implications caused considerable consternation not only among

French authors but among composers and librettists as well. Beaumarchais entered the fray in time to contribute to the new vision of French opera that helped lay the brunt of Rousseau's concerns to rest. In a mock apology that appears in his *Lettre modérée sur la chute et la critique du Barbier de Séville,* Beaumarchais alludes to the controversy surrounding the ideal form of works written for the spoken and the sung theatre, making an unmistakable reference to Rousseau's attribution of the poor quality of French music to the shortcomings of the language: 'Peut-être un jour oserai-je affliger votre oreille d'un Opéra dont les jeunes gens d'autrefois diront que la musique n'est pas *du bon français,* et j'en suis tout honteux d'avance' (Perhaps one day I will dare to afflict your ears with an opera whose music, the young folk of yesteryear would say, is not in good French, for which I am much ashamed).[2] His evocation of 'les jeunes gens d'autrefois' clearly refers to those who participated in the *Querelle des Bouffons.* By feigning concern that his music may not be in good French, Beaumarchais calls attention to the counterintuitive nature of Rousseau's argument. Like Diderot and Cazotte, Beaumarchais disagreed with Rousseau's attribution of the shortcomings of French opera to the French language instead of to French poets and composers, yet he shared Rousseau's musical ideal. The genesis of Beaumarchais's works – his *drames,* his *parades,* his comedies, and his opera – have long been a subject of scholarly interest. Their diversity resulted, in large part, from his own rethinking of generic categories in the spoken and the sung theatre, as the prefaces to his works reveal. The form Beaumarchais assigned to his Figaro comedies and his opera *Tarare* constitute two distinct approaches to theatrical reform that stemmed from his search for an ideal combination of language and music *within* the French tradition.[3] His efforts to incorporate music into his plays (rather than narrative) culminated in the creation of two musical tableaux on the stage of the Comédie-Française which, ironically, were far more successful than those that Diderot had originally prescribed.

Beaumarchais's first attempt to write for the theatre was in the dramatic, not the comic vein. Diderot had laid out his theory of the *drame,* a new genre midway between tragedy and comedy, in a treatise entitled *De la poésie dramatique* and illustrated the concept in his play *Le Père de famille.* His play inspired Beaumarchais to complete his own initial attempt at the new genre, *Eugénie,* which he defended in his *Essai sur le genre dramatique sérieux* of 1767 that served as a preface.[4] In his essay Beaumarchais responds to the critics of the new genre by defending the right of the French public to decide for itself what kind of staged performances it wishes to attend. The following rhetorical question, written in reference to the *drame*, is reminiscent of Cazotte's defence of the right of the French to attend their own opera: 'N'est-il pas aussi hasardé de soutenir que le jugement du public ému est faux et mal porté qu'il le serait de prétendre qu'un genre de spectacle dont toute une nation aurait été vivement affectée, et qui lui plairait généralement, n'aurait pas le degré de bonté convenable à cette nation?' (Is it not just as risky to maintain that the judgment of the aroused public is false and misguided as it would be to assert that the kind of spectacle that had vividly affected an entire nation and that pleased it in general is not good enough for the nation?).[5] Once Beaumarchais takes up the cry, the democratic overtones of Zerbin's complaint that philosophers were allowed to overrule the common sense of the people in matters of taste become more apparent. Arguing against the notion that public opinion should be moulded by the intellectual elite, Beaumarchais makes a vital distinction between matters of taste in the realm of the theatre, and the rest of public life:

Je conviens qu'une vérité difficile sera plutôt rencontrée, mieux saisie, plus sainement jugée par un petit nombre de personnes éclairées que par la multitude en rumeur, puisque sans cela cette vérité ne devrait pas être appelée difficile; mais les objets de goût, de sentiment, de pur effet, en un mot de spectacle, n'étant jamais admis que sur la sensation puissante et subite qu'ils produisent dans tous les spectateurs, doivent-ils être jugés sur les mêmes règles?

[I admit that a difficult truth would be more easily met, better grasped, more soundly judged by a small number of enlightened people than by the murmuring multitude, because otherwise it would not be considered difficult, but should matters of taste, of sentiment, of pure effect, in a word, of spectacle, never being admitted except on the basis of the power-ful and sudden sensation that they produce in the spectators, be judged according to the same rules?][6]

Beaumarchais's defence of the people's right to choose is in keeping with his call for freedom of expression and the ongoing battle against censorship that he waged in his prefaces and his plays. Later he would demonstrate his capacity to use public opinion to his advantage in his struggle to overcome the king's opposition to the staging of his works.

In *Le Mariage de Figaro*, Figaro attests to the difficulties awaiting those who seek to reform the sung and spoken theatres when he lists them among the subjects that were censored at the time: 'Il s'est établi ... un système de liberté ... de la presse; et ... pourvu que je ne parle en mes écrits, ni de l'autorité, ni du culte, ni de la politique, ni de la morale ..., ni de l'opéra, ni des autres spectacles ... je puis tout imprimer librement' (A free-market principle has taken over ... which even extends to the press, and ... provided I refrain in my articles from mentioning the government, religion, politics, morality ... opera or any other kind of theater ... I am free to publish whatever I like).[7] The prerevolutionary rumblings that go undetected when uttered by Cazotte's characters thus become quite audible in Figaro's famous tirade. In effect, Beaumarchais exhorted the French public to define and defend its national taste rather than cede to authority or drift on the changing winds of international fashion.

The period in which Beaumarchais conceived his theatrical works and, in many ways, the form that those works assumed, hearkens back to that of Molière's theatrical innovations, which also involved the integration of words and music, towards the end of the seventeenth century. Molière's works, like Beaumarchais's, arose at a moment of generic flux. When collaborating with Lully, Molière drew upon ballet, orchestral music, and spoken dialogue to create the *comédies-ballets* that became the forerunner of the *opéra-comique*.[8] The comedies of Molière and Beaumarchais stemmed from a similar blend of the French and Italian traditions, and followed a comparable trajectory from popular to high art, resulting in a rare composite of the comic and dramatic for which Hugo would later laud them in his *Préface de Cromwell*.[9] An avid reader of Molière, whose plays were performed in the Beaumarchais household at a time when they were no longer produced on the stage of the Comédie-Française, Beaumarchais clearly had his predecessor in mind when writing his comedies. Act III, scene iv from *Le Barbier*, in which Lindor, passing for Bazile's pupil, gives Rosine her singing lesson, bears a striking resemblance to Act II, scene v of Molière's *Le Malade imaginaire*, in which Angélique's lover Cléonte disguises himself as her music teacher and they express their love in a 'petit opéra impromptu.'[10] Bartholo's request that Rosine sing a ditty from his youth in the same scene from *Le Barbier* also resembles Act I, scene ii from *Le Bourgeois gentilhomme*, in which M. de Pourceaugnac displays a similar longing for the songs of yesteryear. Beaumarchais was the first to bring a comparable blend of music and dialogue to the Comédie-Française since

Molière's *comédies-ballets* of a hundred years before, yet he used the musical numbers within his comedies to dramatically different effect.

The trajectory that led from Molière's to Beaumarchais's comedies was long, intermittent, and complex. Though the various combinations of words and music or forms of sung and spoken comedy that arose in the intervening period were frequently indebted to the Italian tradition, they became and remained peculiarly French. Eighteenth-century comic opera was an outgrowth of the *comédies-ballets* that Molière and Lully had originally composed as a form of court entertainment. Once Molière died and Lully began to collaborate with Quinault, it survived as a means of parodying the grander *tragédie en musique* that flourished under the sanction of Louis XIV. *Pièces en vaudevilles,* as they were known at the time, interspersed *vaudevilles* with spoken dialogue characterized by a salty, even crass sense of humour that appealed to people from all walks of life and was used by fair performers to compete with the Italians for the favour of the aristocracy as well as the rabble. They were first given the name *opéra-comique* in 1715 under Louis XV and were gradually made palatable to more refined tastes.[11] A specifically French form of comic opera thus already existed in 1752 when the Italian troupe that helped reify the opposing sides of the *Querelle des Bouffons* performed Pergolesi's *La Serva padrona* between two acts of Lully's *tragédie en musique, Acis et Galathée.* Though the French referred to *La Serva padrona* as an opera buffa, it was, more accurately, an intermezzo, consisting of one act with only two to three characters. This economy of style set it apart from the French *opéra-comique,* as did the fact that it employed recitative rather than spoken dialogue.[12] When Rousseau wrote *Le Devin du village* – which, it will be remembered, was taken to be a contribution to the French side of the *Querelle des Bouffons* until his *Lettre sur la musique française* suggested otherwise – he borrowed the reduced number of characters and the continuous musical line from the Italian form.[13] Despite the public outcry that his letter provoked, the simplicity of composition and pastoral theme that characterized Rousseau's comic opera became the model for the French *opéras-comiques* of the latter half of the century.[14]

The seed of Beaumarchais's first comic work lay in another combination of words, music, and pantomime, which bore a certain affinity to the *comédie-ballet* and the *opéra-comique.* The *parade* was a popular form of farce that was often used outside theatres to attract audiences. It, too, interspersed *vaudevilles* with dialogue that parodied common speech and proved entertaining to spectators from all walks of society.[15] As the *parade* moved from outside the theatres into the salons and onto the stage, the parodies of common speech became more precise and the bawdy banter more refined, until all that was left of the original form was a certain lusty humour unknown to the comedies written along more conventional lines and antithetical to the moral tone of the *drame*.[16] The history of the *parade* thus bears a strong resemblance to that of the *opéra-comique*. The first recognizable sketch of Beaumarchais's *Barbier de Séville* was in the form of a *parade* entitled *Le Sacristain*.[17] Beaumarchais's initial impulse when attempting to stage the work, to recast it as an *opéra-comique* and submit it to the Théâtre-Italien, was therefore, in a sense, quite consistent. The Théâtre-Italien's refusal to stage the work (purportedly because their lead singer had previously been a barber) was a critical decision in the history of the theatre, however, for it prompted Beaumarchais to withdraw his opera, revamp it as a play, and submit it to the Comédie-Française.

In his *Lettre modérée sur la chute et la critique du Barbier de Séville* of 1775, Beaumarchais alludes to his decision to transform *Le Barbier* from an opera into a play, and to his change in alliance, as it were, from the Italian to the French theatre. He cites a complaint voiced by a woman who was unable to attend the performance as a result of his decision: 'Vous êtes bien honnête d'avoir été donner votre pièce aux Français! moi qui n'ai de petite loge qu'aux Italiens! Pourquoi n'en avoir pas fait un opéra-comique? ce fut, dit-on, votre première idée' (A fine idea to have gone and given your play to the French! and I who have but a small box at the Italians'! Why did you not make it into a comic opera? It was, so they say, your original intent).[18] 'Français' here refers to the Comédie-Française and 'Italiens' to the Théâtre-Italien. The names of the theatres evoke the different national traditions they represent, calling our attention to the strict division between them, which existed in the realm of the spoken theatre as well as the sung. To the question of why he did not leave his comedy in the form of an *opéra-comique*, Beaumarchais responds not with respect to the *Barbier* in particular, but rather with respect to opera in general. The time to write such works, he claims, is not yet ripe. The reason he provides indicates that his decision to transform his opera into a play was motivated in part by the contrast he observed between the current and the ideal state of the lyric theater: 'Notre musique dramatique ressemble trop à notre musique chansonnière pour en attendre un véritable intérêt ... Il faudra commencer à l'employer sérieusement au théâtre quand on sentira bien qu'on ne doit y chanter que pour parler' (Our dramatic music bears too strong a resemblance to our song music to afford any real interest ... We must begin to employ it seriously in the theatre when we feel that we must sing there only in order to speak). Sharing Rousseau's operatic ideal of declamation modelled on speech, he reproaches contemporary French music for its unnatural ornaments and reprises, exclaiming: 'Au lieu de narrer vivement, tu rabâches!' (Instead of narrating vividly you repeat!).[19] Songs prevent the music from effectively communicating the passion it was thought to represent to the soul of the listener, Beaumarchais claims. Yet poets have begun to master the art of conveying powerful images through concise writing, he states, and composers ought to emulate them. Despite his aversion to the use of song forms in the sung theatre, Beaumarchais nevertheless suggests that they will have to do until the French learn to emulate Rousseau's musical ideal. Addressing his fellow countrymen, Beaumarchais declares: 'Reste, reste aux chansons pour toute nourriture, jusqu'à ce que tu connaisses le langage sublime et tumultueux des passions' (Stick with songs as your sole nourishment until you learn the sublime and tumultuous language of the passions).[20] While at first this exclamation does not appear to respond to the question of why Beaumarchais gave his play to the French rather than the Italian theatre, it does if we consider that he essentially followed his own advice. Dissatisfied with the form of his *opéra-comique*, which had just been rejected and did not conform to his vision for the lyric theatre, he converted it to a play that constituted a veritable showcase for the French *chanson*.

Beaumarchais revamped *Le Barbier de Séville* in 1773, the year that Molière's works were revived in celebration of the centennial of his death.[21] From the first lines of the play, we see Figaro immersed in the activity of song writing, wracking his brain for an 'antithèse' (antithesis) or something 'qui eût l'air d'une pensée' (that sounds as if it might be profound).[22] His disparaging reference to the carelessness of opera librettists suggests that his own poem will be more tailored, and he clearly does not limit himself to the 'gloire' and 'victoire' that was said to comprise the sparse lexicon of operatic lyrics. While the decision to transform an *opéra-comique* into a play would usually have entailed eliminating all but the incidental music, Beaumarchais allowed the *vaudevilles* and *romances*, both characteristic of *opéra-comique*, to remain.[23] The snatches of song that litter *Le Barbier* may thus be considered the vestigial remains of its original form. This explanation does not account for their presence in *Le Mariage*, however, which was destined for the Comédie-Française from the very start. Beaumarchais must have recognized that he had hit upon a formula that was both diverting and dramatically effective, and that music played an essential role in both. His sustained attempts to integrate music into the comic effects and narrative functions of his plays ultimately enabled him to decrease the distinction between the acts (the traditional place for the words) and the *intermèdes* (the traditional place for the music). He had expressed the desire to create a seamless continuum between the *intermèdes* and the acts of *Eugénie* as early as his *Essai sur le genre dramatique sérieux*, when he had been frustrated at his inability to command the audience's attention during the *entr'actes* of his play.[24] The only way to persuade the audience to devote the same attention to the *intermèdes* as it did to the acts, he concluded, was to incorporate the music that was usually played between the acts into the action itself.[25]

Philip Robinson characterizes Beaumarchais's decision to foreground the *vaudevilles* on the stage of the Comédie-Française as nothing short of insolent. By conserving them, however, he was able to introduce a specific brand of musical humour into his Figaro plays and to demonstrate how well-suited this form of musical joke was to the comic theatre.[26] *Vaudevilles* were composed by setting new verses to an old tune. The spectators were expected to remember the original verses, and to derive pleasure from the contrast between the two. The joke, then, resides in the music, which alone calls the original verses to mind.[27] When Count Almaviva enters Doctor Bartholo's house in *Le Barbier de Séville*, pretending to be a drunken soldier in the hopes of chatting with Rosine, he sings a rather unflattering description of Bartholo to the tune of 'Ici sont venus en personne.'[28] The song that was originally set to this tune was comprised of a series of transparent metaphors describing Alizon's private parts ('Elle a aussi une houlette / Un poëlon et une cuvette / Deux gros flacons qu'sont tout rondis / Et y allons, et y allons / Joue violon ta ra la la la la la la' [She also has a trowel / A pan and a basin / Two large well-rounded flasks / And off we go and off we go / Play violin tra la la la la la la]), after which Martin is subjected to the same indignities ('De son côté Martin apporte / Une clef pour ouvrir la porte' [For his part Martin brings / A key to open the door]).[29] Bartholo's irritation when the Count sets his portrait to this tune ('Le chef branlant, la tête chauve, / Les yeux vérons, le regard fauve, / L'air farouche d'un Algonquin' [A nodding brow, a balding head, / Eyes of green, a look of dread, / Ferocious as ten wild Injuns]) is therefore understandable, for not only is the portrait unflattering, but the music highlights the old man's lechery.[30] In *Le Mariage de Figaro*, Beaumarchais uses the *vaudeville* to similar effect. The stage directions indicate that Bazile should sing a song entitled 'La Fauvette' to the tune of the final *vaudeville*. Since the audience hears Bazile's song before the final *vaudeville*, however, it has the impression that the latter is set to the tune of the former, not the other way around. Bazile's song runs as follows: 'Cœurs sensibles cœurs fidèles / Qui blamez l'amour léger, / Cessez vos plaintes cruelles: / Est-ce un crime de changer? / Si l'Amour porte des ailes, / N'est-ce pas pour voltiger?' (Hearts so tender, hearts so faint / Who groan that love is callous, / Cease now your fond complaint / It is no crime to be capricious. / Cupid has wings, Cupid has darts. / Is it surprising he flits among hearts?).[31] The repetition of the tune at the end of the play adds a sense of irony to the final *vaudeville*, in which the characters sing the morals they have deduced from the day's events to the tune of fickle love. It thus subtly prepares the spectator for *La Mère coupable*, putting the lie to the apparently harmonious close of *La Folle journée*.

The disjunction between the words of the *vaudeville*, which belong to the present song alone, and the music, which belongs to the present song and the one on which it is based, allowed the music to have a comic effect that could be distinguished from that of the words. It thus granted the music a voice of its own. While Beaumarchais reproaches the music of the lyric theatre for not narrating vividly enough in his *Lettre modérée* ('au lieu de narrer vivement, tu rabâches!'), the *vaudeville*'s form in a sense allows the music to do just this.[32] When Rosine sings her response to Lindor's profession of love in *Le Barbier de Séville*, all she *says* is, 'Tout me dit que Lindor est charmant, / Que je dois l'aimer constamment' (Fair Lindor's song suggests to me / That I shall love him constantly ...).[33] Fearing her tutor's return, she knows she must be brief, yet she seeks to convey her plight by singing the two verses to the tune of 'Maître en droit' (The Rightful Master), a song from an *opéra-comique* of the same name in which another young lady is forced to marry her tutor against her will.[34] Similarly, when the Count, feigning to be a horse doctor, sings a comparison of their respective medical professions to Bartholo, a general practitioner, he does so to the tune of 'Vive le vin' (Long Live Wine), reminding us that he intends his brash discourse to convince the doctor that he is drunk. The music thus serves, in a sense, as a wink at the audience. Between Acts III and IV of *Le Barbier* Beaumarchais exploits the music's potential to the full by allowing it to narrate the progression of the storm, thus making use of the most universally understood subject of musical mimesis in the eighteenth-century operatic tradition, a subject that required no glossing. Though the wedding ceremony in *Le Mariage de Figaro* closely resembles the traditional *intermède*, it also plays a vital role in the unfolding of the plot. As the peasants dance a fandango Suzanne finds occasion to hand the Count a note in which she fixes the site of their nocturnal rendezvous and Figaro sees the Count prick himself with the pin that seals the note. In this combination of song, dance, and shadowplay, it would be hard to say whether the *intermède* is invading the action or the action the *intermède*. Because it tells us something that the words themselves do not convey, the music can be said to narrate.

Several aspects of Beaumarchais's dramaturgy served to narrow the distance between theatre and the novel still further. Beaumarchais used the term *roman* to describe his drame *Eugénie* as well as his trilogy, 'le roman de la famille Almaviva' (the novel of the Almaviva family).[35] In his *Essai sur le genre dramatique sérieux* he stated: 'Les romans de Richardson ... sont des vrais drames, de même que le drame est la conclusion et l'instant le plus intéressant d'un roman quelconque' (The novels of Richardson ... are real dramas, just as the *drame* is the conclusion and the most interesting moment in any novel).[36] The primary distinction that Diderot drew between the novel and the *drame* was that 'le roman suit le geste et la pantomime dans tous leurs détails; ... au lieu que le poète dramatique n'en jette qu'un mot en passant' (the novel describes gesture and pantomime in every detail; ... whereas the dramaturge makes only a passing reference to them).[37] Yet Beaumarchais's use of stage directions in unprecedented abundance enhanced his move towards narrative continuity.[38] By detailing everything from the costume to the facial expression to the presiding emotion the characters are meant to convey, Beaumarchais came as close as possible to narrative asides designed to govern the reaction of the spectator.[39]

Beaumarchais's musical tableaux are in keeping with the tendencies of his larger dramatic project to straddle the divide between the sung and spoken theatre and the novel. Taking advantage of music's ability to contribute to the comedy and the drama, he combined them with an efficacy that Hugo was later to appreciate. True to the spirit of the *opéra-comique*, he integrated the songs into the action of his comedies and yet as a concession to the spoken theatre he was careful to motivate the singing.[40] The musical numbers thus take the form of short performances within the body of the work in which the characters perform not for the audience but for one another. The unusual combination of theatrical conventions upon which Beaumarchais drew favoured the occurrence of musical tableaux whose presence was not incidental to the progression of the play and whose effect upon the audience was mediated by a beholder. As a result, the musical tableaux in his comedies bear a closer resemblance to the narrative tableaux I have examined thus far than to those that Diderot envisioned for the theatre, for Beaumarchais's beholder is a character in the play rather than a member of the audience.

Of the many musical moments in the Figaro comedies, only two suspend the action long enough to have the combined aural, visual, and emotional effect associated with the musical tableau. The first is Rosine's *ariette* from *Le Barbier de Séville*. This *ariette* is a romance, the form Rousseau originated and popularized in his *Devin du village*, and is set to the original music of Baudron, the first violinist of the Comédie-Française. Robinson explains that no other piece in the two comedies qualifies as an *ariette*, a sophisticated genre which tended to serve as a show-stopper and was deemed singularly out of place in the spoken theatre. Its inclusion was unprecedented on the stage of the Comédie-Française.[41] So great was the public outcry at the first performance that the lead actress refused to sing the song a second time, forcing Beaumarchais to console himself with the following petition in a footnote: 'Sur les théâtres où quelque peu de musique ne tirera pas tant de conséquence, nous invitons tous directeurs à restituer [cette ariette], tous acteurs à la chanter, tous spectateurs à l'écouter, et tous critiques à nous la pardonner, en faveur du genre de la pièce et du plaisir que leur fera le morceau' (In theaters where the occasional use of music does not rouse such high passions, we would encourage managers to include [this *ariette*], actors to sing it, audiences to listen to it, critics to forgive the author, and all to bear in mind what kind of play this is and the enjoyment the piece will give to those who see it).[42] We are hard put to imagine the work without the *ariette*, however, for while the words themselves have little to do with the Count's and Rosine's immediate situation, the song provides the only vehicle for expressing their feelings.[43] Though the scene was clearly inspired by Molière's *Le Malade imaginaire*, the contrast between the plays helps to convey the extent of Beaumarchais's innovation. In *Le Malade imaginaire*, Cléonte, disguised as Angélique's music teacher, gives her a lesson before the combined audience of Angélique's father and the suitor he wishes her to marry.[44] In an effort to convey his feelings and discover his fate, Cléonte gives Angélique a page of musical notation with no words, and the two proceed to improvise a duet in which they are able to speak to each other freely. So transparent are their words, however, that Angélique's father immediately recognizes their relevance to the situation and cuts the lesson short. There is therefore no time for the lovers to be moved by one another's singing or for the spectators to be moved by their romantic exchange. The lovers have, indeed, conveyed as much information and as little emotion as they would have had they been at liberty to speak.

Rosine's *ariette*, which evokes a shepherd's love for a shepherdess, is quite different. As in the scene described above, in Beaumarchais's first musical tableau an onlooker's presence prevents the lovers from expressing themselves freely. Count Almaviva, doubly disguised as Lindor the student and Alonzo the music teacher, proposes to replace Bazile and give Rosine her music lesson. Refusing to allow Rosine to have her lesson in private as accustomed, Bartholo pulls up a chair and settles down to spectate. He thus faces Rosine, who is seated at the harpsichord, the Count looking over her shoulder. Aside from Lindor's name, which appears in the lyrics of the song, the only lines that refer to the immediate situation occur in the reprise: 'Si quelque jaloux / Trouble un bien si doux, / Nos amants, d'accord, / Ont un soin extrême ... / ... De voiler leur transport; / Mais quand on s'aime, / La gêne ajoute encore, / Au plaisir même' (Should some jealous swain / Mar their happy refrain, / Our passionate pair / Would take every care .:. / ... To hide their emotion. / Yet love is not frightened, / For with every commotion / The pleasure is heightened).[45] The lyrics thus call attention to the pleasure that voyeurism affords not the beholder but the object of his gaze. Bartholo does not notice the relevance of the words to the current circumstances, however, for Rosine's singing has lulled him to sleep. He consequently does not interrupt the performance, and the effect of the music is given time to accumulate. The effect of Rosine's song is thus twofold, for while it puts Bartholo to sleep, providing the spectator with a comic alternative, it sincerely moves the Count.[46] Beaumarchais indicates as much not in the words of the play, but in one of the numerous stage directions, in which he describes the pantomime and the musical modulation that is to convey the emotional impact of the tableau: '*Le Comte, pendant la petite reprise, se hasarde à prendre une main qu'il couvre de baisers. L'émotion ralentit le chant de Rosine, l'affaiblit, et finit même par lui couper la voix au milieu de la cadence, au mot* extrême. *L'orchestre suit le mouvement de la chanteuse, affaiblit son jeu et se tait avec elle*' (During the chorus, the Count reaches tentatively for Rosine's hand and smothers it with kisses. The effect is to make her sing more slowly, she falters and her voice breaks in the middle of her phrase at the words 'every care'. The *orchestra, following her lead, also falters then stops when she does*).[47] This instant, in which all comic repartee is momentarily suspended, affects the spectators along with the Count. The spectacle of the heroine's beauty and the sentiment of her song give the audience a foretaste of the greater solemnity Rosine will acquire as the Countess in the *Mariage*. The orchestra's role, in this instance, clearly goes beyond providing background music, in which case the melody would continue even as the singer faltered. To the contrary, the music follows the contours of the character's emotion. Yet Beaumarchais allows the romance to repeat, in accordance with the convention he found so distasteful on the lyric stage, indicating that he remained fully committed to exploring the French song's dramatic potential.

Whereas in the *Barbier*, the reader is obliged to identify the musical tableau according to its salient features, in the *Mariage* Beaumarchais identifies it for us in another of his stage directions that describes the spatial arrangement in detail: '*La Comtesse, assise, tient le papier pour suivre. Suzanne est derrière son fauteuil, et prélude en regardant la musique par-dessus sa maîtresse. Le petit page est devant elle, les yeux baissés. Ce tableau est juste la belle estampe d'après Vanloo, appelée* la Conversation espagnole' (*The Countess, who is seated, holds the paper and follows the words. Positioned behind her chair, Suzanne plays the introduction, reading the music over the Countess's shoulder. Chérubin stands facing them, head lowered. This composition is an exact replica of the print after Vanloo entitled:* The Spanish Conversation).[48] Robinson has suggested that the staged tableau resembles that of Van Loo less in the precise arrangement of its characters than in a certain blend of 'impertinence' and 'naïveté.' Yet the arrangement of the characters is also true to Jacques Firmin Beauvarlet's print of Carle Van Loo's painting, displayed in the Salon of 1755. The painting, which is variously known as *The Spanish Conversation*, *The Spanish Concert*, or simply *The Concert*, was said to depict a 'pretty woman giving a music lesson to a little girl' (figure 5).[49] The tableau that results from this arrangement resembles the variety that Diderot wished to bring to the stage for it signifies simultaneously and is internally dynamic. The Countess, for one, fully anticipates that the moment she hears Chérubin sing is likely to be emotionally charged. To Suzanne's suggestion 'Faisons-lui chanter sa romance' (Let's make him sing that song he wrote) she can only muster the distracted reply: 'Mais, c'est qu'en vérité, mes cheveux sont dans un désordre ...' (No, but really, my hair is such a mess ...), suggesting that romance is in the air.[50] Chérubin likewise betrays the state of his emotions by blushing and trembling uncontrollably. The mutual feelings of

Chérubin and the Countess form an undercurrent that runs throughout the *Mariage*, in anticipation of the final chapter in the 'roman de la famille Almaviva,' *La Mère coupable*, in which the fruit of their clandestine affair will be revealed. In keeping with the tableau of Van Loo the Countess takes up her position vis-à-vis Cherubin, Suzanne strumming her guitar and looking over her shoulder in a grouping that mirrors that of the Count, Rosine, and Bartholo around the harpsichord in the previous play. Once again, the song takes the form of a romance with several stanzas.[51] Like Rosine's song, the words themselves are not precisely suited to the situation and do little to further the intrigue. The only telltale verses are, indeed, those which run, 'J'avais une marraine / que toujours adorai' (I had a godmother / Whom I loved most tenderly).[52] Chérubin's romance was traditionally shortened when staged, however, and these are the very words at which the Countess interrupts Chérubin's singing during the performance. This interruption conveys the function of the romance, for it suggests that the Countess has understood the import of the verses. Chérubin's song, though technically a romance, was set to the music of 'Malbrough s'en va-t-en guerre.' It thus likewise conformed to the definition of the *vaudeville*. Though the words of Chérubin's romance convey little, the original words were sung by a page to his mistress announcing the death of her husband.[53] The music, not the words, thus provides the parallel to the immediate situation, for the Countess has grounds to suspect that Chérubin might wish such a fate on the Count. Understanding the song's reference and therefore its import, the Countess cuts it short, fearing, perhaps, that Chérubin will feel unduly encouraged or she herself be persuaded to listen. The music has nevertheless exerted its influence, and once Chérubin has finished, the Countess observes: 'Il y a de la naïveté ... du sentiment même' (Very simple, very charming ... and in fact rather touching).[54] As in the tableau of the *Barbier*, the audience is presented with two possible responses to Chérubin's song: that of Suzanne, who mercilessly recommences her teasing, and that of the Countess, who absently fondles the ribbon Chérubin had stolen from her, the symbol of their mutual bond. Once again a potentially comical moment is rendered irresistibly poignant and the audience is given a foretaste of the denouement to the Countess and Chérubin's illicit affair in the third play of the trilogy. While the words of the song do little to further the plot, the singing itself and the musical accompaniment enable us to read the story of the characters' hearts and to share in their sentiment. Momentarily suspending the action, Beaumarchais's musical tableaux enable the characters and the audience alike to attain a new emotional level. By giving the spectator and reader alike a choice of beholders with whom to identify (Bartholo/ the Count, Suzanne/the Countess), Beaumarchais enhanced the blend of comedy and drama that is at the heart of his Figaro plays.

As we have seen, Beaumarchais brought his plays far closer to narrative by eliding the distinction between the action and the entr'actes, by adding copious stage directions that resemble narrative asides, and by giving the music a narrative voice as well as a role in the comedy and drama. The musical tableaux that the staged nevertheless converge with the structure of the play within the play that Forestier describes.[55] Though today we are more likely to read the play than to see it performed, eighteenth-century audiences heard the music just as clearly as the characters on stage did, and were equally susceptible to its cumulative effect. While Diderot called upon the reader's imagination to fill in the interstices of the Nephew's pantomime of music and Cazotte tempted the reader to recreate the performance if he dared, Beaumarchais exposed his audience directly to the tunes that toyed with his character's affections. By arranging the characters so as to resemble the tableau of Van Loo, Beaumarchais quite literally infused the tableau with music, seating the inscribed beholder on stage. Interestingly enough, when his Figaro comedies made their successful transition to the opera, Rosine's and Chérubin's songs became examples of what Carolyn Abbate has called phenomenal as opposed to noumenal music.[56] The tableau structure is thus, in a sense, preserved in the plays' operatic form, for the audience is momentarily released from sustaining the fiction that song is speech, aware that the characters on stage also hear the songs as music.

Chérubin's song is an excellent example of Beaumarchais's awareness of the popular appeal of French songs and of his ability to use public opinion to his advantage. Adept at setting the public against the king and his censors through well-timed readings and ill-timed cancellations, Beaumarchais had Chérubin sing his song to the tune of 'La Malbrough' not only because the story provided a witty commentary on the state of the Countess and Chérubin's affections but also because the music was all the rage at the time. Well aware of how to manipulate a crowd, he used the song as a sort of advance publicity, circulating it in the streets of Paris before the play had been approved in an attempt to curry popular favour. After three years of resistance and more than the usual number of censors, Louis XVI was ultimately obliged to give way to popular demand.[57] The bittersweet effect of Chérubin's setting new words to old music is undeniable. More important, however, the audience loved it. While Rosine's romance had threatened to stall the performance, Cherubin's ensured its success. When the curtain rose for the first performance, the house was full, the appreciation unmitigated, and the *Mariage* netted more proceeds than any other play in eighteenth-century France.[58]

Beaumarchais's irreverent use of French *chansons* on the stage of the Comédie-Française and his willingness to use their popularity to win public support for the staging of his plays echoes the cry of French music for the French that dates back to the *Querelle des Bouffons*. Faced with Rousseau's doubt that the French language could convey music, Diderot replaced language with gesture on the level of the story and Cazotte rendered the language of the story impossible to determine. Beaumarchais went still further, however, boldly setting the French language to such an intoxicating tune that he set all Paris a-whistling.[59] Far from conceding that French was not suited to a musical setting, therefore, Beaumarchais's comedies suggest that music is an integral part of French humour, sentiment, and storytelling. Aware of the linguistic aspect of the aesthetic controversies, Beaumarchais did not choose to obviate the question of the language of the story. Instead, every development in his comedies, whether of costumes, stage directions, the characters' references, or the musical allusions themselves, confirms that the language of the story is Spanish despite the fact that the plays are written in French. Beaumarchais treats this anomaly lightly, first acknowledging, then promptly dismissing it in one of the most entertaining passages of his *Lettre modérée*:

> Des connaisseurs ont remarqué que j'étais tombé dans l'inconvénient de faire critiquer des usages français par un plaisant de Séville à Séville, tandis que la vraisemblance exigeait qu'il s'étayât sur les mœurs espagnoles. Ils ont raison; j'y avais même tellement pensé, que pour rendre la vraisemblance encore plus parfaite, j'avais d'abord résolu d'écrire et de faire jouer la pièce en langage espagnol; mais un homme de goût m'a fait observer qu'elle en perdrait peut-être un peu de sa gaieté pour le public de Paris, raison qui m'a déterminé à l'écrire en français.

> [Connoisseurs have remarked that I fell into the trap of having a wit from Seville criticize French custom in Seville, whereas verisimilitude would require that he defend Spanish custom. They are right, and I was so

convinced of this that in order to render my play even more plausible I originally resolved to write and stage it in Spanish, but a man of taste brought it to my attention that it would thereby lose a bit of its appeal for the Parisian public, which persuaded me to write it in French.][60]

The only portion of Beaumarchais's comedies that can be said to be in French on the level of the story are therefore the songs themselves. Rosine's romance and Bazile's *séguedille* aside, the music is derived almost entirely from French tunes. Both the old and the new versions of the song lyrics are also in French, the old being those of the original French tune, the new being those that are sung in the context of the play (in Spanish on the level of the story but in French on the level of the discourse). The double set of lyrics, whose irony lies in their contrast, thus offers a lasting testimony to the capacity of the French to set their language to their music – to their great satisfaction. Beaumarchais's success in bringing French music back into the theatre and into the tableau itself provided a convincing counterexample to Rousseau's claim that the French language was unmusical. Though he restricted himself to song forms for the purposes of the spoken theatre, Beaumarchais came as close as possible to realizing his musical ideal within these self-imposed limits. He would discard these constraints as soon as he deemed the French to be ready for operatic reform.

Seventeen hundred and seventy-three was not only the year of Moliere's revival at and Beaumarchais's resolution to write for the Comédie-Française; it was also the year of Christoph Willibald Gluck's arrival in Paris.[61] Several ties bound Gluck to the cause of French operatic reform. The German composer had received the greater part of his musical training at the Burgtheater, where he was in charge of revamping French *opéras-comiques* for Viennese audiences.[62] The *opéras-comiques* most often performed in Vienna included Rousseau's *Le Devin du village* as well as works based on libretti by Sedaine who, along with Diderot and Beaumarchais, was one of the most successful authors of the *drame*.[63] Giacomo Durazzo, the director of the Burgtheater who commissioned several of Gluck's Viennese works, remarked that *Le Devin du village*, among others, 'nous [fait] voir qu'on peut créer un nouveau genre de Musique, imitée des Italiens, sans assujettir les paroles Françoises à des sons qui leur sont totalement étrangers' (shows us that we can create a new genre of music based on the Italians' without subjecting French words to sounds that are completely foreign to them).[64] Calzabigi, the librettist for several of Gluck's early works, had lived in

France during the thick of the *Querelle des Bouffons*, and had communicated the philosophes' views concerning operatic reform to Gluck in the course of their collaboration.[65] Convinced that French, not Italian, was the language that most closely approximated the Greek ideal of the lyric theatre, Gluck undertook the assiduous study of the French language, its cadences, its authors, and the tradition of the *tragédie en musique*.[66] He came to Paris in the hopes of reforming French opera not by having recourse to an Italian style, but rather by drawing upon the strengths of the French lyric tradition, remaining true to its language, and taking into account the reform principles expressed by those who professed to have the interest of the French at heart. According to Du Roullet, who translated Calzabigi's Italian libretti into French and wrote the libretto for Gluck's *Iphigénie en Aulide*, while Gluck was convinced that the inferior quality of French libretti was responsible for the relative poverty of French opera, he did not believe it was the fault of the language but rather of the poets. Du Roullet added that Gluck 's'est indigné contre les assertions hardies de ceux de nos écrivains fameux qui ont osé calomnier la langue française, en soutenant qu'elle n'étoit pas susceptible de se prêter à une grande composition musicale' (resented the brash assertions of those of our famous authors who dared to criticize the French language, maintaining that it was ill-suited to lend itself to a great musical composition).[67]

Gluck turned his indignation to good effect. Rather than critiquing the critics of the French language in turn, he resolved to pay attention to what, precisely, Rousseau found to criticize and then to rectify it. Though it is not known whether the preface to *Alceste* was written by Gluck or Calzabigi, it expresses what they together strove to achieve in the first operas they brought to Paris. The following manifesto emphasizes the importance of reforming both the musical *and* the lyric line:

> Lorsque j'entrepris de mettre en musique l'opéra d'*Alceste* ... je cherchai à réduire la musique à sa véritable fonction, celle de seconder la poésie, pour fortifier l'expression des sentiments et l'intérêt des situations, sans interrompre l'action et la refroidir par des ornements superflus ...
>
> Voilà mes principes; heureusement le poëme se prêtoit à merveille à mon dessein; le célèbre auteur de l'*Alceste*, ayant conçu un nouveau plan de drame lyrique, avoit substitué aux descriptions fleuries, aux comparaisons inutiles, aux froides et sentencieuses moralités, des passions fortes, des situations intéressantes, le langage du cœur et un spectacle toujours varié. Le succès a justifié nos idées.
>
> [When I undertook to set the opera *Alceste* to music ... I sought to reduce

the music to its true function, that of seconding the poetry, to reinforce the expression of the sentiments and the interest of the situations, without interrupting the action or cooling it by means of superfluous ornaments ...

These are my principles; fortunately the poem lent itself beautifully to my purpose; the famous author of *Alceste*, having conceived of a new model for lyric drama, had replaced the florid descriptions, useless comparisons, and cold and sententious morals with strong passions, interesting situations, the language of the heart and an ever-varied spectacle. Success has justified my ideas.][68]

Stripping the libretto of all florid language and the music of all superfluous ornamentation, Calzabigi and Gluck sought to convey the essence of the dramatic situation. The two reforms were interdependent. The composer was able to subject the music to the poem more effectively because the poet had improved the poem itself. Gluck's operas were thus an attempt to rethink the relationship between music and language in response to Rousseau's critique. In a letter addressed to the editor of the *Mercure de France*, Gluck suggests that Rousseau would have been his ideal partner in the reform of French music and libretti:

Avec l'aide du fameux M. Rousseau de Genève, que je me proposois de consulter, nous aurions peut-être ensemble, en cherchant une mélodie noble, sensible & naturelle, avec une déclamation exacte selon la prosodie de chaque Langue & le caractère de chaque peuple, pû fixer le moyen que j'envisage de produire une musique propre à toutes les nations, & de faire disparoître la ridicule distinction des musiques nationales.

[With the aid of the famous Mr Rousseau of Geneva, whom I intended to consult, we might together, by seeking a noble, sensitive, and natural melody, with a declamation that conforms exactly to the prose of each language and the character of each people, have discovered the means I envision of producing a music suited to all nations, and of eliminating the ridiculous distinction between national musics.][69]

In this passage, Gluck emphasizes the importance of purifying music and declamation alike, a dual challenge to which Gluck, Rousseau, Beaumarchais, and Salieri, among others, sought to respond.

In the years since the *Querelle des Bouffons*, the perception of Rousseau's attack on the French language had clearly started to change. Indeed, rather than being ostracized for his criticism of the language, he was starting to be hailed as the initiator of its reform. When Marie-Antoinette invited Gluck to Paris, the performance of his opera *Iphigénie en Aulide* touched off the century's third set of debates on the subject of the French opera, this time known as the *Querelle des Gluckistes et des Piccinnistes*.[70] Ironically, Rousseau entered the quarrel as a *Gluckiste*, that is to say, on the side of French operatic reform. In his 'Observations sur l'Alceste de Gluck' Rousseau defined the problem that faced the lyric theatre in more general terms than he had previously used: 'C'est un grand et beau problème à résoudre, de déterminer jusqu'à quel point on peut faire chanter la langue et parler la musique. C'est d'une bonne solution à ce problème que dépend toute la théorie de la Musique Dramatique' (It is a great and beautiful problem to solve to determine to what extent one can make language sing and music speak. The entire theory of dramatic music depends on a good solution to this problem).[71] Rousseau's solution to this problem was to allow the language and the music to speak in turn, a solution he sought to exemplify in his work *Pygmalion*. Dissatisfied with the provisional blend of French and Italian styles that he had come up with in his *opéra-comique*, *Le Devin du village*, he attempted to write a work in which the music would arise from and yet not accompany the words. He introduced the term *mélodrame* into the French language to describe his *Pygmalion*, in which spoken libretto alternates with musical passages by Coignet.[72] In an interpolated passage in his 'Observations sur l'Alceste de Gluck,' Rousseau's editors contend that he wrote his *mélodrame* in an attempt to compensate for the insufficiencies he perceived in the French language:

> Persuadé que la langue française, destituée de tout accent, n'est nullement propre à la musique et principalement au récitatif, j'ai imaginé un genre de drame, *dans lequel les paroles et la musique, au lieu de marcher ensemble, se font entendre successivement, et où la phrase parlée est en quelque sorte annoncée et préparée par la phrase musicale. La scène de* Pygmalion *est un exemple de ce genre qui n'a pas eu d'imitateurs. En perfectionnant cette méthode, on réunirait le double avantage de soulager l'acteur par de fréquent repos, et d'offrir au spectateur français l'espèce de mélodrame le plus convenable à sa langue.*

> [Persuaded that the French language, destitute of all accent, is not at all appropriate for Music, and principally for recitative, I have devised a genre of Drama *in which the words and the Music, instead of proceeding together, are made to be heard in succession, and in which the spoken phrase is in a way announced and prepared by the musical phrase. The scene 'Pygmalion' is an example of this genre of composition, and it has not had imitators. By perfecting*

this method, one would bring together the double advantage of relieving the Actor through frequent rests and of offering to the French Spectator the type of melodrama most suited to his language.][73]

Though Rousseau was willing to participate in the reform of French opera, the very form of his *mélodrame* continued to signal that he considered the French language to be a hindrance to musical expression.

Beaumarchais was fully aware of the controversy surrounding the reform of the lyric theatre as several of Figaro's comments suggest. In *Le Barbier de Séville*, Figaro states that *opéras-comiques* are a dime a dozen, and libretti, on the whole, rather poor. In the midst of editing a song lyric he remarks: 'Nos faiseurs d'opéra-comiques n'y regardent pas de si près. Aujourd'hui, ce qui ne vaut pas la peine d'être dit, on le chante' (The people who write comic operas don't worry about little things like that. These days what's not worth saying gets set to music).[74] Beaumarchais was thus clearly aware of the relative poverty of opera libretti, which Diderot had noted before him. In his *Lettre modérée*, written shortly thereafter, Beaumarchais indicates that the poetic reform is well under way, however, and that his principal concern lies with the music. Holding poetry up as an example, Beaumarchais playfully attempts to shame the music into following suit: 'Le poète se tue à serrer l'événement, et toi tu le délayes! Que lui sert de rendre son style énergique et pressé si tu l'ensevelis sous d'inutiles fredons?' (The poet kills himself in an effort to tighten the plot, and *you* diffuse it! What is the use of his rendering his style rapid and energetic if you bury it beneath useless trills?).[75] As we saw above, Beaumarchais concluded his *Lettre modérée* by saying that the French should content themselves with staging songs until such time as poetry resembles speech and music becomes more natural. His evocation of the language of the passions, his analogy between song and speech, and his desire for music to imitate nature were reminiscent of the Rousseauian rhetoric that had coloured the controversy surrounding French opera ever since the 1750s. Two decades later, the time was apparently ripe to abandon the songs whose dramatic effect he had exploited in his comedies and to move in the direction of operatic reform.

Though Beaumarchais did not contribute directly to the *Querelle des Gluckistes et des Piccinnistes* the preface to his opera *Tarare* and the form he assigned the work reflect the issues that were debated at the time. Picking up where his *Lettre moderée* left off, Beaumarchais openly aligns himself with Gluck and Calzabigi's reforms in the preface to his opera, and therefore (implicitly) with those of Rousseau. In his preface, addressed 'Aux abonnés de l'Opéra qui voudraient aimer l'opéra' (To the opera subscribers who want to like opera), he proposes to examine 'l'action de la poésie sur la musique, et la réaction de celle-ci sur la poésie au théâtre' (the effect of the poetry on the music and the reaction of the music to the poetry in the theatre); in other words, the reciprocal effect of music and language.[76] Unlike Gluck, Calzabigi, and Rousseau, however, Beaumarchais reserves his criticism for the music alone. Seeking an explanation for his boredom at the opera, he observes: 'Il y a trop de musique dans la musique du théâtre, elle en est surchargée; et pour employer l'expression naïve ... du célèbre chevalier Gluck, notre opéra pue de musique: *puzza di musica*' (There is too much music in theatre music, it is overpowering. To use the naive expression of the famous chevalier Gluck, our opera stinks of music: *puzza di musica*).[77] Sharing Gluck and Calzabigi's impatience with *ritournelles*, he accuses the musician of thwarting the poet's efforts to arrive at a more direct form of expression by obliging the singer to repeat himself at the end of a phrase.[78] So staunch is his faith in French poetry that he suggests it should serve as a model for musical reform, calling for composers to '[s]implifier le chant du récit ... le rapprocher de la parole' (simplify the story's song ... bring it closer to speech).[79] Music should provide not ornamentation but energy of expression, and the poem and the music, rather than working at cross purposes, should reinforce one another. He therefore wishes to render the music as simple, natural, and concise as the poetic line. Beaumarchais thus echoes the concern that Gluck and Calzabigi expressed in the 'Préface à Alceste' – economy of language and economy of music – yet rather than requiring that concessions be made on both sides he suggests that it is up to the composer to adhere to the poet's standard.[80]

Beaumarchais's plans for his own opera indicate that he was persuaded of the affinity between Gluck's ideas and his own, for when writing the libretto for *Tarare* he contacted Gluck in the hopes of persuading him to write the music. Protesting that old age and fatigue would prevent him from pursuing the project, the composer recommended his student Salieri for the job.[81] In his preface to the work Beaumarchais pays tribute to Salieri's adept rendering of the score and refers with pride to 'le système de Gluck, de Salieri, ... le mien!' (the system of Gluck, Salieri, ... mine!).[82] His insistence that music should emulate poetry and his persistance in writing his libretto in French despite the purported drawbacks indicate that he fundamentally disagreed with Rousseau's categorical condemnation of the language. Yet he agreed with Rousseau's suggestion that a national music should conform to the particularities of the national tongue, however imperfect. This concession, which Rousseau made as early as his *Lettre sur la musique française*, ultimately prevailed, for as we have seen Rousseau himself eventually began to explore what little potential the French language had.[83] Like Rousseau, Beaumarchais used the term *mélodrame* to refer to his ideal for the lyric theatre, yet the combination of words and music that he proposed differed slightly from what Rousseau had in mind. Rousseau chose to alternate language and music in order to avoid subjecting either sign system to the constraints of the other. Beaumarchais proposed, to the contrary, that the music should cleave entirely to the logic and cadence of the poem, in keeping with Salieri's watchword: *prima la parola, poi la musica*. Even as he responded to the aesthetic problem that his predecessor framed ('jusqu'à quel point [peut-on] faire chanter la langue et parler la musique'), therefore, Beaumarchais continued to find the French language for more *chantant* (tuneful) than Rousseau ever had.

Four full decades after the fateful day when Rousseau released his *Lettre sur la musique française* his critique of the French language continued to inspire authors, composers, and librettists alike to undertake the study of the language's strengths and weaknesses in order to gain a better understanding of their undervalued arts. As a result, they began to experiment with different combinations of words and music, drawing upon musical aesthetics to enhance the language in an effort to revitalize their plays, their operas, and their literary texts. Several stories attest to Rousseau's appreciation of Gluck's operas, which were written with his criticism in view. One reports that Rousseau, after having openly expressed his admiration for Gluck's work, received a visit from him and promptly showed him the door, accusing the composer of having written his operas for the sole purpose of proving him wrong.[84] Another relates, to the contrary, that Rousseau elected to recant his views publicly, stating: '[L]e zelé partisan du nouveau système; [Rousseau] a déclaré ... qu'il s'était trompé jusqu'à présent; que l'opéra de M. Gluck renversait toutes ses idées et qu'il était aujourd'hui très convaincu que la langue française était aussi susceptible qu'une autre d'une musique forte, touchante et sensible' (A zealous partisan of the new system, Rousseau has declared that he was mistaken, that Gluck's opera put the lie to all of his ideas and that he was now quite convinced that the French language is as susceptible as any other to strong, touching, sensitive music).[85] Finally, Jean Pappas reminds us that when asked late in his career whether he was still opposed to French opera, Rousseau responded by intoning a passage from Gluck's *Orphée et Eurydice* that had moved him to tears.[86] At the end of his career, then, Rousseau found himself obliged to concur with his opponents' stance that, given a good poem, the French language could be set to as fine a piece of music as any other. In all likelihood, at this point he would have agreed with Cazotte's assertion of yore that 'le Dictionnaire [n'est] pas si étroit que M. Rousseau se l'imagine.'[87] With this concession, the controversy of the previous several decades was effectively laid to rest, reminding us of the Nephew's famous last words: 'Rira bien qui rira le dernier' (He laughs best who laughs last).[88]

Rousseau's *Lettre sur la musique française* catalyzed a defence of the French language by three authors whose political and aesthetic convictions are not traditionally associated. The stance that Diderot, Cazotte, and Beaumarchais assumed during the debates was characterized not by a penchant for the status quo, but by the conviction that all aesthetic permutations had not yet been exhausted, that the French language could be enriched by infusing it with foreign languages, alternate sign systems, and the sister arts, and that the French public knew its own mind. Their defence of the national language and their suggestion that to attack it was unpatriotic proved to be progressive, not reactionary, for it did not prevent them from heeding the import of Rousseau's statements and experimenting with possible solutions to the problems he identified. Their response to Rousseau's negative characterization of the French language and music helped keep alive the notion that libretti could be rendered more natural and meaningful and that music could be adapted to the lyric line until such time as composers and librettists could turn their theory into practice. Not content to parry Rousseau's thrust in the letters they wrote during the opera debates and the prefaces to their works, Diderot, Cazotte, and Beaumarchais carried their defence of the language into the body of their literary texts. As the *Querelle des Gluckistes et les Piccinnistes* was brewing, Diderot revised *Le Neveu de Rameau* (1762–79), Cazotte wrote three successive versions of *Le Diable amoureux* (1772, 1774, 1776), and Beaumarchais converted *Le Barbier de Séville* from an opera into a play (1773).[89] The ingenuity of their solutions to the problem of how to convey music via the French language enabled these authors to enhance their texts considerably, leaving a literary legacy rife with aesthetic and ideological potential. Because

their responses to Rousseau's question were separately and simultaneously conceived, they neither acknowledged nor sustained the influence
of one another's writings. The Romantics were quick to recognize the
originality of their textual innovations, however. We must ask ourselves,
therefore, whether the history of the revitalization of French narrative,
the birth of fantastic fiction, the rise of the Romantic drama, and the
reform of opera would have been the same if Rousseau had chosen to
keep his letter in his briefcase.

The implicit response to Rousseau's question of how, or whether,
music can be conveyed via the French language can be found in the
musical tableaux of these three authors, tableaux that are arguably the
most aesthetically innovative passages of their texts. By inscribing a
beholder in their works, Diderot, Cazotte, and Beaumarchais gave their
readers a model for their affective participation in the text. As we watch
the Philosopher listen to the Nephew we alternately maintain our critical
distance or are moved to sincere admiration. As we watch Alvare listen
to Biondetta we hesitate between natural and supernatural explanations
and feel the tension between virtue and eroticism. As we watch Bartholo
and the Count listen to Rosine or Suzanne and the Countess listen to
Chérubin we sustain both the comic and the dramatic effect of the play.
In each instance the tableau favours simultaneity over sequentiality,
reaction over action, movement over stasis, and acts as a *mise en abyme*
of the relationship between text and reader. In the play within the play,
however, our tendancy to understand the internal spectacle as theatre
along with the characters enhances our ability to accept the external
spectacle as real.[90] In the musical tableau, to the contrary, we are not
inclined to understand the internal performance as merely staged. The
invidious aspect of these musical moments is that they invite true belief
on the part of the character and the reader alike. The Philosopher is thus
at risk of condoning the Nephew's philosophy, Alvare is at risk of losing
his soul, and the French were at risk of accepting the use of song on the
stage of the Comédie-Française. The musical tableau, which enabled
Diderot to play upon the structure of mimesis, thus also works in
tandem with the mechanism of sensibility, with salutory or sinister
consequences depending on the context. Taking advantage of the
tableau's tendency to invite rather than suspend belief, these authors
were able to continue their resistance to the political implications of
Rousseau's statements on a far more subtle level. By choosing an alternate
sign system, refusing to designate a language, or claiming to use a
foreign language on the level of the story, they enhanced the reader's

capacity to believe in the musical moments while continuing to write their narratives in French. Their tableaux thus ultimately imply that the French language is as capable of conveying music as any other. Diderot freed up the level of the story, Cazotte penetrated the level of the discourse, and Beaumarchais bridged the remaining distance between fictional and factual beholders. This trajectory led inexorably to the singular relationship between spectators and the stage during the French Revolution, when Beaumarchais once again displayed this ability to cater to (or control) the masses by changing the ending of *Tarare* three times to accommodate the shifting political winds.[91] The collapse of the distinction between nature and art and between performer and beholder was followed by what Johnson has called 'a collapse of dramatic fiction into political reality.[92] The distribution of song sheets to the members of the audience elided the difference between stage and street, between actors in a theatre and citizens in a republic.[93] Because the tableau structure and the mechanism of sensibility encouraged the audience to accept the fictional as real and react accordingly, art was increasingly held accountable for its political message. Throughout the years of social upheaval that followed close on the heels of aesthetic debate, music continued to be held in suspicion for its dual capacity for sincerity and subversion and language was used to bind it firmly to the fate of the nation.

PART TWO

Music and Morality
La Querelle des Femmes

4 Charrière's Exercises in Equivocation

Jamais il ne fut plus aimable musicienne ...

[There was never a nicer musician ...]

Charrière, *Caliste, ou Lettres écrites de Lausanne*

Isabelle de Charrière, Rousseau's contemporary and reader, was privy to the cult that arose after his death, yet maintained a more equitable view of his life and writings than did some of his younger enthusiasts.[1] More than once she took up pen in his defence, but careful readings of her works indicate that she never wholeheartedly embraced his ideas on women, marriage, and education.[2] Though Dutch by birth (*née* Belle van Zuylen), Charrière learned French at an early age, and used it in her conversation, correspondence, and literary texts practically to the exclusion of her native tongue.[3] She read widely in the French and classical traditions and promptly consumed each of Rousseau's works as they appeared. Though her family took up residence in Rousseau's native Switzerland, where she remained after her marriage, she kept abreast of the political, artistic, and musical scene in Paris via her correspondence. Schooled in philosophy, math, physics, foreign languages, classical texts, and musical notation from an early age, she bore a close resemblance to the 'femmes à grands talents' (talented women) that Rousseau despised.[4] When James Boswell, one of Charrière's suitors, offered to show a sample of her poetry to Rousseau Charrière declined his offer and sent him the following verses that summarize Rousseau's anticipated response:

Un peu de vers et de Philosophie
Avec Rousseau me brouilleroit.
A tout venant il crieroit
Non, ce n'est pas là ma Sophie
Fille à brochures et Billets,
Qui ne fit onc manchettes ni lacets,
Ni Savonnage ni Purée
Mais des Contes et des Portraits
En un mot Fille un peu lettrée
Doit rester Fille à jamais.

[Some verses and philosophy
Would estrange me from Rousseau.
To each passerby he would cry
No! That is not my Sophie
A maid of brochures and letters
Who never made cuffs or braid
Soap or purée
But fairytales and portraits
In a word a maid of letters
Will remain a maid forever.][5]

The last couplet is a direct reference to Rousseau's words, taken from the defamatory passage in *Emile* that reads: 'Toute fille lettrée restera fille toute sa vie, quand il n'y aura que des hommes sensés sur la terre' (Every maid of letters will remain a maid all her life as long as there are sensible men on earth).[6] Aware that she herself did not remotely correspond to the ideal of womanhood that Rousseau outlined in his treatise on education, Charrière took issue with such an ideal in several of her texts. Her single-minded dedication to the art of musical composition, in which she surpassed her female contemporaries, rendered her particularly sensitive to the stigma against women's musical education. Evidence of this stigma, which can be detected in Rousseau's writings, was widespread in eighteenth-century French society, as I will demonstrate in the following pages. Aware of the moral quandary at the heart of musical performance and its implications for women, Diderot, Cazotte, and Beaumarchais had treated the subject in a sympathetic, albeit cavalier manner. The morality of music thus constituted neither the central concern nor the most innovative aspect of their musical tableaux. Charrière, Cottin, Krüdener, and Staël, on the other hand, wrote specifically against the association between music and immorality in the public imaginary and the consequences of such an association for women. Grasping the significance of the tableau's persuasive power, these authors stripped the musical tableau of its aesthetic trappings, converting it into an effective weapon of social resistance and obliging their readers to acknowledge the moral fortitude of their musical heroines. While Charrière subtly resisted Rousseau's characterization of women's role in society throughout her literary works, the musical tableaux in *Caliste, ou Lettres écrites de Lausanne* provide particularly striking testimony to a woman's ability to cultivate her musical sensibility without the sensual overtones that her talents were thought to entail.

Charrière expressed her most open opposition to Rousseau's views in her *Courte réplique à l'auteur d'une longue réponse* of 1789. The *Courte réplique* was a reply to the abbé de Champcenetz, who had criticized Germaine de Staël's *Lettres sur les ouvrages et le caractère de J.-J. Rousseau* for being insufficiently critical of their subject.[7] Charrière took up Staël's defence by writing in her name, possibly out of female solidarity, possibly from a desire to demonstrate to Staël how she ought to have expressed herself. So effective was the ruse that, until recently, the pamphlet was attributed to Staël herself.[8] Shielded by what Jacqueline Letzter has aptly termed a feat of literary ventriloquism, Charrière was more pointed in her critique than she might otherwise have been.[9] Stating, solemnly, 'J'ose faire à Rousseau un ... reproche' [I dare to reproach Rousseau], Charrière rejected the separate programs of education for men and women that he proposed in *Emile*, calling attention to his double standard: '[Il] ne veut pas que les parens ou Instituteurs d'un jeune homme prennent sur eux de plier son caractère au joug de la société ... et il veut qu'on plie d'avance au joug la jeune femme' (He does not want the parents or tutors of a young man to undertake to bend his character to the yoke of society ... and they want us to bend a young woman to this yoke in advance).[10] Women may find it more beneficial to be adequately prepared for encountering life's various pitfalls, she suggested, than to be preserved in a state of childlike innocence.[11] While Charrière ultimately refrained from specifying in the pamphlet whether children should be fully prepared for what lies ahead or simply be allowed to remain children, she stipulated that, regardless of what is decided, the same decision should apply to both sexes. She was thus in favour of equal education for men and women and held that instruction, not naivety, would most effectively enable a woman to defend her virtue.

Disagreement with Rousseau's views forms a current of dissent that runs throughout Charriere's literary works. In *Sainte-Anne* she depicts three women, two of whom have received formal instruction and one of whom has learned through natural assimilation, the educational approach Rousseau had recommended for Sophie, Emile's female counterpart. Though the story is often read as a celebration of Rousseau's ideal of female innocence, Letzter observes that by enabling all three female characters to find husbands in the end Charrière suggests that women's education is *not* incompatible with marriage.[12] In her *Lettres de Mistress Henley*, she goes a step farther, implicitly reexamining the marriage of a couple that bears a striking resemblance to Julie and Wolmar and questioning whether being governed by a man's reason necessarily ensures a woman's happiness.[13] In her *Caliste, ou Lettres écrites de Lausanne*, the two-part work that I examine here, Charrière's resistance to the cultural association of music, women, and immorality that Rousseau helped perpetuate is equally subtle, yet she invests her heroine with a means of combating prejudicial public opinion that is reminiscent – or indicative – of her own approach to social reform.

Charrière considered Rousseau – as he considered himself – to be first and foremost a musician, if not by virtue of his compositions then by virtue of his sensibility and his musical ear. In a literary fragment entitled 'De Rousseau' Charrière asks:

> Qu'est-ce qui l'a rendu ... le digne objet de tant d'enthousiasme ...? Qu'est-ce? Son oreille, oui, la sensibilité de son oreille. Peut-être l'a t'elle fait auteur, mais surement elle l'a fait l'auteur et même l'homme qu'il a été. C'est elle qui a dicté son stile .... Dès sa plus tendre enfance les sons, les chants, la mélodie eurent un grand pouvoir sur lui mais il n'aprit que tard & lentement un art qu'il idolatroit & pour lequel je croirois qu'il eut moins de talent que de passion.

> [What rendered him ... the worthy object of such enthusiasm ...? What? His ear, yes, the sensitivity of his ear. Perhaps it made him an author, but surely it made him the author and even the man that he was. It dictated his style ... Ever since his most tender youth sounds, song, and melody had great power over him, but he only learned later and slowly an art that he idolized and for which, I believe, he had less talent than passion.][14]

Despite Charrière's appreciation of Rousseau's musical ear, when it came to matters of musical taste she once again only selectively adhered to his views. She shared his preference for the Italian over the

French tradition, yet preferred serious to comic opera.[15] She was convinced that the Italian language was fundamentally more lyrical than French, yet like Diderot, Cazotte, and Beaumarchais, she believed that a sufficiently gifted librettist should be capable of overcoming the difficulties of a French musical setting. In a letter to her correspondent Chambrier d'Oleyres, who kept her abreast of the *Querelle des Gluckistes et des Piccinnistes* and assisted her in her efforts to publish her works, she makes her position clear:

> Il faut beaucoup de soin je l'avoue quand on fait des vers en françois pour les chanter, mais n'importe. Ce n'est pas toujours ce qui est facile qui reussit le mieux. La difficulté tend l'esprit, & force l'industrie à s'aiguiser à se tourmenter pour chercher des ressources ... Si les poetes avoient été un peu plus musiciens il y auroit eu quelques reproches de moins à faire aux opera françois.

> [When one writes verses in French it takes a great deal of care, I admit, to sing them, but no matter. Easy things are not always the most successful. Difficulty sharpens the wits and forces industry to stimulate and torment itself in order to find the necessary resources ... If the poets had been more musically inclined we would have less to reproach French opera.][16]

Charrière's opposition to the position Rousseau had taken during the *Querelle des Bouffons* demonstrates her faith in her own musical training and powers of discernment. She nevertheless considered Rousseau to be the model of someone who, by dint of sheer passion and determination, had managed to acquire the rudiments of the musical arts at a relatively advanced age.

Charrière's own musical education began under her mother's tutelage.[17] Once married, she attempted to draw upon the resources at her disposal in order to pursue her study of music, but found them to be sorely lacking. Her restrictive circumstances gave rise to frequent expressions of frustration in her correspondence. Charrière was one of the few in her immediate circle to invite persons of some renown to visit her at Colombiers, but had difficulty getting accomplished musicians to come her way. The musicians who resided in the area were, to her mind, 'tant de demi talens qui ont peine à vivre' (so many semi-talents who can barely scrape together a living).[18] When the opportunity to go to Paris presented itself she seized it, devoting her stay almost entirely to musical composition and nights at the opera. One of the two remaining letters from this period, which lasted from 1787–8, attests to her intense musical activity:

> Vous demandez quelle est ma maniere de vivre ... tous les jours six ou huit ou dix heures à mon clavecin; ce n'est pas un gout c'est une fureur. Tous les jours je fais un menuet un allegre ou un andante ... je ne fais autre chose [que la musique] ayant pour cela le plus admirable secours dans la personne d'un jeune compositeur allemand. On a gravé de moi, ou de nous 9 sonates de Clavecin, on en grave 6 autres, il y en a plusieurs encore à graver, & je viens de faire des trio de violon ... sitot que je me leve & jusqu'a minuit ou une heure il n'est plus question que de musique.

> [You ask me what my life is like ... every day six or eight or ten hours at my harpsichord; it isn't a penchant it's a fury. Every day I compose a minuet, an allegro, or an andante ... I do nothing other [than music] receiving the most admirable assistance in the form of a young German composer. Nine of my, or our, sonatas for harpsichord have been printed, six are being printed, there are still more to print, and I have just composed some trios for violin ... From the moment I get up until midnight or one o'clock there is talk of nothing but music.][19]

Upon her return to Switzerland, Charrière actively sought out some of the most celebrated musicians of Europe in the interest of furthering her study of recitative and collaborating with them on the scores of the nine *tragédies en musique* for which she wrote the words and substantial portions of the music. Though none of the music for Charrière's operas has survived, her sonatas, romances, and minuets are still played today.[20]

Charrière was exceptional among the women of her period for daring to try her hand at tragic opera. While increasing numbers of women had begun to stage their operas successfully in Paris towards the end of the century, they confined themselves almost exclusively to *opéras-comiques* with spoken dialogue, for their musical education rarely prepared them to write recitative.[21] Charrière was highly unusual in wanting to overcome this obstacle. Unwilling to confine her musical aspirations to the presiding notion of what befitted or was within reach of her sex, she set her sights high, hoping to attract the attention of Cimarosa, Salieri, Mozart, or Zingarelli. Her interest in Salieri's music, and her desire to collaborate with him on her opera *Les Phéniciennes*, was sparked by her enthusiasm for his setting of Beaumarchais's *Tarare*, which she would have had the opportunity to hear while in Paris.[22] Zingarelli, who later taught Bellini and was a composer in his own right, consented to come to Colombiers several times to assist Charrière in her study of recitative and to collaborate with her on her operas. Charrière's account of her conflictual relationship with Zingarelli indicates, however, that the composer was inclined to share his contemporaries' notions as to what a woman should and should not compose:

> Zingarelli me trouvoit trop hardie de prétendre a faire jamais autre chose que des romançes et quand malgré lui je me suis élevée un peu plus haut, surpris, tantot de mon ignorance, tantot de ce que malgré mon ignorance je faisois parci par là des choses qu'il etoit forçé de trouver belles et jaloux pour ainsi dire pour son art qu'il trouvoit devoir etre étudié de longue main, il se mettoit de très mauvaise humeur contre moi. J'ai escamotté ses avis parmi ses invectives. Jamais je n'ai osé ecrire deux nottes en sa présence.

> [Zingarelli found me too bold in aspiring to write something other than romances and when, despite him, I raised myself somewhat above them, surprised first at my ignorance and then at the fact that, despite my ignorance, I managed to do things here and there that he found beautiful, and jealous, so to speak, of his art, which he thought should be studied for a long time, he was very annoyed with me. I grasped his opinion from among his invectives. I never dared to write two notes in his presence.][23]

Charrière's choice of words is telling, for in saying that she occasionally aspired to 'rise above' the romance, she indicates that she adhered to the reigning opinion that the *tragédie en musique* was hierarchically superior to comic opera, thus disparaging the song-form and operatic genre with which Rousseau was most closely associated. Her determination to write in the tragic vein despite the difficulties she encountered illustrates her resistance to the notion that women should limit themselves to so-called feminine artistic genres. In a letter to a friend whose daughter had expressed the desire to become an artist, Charrière wrote:

> Nous souhaitons ardemment qu'elle devienne peintre, là tout de bon peintre, *Mahler* plutôt que *Mahlerin*. De petits portraits en miniature, ne nous satisferoient pas … Qu'elle apprenne de bonne heure … tout le mechanisme, tout le matériel de l'art. Dans le genre du paysage, une

femme ne rencontre pas plus d'obstacles qu'un homme, de petites figures *habillées* suffisent, et l'on n'a nul besoin de salle de peinture, de modèle nu, pour apprendre à très bien dessiner les animaux.

[We ardently wish her to become a painter, a bona fide painter, a *painter* not a *paintress*. Little miniature portraits will not satisfy us ... May she learn early ... the technique, the material aspect of the art. In the genre of the landscape, a woman does not encounter more obstacles than a man. Some small clothed figures suffice, and one does not need an artist's studio or a nude model to learn to draw animals well.][24]

Aspiring to compositional heights, Charrière agonized over the composition of recitative, turning to Zingarelli and to Rousseau's *Dictionnaire de musique* for assistance, and complaining bitterly of 'recitatifs que je chante bien dans mon lit mais que je ne sais pas notter ou du moins que je notte fort peniblement tandis que ces Messieurs ecrivent cela comme j'ecris une lettre' (recitatives that I sing well in bed but that I do not know how to notate or at least that I have great difficulty in notating whereas these gentlemen toss them off like I write a letter).[25] The contrast she draws between the difficulty she experienced in writing recitative and the relative ease with which her male counterparts could dispatch it reflects in part not a difference in talent, but a difference in musical training.

Given the nature of Charrière's musical aspirations, her expectations of women artists, and the obstacles she encountered en route to becoming one herself, she may well have been sensitive to a passage in the fifth book of Rousseau's *Emile*, in which the author claims that there is little point in exposing girls to the finer points of musical notation. When discussing women's education, Rousseau treats the question of their music making in ambiguous yet suggestive terms. He attests, first of all, to the view of many moralists and educators who, he claims, do not wish young women to learn either singing or dancing because they are persuaded that '[l]es chansons profanes sont autant de crimes; la danse est une invention du Démon; une jeune fille ne doit avoir d'amusement que son travail et la priére' (profane songs are criminal, dance is an invention of the devil, the only amusement in which a young girl should indulge is work and prayer). Rousseau scoffs at this view, indicating that he believes such arts to be more appropriate for women than for men ('à qui veulent-ils donc qu'on les apprenne? Aux garçons?' [to whom do they want us to teach them? To boys?]) and that he fears that undue restraint during childhood will lead women to try to escape such confines once married.[26] Rousseau stipulates, however, that such a pursuit should at no point become anything other than a simple pastime, for he does not expect young women to learn composition but merely to carry a tune. Herein lies a key difference between the musical education Rousseau envisions for Emile and for Sophie. While Rousseau does not wish to belabour a young man's musical instruction – 'enseignez-la [musique] comme vous voudrez pourvu qu'elle ne soit jamais qu'un amusement' (teach [music] however you wish provided that it never becomes anything more than a form of amusement) – he nevertheless envisions teaching Emile the art of *solfege*. Sophie, on the other hand, is not to be initiated into this body of knowledge, for her musical aptitude is 'un gout plustôt qu'un talent; elle ne sait point déchiffrer un air sur la note' (a taste more than a talent; she cannot sight-read a song).[27]

When discussing Sophie's music lessons, Rousseau reveals his awareness of the illicit nature of such an arrangement. He starts out innocently enough, declaring that no two students should be taught music in the same way. While one might assume that Rousseau has in mind differences in aptitude and musical sensibility – the capacity of one student to memorize and another to improvise; the ability of one to execute and another to create – he puts quite another spin on the matter: 'On ne me fera jamais croire que les mêmes attitudes, les mêmes pas, les mêmes mouvemens, les mêmes gestes, les mêmes danses conviennent à une petite brune vive et piquante et à une grande belle blonde aux yeux languissans' (I will never be persuaded that the same attitudes, the same steps, the same movements, the same gestures, the same dances are suitable for a vivacious, zesty young brunette and a big beautiful blond with languorous eyes).[28] What, one might wonder, does the colour of a girl's hair and the look in her eye have to do with the quality of her dancing? While 'piquante' and 'languissans' do, to some extent, convey rapidity of bodily movement, they are nevertheless highly charged words that are more likely to be applied to the description of a mistress than a musician. Rousseau is clearly aware of the suggestive nature of his own statement, for he suddenly raises the question: to whom is it safe to entrust a young girl's musical education? Transiting imperceptibly into a discussion of her dance instructor, he remarks: 'Je ne sais s'il faut qu'un maitre-à-danser prenne une jeune écoliére par sa main délicate et blanche, qu'il lui fasse accourcir la jupe, lever les yeux, déployer les bras, avancer un sein palpitant; mais je sais bien que pour rien au monde je ne voudrois être ce maitre-là' (I don't know if a dance master should take a young student by her delicate white hand, if he should have her shorten her skirt, raise her eyes, extend her arms, hold out a beating breast, but I know that nothing in the world would make me want to be in the dance master's shoes).[29] It is clear from his discussion, in which Rousseau characterizes a young girl's exposure first to music then to dance, that he would not wish to have his capacity to resist temptation put to the test by undertaking to instruct one of these enticing young women in the musical arts. Though he hesitates before exposing Sophie to such a compromising situation, Rousseau nevertheless savours the notion of affording such a 'voluptuous' moment to Emile, for whom he reserves the pleasure of putting the final touches on Sophie's musical education:

> C'est à présent ... [qu'] Emile commence à sentir le prix des talens agréables qu'il s'est donnés. Sophie aime à chanter, il chante avec elle; il fait plus, il lui apprend la musique. Elle est vive et légére, elle aime à sauter, il danse avec elle, il change ses sauts en pas, il la perfectionne. Ces leçons sont charmantes, la gaité folâtre les anime, elle adoucit le timide respect de l'amour; *il est permis à un amant de donner ces leçons avec volupté; il est permis d'être le maitre de sa maitresse.*

> [At this point ... Emile starts to sense the value of the agreeable talents he has acquired. Sophie likes to sing, he sings with her. He goes further, he teaches her music. She is light and vivacious. She likes to jump, he dances with her; he transforms her jumps into steps and perfects them. These lessons are charming and are animated by the playful fun that softens love's timid respect. *A lover is permitted to give lessons voluptuously; he is allowed to be the master of his mistress.*][30]

Rousseau thus alerts his readers to the differing standards for women and men's musical education, to the undesirability of women's presuming to excel in the art, to the potential dangers of private lessons, and to the pervasive sensuality of lovers' musical moments.

Though Charrière may have found Rousseau's opposition to her desire to pursue her passion somewhat troubling given the sincerity of her admiration for his musical sensibility and self-training, his stance was quite characteristic of the times. The debate as to whether, and to what extent, women should cultivate their musical talents intensified across Europe in the course of the eighteenth century, yet the association between women, music, and immorality was particularly prevalent in France.[31] This association dates back to antiquity, when the Greek *hétaïres*, or educated courtesans, were renowned for their musical accomplishments.[32] At the beginning of the eighteenth century, Clement XI renewed the papal decrees that precluded women from participating in musical activities in church, on the stage, or at home, offering the following rationale for his decision: 'On sait bien qu'une beauté qui chante au théâtre et veut cependant préserver sa chasteté ne se conduit pas autrement que celui qui voudrait sauter dans le Tibre sans se mouiller les pieds' (As we well know, a beauty who sings in the theatre but wants to preserve her chastity is no different from one who wants to jump in the Tiber without getting her feet wet).[33] The papal injunction both attested to and helped perpetuate the stigma against women's musical pursuits. The decree did not affect Protestant countries such as Germany and England, however, where women were occasionally allowed to sing in church. The English, moreover, had recourse to boys' choirs and the Italians to castrati to provide the high register in church or on stage. The case in France was somewhat different. As a Roman Catholic country, France sustained the full weight of the papal injunctions and women were forbidden to sing in church. But because the French had no boys' choir tradition and found the idea of castration abhorrent, Louis XIV granted Lully special dispensation to allow women to sing on the operatic stage. As Lully's students gave lessons in turn, educational opportunities for musically inclined young women started to multiply, and as the size of operatic choruses gradually increased in the course of the century, so did the professional venues that women were at liberty to explore.[34]

Freedom came at a price, however, for while the opera afforded women a means of pursuing musical careers, its public venue and low recruitment standards served only to enhance the age-old association between music and immorality. Recruitment standards at the Académie Royale de Musique were not particularly high, especially where singers were concerned: 'Les femmes qui possédaient une belle voix firent quelques études pour être admises à l'Opéra; d'autres s'y présentèrent avec les seuls avantages qu'elles tenaient de la nature et ne réussirent pas moins' (Women with beautiful voices studied a bit in order to be admitted to the Opera. Others showed up only with their natural endowments and were just as successful).[35] Women were primarily needed not for starring roles but to add sound and colour to productions by filling out the chorus. These women received similar salaries to their

male counterparts, yet they risked being disowned by their families for
fear that not only their own reputations but also those of their siblings
would be compromised, and that their chances of marriage would
decrease.[36] Though marriage was often beyond their reach, their stage
appearances afforded excellent opportunities to meet potential patrons,
as the following excerpt from a farcical set of amendments designed for
the Académie Royale indicates:

Article XXVI:
Item très solennellement
Prononçons une juste peine
Contre le ravisseur qui vient insolemment
L'or en main dépeupler la scène,
Taxe pour chaque enlèvement
Et le tarif incessamment
Public dans tous les domaines.
Cette taxe imposée à raison du talent,
De la beauté surtout, tant pour une danseuse,
Tant pour une chanteuse,
Rien pour celles des chœurs, nous en ferons présent.

[Item. Let us very solemnly
Pronounce a just punishment
Against the ravisher who comes insolently
Gold in hand to depopulate the stage,
A tax for each kidnapping
And the tariff incessantly
Publicized in every domain.
This tax imposed in proportion to talent
And particularly to beauty, so much for a dancer,
So much for a singer,
Nothing for the choristers, we'll throw them in for free.][37]

A predecessor of the chorus girl of American Broadway fame – characteristically found under the patronage of a 'Big Daddy' – the 'fille
d'opéra' (show girl) was a woman of unexceptional talent in need of
financial assistance and consequently willing to become a 'femme
entretenue' (kept woman).[38] An anecdote from the records of one of the
first girls' schools, headed by Madame de Maintenon, attests to how
women who sang at the opera were commonly perceived. At a produc-

tion of Racine's *Esther* performed by the young ladies of Saint-Cyr, an onlooker, struck by the beauty of one of the pupils, remarked: 'Si c'était une fille d'opéra, j'y mettrais n'importe quel prix' (If she were a show girl I'd pay whatever it took).[39] The reputation for loose morals proved to be infectious, and extended from the *filles* right up through the director of the Opéra-Comique, la Montansier, who was known to deploy all 'les talents d'une hétäire grecque' (the talents of a Greek courtesan).[40] Jacqueline Letzter and Robert Adelson recount that Julie Candeille, a successful opera singer and composer, perceived and objected to the common characterization of herself and her peers, protesting that 'whereas it might be true that theatrical women were sometimes bad wives because the intensity of their public lives left them little time for domestic duties, for exactly the same reason, it was unlikely that they would engage in extra-marital affairs.'[41]

Though women risked sullying the churches in which they sang and risked being sullied by the stage, music nevertheless became a standard component of their education in the course of the century, one that they could exercise for the amusement of family and friends in the privacy of the home or the semiprivate venue of the salons. The establishment of the first mixed orchestras and the proliferation of keyboard instruments opened up new, less stigmatized professional paths for women who wished to pursue the musical arts. By the end of the century, however, the value of women's musical training was once again called into question. The tone of the debate differed somewhat in England and France, a phenomenon worth exploring, particularly since Charrière, Cottin, and Staël chose England as the setting of their novels. In England musical aptitude served as a guarantee that a woman had not been idle in her childhood, and had thus had no time to give way to temptation. Her music lessons were thought to safeguard her chastity, increasing her value on the marriage market.[42] Those who questioned the value of music lessons claimed that they were simply an excuse to keep young women busy, and that one could obtain the same end by having them study something more likely to improve either their mind or their home economics.[43] In France, to the contrary, music was thought to have such a hold on the senses that a lesson or performance constituted the moment when a woman was most likely to go astray. Contemporary caricatures reveal this discrepancy in the public perception of women musicians in England and France. The English sketches that Richard Leppert reproduces in *Music and Image* mock those women who preen themselves on their musical accomplishments, acquired at great expense, while displaying relatively little talent (figure 6).[44] The French captions that Marcel Vilcosqui cites in his unpublished study of women in eighteenth-century French music, however, inevitably associate music with love making and are occasionally downright bawdy.[45] This discrepancy is equally apparent in contemporary literary texts. In Thomas Middleton's *Michelmas Term* a father's order 'get thee to thy virginals' carries with it the sense that he considered the instrument a safeguard of his child's virtue and her 'proper place.'[46] Quite different are the scenes in Riccoboni's *Le Marquis de Cressy*, Diderot's *La Religieuse*, and Laclos's *Les Liaisons dangereuses*, where a harp or a harpsichord can lead to a girl's undoing.[47] Contemporary English novels, such as those of Jane Austen, that featured musically accomplished young women tended to end in matrimony; French novels featuring similar characters ended with their social demise and death. It seems, therefore, that women's musical activities, even in the home where they received social if not ecclesiastic sanction, were affected by the negative connotations of a taste for public display, the intimacy of private lessons, and the association of musical sensibility with the pleasure of the senses. In his book *Men, Women and Pianos*, Arthur Loesser associates the public perception of music in England with economics and in Germany with idealism but does not provide a watchword for France. The watchword I would venture is sensuality. Loesser notes that the English named the virginal for the young ladies who played them.[48] Suffice it to say that had the French harpsichord been named according to the same criteria, it would probably have been dubbed the 'nubile.' In her 1799 treatise entitled *Strictures on the Modern System of Female Education*, the English educational reformer Hannah More deplored a 'system which, regardless of aptitude, "erected the whole sex into artists."'[49] Across the channel Charrière, Cottin, Krüdener, and Staël instead protested against the fact that women were unable to become musically adept with impunity. Their writings thus call into question not only the social perception of women playing music, but the social status of music itself.

While critics have recently devoted much attention to the central role music played in Charrière's life, the role of music in one of her most celebrated literary works has received virtually no attention.[50] Just before she left Colombiers for Paris to dedicate herself to composition, Charrière produced part two of her epistolary novel *Caliste, ou Lettres écrites de Lausanne*.[51] Its date of publication, prior to 1787, indicates that the story cannot have been inspired by her most intense period of musical production, yet it may have been suggested by her previous visits to France and England, her observation of her social surroundings in Holland and Switzerland, her correspondence with friends in Paris who kept her abreast of the musical scene, her extensive knowledge of French literature, and her reading of Rousseau.[52] The first part of Charrière's *Caliste, ou Lettres écrites de Lausanne* is comprised of a series of letters written by a Swiss woman to her cousin. In them, she describes how she raised and educated her daughter Cécile and recounts her efforts to find Cécile a suitable husband. The second part is comprised of several letters from an English gentleman named William (the companion of the young man who has shown an interest in Cécile) to Cécile's mother. In them, he tells the tale of a talented Englishwoman named Caliste whom he once loved. The reader is thus invited to compare the stories of the two women: one ordinary, the other exceptional. Cécile's education closely corresponds to Rousseau's recommendations, except that Cécile learns to read and write 'dès qu'elle a pu prononcer et remuer les doigts; pensant ... que nous ne savons bien que ce que nous avons appris machinalement' (as soon as she could speak and move her fingers, thinking ... that we only know well what we have learned by rote).[53] Rousseau was against rote learning, insisting that he wished to fill children's heads with ideas, not words, and specifically recommending that parents delay teaching their children to read and write until they have learned to explore the world around them and to exercise their judgment. In all other aspects, however, Cécile's education closely resembles that of Sophie. She is taught by a relative, learns music from the local organist, devotes special attention to the useful, graceful arts of sewing and making lace, and absorbs only so much worldly wisdom as can be gleaned from the maps on the walls and the books on the shelves. Caliste's education is a study in contrast, the singularity of her upbringing thrown into relief by its juxtaposition to that of Cécile. Though her studies are also comprised of the fine arts and 'tous les ouvrages de femme' (woman's work), Caliste displays unusual aptitude and proceeds to go much further, eventually reaching a level of accomplishment that Rousseau would not necessarily have condoned.[54]

From the very start of Caliste's story, the reader has the impression that her talents, which open up rare opportunities for education and social advancement, are also the source of her downfall. Her mother, who was abandoned by Caliste's father and left financially destitute, destined Caliste for the stage from a young age, 'voulant tirer parti de sa figure, de ses talents, et du plus beau son de voix qui ait jamais frappé une oreille sensible' (wanting to take advantage of her face, her talents, and of the most beautiful voice that has ever struck a sensitive ear).[55] It is unclear from this description whether Caliste's singing or speaking voice had attracted her mother's attention. She would have had need of both, however, to incarnate the role of the heroine in Nicholas Rowe's *The Fair Penitent* for whom she is named. *The Fair Penitent* was performed in London throughout the eighteenth century, and Charrière would have had occasion to see it when she went there in 1767. The close association between Caliste and her role helps explain why Charrière chose England as the setting of the second part of her novel. The play included two musical numbers written into the script, the latter of which is sung by the character of Calista.[56] A contemporary advertisement for the play offered, in addition, 'Four Entertainments of Singing (entirely new) ... to which will be added, the Nightingale Song ... The Instrumental Musick Compos'd by Signior *Iacomo Greber.*'[57] Such musical interludes were customary for the English stage. As Jane Girdham attests: 'An evening's entertainment at a London theatre normally consisted of two substantive pieces, interspersed with various songs, dances, and other light forms of entertainment.'[58] Actresses were regularly screened at the time for their singing talents, and were not likely to be hired if they had none, for those who were primarily actresses were required to sing, and those who were primarily singers were required to act.[59] When Caliste's mother destined her for the stage, therefore, she presumably sought to profit from both her singing and her speaking voice, which, as William observes, were practically indistinguishable: 'J'ai toujours trouvé qu'elle jouait et chantait comme on parle ou comme on devrait parler' (I always found that she played and sang like one speaks or should speak).[60] Caliste thus possesses the gift of declamation that contemporary French society mourned as one of the lost Greek arts and that Rousseau held up as the model to which French composers and librettists should aspire.

Unfortunately, Caliste's gift of declamation is not the only one of her characteristics that hearkens back to the Greeks, for her fate also resembles that of the *hétaïres*, or educated courtesans renowned for their musical accomplishments.[61] In keeping with the false amendments written for the Académie Royale de Musique, cited above, the first time Caliste appears on stage – in the role of a fallen woman whose transgression brings misery and death on herself and her loved ones – she is spotted by an English lord who promptly inquires about her purchase. Though the mother's sale of her daughter is, indeed, salacious, Lord L***'s intentions seem somewhat more honourable. In buying Caliste from her mother, he in effect rescues her from the stage, thereby enabling her to cultivate the talents he finds so captivating. He sends her to a Parisian convent to complete her education and then takes her to Italy to add the finishing touches. William, who courts Caliste several years after Lord L***'s death, draws our attention to the talent he finds most exceptional when he exclaims: 'Jamais il ne fut plus aimable musicienne' (There was never a nicer musician). Though Caliste was primarily educated in Paris, William asserts, when describing her musical talent, 'ce degré de perfection et de facilité, ce ne fut pas à Paris qu'elle l'acquit, ce fut en Italie' (it was not in Paris but in Italy that she acquired this degree of perfection and facility).[62] Her musical sensibility, in its Italianate purity, simplicity, and authenticity, is thus eminently Rousseauian. While Charrière gives Cécile the education Rousseau recommended to Sophie, therefore, she grants Caliste the musical skill and sensitivity that Rousseau idealized but deemed inappropriate for women.

Caliste is not immune to the consequences of the precocious talent she displays. Though it is impossible to say whether she was purchased for her musical gifts or became a musician by virtue of her purchase, the two remain inextricably linked in the minds of the surrounding society. Lord L*** refuses to marry Caliste on the grounds that his love speaks for itself and he has no fortune to leave her, thus compromising her in the public eye. Were she not to take precautions she would jeopardize her reputation not because of her questionable past but because morals and music do not mix. Twice a week Caliste gives a dinner for the musicians who perform at her house. 'Avec une autre que Caliste,' William remarks, 'ces soupers eussent été froids, ou auraient dégénéré en orgies; avec elle, ils étaient décents, gais, charmants' (With anyone other than Caliste, these suppers would have been cold or would have degenerated into orgies. With her they were decent, gay, and charming).[63] We understand from this remark that Caliste managed to keep the dinners decent despite the questionable company. Caliste draws a key distinction between music and moral degeneracy when she writes William that she had enabled a singer 'qui s'était dégoûtée du théâtre' (who was disgusted with the theatre) and a musician 'honnête homme' (gentleman) to marry. Though Caliste does not share her suitor's bias against the company of musicians, she nevertheless finds it necessary to emphasize the singer's abhorrence for her profession (which is clearly to her credit) and the musician's honesty (which is by no means a matter of course) before admitting that she had conjoined them in the sanctity of marriage. Poor, yet unsullied by their talents, the singer and the musician help Caliste train young orphan girls in the musical arts. Here again, the widespread disapprobation of musical education for financially disadvantaged young women comes to light, for Caliste writes: 'On m'a dit que je les préparais au métier de courtisane' (I was told I was preparing them to be courtesans). Caliste immediately detects and rejects the prejudicial statement and draws a vital distinction between a young woman's ability to deploy her musical talents and her decision to use such talents to attract illicit attention. Poverty, good looks, and the big city will be responsible for her pupils' being reduced to such an extreme, Caliste insists, not their knowledge of music: 'J'ai fait remarquer que je les prenais très pauvres et très jolies, ce qui, joint ensemble et dans une ville comme Londres, mène à une perte presque sûre et entière, sans que de savoir un peu chanter ajoute rien au péril' (I pointed out that I took them on very poor and very pretty, which, taken together in a city like London, leads to almost inevitable and complete ruin; knowing how to sing adds nothing to the peril). Music is, indeed, more likely to break than to bring about their fall, she suggests, responding to her accusers that 'il valait encore mieux commencer et finir comme moi, qu'arpenter les rues et périr dans un hôpital' (it was better to begin and end as I had than to roam the streets and die in a hospital).[64]

Caliste's remarks suggest that she attributes her social ascent rather than her demise to her knowledge of music, and she goes to great lengths to ensure that those around her will come to the same conclusion. Faced with opposition to her giving music lessons to orphan girls, Caliste backs her claim that music will not degrade them further by teaching them to sing only those songs whose intent cannot possibly be misconstrued. She translates the choirs of *Esther* and *Athalie*, two plays that Racine wrote at Madame de Maintenon's request for the girls of Saint-Cyr. Though the crass comments of a nobleman and the protests of a prudish abbé eventually obliged Madame de Maintenon to ban all staged musical productions as morally unsound, these two plays were nevertheless commissioned with the specific intent of providing the girls with an innocent means of developing their talents.[65] Caliste also has Psalms 103 and 104 set to music for them, a choice which is clearly more redolent of the convent than the street. Hymns of mercy, forgiveness, and a celebration of God's works, the psalms end with the words 'Je chanterai l'Éternel tant que je vivrai, / Je célébrerai mon Dieu tant que j'existerai. / Que mes paroles lui soient agréables!' (I will sing the Eternal as long as I live, / I will celebrate God forever / Let my words be agreable unto Him).[66] Upon hearing such verses, the reproaches of Caliste's compatriots would, presumably, have died on their lips.

The decency that prevails throughout Caliste's dinner parties and music lessons clearly makes a favourable impression on William, yet he is not the only one whose good opinion Caliste hopes to earn. As William remarks, 'Elle savait se faire respecter' (she knew how to command respect).[67] What is, perhaps, less evident is that she uses her musical arts to gain the public esteem she covets. Combining her musical talents with her social sense, she slowly but surely starts to dissociate musicality from immorality in the public imaginary. Accustomed to conducting herself with dignity in a society that tends to look at her askance as soon as she turns her back, Caliste explains that she had contracted '[l']habitude d'arranger pour les autres mes actions, mes paroles, ma voix, mes gestes, jusqu'à ma physionomie' (the habit of arranging my actions, my words, my voice, my gestures, even my physiognomy for others), masking her emotions behind the outer semblance of respectability.[68] She draws upon the same sense of propriety when planning musical events. Her own sensibility and attentiveness are enough to earn the deference of the musicians she invites to her home to perform. She is more resourceful, however, when it comes to winning the respect of those members of society who are less musically inclined. Twice a week she holds concerts at her house, given by the most renowned musicians of Europe, yet attendance is by invitation only, tendered to members of the first families. She makes it clear to children who presume to enter unbidden that they are taking a liberty which she will not allow them to repeat. By insisting that the sanctity of her home be respected, by ensuring that invitations to her home are highly prized, she increases her own value in society's eyes. She displays additional finesse by inviting exclusively men, which, far from being an indication of a licentious preference for their company, is rather a mark of the quality of the concert and of her desire to share it with trained ears alone.[69]

Reading the description of Caliste's musical activities, one would almost conclude that she hosts concerts, performs, and listens to music for the sole purpose of enhancing her image in the public eye. Her resolution to dedicate her talents to the improvement of her social situation, far from being self-serving, is lent a certain urgency by the fact that Caliste has no assigned niche in society. Though she is reputed to be of decent extraction, her name was kept from her, suggesting that she was, in all likelihood, illegitimate. The English lord who rescued her from the stage, saving her from a worse fate, educated and loved her, but also refused to give her a name. As a result, she is caught between the different social echelons.[70] She possesses enough talent, cultivation, dignity, and high-mindedness not to wish to become again what she was before, namely a kept woman. She thus abjures the role of courtesan or mistress. Because she was once considered such, however, William's father disapproves of his son's desire to marry her. Marriage remains a possibility, one of which she will avail herself, yet Caliste is prevented from combining marriage and happiness. Forced to choose between dishonourable love, marriage for love, or marriage for the sake of appearances, Caliste spurns the first, is denied the second, and consequently opts for the third.[71]

The gravity of Caliste's situation is even more striking when we consider that even if society were redesigned along the utopian lines that Cécile's mother outlines in the first part of *Caliste, ou Lettres écrites de Lausanne*, there would be no place for Caliste. The utopia in part one has been described as matrilineal and a meritocracy.[72] What better arrangement, then, for a talented woman? Yet critics tend to overlook the fact that the two terms do not apply to the same members of society. Cécile's mother plans to divide society into three classes: an upper class comprised of the nobility, a middle class comprised of ranked officers and those who have distinguished themselves by a contribution to society, and a lower class comprised of the people ('le peuple'). Each class will select deputies based on their merit to serve on the national council, and their offspring will become members of the nobility. Merit therefore serves as a means of social advancement, yet the ranked officers and deputies are men. The utopian society is thus a meritocracy for men. Women are advantaged because men can marry into their class, and therefore meretricious men from their own as well as the lower classes may seek their hand.[73] Women are therefore a means of social advancement for men, and stand to benefit in turn as their own statistical chances of marrying a man of merit increase. Nowhere, however, does Cécile's mother indicate that women are able to improve their own social circumstances either through merit or through marriage. While a man may aspire to win the hand of a woman above his station, women are not upwardly mobile. Nor does Cécile's mother

1. The Inscribed Beholder. *Belisarius Begging for Alms* by Jacques Louis
David. Courtesy Réunion des Musées Nationaux / Art Resource, NY.

2. Music as Absorptive Activity. *The Music Lesson* by François Boucher. Courtesy Réunion des Musées Nationaux / Art Resource, NY.

3. Performer and Beholder. 'Through the Keyhole,' attributed to Clément-Pierre Marillier, from *Le Diable amoureux* by Jacques Cazotte (1772).

4. The Music in the Text. 'Biondetta's Barcarole,' attributed to Clément-Pierre Marillier, from *Le Diable amoureux* by Jacques Cazotte (1772).

5. 'La belle estampe d'après Vanloo.' *The Concert* by Carle Van Loo.
Courtesy Scala / Art Resource, NY.

6. Music as Innocent (Inadept) English Pastime. *Farmer Giles & his Wife shewing off their daughter Betty to their Neighbours, on her return from School* by James Gillray (1809). Courtesy Yale Center for British Art, Paul Mellon Collection.

7.   Portrait of the Author as Musician. *Corinne at Cape Miseno* by François Gérard. Courtesy Musée des Beaux-Arts de Lyon, © Studio Basset.

8. Corinne's Musical Heritage. *The Cumaean Sibyl* by Domenichino.
Reproduced by permission.

concern herself with the fate of the illegitimate. Caliste, whose father has given her no name, who belongs to the lowest class on her mother's side, and who is, in effect, excluded from the class system by virtue of her implied illegitimacy and her degrading purchase, would therefore be unable to rely upon either her musical talents or a loveless marriage to improve her social situation in the posited utopia.[74]

Ironically, then, Caliste fares better in her own society than in the utopia that Cécile's mother envisions. Yet she considers the fate to which society has condemned her with 'une sorte d'étonnement mêlé d'horreur' (a sort of surprise mixed with horror).[75] Longing for love and respect, if she cannot have the former she is determined to earn the latter. If her talents and a marriage of convenience are the only recourses that contemporary society affords, she will avail herself of them. The musical tableaux in the text bear the mark of Caliste's determination. Though Charrière admired Rousseau's musical sensibility, which she was careful to instil in her heroine, and though she was presumably capable of musical description given the extent of her training, her tableaux are practically devoid of both. Instead, they serve as highly sophisticated strategic devices. Charrière does not take up the terms of the contemporary musical controversies, nor does she experiment with alternate means of conveying music through text. Instead she deemphasizes the musical content and minimizes the beholder's affective response. The descriptions of Caliste's music and its effect on the listener are discrete, sometimes accorded little more than an adjective. Subtly sketched in Charrière's characteristically understated prose, they nevertheless achieve their aim, which, unlike the tableaux we have seen thus far, is social rather than aesthetic.

The musical tableaux in Charrière's text are, in a sense, staged, for Caliste uses them expressly to influence her beholder's actions and to manipulate his sensibilities. Unlike Biondetta, however, she does so for noble ends. Aware, since her fateful stage debut, that she can use her musical talents to attract men's attention, Caliste becomes equally adept in using them to repel their advances. As William remarks, 'Elle opposa ... l'amour à l'amour; maîtrisant le sens par le cœur ... faisant oublier sa personne à force de me faire admirer ses grâces, son esprit, et ses talents' (she opposed ... love with love, mastering the senses with the heart ... making me forget her body and admire her grace, her mind, and her talents).[76] She expertly tempers one effect with the other until the beholder approaches a state of frenzy without daring to act on inclination.[77] Such instances often arise when Caliste and William find themselves alone after dinner. According to William, 'l'heure qui suivait le souper était, quand nous étions seuls, la plus difficile à passer' (the hour following dinner was the most difficult to pass when we were alone). The reader is left wondering whether the lovers find the hour difficult to fill because the day has been long and conversation starts to wane or because they are experiencing particular difficulty keeping their desire within bounds. At such moments, Caliste summons a cellist to entertain them, and the exasperation that William expresses at having to share her company with another suggests that desire and not boredom is responsible for the difficulty of the hour. The description of the cellist, though brief, is riveting. Referred to as 'ivrogne, crasseux' (drunk, dirty) and a 'petit gnome' (little gnome), he surges forth from the earth like a 'mauvais génie' (bad spirit), adding an air of enchantment to the haunting admixture of cello, harpsichord, and voice that fills the room as Caliste accompanies him on her instrument. William's attention, along with the reader's, is immediately drawn towards the centre of the room. Disturbed by the presence of the cellist yet not wanting to be the one to leave, William is subject to conflicting impulses and does not know whether he is coming or going. No sooner does he make a movement in the direction of the door than he is stopped by a smile. Refusing to sit, he stands in the doorway, his hat on his head, suggesting that his departure is imminent, but mesmerized by their performance despite himself. Complaining bitterly, he usually capitulates, seizing an instrument himself and joining in the concert until Caliste packs him off along with the musician. While the experience is frustrating, the memory of such evenings is 'délicieux' (delicious), and Caliste achieves her end.[78] She manages to retain her lover, thus enabling them to spend the evening together, yet rests assured that in the presence of the musician her virtue will not be compromised, regardless of the music's allure.

The next musical tableau is sketched even more rapidly, hardly leaving the necessary time for a full impact on the reader and yet clearly having a significant effect on the beholders in the text. In the second tableau, a third party, this time in the guise of a rival, once again disturbs Caliste and William's intimacy. The gentlemen thus find themselves in agreeable proximity to the object of their affections, yet they are unable to speak their minds freely in one another's presence. In an attempt to convey her own inclinations and appeal to their better feelings, Caliste has recourse to her music. Intensely aware of the delicacy of her situation, she makes her musical selection with care. Confronted with William, the man she loves but cannot marry, and M. de Norfolk, the man who may win her hand but not her heart, she rises to the occasion and makes a last valiant attempt to combine love with respectability. M. de Norfolk requests that she sing French and Italian arias to her own accompaniment. Judging that William will find such a performance too familiar to be of interest, Caliste decides to ask his help in writing the words to some original romances that she proposes to set to music. She thus selects a genre well suited to affairs of the heart and affords herself and William the pleasures of collaboration while displaying a talent for composition, which was thought to be superior to that of execution. Once again, Caliste's performance is highly strategic: by disclosing her full arsenal of musical talent she hopes to retain the attention of her fallback while making a last-ditch attempt to convince her vacillating lover to marry her despite his father's opposition. Yet try as she might to persuade William that this unusual display of talent is for his benefit alone, he presumes that she is performing for his rival. Obliged to interpret the meaning of her music in the absence of any accompanying explanation, both men mistake her intent, and while William gives vent to a jealous tirade, his rival asks for Caliste's hand. Though she wields her talents to the best of her ability, Caliste falls prey to the inscrutability of music's meaning and unwittingly sacrifices her last chance for love to the respectability she has long sought.[79] Silencing William's protest at her having revealed her talents to another, she states, 'C'est bien ... de leur part le chant du cygne' (clearly it is ... their swan song), suggesting that now that the die has been cast she has no further use for her music.[80]

Caliste thus empties music of its aesthetic content, retaining only its ability to attract, to repel, or to maintain appearances. This tactic reaches an exaggerated extreme at certain key moments of the narrative. In one, William, his frustrated desire having reached a point he can no longer withstand, lifts her up bodily from behind her harpsichord and announces, ominously, 'Finissons' (let's put an end to it).[81] The only indication that music plays a part in the scene is Caliste's position behind her harpsichord. Her instrument thus becomes a concrete version of the music she uses to keep her lover in the vicinity and yet at bay. He must literally sidestep the harpsichord interposed between them in order to approach her physically.[82] In another, Caliste and William happen to meet at a performance of The Fair Penitent after Caliste has married William's rival.[83] Though the theatre and the opera often served a social function in eighteenth-century narratives, providing an arena in which couples could rendezvous in boxes or study one another from afar, seldom did characters enact these scenes with such complete indifference as to what was transpiring on stage. No overtones of either song or declamation reach our ears. Here the theatre is purely a *lieu de rencontre*. Caliste recounts how she managed to begin her married life without revealing that she was still in love with another man. As much for herself as for her husband, she cast off all vestiges of her previous existence so that he would not suspect and she would not remember: 'Les habits que je portais, la musique que je jouais, ne fûrent plus les mêmes' (The clothes I wore, the music I played, were no longer the same).[84] Her phrasing is significant, for in this instance as in so many others, she seems to be wearing her music like her clothes, making musical selections that mask her true sentiment with an eye to what propriety demands.

At the end of the novella Caliste employs her musical talents and taste in a manner that is equally effective, and yet as she is near death's door and arguably past the point of strategizing, the third musical tableau casts no further doubt upon the sincerity of her intent. Caliste's husband, not William, describes this last tableau, thus removing even the implicit impurity of an unsanctified sentiment from the account. Sensing that her final hour is approaching, Caliste arranges her closing concert in view of the solemnity of the occasion, choosing purely religious music, including Handel's *Messiah*, an Italian *Miserere*, and Pergolesi's *Stabat Mater*.[85] The music provides the only continuum during the shifting scene that depicts Caliste's last movements. Gradually drifting into a fuller concentration on the music itself and a waning awareness of her surroundings, Caliste closes her eyes as the music draws to a close, providing a seamless transition into what can only be described as her death and transfiguration.[86] This tableau, is, in a sense, double, for the musical performance affects its primary beholder, Caliste, while the spectacle of Caliste's absorption in turn affects those around her. Her husband and the faithful servant to whom she gives her last request are less attentive to the music itself than they are entranced by her preparatory ritual. All eyes are focused upon her quiet resolution of her remaining orders of business, the thought she devotes to each of those who are dear to her, her silent prayer, and her barely perceptible response to the concert taking place before her. Her manner of dying has a decisive effect upon those who are present, for while her husband concedes that '[a]insi a fini ... Caliste, les uns diront comme une païenne, les autres comme une sainte' (thus ended ... Caliste, some say like a pagan, others like a saint), he adds that the cries of all who had loved and served her 'disent mieux que des paroles ce qu'elle était' (say better than words what she was).[87] The sanctity of the music thus ultimately outweighs all suggestion that her passing was anything other than holy, and with her dying breath Caliste finally manages to swing the balance of public opinion in her favour.

Charrière's musical tableaux differ from what I have described as the musical scenes characteristic of the French literary tradition not in their aesthetic complexity – though they still take the form of music performed for a beholder inscribed within the text – but rather in the nature of their effect on the beholder and in the heroine's refusal to employ them as seduction scenes. Jean Rossard notes Charrière's tendency to exploit the 'recipe' of sentimental literature:

> Caliste ne réconcilie pas la raison et le sentiment, l'état de nature et l'état social, le relatif et l'absolu, l'égoïsme et le plaisir. Caliste démontre, au contraire, par l'absurde – la mort – leurs contradictions insurmontables. Mais, afin de souligner le vide de cette littérature sentimentale, l'auteur en utilise les recettes.

> [Caliste does not reconcile reason and sentiment, the state of nature and of society, the relative and the absolute, egotism and pleasure. Caliste demonstrates, to the contrary, through the absurd – death – their insurmountable contradictions. But in order to emphasize the emptiness of this sentimental literature, the author uses its recipes.][88]

Similarly, Charrière employs the 'recipe' of the musical seduction scene, but modifies the outcome and has the woman call the shots. Caliste uses her music to seduce the beholder into honouring her request that he love her from a distance. She thus takes control of the incontrollable ('insaisissable') effect her music has on the beholder and uses it to defend her virtue. By downplaying the aesthetic content of the musical tableaux, Charrière calls attention to the social stakes with which women musicians were obliged to contend. Unlike Diderot, Cazotte, and Beaumarchais, whose works were savoured primarily by authors and composers of the following century, Charrière's Caliste had a marked impact upon her contemporaries. The changes Charrière brought about in the literary depiction of women musicians and in the musical tableau were therefore of the utmost importance. Charrière read, respected, and took issue with Rousseau. Regardless of whether her awareness of the stigma women faced if they sought to excel in music stemmed from the suggestive passages in Rousseau's *Emile*, her broader knowledge of French literature, her observation of society, or her personal experience, she chose to represent such prejudice in the society depicted in her novel and to arm her heroine against it. Initially allowing the suspicion to linger that music may, in part, be responsible for Caliste's fall, Charrière ultimately has her heroine reject such an interpretation of her existence, insisting that society alone is responsible for her fate and that music merely renders her situation tolerable. Caliste uses music to combat society's preconceived notions, gradually winning the esteem of the public, her potential father-in-law, her husband, and finally of the man who refused to marry her. She clearly intends, moreover, to continue her mission past the grave, for she leaves behind a legacy of poor orphan girls whom she has trained to use their musical talents to improve their social condition and, slowly but surely, to win society's respect for their profession.

Charrière's construction of her musical tableaux is in keeping with the system of political tactics that has been identified in her texts. Letzter uses the term 'tactic' rather than 'strategy' to describe Charrière's machinations, citing Michel de Certeau's distinction between the terms: 'Alors que les stratégies sont des manœuvres légitimes déployées par ceux qui détiennent le pouvoir, les tactiques sont les ressources de ceux qui n'ont ni pouvoir, ni légitimité propres et ne possèdent que de faibles moyens' (While strategies are legitimate manoeuvers employed by those who hold power, tactics are the recourse of those who have neither power nor legitimacy and possess only feeble means).[89] Tactics are thus the strategies of the disenfranchised. The particular tactic that Letzter deems characteristic of Charrière's work is that of tacking, a metaphor drawn from Charrière's *Les Trois femmes* in which one of the characters cautions: 'N'excitez pas de grand mouvement dans les esprits; n'essayez d'arriver au mieux possible que par degrés; il faut se contenter de louvoyer' (Do not attempt to revolutionize thinking; try to attain the best by degrees; one must be content to tack).[90] This is the tactic that Charrière employed to combat Rousseau's ideas with relative impunity during the time of the escalating author cult.[91] The latent tendencies that critics have identified in Charrière's life and work thus amount to a coherent system of literary politics.

Caliste's practice of constantly assessing the barometre of her suitors' affections – sustaining their interest by deploying her talents, yet changing tack to appease their mounting frustration and offering them her music in place of herself – closely resembles the tactics that Charrière herself employed. By endowing Caliste with a strong moral code and persuading the reader that, were it not for her mother's decision to sell her for profit, Caliste would never have gone wrong, Charrière creates a heroine who, along with her pupils, serves as living proof that music and morality are not incompatible, providing an exception to Rousseau's rule. Letzter has observed that Charrière 'attached little moral weight to female modesty and chastity.'[92] Her decision to endow her heroine with a strong moral code thus stems not from a conviction that women have a social responsibility to conduct themselves according to that code, but from the realization that doing so was the only way for Caliste to dissociate musicality from immorality, setting herself up in opposition to the *idées reçues* that structured contemporary society and the conventional musical scenes of the French literary tradition. Convinced that '[l]a plume est une arme' (the pen is a weapon), Charrière sought to influence public opinion with her pen much as Caliste did with her instrument.[93]

Although Caliste dedicated her music and Charrière her writing to similar ends, I do not wish to suggest that the one is merely a stand-in for the other. Critics tend to read the plight of the struggling woman musician as a covert allusion to the author's own struggle to become a writer, yet Charrière encountered more obstacles as a composer than as an author. To read Charrière's defence of Caliste's right to cultivate her music with impunity as a metaphor for a woman's right to write would therefore be reductive. Her representation of the pervasive association of music and immorality in her novel is too historically accurate to have been merely metaphorical. Charrière's preoccupation with the shortage of musical resources in her own immediate surroundings, her admission that she devoted more time to music than to any other pursuit, and her frustration at having neither the freedom nor the training required to compose music of the same caliber as men render it unlikely that she would have drawn attention to the social stigma against women musicians as an indirect means of addressing the challenges that faced women authors, from which she did not suffer as acutely, or women artists, whom she did not aspire to become.

5 Cottin, Krüdener, and Musical Mesmerism

[I]l faut rester insensible, ou se laisser émouvoir outre mesure; ou [la musique] est le vain bruit d'une langue qu'on n'entend point, ou c'est une impetuosité de sentiment qui vous entraine, et à laquelle il est impossible à l'âme de résister.

[One must remain insensible or allow oneself to be moved beyond measure; either [music] is the empty noise of a language you do not understand, or it is an impetuosity of sentiment that pulls you along, and that it is impossible for the soul to resist.]

Rousseau, *Julie, ou la Nouvelle Héloïse*

Though their novels were immensely popular in their day, Sophie Cottin and Barbara Juliana von Krüdener have since fallen into comparative oblivion. Recent attempts to revive them have largely been devoted to biographical accounts and surveys of their literary production.[1] I wish, instead, to draw attention to the literary merit of their works by analysing their form and content, focusing upon two in particular, namely Cottin's *Malvina* (1800) and Krüdener's *Valérie* (1803). There are several reasons for treating Cottin and Krüdener's works in the space of a single chapter. While neither author was sufficiently engaged in the political or aesthetic controversies of her time to permit extensive analysis of her works along these lines, they were both acutely aware of the expectations of the reading public. Unlike Charrière, who was critical of Staël's *Lettres sur les ouvrages et le caractère de J.-J. Rousseau*, Cottin and Krüdener enthusiastically seconded Staël's youthful expression of admiration for Rousseau's writing. Avid readers of his *Julie ou la Nouvelle Héloïse*, they embraced his precepts more fully than did Charrière and Staël, preferring not to take issue with his views on women's role in society or the education of young girls. Nor did they seek to acquire knowledge that Rousseau considered inappropriate for women, either in the extensive study of politics and musical composition, as did Charrière, or in the sophisticated understanding of contemporary aesthetic controversies and philosophical movements, as did Staël. Instead they received an education far more characteristic of the women of their generation. Cottin read widely in the English tradition and was well acquainted with the novels of Richardson while Krüdener possessed a broad reading knowledge of the German tradition, particularly the works of Goethe.[2] They benefited, moreover, from the inspiration afforded by the novels, correspondence, and friendship of Bernardin de Saint-Pierre, Chateaubriand, and Staël.[3] Thus, while they chose not to address the political upheaval that directly affected their lives, they nevertheless displayed a marked sensitivity to the literary tastes and prevailing beliefs of their generation.[4] Their novels struck a sympathetic chord among their readers and had a palpable impact upon the Romantics who found their novels to be more palatable than those of Charrière and Staël.[5] Cottin and Krüdener are interesting, therefore, in that they adhered, quite unapologetically, to the post-Revolutionary cult of Rousseau and were more closely in tune with what might be described as popular culture. Their evocation of music in their novels runs the gamut from scenes characteristic of the French, English, and German literary traditions to tableaux that reveal a keen understanding of the mechanism of sensibility as well as an awareness of the underlying affinity between sensibility and the faith in music's healing powers that became increasingly pronounced in the latter part of the century.

Notions of music's therapeutic powers date back to Renaissance associations between universal harmony and physical harmony, or health.[6] Yet the eighteenth century saw the publication of the first scientific treatises in Italy, England, and France investigating music's salutary effects, both physical and spiritual, particularly in cases of melancholy or madness.[7] Popular movements in pseudoreligion and pseudoscience alike were also interested in music's power to catalyze connections between the senses and what lay beyond. Louis-Claude de Saint-Martin, who distinguished between artificial (worldly) and natural (otherworldly) music, held that vocal music gives rise to moments of insight in which humans can achieve heightened awareness of the divine.[8] Franz Anton Mesmer used the sounds of the pianoforté and the glass harmonica to help magnetize his patients, healing their physical or mental ailments via the power of suggestion.[9] These precursors of modern music therapy made the connection between music, the psyche, and the soul. Once again, evidence of this contemporary trend can be seen in Rousseau's writings, which in turn helped catalyze such convictions.[10] In part I, letter XLVIII of *Julie ou la Nouvelle Héloïse*, which I discussed in the introduction, Saint-Preux relates his conversion experience from French to Italian music and envisions a tableau in which Julie, and not the castrato, would ravish him with her song.[11] He also, however, provides a detailed explanation of the mechanism of musical sensibility – with clear parallels to Rousseau's notion of identification or *pitié* – as well as of the paradigm shift that occurred in the latter half of the century from the association between music and the senses to the association between music and the soul.[12] Before launching into an explanation of his current convictions, Saint-Preux alludes in passing to his prior persuasion:

> La musique n'est qu'un vain son qui peut flatter l'oreille et n'agit qu'indirectement et légèrement sur l'âme: l'impression des accords est purement mécanique et physique; qu'a-t-elle à faire au sentiment, et pourquoi devrais-je espérer d'être plus vivement touché d'une belle harmonie que d'un bel accord de couleurs?

> [Music is but an empty sound that can flatter the ear and acts only indirectly and faintly upon the soul. The impression of chords is purely mechanical and physical; what has it to do with sentiment and why should I expect to be more moved by a beautiful harmony than by a beautiful combination of colors?]

Abjuring the sensationalist notion that music acts primarily on the senses as well as any lingering suspicion that painting is more powerful, Saint-Preux goes on to describe the relationship between music, the passions, and the heart that he has only recently come to appreciate:

> Je n'apercevais pas, dans les accents de la mélodie appliqués à ceux de la langue, le lien puissant et secret des passions avec les sons; je ne voyais pas que l'imitation des tons divers dont les sentiments animent la voix parlante donne à son tour à la voix chantante le pouvoir d'agiter les cœurs et que l'énergique tableau des mouvements de l'âme de celui qui se fait entendre est ce qui fait le vrai charme de ceux qui l'écoutent.

[I did not perceive in the accents of melody applied to those of language the powerful and secret connection of the passions with the sounds; I did not see that the imitation of the various registers by which sentiments animate the speaking voice confers in turn on the singing voice the power to stir hearts and that the performer's energetic tableau of the movements of his soul is what constitutes the true charm of the listeners.][13]

Here Rousseau echoes Diderot's original association of the tableau with the soul of the artist in his *Lettre sur les sourds et muets*, linking it not to all art forms but to music in particular. Upon hearing Italian music, Saint-Preux recaps his recent discovery, saying: 'Le plaisir ne s'arrêtait point à l'oreille, il pénétrait jusqu'à l'âme' (The pleasure did not stop at the ear, but entered the soul).[14] He thus draws a key distinction between the understanding of music's effects on the senses that remained prevalent around mid-century and the understanding of music's effects on the soul that increasingly came to the fore with the advent of Romanticism. Unlike the authors of the previous generation, Cottin and Krüdener respond less to the distinction Saint-Preux draws between French and Italian music than to the connection he establishes between music and the soul. Cheryce Kramer characterizes the difference between the Enlightenment and the Romantic understanding of music as a shift in interest from its physiological to its psychological effects, from its appeal to the senses to its appeal to the emotions and the intellect.[15] While Cottin and Krüdener's tableaux certainly reflect this shift, they go beyond music's effects on the senses, the intellect, and the heart – beyond, in a sense, both its physical and its psychological effects – and attempt to penetrate the mystery of the interconnection between mind, body, and soul itself. Their interest can, I believe, be attributed, on the one hand, to the care with which they read Rousseau's writings and, on the other, to their awareness of the increasingly widespread use of music in mysticism and medical science to contest the hold that sickness, death, madness, and the forces of the occult exercised over the soul of the listener. Though neither Cottin nor Krüdener explore music's relationship to mysticism or medicine in depth, their tableaux suggest that music has the power to heal, hypnotize, or exorcize the listener. It seems, therefore, that they were as acutely aware of trends in pseudo-religion and pseudoscience as they were of those in popular fiction.

Sophie Cottin was inspired to return to Rousseau's writings after reading Staël's *Lettres sur les ouvrages et le caractère de J.-J. Rousseau* in 1789.[16] Her disavowal (or disobedience) of his precepts for women's education and role in society is even more understated and difficult to discern than that of Charrière and Staël. She repeatedly read the final – and more virtuous – volumes of Rousseau's *Julie*, to which her first novel *Claire d'Albe* has frequently been compared.[17] While both novels feature a love triangle, they differ in that Cottin's heroine does not manage to sublimate her passion and, consequently, is never absolved of her adulterous affections.[18] Such an ending may have been prompted by the conviction, shared by many of Rousseau's readers, that Julie should have suffered for her sins.[19] Yet it also conveys an image of unbridled female passion that Rousseau refused to portray in his novel.[20] Cottin's message thus remained somewhat open to interpretation. For the same reason that they appealed to a broad audience her novels tended to receive mixed reviews, for while seeming to adhere to the notion that women should remain in obscurity she described her heroines' affections in terms that surpassed the amorous frenzy of characters depicted by some of the more licentious authors of the time. Accordingly, some of her readers heralded her novels as authentic while others condemned them as scandalous. Mme de Genlis, notably, wrote the following in her essay *De l'influence des femmes sur la littérature*:

> *Claire d'Albe* est d'une immoralité révoltante. L'amour y est furieux et féroce ... L'héroïne se livre sans pudeur à des emportements effrénés et criminels ... *Amélie Mansfield* est passionné jusqu'à la fureur ... Ce n'est pas peindre l'amour, c'est peindre la rage semblable à celle que les animaux féroces éprouvent dans une certaine saison de l'année.

> [*Claire d'Albe* is revoltingly immoral. In it, love is furious and ferocious ... The heroine gives way immodestly to frenetic and criminal excesses ... *Amélie Mansfield* is passionate to the point of fury ... This is not painting love; it is painting rage akin to that which ferocious animals feel during a certain season of the year.][21]

Catherine Cusset and Colette Cazenobe recognize the tension between virtue and eroticism in Cottin's writings, yet they infer from it opposite notions of her authorial strategy. Cusset argues that Cottin was aware of the tension but that she wrote passionate novels with the ultimate aim of denying, or purifying, the violence of passion, thus using the sin to cure the sinner. Cazenobe suggests, to the contrary, that the tension arose from an abnegated conflict between the predominant moral code and Cottin's personal inclinations, saying, 'Mme Cottin n'a pas osé écrire vraiment le livre qu'elle portait en elle, mais son discours moral et didactique ne parvint pas non plus à le dissimuler tout à fait' (Madame Cottin did not really dare to write the book that she carried within her. Nor, however, did her moral, didactic discourse succeed in masking it entirely).[22] This conflict, among others, renders Cottin's works interesting, for it suggests that she may have harboured convictions about female passion and creativity that can be detected in her writings but that she would not avow. This tension was characteristic at the time of women who loved and of women who wrote, for both acts were considered infringements of female modesty.[23] In Cottin's case, she had difficulty resolving either conflict, and the moralizing bent of her works may well have served as the expiation of both.

In her correspondence, Cottin proclaimed her adherence to the conviction Rousseau espoused in *Emile* that a woman's highest calling and designated social role is that of wife and mother. She approved, moreover, the education of Sophie, which some of her more outspoken contemporaries found unduly restrictive.[24] Cottin did not consider her own act of writing to be in defiance of Rousseau's principles. While she agreed that under ordinary circumstances a woman's vocation is, first and foremost, to be a wife and mother, the premature death of her husband and her incapacity to bear children justified her own divergence from this path, obliging (or enabling) her to have recourse to another – implicitly less fulfilling – act of creation.[25] Her writings thus reveal an unsettling ambivalence towards women authors, whom she wrote against despite the fact that she was one. While Cottin did not claim authorship of her first novel, her identity was revealed before she wrote her second. Stripped of her anonymity, she increasingly sought to bring her narrative in line with her personal convictions. Accordingly, the heroine of *Malvina*, a book she claimed was meant to be a correction of *Claire d'Albe*, suffers not from the constraints of her role as wife and mother but from the guilt that accompanies her inability to fulfil her dual role. Cottin's second novel is thus considered more Rousseauian than her first, for though its plot differs more dramatically from that of Rousseau's *Julie*, its moral is more in keeping with his principles on society and education.[26]

The first edition of *Malvina* features a discussion of women authors that takes place between the heroine and a secondary character named Mistress Clare, who engages in the questionable activity of novel writing. Malvina broaches the subject by voicing the opinion that writing simply takes time away from a woman's responsibilities and asking what is the good of writing educational books if it comes at the expense of one's own child's instruction?[27] At first, Clare seeks to justify her writing by explaining that because she has neither husband nor children, it does not detract from her other responsibilities. Like Cottin, she therefore considers herself to be an exception to the rule. She stipulates, however, that only those women who find themselves in her situation can allow themselves the luxury of engaging in such an activity. At this point, one might argue that the reasons Malvina and Clare provide for disapproving women's writing reflect less on women per se than on the act of writing itself, for men's writing may also be suspected of detracting from their civil responsibilities. Clare goes on to distinguish, however, between the act of writing, which she claims is no more harmful than any other pastime, and the decision to publish, which exposes the author to public opinion. This act, she insists, is a problem for women alone, for whereas the public sphere is men's natural domain, Clare expresses the belief that women should keep a low profile: 'Qu'une femme écrive un roman, apprenne une science, ou travaille à l'aiguille, cela est fort égal, pourvu qu'elle reste dans son obscurité' (That a woman write a novel, learn a science, or do needlework, is one and the same provided that she remains in obscurity).[28]

Whereas the reader initially expects Malvina to criticize and Clare to defend the vocation of women authors, Clare soon demonstrates the same oddity that Cottin displays in seeming to accuse herself. While she attributes a more natural capacity for writing novels to women than to men, the reason she gives – that love is 'l'histoire de leur vie, tandis qu'il est à peine l'épisode de celle des hommes' (the story of their life, while it is hardly an episode in that of men) – is less to their credit. Ultimately, Clare casts off all pretence of making a favourable argument for women's aptitude, characterizing the novel as the lowest of the literary genres and consequently the only one within women's reach, and stating categorically: 'Les femmes n'ayant ni profondeur dans leurs aperçus, ni suite dans leurs idées, ne peuvent avoir de génie' (Women, who have neither depth in their observations nor order in their ideas, are incapable of genius). This statement is remarkably similar to Rousseau's disparaging remarks about female genius in his *Lettre à d'Alembert* and is diametrically opposed to Charrière's frustration with the fact that women's education enabled them to excel in the subordinate genres but not to aspire to the heights of artistic creation.[29] In a sense, however, Mistress Clare holds women to a higher standard than did many of her contemporaries, rejecting the notion that Charrière and

Staël shared that women are held back by the lack of equal educational opportunities:

> On a beau rejeter cette vérité démontrée par les faits, sur le genre de leur éducation, on a tort; car, combien n'a-t-on pas vu d'hommes nés de parens misérables, de la plus basse extraction, entourés de préjugés, sans ressources, sans moyens, plus ignorans que la plupart des femmes, s'élever eux-mêmes, par la force de leur génie, du sein de l'obscurité jusqu'à la palme de la gloire, éclairer leur siècle, et percer jusques dans l'immense avenir: nulle femme, que je sache, n'a encore fait ce chemin.

> [In vain do we attribute this truth, upheld by the facts, to the nature of their education; we are wrong, for how many men have we seen born of miserable parents, of the lowest extraction, surrounded by prejudice, without resources, without means, more ignorant than most women, raise themselves, by dint of their genius, from the breast of obscurity to the palm of glory, enlightening their century, and acceding to the immense future. No woman, that I know of, has yet traversed this distance.][30]

Clare does not, however, entertain the possibility that the very notion that women should remain in obscurity, a notion ingrained in them from an early age, might curtail their creative powers and prevent them from attempting to improve their situation. In case the reader has any doubt as to whether Cottin is speaking through her character, she chooses this moment to intervene, seconding Clare's words in a footnote:

> Non, aucune, pas même cette Sapho toujours citée par les défenseurs de la gloire littéraire de notre sexe; car, lors même qu'elle ne devrait pas sa célébrité autant aux malheurs de sa passion qu'à l'éclat de ses talens, il n'en résulterait pas moins que ses talens se sont bornés à peindre avec chaleur ce qu'elle éprouvait, et certes, je suis loin de refuser celui-là aux femmes. Mais qu'on m'en cite une qui ait tracé un ouvrage philosophique, une pièce de théâtre, enfin, une de ses productions vastes qui demandent une méditation longue et réfléchie, et qui puisse se mettre au niveau de celles de nos littérateurs de la seconde classe?

> [No, not one, not even this Sappho, ever cited by the champions of the literary glory of our sex, for even if she did not owe her fame as much to the misfortune of her passion as to the brilliance of her talents, her talents

would nevertheless be restricted to painting what she felt with warmth, and far be it from me to refuse women that. But name me one who has conceived of a philosophical work, a play, one of those vast productions that requires long, sustained meditation and who can be placed on a par with our second class authors.][31]

Cottin rendered our efforts to reconcile her identity as a woman author with her views on women all the more complicated by eliminating her discussion of women authors in subsequent editions of her novel, presumably out of consideration for her predominantly female readership.[32] She did not, however, eliminate the occasional asides in her novel, which tend to reinforce the impression that she harboured a deep-seated ambivalence towards her sex. Though Malvina passionately takes up the defence of fallen women, whom she characterizes as victims rather than predators, the facts quickly put the lie to her speech, exposing her naivety, when Kitty Melmor proves to be just as brazen as Edmond, her supposed seducer.[33] Later, the narrator castigates Malvina for giving false hopes to Edmond's rival M. Prior, questioning her motives for doing so and undercutting the reliability of the heroine with the exclamation: 'Malvina avait l'âme si pure! mais elle était femme, et ce mot me rend tous mes doutes' (Malvina had such a pure soul! But she was a woman, and this word restores all my doubts).[34] Ultimately, however, Cottin seems to espouse a quintessentially Rousseauian belief in the absolute yet relatively unhierarchical division of the sexes, with respect to both their nature and their social role. Citing Chamfort, she stipulates in her footnote that 'il semble que, dans le partage des deux sexes, les femmes eurent une case de moins dans la tête, et une fibre de plus dans le cœur' (it seems that in the division of the sexes, women have one less compartment in the head and one more string to the heart).[35] This distinction has implications for notions of male and female fidelity. Men, Cottin claims, who are inclined to love with their senses rather than their heart, are capable of being unfaithful without being inconstant. Citing Saint-Preux as an example of this dual capacity, she explains:

> Cette différence qui existe entre la manière d'aimer des deux sexes n'est point rappelée ici comme un reproche, mais comme une simple observation des lois générales de la nature; car cette moitié du monde à qui elle dit: *sois homme*, reçut avec la sensibilité un mélange d'ambition et de gloire; mais celle à qui elle dit: *sois mère* dut être formée toute d'amour.

[This difference in the way that the two sexes love is not recalled here as a reproach, but rather as a simple observation of the general laws of nature, for the half of the world to which she says 'be man' receives along with sensitivity a mixture of glory and ambition, but that to which she says 'be mother' must be formed entirely of love.][36]

Woman is thus condemned to love the faithless and, at first glance, her lot seems rather unfortunate. Yet because she is destined for motherhood and comes equipped with an extra heartstring, the effect of love upon a woman is to 'exalter sa délicatesse jusqu'à la plus céleste pureté, son dévouement jusqu'à l'héroïsme' (exalt her delicacy to the most celestial purity, her devotion to heroism).[37] The sensibility of Cottin's heroines – which, towards the end of the century, had come to be prized above the ability to exercise one's reason – is the very source of their heroism. Women's love for and solidarity towards other women in Cottin's novels is just as strong, stronger even, than the overpowering passion they feel for men. Malvina's lover, for instance, is jealous not of her first husband but of her childhood friend. Samia Spencer contrasts the heroines of Cottin's novels, whose pursuit of love and happiness 'is generally linked to a higher and more noble goal,' to the heroes who 'appear to have no particular purpose or mission in life.'[38] While L.C. Sykes views this as a weakness in Cottin's ability to conceive the masculine subject, remarking that 'Mme de Krüdener sait ... saisir dans la psychologie masculine des nuances qui ont toujours échappé à Mme Cottin' (Madame de Krüdener knows how ... to seize nuances in masculine psychology that always escaped Madame Cottin), it can also be interpreted as a *parti pris*.[39] Though Cottin ostensibly believed that women should remain in obscurity, her heroines quail at nothing.[40] Her novels are thus a tribute to 'ce chef-d'œuvre d'amour, le cœur d'une femme' (this masterpiece, a woman's heart).[41] I suggest, therefore, that Cottin's acceptance of woman's place in society, prioritization of her responsibilities, and deprecation of her creative genius does not necessarily imply that she underestimated or did anything short of glorifying woman's character, particularly her moral fortitude. In the realm of music, whose association with immorality prevented women from developing their talents, this positive representation of women's sensibility proved to be invaluable.

Cottin pursued musical studies somewhat further than Rousseau would have liked, for after she was widowed at age twenty-three she undertook the study of harmony and composition that he advised against in Book V of his *Emile*.[42] She was, moreover, clearly aware of the French literary trope of the musical seduction scene, for her use of music in her novels is, for the most part, extremely conventional. Jean Rossard numbers the love scenes that transpire before Claire's harp in Cottin's first novel, *Claire d'Albe*, among '[l]es lieux communs du genre romantique' (the commonplaces of the romantic genre), and Cazenobe observes of Cottin's third novel, *Amélie Mansfield*, that 'Entre Amélie et M. Mansfield, la musique a été perverse entremetteuse' (Music served as a perverse procuress for Amélie and Mr Mansfield).[43] In *Malvina*, however, Cottin takes the reader on a journey from musical scenes characteristic of the English and French traditions to a truly original musical tableau that explores the connection between music and the sensitive soul and draws upon contemporary trends in medical science. Like Cottin herself, Malvina is obliged to take refuge in England during the Revolution. She does not return to France in time to recover her title and property, however, electing instead to remain by the deathbed of her childhood friend. Entrusted with the guardianship of her friend's child, Fanny, she takes up residence in the Scottish castle of one of her few remaining relatives, one Mistress Birton. When giving Malvina a tour of her castle, Mistress Birton shows her a room dedicated entirely to musical instruments, none of which she plays. Instead, the instruments represent her social status as well as any rarified painting or piece of furniture.[44] It is up to Malvina and her future love interest, Edmond Seymour, to put the room to its proper use. The couple has not yet met when Malvina ventures forth from her rather reclusive existence in an isolated wing of the castle and relocates the music room. Happening upon a book of French romances, she seats herself at a harp and starts to accompany her singing. 'Tout à coup les doux sons d'une flûte vinrent se mêler à sa voix' (Suddenly the sweet sounds of a flute came and mixed with her voice) and Malvina turns to see Edmond for the first time.[45] Though Cottin has already devoted the first hundred pages of her narrative to Malvina, she chooses this moment to provide the first physical description of her heroine. Initially placing the reader in the position of Malvina, who hears Edmond's flute before seeing him, she then places us in the position of Edmond, who is attracted by Malvina's voice before sustaining the full effect of her beauty as she turns round to discover the source of the sound: 'Il entend de loin Malvina, il s'approche, écoute, et cette voix retentit jusqu'à son cœur et lui apprend qu'il en a un! il entre, elle se retourne, et le charme s'achève' (He hears Malvina from afar, he approaches, listens, and this voice echoes in his heart and teaches him that he has one! He enters, she turns, and the charm is complete).[46] Cottin thus plays upon the perspective from which the scene is viewed as well as the sound effects by which it is accompanied. She draws a clear distinction, however, between the impact Malvina's charms have on Edmond's senses and the appeal that her voice makes to his heart. In a letter to his friend, to whom he is in the habit of recounting his romantic escapades, Edmond vividly recalls the impression he sustained, declaring 'Malvina m'a changé, ami; elle a éveillé en moi des sensations qui m'étaient inconnues: elle a fait résonner dans mon cœur des cordes muettes jusqu'à présent' (Malvina has changed me, my friend. She has awakened unknown sensations in me; she has made chords resonate in my heart that were mute until now).[47]

Cottin cleverly incorporates elements of both the French association between music and sensuality and the English association between music and social standing into the musical scenes in her novel. Mistress Birton's use of instruments as one of the many status symbols displayed in her home, suggesting that she still covets the recognition of the society she has purportedly left behind, bespeaks the role that the piano played in the contemporary English bourgeois household. When Malvina catches Edmond in a tête-à-tête with the young Kitty Melmor, the amorous nature of their conversation is represented by the harp standing behind them, in keeping with the frequent allusions to music's illicit overtones in France. Yet Cottin renders even this most conventional of symbols visually interesting by situating Mistress Birton, who dislikes her nephew's philandering, where she can contemplate the scene in the mirror:

En entrant dans le salon, [Malvina] aperçut miss Melmor debout devant une harpe; sir Edmond, assis auprès d'elle, lui parlait bas d'un air animé; et mistriss Birton, assise devant la cheminée, tenait un livre à la main, et, tout en feignant de lire, regardait dans la glace ce qui se passait derrière elle, et décidait dans son âme la destinée future de miss Melmor.

[When she entered the salon, [Malvina] perceived Miss Melmor standing before a harp. Sir Edmond, seated next to her, spoke softly to her with an animated expression. Miss Birton, seated before the fireplace, held a book in her hand and, while pretending to read, watched what was taking place behind her in the mirror, deciding in her soul the future fate of Miss Melmor.][48]

Though no note is played and no emotion conveyed, Cottin nevertheless demonstrates her ability to layer visual effects by depicting Malvina
as she watches Mistress Birton surreptitiously observe the couple. Later,
Cottin evokes the suspect nature of the teacher-pupil relationship in the
private space of the lesson when Kitty's mother, who seeks to avenge
her daughter by tarnishing Malvina's reputation in turn, casts doubt
upon the reasons for the priest M. Prior's daily visits to Malvina's room,
stating suggestively: 'Il prétend ... que c'est pour lui donner des leçons
(Dieu sait de quoi?)' (He claims it is to give her lessons [God knows in
what?]).[49]

In a scene that bears a striking resemblance to the work of her contemporary Jane Austen, indicating that the two may have drawn upon
similar literary sources, Cottin enhances her characterization of the
women who inhabit the castle by contrasting their various kinds and
degrees of musical aptitude.[50] Kitty Melmor is as accomplished an
'executrice' as she is a strategist in love, yet her playing, like her love
affairs, lacks soul.[51] Mistress Birton prides herself on her musical appreciation as she does on her possession of a room full of instruments, but
cannot bear to listen any more than she can play.[52] Her inability to stay
seated for the duration of a musical performance is just another sign
that her sensibility is purely for show. Malvina alone displays the pre-
cious combination of a sensitive ear and good taste and though she
lacks Miss Melmor's technical skill she is able to give a pleasing turn to
the most difficult passages.[53] In the midst of the scene, which suitably
enhances the British setting of the story, Cottin suddenly makes one of
her rare references to contemporary France, for while looking through
Mistress Birton's store of sheet music, Malvina happens upon a collection of French operas. In a brief exchange, Malvina, Kitty, and Edmond
neatly recap the debate as to the superiority of French versus Italian
opera that had divided Parisian public opinion in the years 1752–4 and
again in 1777–9:

Quoi! vous avez ici Armide, Alceste, Œdipe, tous ces immortels chefs-
d'œuvre de notre scène? s'écria Malvina en parcourant les cahiers qui
étaient devant elle. O chère mistriss Birton! on voit bien que vous avez le
cœur toujours un peu français. – Pour moi, reprit miss Melmor dédai-
gneusement, je ne connais rien de plus triste et de plus froid que cette
langue, et je ne pense pas qu'on puisse jamais rien dire d'aimable avec
elle. – Priez madame de Sorcy d'en prononcer quelques mots, répondit sir
Edmond, et je suis sûr que votre incrédulité cessera.

[What! You have here *Armide, Alceste, Œdipus*, all of these immortal masterpieces of our stage? Malvina cried, leafing through the notebooks before her. Oh! dear Miss Birton, it is clear that your heart is still a bit French.
– As for me, Miss Melmor responded disdainfully, I know of nothing more
sad and cold than this language and I do not think that anyone can ever
say anything nice in it. – Ask Madame Sorcy to pronounce some words of
it, replied Sir Edmond, and I am sure you will cease to disbelieve.][54]

While this passage reveals that the operas of Gluck rather than those of
Lully or Rameau had come to represent the French tradition by the end
of the century, Cottin nevertheless hearkens back to the statement that
polarized public opinion in the 1750s when she has Miss Melmor reiter-
ate Rousseau's complaint that the French language is unmusical.[55] Cottin
may have derived her familiarity with Rousseau's critique of the French
language from her reading of *Julie*, for Saint-Preux briefly alludes to it
in his letter, attributing the following explanation to the castrato who
initiates him into the mysteries of Italian opera:

C'est en ceci que consiste l'erreur des Français sur les forces de la musique. N'ayant et ne pouvant avoir une mélodie à eux dans une langue qui
n'a point d'accent, et sur une poésie maniérée qui ne connut jamais la
nature, ils n'imaginent d'effets que ceux ... qui ne rendent pas les sons
plus mélodieux mais plus bruyants.

[In this consists the Frenchmen's error on the strengths of music. Having,
and being able to have, no melody of their own in a language devoid of
accents, and for a mannered poetry unakin to nature, the only effects they
imagine are those ... that make the sounds not more melodious but more
noisy.][56]

Cottin's familiarity with the eighteenth-century opera quarrels goes
beyond the scope of Saint-Preux's letter, however, for she has Edmond
attenuate the effect of Kitty's observation by reminding all present,
including the reader, of their eventual outcome, namely that when
rendered by a gifted musician who is sensitive to its subtle inflections,
the French language is as appealing as any other. This interplay of
tropes borrowed from the English literary and the French musical traditions suggests that Cottin possessed a far broader cultural awareness
than that with which she has previously been credited.
  The evidence of Cottin's familiarity with contemporary musical cul-

ture is confirmed in the course of a second evening of musical entertainment, when Mistress Birton requests that Edmond sing to distract them from the news of his imminent departure. Knowing Malvina's taste for French music, Edmond asks his aunt to bring them her new collection of French romances and agrees to sing in order to put Malvina's affections to the test. Steering her into the music room, Edmond persuades Malvina to accompany him on the piano. He takes advantage of his aunt's momentary absence to intone the final aria of Gluck's *Armide*, laying particular emphasis on the words 'je vais vous quitter' (I will leave you). Malvina, who has been singularly distracted ever since Edmond announced his impending journey, is quickly reduced to tears, betraying the state of her affections. Losing not a moment, Edmond makes a frank declaration of his passion and receives enough of a response from Malvina to sustain his hopes. Their momentary exchange is interrupted, however, by the arrival of M. Prior, Edmond's rival, whose suspicions are promptly aroused. Mistriss Birton returns, preventing a confrontation, but the general embarrassment causes everyone to play out of sync or to sing off key and what had the potential to become a moving musical tableau rapidly disintegrates into a rather comical musical scene. Just as the concert is breaking up, however, Mistress Birton notes that one of the French romances was written by a woman, at which M. Prior snatches it up, proclaiming that Malvina must and shall pay tribute to one of her compatriots. This seeming absurdity is, in fact, a reference to the growing number of works by women composers in the years 1770 to 1820 that Letzter and Adelson have recently documented in their book *Women Writing Opera*.[57] Cottin, who lived on the outskirts of Paris and remained abreast of the current controversies about women who loved and women who wrote, may well have been aware of the trend and have formed an opinion of women composers as she had of women authors. The narrator's deprecation of the song lyrics – 'Ces paroles, toutes mauvaises qu'elles étaient ...' (These words, as bad as they were...) – is consistent with Cottin's desultory view of women's creative powers and, like her critique of women authors, was suppressed in subsequent editions of the novel.[58] Yet the song lyrics, which express a gentle reproach to a departing lover, strike a sympathetic chord, causing Malvina's voice to fail her. Cottin thus maintains her position both on the mediocrity of women's intellectual capacity and on the superiority of their sentiment.[59]

Throughout her novel, therefore, Cottin demonstrates her ability to play upon visual and musical effects and to blend elements of the French and English literary traditions. Though she comes quite close to the construction of a tableau, its efficacy has, thus far, been thwarted by the secondary characters. Yet by endowing Malvina with a profound sensibility, evident in the sincerity of her emotional response to music, Cottin has laid the groundwork for a truly exceptional musical tableau that the doctor uses to bring Malvina back to her senses towards the end of the novel. Malvina and Edmond have been married in secret despite the concerted efforts of Mistress Birton and Kitty Melmor, who are determined to destroy the couple's happiness. With revenge in their hearts, Edmond's aunt secures legal guardianship of Fanny, the child Malvina promised to raise, while Edmond's ex-mistress succeeds in rendering him unfaithful. Simultaneously deprived of her husband and her child, Malvina loses all touch with reality and it is in this sorry state that Edmond finds her when he returns, child in hand, wise to the machinations of their enemies, and ready to renew his vows. Earlier in the novel, Cottin had alluded to the persistent association of medicine and magic in the public imaginary. In a chapter entitled 'Accusation de magie' (Accusation of Magic) the inhabitants of the castle widely assume that Malvina has had recourse to sorcery in order to cure Edmond's persistent fever.[60] Yet the doctor himself pays no heed to the rumours, persuaded that Edmond recovers thanks to Malvina's attentive care but otherwise by natural means. Now, however, the doctor himself proposes to use music to cure Malvina.[61] Thus while Cottin relegates the ability to appeal to the sufferer's soul through magic to the realm of folk belief, she invests the ability to appeal to the sufferer's soul through music with all the authority of medical science.

Once a day, on the hour at which her madness first struck, Malvina regains some semblance of consciousness and paces the garden awaiting her death. In light of this peculiarity, the doctor choreographs an elaborate musical tableau. On the evening in which the cure is to be effected, her family and friends gather in the twilight, concealed behind the bushes so that they may see without being seen. Though initially we are arrested by the spectacle of Malvina's absorption, the doctor has Clare play a few chords on an organ in an effort to attract Malvina's attention. The effect is immediate, for Malvina suddenly stops to listen, the first sign that she is vaguely aware of her surroundings. The doctor then asks Clare to sing a song that Malvina knows well. Striking some preparatory chords on the harp, Clare notes that Malvina once again stops to listen. Clare then sings a ballad of Malvina's own composition, in which she implores Edmond to return so that she can see him before she dies, assuring him that her love will end with her life.[62] Though Malvina recognizes the song as hers, she is puzzled by the fact that she is not singing, an indication that her surroundings may be distinct from the all-consuming internal agony upon which her faculties are focused. In an effort to locate the origin of the voice, Malvina begins to sing herself, appropriating the words of her song yet rendering their meaning all the more poignant with the tone of voice that she employs:

> Alors, comme frappée d'une nouvelle idée, elle élève la voix, et recommence la même romance que mistriss Clare vient de chanter; que dis-je? la même? ah! ce ne l'était plus! son expression a quelque chose de si plaintif, qu'elle fait pleurer chacun de sa peine; mais en même temps son accent est si doux et si tendre, qu'il pénètre toute l'âme et y suspend la douleur.

> [Then, as though struck by a new idea, she raises her voice and begins the same romance that Miss Clare just sang. What am I saying? the same? Ah! such was no longer the case. Her expression has something so plaintive that she makes everyone cry from her pain, but at the same time her accent is so sweet and tender that it penetrates the soul, suspending sorrow.][63]

Malvina thus transforms the song into one that touches yet sustains the listener, transforming the scene into a two-way tableau in which Clare's rendition of the song arrests Malvina's attention and Malvina's rendition of the song moves the onlookers to tears. At this point, Malvina's adoptive child, unable to contain her impatience any longer, starts calling for her mother. Malvina does not recognize Fanny but at the sound of her voice she suddenly recalls that the child was taken from her by force. While not yet fully aware of her surroundings, Malvina nevertheless begins to make her way back from madness to memory.

The return of her child is not all that is required before Malvina can recover or die in peace. Once she remembers the source of her sadness she is able to articulate the desire to see Edmond again. No sooner has she expressed the wish than the sounds of a flute beckon her to a nearby grove. Malvina associates the instrument with Edmond and, recalling the day they first met, when the sound of the flute preceded the sight of her lover, she describes the music's effect:

> Entendez-vous, dit-elle d'une voix basse et tremblante, entendez-vous cette ravissante harmonie? c'est lui qui la cause; de même elle le précéda

lorsqu'il m'apparut pour la première fois ... Oh! je vous en conjure, ne parlez pas, continua-t-elle, en voyant que le docteur ouvrait la bouche pour répondre; qu'aucun autre son ne se mêle à ces sons harmonieux! Si vous saviez le bien qu'ils me font! comme ils rafraîchissent mon sang, raniment mon esprit et attendrissent mon cœur!

[Do you hear? she said in a low, trembling voice, do you hear this ravishing harmony? It is he who causes it, just as it preceded him when he appeared to me for the first time ... Oh! I beg of you, do not speak, she continued, noticing that the doctor was opening his mouth to respond. Let no other sound mix with these harmonious ones. If you only knew what good they do me, how they refresh my blood, reanimate my spirit and soften my heart!][64]

The patient thus affirms what the doctor could only suspect, that music helps revive the vital link between her mind and her heart. Fearing disappointment, Malvina wavers on the brink of the little wood, not daring to enter lest Edmond not be there, when he starts to sing, in a voice she knows well, a song of reconciliation and reassurance that his love had never ceased. Malvina visibly concentrates upon each word in an effort to grasp its full meaning, and the joy and relief the lyrics call forth can be seen in her expression as she takes the final step into the wood, recognizes her husband, proclaims her love for him, and falls senseless at his feet. The silence of the onlookers is complete as they direct their attention towards Malvina's reactions and her own response is beyond catharsis as the music touches the very core of her being. Though her soul makes the long journey back to the living, her heart and mind have been overtaxed. She regains consciousness long enough to bid farewell to her loved ones, but her life lasts only a few more pages.

Despite the repeated attempts of the secondary characters in the novel to besmirch Malvina's reputation by depicting her as a seductress and driving Edmond wild with jealousy, her final moments provide incontrovertible proof of her purity as music restores her faculties without a hint of eroticism. Cottin thus casts the connection between music and the passions in a positive light, interpreting passion not as sensuality but as true love, which is perfectly compatible with morality. She thereby proposes a solution to the problem of how to portray a musically inclined romantic heroine while preserving her from the stigma that her heightened sensibility implies. Though Malvina falls prey to the elaborate schemes of a duplicitous society, her own behaviour is beyond reproach, making her a character to emulate rather than pity or condemn. While Cottin evokes music's association with social status, sensuality, and sensibility throughout the first scenes of her novel, she empties the art of all its suspect connotations in her final tableau, preserving only music's privileged link to the mind, the heart, and, ultimately, the soul of the listener.

Krüdener drew upon a somewhat different literary background than did Cottin. Born in Russia, she learned German and French at an early age and lived in Germany and Italy before going to Paris in 1787 and again in 1802.[65] It was during her second sojourn in Paris that she wrote *Valérie*, her only truly successful novel, which was heralded as another *Julie, Werther*, or *Delphine* when it appeared in 1803.[66] Though based on an incident in Krüdener's life, the scenario – that of a young man in love with his friend's wife – is similar to that of Rousseau's *Julie* and of Goethe's *Werther*.[67] While *Claire d'Albe* was thought to be a racier version of *Julie*, *Valérie* – like *Malvina* – has been dubbed a cleaned up version of both.[68] Like Cottin, however, Krüdener was suspected of having 'justified vice under the label "virtue,"' enabling author and reader alike to enjoy the pleasures of the two with impunity.[69] Whereas her contemporaries' views on women have been the subject of heated debate, critics have paid relatively little attention to those of Krüdener, possibly because she neither spoke out against women authors, as did Cottin, nor was in a position to have done more for their cause, as was Staël. Krüdener writes of herself that she 'se mêle peu de politique' (concerns herself little with politics), an admission that Francis Ley confirms, observing: 'Avec Mme de Krüdener, Mme de Staël ne parla que peu de politique; son auditrice n'y entendait rien' (With Madame de Krüdener, Madame de Staël spoke but little of politics, for her interlocutor understood nothing).[70] Krüdener vied with Staël for literary laurels, however, and was intensely pleased with the popular success of *Valérie*.[71] She was not, therefore, such a devotee of Rousseau as to feel she had to justify her writings, or that a woman's name should necessarily remain in obscurity. Yet certain passages in *Valérie* suggest that she shared Cottin and Staël's conviction that love is the focal-point of a woman's existence. According to Gustave, the antihero of her novel, 'Le ciel, pour dédommager les femmes des injustices des hommes, leur donna la faculté d'aimer mieux' (Heaven gave women a greater ability to love to compensate them for the injustice of men).[72] Gustave's mother claims, moreover, that while men are obliged to tend to their ambitions, women have the more glorious destiny:

> Puissance divine! tu nous laissas l'amour; et l'amour sous mille formes, enchante nos jours! Nous aimons en ouvrant les yeux à la lumière, et nous donnons toute notre âme d'abord à une mère, ensuite à une amie, toujours aux malheureux; ainsi de plaisirs en plaisirs nous arrivons à l'enchantement d'un autre amour; et tout cela n'a fait que nous apprendre mieux le devoir pour lequel nous fûmes créées.

> [Divine power! you left us love and love, in a thousand forms enchants our days. We love when opening our eyes to the light and we give all our soul first to a mother, then to a friend, and always to the unhappy; thus from pleasure to pleasure we reach the enchantment of another love, and all that only taught us better to know the end for which we were created.][73]

The quasi-autobiographical basis of her novel suggests that Krüdener may have inwardly echoed her character's grateful words, which she certainly did not seek to contradict. Krüdener thus seems to have accepted the separation of spheres without envying men their lot.

Krüdener makes no mention of music in her recollections of her childhood activities. In all likelihood, she gleaned what she knew of the art from her extensive travels through Germany, Italy, and France.[74] She was a skilled dancer, however, and her salon performance of the dance of the shawl was the model not only for the dance in *Valérie* but for the dance in Staël's *Delphine*, as well as for Corinne's *tarantelle*.[75] Krüdener's relatively brief exposure to Parisian society would not necessarily have provided her with an extensive background in the aesthetic controversies of the French eighteenth century. She was, however, exposed to several authors who were deeply devoted to the musical arts, and was, notably, aware of the letter from Saint-Preux to Julie in which Rousseau evokes music's power over the soul of the listener. Her familiarity with the German literary and philosophical tradition and her affiliation with mystic sects render the language of her text somewhat more spiritual than that of her contemporaries, and it is clear that her male protagonist, Gustave de Linar, relies on music less to preserve his morality than to ensure his salvation. Beatrice Guenther has described Krüdener's novel as a female *Bildungsroman*, yet Krüdener initiates the reader more fully into Gustave's emotional depths and it is he, not Valérie, who ultimately learns the lesson of the story, namely to distinguish the ideal of woman that he has preserved since childhood from Valérie herself.[76] When gauging the morality of the novel as a whole a distinction must be made, moreover, between the virtue of the hero and that of the heroine, for while the love-struck Gustave founders in a turmoil of adulterous passion, he takes elaborate steps to ensure that his sentiment does not reflect negatively on its object, enabling Valérie to sail the waters of untroubled innocence. In the following pages I will examine Gustave's approach to preserving the sanctity of his feminine ideal, for he constructs a series of musical tableaux in order to maintain the distinction between the inherent virtue of Valérie's sensibility and the corrupt nature of his own.

An epistolary novel, *Valérie* is comprised of the letters that Gustave writes to his childhood friend when he leaves his native Stockholm for Germany after the death of his father. There he takes up residence with his father's friend the count. Continually thrown together with the count's young bride Valérie by virtue of their similar age and affinities, Gustave soon finds himself torn between loyalty to his 'second father' and a mounting affection for the count's wife. Throughout the novel, Krüdener consistently differentiates between the nature and intensity of the young protagonists' artistic sensibilities. Both Valérie and Gustave are musically inclined, Gustave displaying a predilection for the violin while Valérie prefers the guitar. Gustave proves to be still more adept at the guitar than Valérie, however, and while Valérie is moved by the sound of music, Gustave is quite literally overcome.[77] Like Malvina, Valérie is noted for her acute sensibility and her melancholy temperament. Yet while Gustave is enchanted by what he considers to be Valérie's better nature, Krüdener clearly portrays him as the more sensitive and melancholy of the two. Whereas Cottin evokes the opposition between French and Italian music, Krüdener chooses to investigate a similar contrast between the Germanic and Romantic temperaments. She thus completes the map of Europe, in a sense, that Staël would subsequently explore. Both Gustave and Valérie are of Swedish extraction and though Gustave is highly appreciative of the German countryside, he describes Italy and all it stands for as 'dangereuse pour moi' (dangerous for me). A brief scene in which the two attend the Italian opera is enough to give us a foretaste of the dangers Gustave will encounter when he assumes the position of the beholder in a musical tableau. Seated with Valérie behind a screen, as she does not wish to be in the public eye, Gustave takes advantage of their moment of intimacy to indulge the fantasy that she belongs to him. As Valérie, 'transportée de cette musique' (transported by this music), maintains her ethereal purity, Gustave falls into a sensual delirium, in which he sustains the full effect of the contrasts of light and shadow, the ladies' dresses, the dimly lit opera box, and 'la voix enchanteresse de David qui nous envoyoit des accens passionnés; cet amour chanté par des voix qu'on ne peut imaginer, qu'il faut avoir entendues, et qui, mille fois plus ardent encore, brûloit dans mon cœur' (the enchanting voice of David that sent us passionate accents; this love sung by voices that one must have heard to imagine, and that burned in my heart a thousand times more ardently). While these combined 'voluptés' afford mere sensual pleasure to the Italians, Gustave insists that the novelty of the experience heightens his awareness and enables him to invest the scene before him with the power of his imagination by bringing his soul into play.[78]

Krüdener reinforces the distinction between her characters' affective responses to music during Valérie's dance of the shawl. A form of musical tableau, Valérie's dance, like the Nephew's antics, is comprised of gesture set to music that is slightly out of earshot. The resulting arrangement bears a strong resemblance to Marillier's depiction of Alvare and Biondetta in Cazotte's *Diable amoureux*. Attracted by the strains of music that he hears from afar, Gustave arrives outside the window of the dance hall in time to see Valérie start to dance to the tune of a violin. Characterizing her dance as 'un langage éloquent puisé dans les mouvemens de l'âme et des passions' (an eloquent language that arose from the movements of the soul and the passions), Gustave furnishes a description that subtly transits from the purity of Valérie's own state of mind to the disturbing effect of her dance on the beholder: 'c'est elle qui, à la fois décente, timide, noble, profondément sensible, trouble, entraîne, émeut des larmes, et fait palpiter le cœur' (it is she who, decent, timid, noble, profoundly sensitive, troubles, leads, provokes tears, and makes your heart beat). His description thus simultaneously preserves her innocence and reveals how close he comes to losing his own. While Valérie's dance 'trahit l'âme en cherchant à voiler les beautés du corps' (betrays the soul while seeking to veil the beauties of the body), Gustave does not seem to know which he finds more seductive.[79] Stifling a cry, he opens his arms to embrace the air and, as Valérie nears the window, he passionately kisses the glass. The reader is presented with the compelling image of Gustave, his ardor aroused, outside in the night looking in through the window while Valérie, on the other side of the glass, surrounded by light and applause, remains blissfully unaware of his presence. When Valérie seeks to refresh herself by breathing the night air, Gustave does not allow her to open the window, holding it shut as though he fears she will inhale the strength of his desire along with the breeze. Though the music accompanies Valérie's gestures rather than her voice, Gustave clearly shares Saint-Preux's susceptibility to 'Je ne sais quelle sensation volupteuse' (some unknown voluptuous sensation) that accompanies an exquisite musical passage.[80] For Gustave, music is *both* the voice of passion that stirs the senses *and* the sound that goes straight to the sensitive soul, whereas for Valérie it is but the latter. With difficulty, yet with tremendous resolve, Gustave concentrates all his efforts on shielding the unsuspecting object of his adulation from the fervour of his feelings.

In search of a language through which to express his love for Valérie without making her aware of his feelings, Gustave draws on his talent as an artist and a musician to design what he describes alternately as a 'tableau' and a 'miroir magique' (magic mirror). In honour of Valérie's birthday he commissions a painter to decorate the dance hall with scenes from her youth that depict the Swedish countryside. As Valérie admires her familiar surroundings a curtain rises, revealing a troop of young girls busily sewing away, among whom Valérie's likeness can readily be distinguished. The girls, who are dressed like Swedish peasants, have been trained at the Mendicanti conservatory, and sing ballads composed expressly for Valérie: 'Les voix ravissantes des filles des Mendicanti, le talent de ces artistes fameux, la sensibilité de Valérie, contagieuse pour les autres, tout fit de ce moment un moment délicieux' (The ravishing voices of the Mendicanti girls, the talent of these famous artists, Valérie's sensitivity, contagious for others, everything made this moment a delicious one).[81] Though the tableau represents the landscape in which both Valérie and Gustave were raised, it is intended to recall the day on which Valérie's husband first espied her. Transported back in time, she and the count spend a few moments quietly reminiscing before Valérie escapes to the darkness of the adjoining room to shed a nostalgic tear.[82] Thus while Gustave demonstrates his sensitivity to Valérie's feelings by depicting the scenes and evoking the memories she is most likely to cherish, he designs the tableau to ensure that her thoughts are directed not towards himself but towards her husband. This strategy is consistent with Gustave's declaration that he would cease to love Valérie should she cease to love the count, suggesting that he loves her for her virtue alone.

While Valérie is as acutely aware of Gustave's sensibility as he is of hers, she remains ignorant – or innocent – of her ability to catalyze his reactions, particularly through musical means. Whereas Gustave strives to protect Valérie from the insidious effects of his passion, consciously deflecting her thought from himself to more suitable objects, Valérie unwittingly exposes Gustave to the pain that will prove to be his undoing. When forced to take to her bed in excessive prelabour pains, she summons Gustave and asks that he play some music to distract her. Gustave quails at this suggestion and wonders aloud to his friend in a letter: 'Savoit-elle, Ernest, qu'il falloit me distraire moi-même et me tranquilliser?'[83] (Did she know, Ernest, that I myself needed to be distracted and tranquillized?). Though Valérie intends the music to be reassuring, she does not anticipate that what is her antidote may be her companion's poison. In this passage Krüdener tips her hat to the source of her inspiration, for Gustave notes in passing that the words and music of the romance Valérie asks him to sing were written by Rousseau. Obediently seating himself at the piano, he starts to sing:

Après neuf mois de mariage, Instans trop courts!
Elle alloit me donner un gage
    De nos amours.
Quand la Parque, qui tout ravage,
    Trancha ses jours.

[After nine months of marriage, moments too short!
She was going to give me a sign
    Of our love.
When Fate, who ravages everything,
    Cut her days short.][84]

The words' unexpected relevance to the immediate circumstances render Gustave's situation unbearable. Fearing that Valérie will die in childbirth, he is ready to faint from fright. The morbid image of the song, sung to the tune of Valérie's cries, are enough to send him running for the door. The music that was intended to soothe the listener thus only serves to torture the musician. Gustave does not stop running until he reaches a church where he falls down in fervent prayer, despite the fact that he has no business there, not being Catholic. The suggestion that his love for Valérie approaches his reverence for the divine is troubled, however, by the fact that he asks God first for forgiveness and then for Valérie to return his passion in a singular mixture of sanctity and sin.

Though Gustave wishes to preserve the difference in the nature of their musical sensibilities, he does not profess to understand it. While he and his idol seem to share the same soul, her affections run clear and pure while his drive him to distraction. The two are increasingly thrown together after Valérie's miscarriage by the court's express request that Gustave keep her company while he is away on business. Gustave becomes acutely aware of the difference between them when Valérie starts to sing in a gondola as they await her husband's return. Gustave berates the Italian climate, which only exacerbates 'le feu honteux qui me dévore' (the shameful fire that devours me).[85] Consumed by his passion, he wonders how Valérie can remain so calm, unable to fathom how she is capable of such a neat separation of sense and sensibility:

> Pourquoi chante-t-elle ainsi, si elle n'aime pas? Où a-t-elle pris ces sons? Ce n'est pas la nature seule qui les enseigne, ce sont les passions. Elle ne chante jamais, elle n'a pas appris à chanter; mais son âme lui a crée une voix tendre, quelquefois si mélancoliquement tendre ... Malheureux! je lui reproche jusqu'à cette sensibilité sans laquelle elle ne seroit qu'une femme ordinaire, cette sensibilité qui lui fait deviner des situations qu'elle est peut-être loin de connaître.

> [Why does she sing thus if she does not love? Where did she find such sounds? It is not nature alone that teaches them, it is the passions. She never sings, she did not learn to sing, but her soul gave her a tender voice, sometimes of such melancholy ... Miscreant! I reproach her even for this sensitivity without which she would be but an ordinary woman, this sensitivity that enables her to intuit things that she may be far from knowing.][86]

Gustave is perplexed yet charmed by Valérie's ability to provoke but not participate in his extremes of passion. He is convinced, moreover, that she is blissfully unaware of her power. Valérie's ability to trigger the tableau mechanism without realizing its potential effect on the listener is thus further proof of her innocence. Not wanting to taint the incarnation of his childhood ideal, lest he stop loving her, Gustave invents an elaborate means of exorcising the sensual side of his affections so as not to endanger Valérie's virtue.

Realizing that he cannot hope for Valérie's assistance in saving his soul from his senses, Gustave makes the extraordinary decision to design a musical tableau in which he himself will assume the place of the beholder in order to sustain its salutary effects. Earlier in the novel he had espied a young woman named Bianca who resembles Valérie from the colour of her hair to the sound of her voice. Recalling this physical resemblance he inquires into her background and soon discovers that she is perfect for the role he wishes her to play. Because Bianca is single he need not worry that his feelings for her – like those he harbours for Valérie – will be adulterous. A composer's daughter, Bianca is well trained in music, though she owes her talent to her training rather than to her sensitive soul. While Bianca's aristocratic godmother provides her with clothing fit for polite society, her lower-class origins alleviate Gustave's concern about compromising her virtue. Conscious of class differences, he would be ashamed to associate Valérie, even in thought, with the 'spectacles' to which he feels free to escort Bianca. One day, when in a gondola together, Gustave asks Bianca – innocently enough – to sing a romance that Valérie has often intoned entitled 'T'amo più che la vita.' Persuaded that Gustave is attracted to her, Bianca sings with particular affect and succeeds in arousing Gustave's senses: 'Sa voix entra dans tous mes sens; j'éprouvois une inquiétude délicieuse, un besoin d'exhaler l'oppression de ma poitrine ...' (Her voice penetrated all of my senses; I felt a delicious nervousness, a need to exhale the oppression in my chest ...).[87] Her voice is devoid of the essence that renders Valérie's unique, however: 'Elle a des sons de Valérie, mais aucune de ses inflexions: et où les auroit-elle prises ces inflexions, ces leçons que donne l'âme' (She has Valérie's sounds but none of her inflections. And where would she have acquired these inflections, these lessons given by the soul).[88] Aware of the illusion of his senses, Gustave compares Bianca's song to that of the Sirens and does not for a moment mistake the sensations he sustains for true love. Despairing of ever obtaining the object of his affection, he weeps in utter dejection, yet is encouraged by the thought that he is capable of being attracted to another. The next day, therefore, he proceeds in a more premeditated fashion.

Taking full advantage of the superficial resemblance between the two women, Gustave undertakes to procure a few fleeting moments of happiness at no cost to his paragon. Having purchased a sky-blue shawl identical to the one that Valérie wore for her dance, he enters Bianca's chambers, requests that she remove all other decoration, casts the shawl over her shoulders, and crosses the room. Facing her in the dim light he half-closes his eyes, asking that she bow her head to enhance the resemblance. Only then does he repeat his request that she sing Valérie's romance, softly so as to resemble the untrained voice of his idol. The effect is immediate: 'Mon imagination se monta à un point incroyable; la réalité étoit disparue, le passé revivoit, m'enveloppoit; la voix que j'entendois m'envoyoit les accens de l'amour; j'étois hors de moi; je frissonnois, je brûlois tour à tour' (My imagination was fired up to an incredible extent. Reality had vanished, the past revived and enveloped me. The voice that I heard sent me accents of love. I was beside myself, I shivered and burned in turn).[89] This time the illusion is complete. Interpreting Bianca's glance as one charged with passion, Gustave imagines that she shares his emotion, crosses the room, and takes her in his arms with a cry of 'Valérie!' We can only guess to what extremes his imagination would have led him if they were not at that moment interrupted by Bianca's brother-in-law, at which Bianca stops her song, throws off the shawl, and promptly resumes her own garb. The illusion destroyed, Gustave is left with incontrovertible proof that Bianca is devoid of the depths he attributes to his heroine, for 'Bianca étoit là comme une marionnette qui ne se doutoit nullement de mon âme, et qui, dans l'atmosphère d'une passion brûlante, n'étoit pas même susceptible de la moindre contagion' (Bianca was there like a marionnette who did not remotely suspect my soul and who, in the atmosphere of burning passion, was not susceptible to the least contagion).[90] The ruse has worked, however, for Gustave momentarily experienced the plenitude of desire that he can only feel for a sensitive soul, free from the awareness that his imagination alone has furnished the soul Bianca lacks, and free from the fear that the force of his desire will mar his idol's perfection.

Gustave's tendency to be carried away by the powerful combination of music and imagination anticipates Nathaniel's infatuation with Olympia, the automaton in Hoffman's *Der Sandman*, and Jimmy's reconstruction of Judy as Madeleine in Hitchcock's *Vertigo*. It is reminiscent, moreover, of the moment in Saint-Preux's letter to Julie when, caught up in the performance, he suddenly loses all sense of the performer and is able to give full reign to his imagination. As I discussed in the introduction, once initiated into the beauties of Italian opera, Saint-Preux describes the effect of musical passages that both paint and excite the violence of the passions:

Je perdais à chaque instant l'idée de musique, de chant, d'imitation; je croyais entendre la voix de la douleur, de l'emportement, du désespoir; je croyais voir des mères éplorées, des amans trahis, des tyrans furieux, et dans les agitations que j'étais forcé d'éprouver j'avais peine à rester en place.

[I lost at every moment the notion of music, song, imitation; I thought I was hearing the voice of grief, rage, despair; in my mind's eye I saw mothers in tears, lovers betrayed, furious Tyrants, and in the agitations I was forced to experience I could scarcely keep still.][91]

Equally susceptible to emotional extremes, Gustave is nevertheless careful to hide from Valérie the intensity of feeling that Saint-Preux hastens to recount to Julie. Rather than risk allowing his passion to tarnish its object, he has recourse to Valérie's alter-ego, the lower-class street-singer. Sensuality is good enough for Bianca of the trained voice who frequents 'spectacles' and is willing to fulfil Gustave's fantasies. Not so with the lady of class whose musical ear is attributed to her innate sensibility and whom he can but love from afar. Gustave projects his sensual urges onto the one in an attempt to preserve the innocence of the other. Yet the resemblance between the two women must be complete before Gustave can fully participate in the tableau before him. Just as a more conventional lover might pay for the services of a prostitute so as not to sully the lady of his dreams, Gustave constructs a musical tableau that enables him to give vent to the full range of his feelings without debasing his idol.

Gustave's calculated construction of a musical tableau that allows him to release his pent-up energy carries all the force of orgasm or self-sacrifice. Yet Krüdener ultimately chooses to immolate Gustave, not Valérie, to the powerful association between musicality and sensuality in the male imaginary. Like Cottin, she calls the reader's attention to the various connotations of musical ability, using it as a sign of social status, of pride in performance, of a passionate nature, of dubious morals, and of sacrosanct ideals. Both authors then proceed to separate the wheat from the chaff. Systematically eliminating any suggestion of sensuality from their depictions of their heroines, they posit the existence of an ideal woman who possesses a soul susceptible to music yet impervious to its nefarious effects. In view of the widespread association between music and immorality, the invention of this character was of inestimable importance, for the charge of immorality prevented women from venturing into a domain for which they might otherwise have been suited. The creation of exemplary female characters who were capable of playing music without succumbing to its allure was a crucial step if women were one day to try their hand at a performance or composition that ventured beyond the narrow confines prescribed to their sex.

Cottin and Krüdener had a finger on the pulse of their literary generation. Their novels are of interest precisely because they took relatively little interest in contemporary aesthetics and politics, read widely in the French, German, and English literary traditions, embraced recent trends in mysticism and music therapy, and did not take particular exception to Rousseau's characterization of woman's nature, her creative capacities, her education, or her social role. They are thus, in a sense, more representative of their age than Charrière and Staël, who were exceptions to the rule. Their works contributed, moreover, to the transition between the two. Inspired by Staël's *Lettres sur les ouvrages et le caractère de J.-J. Rousseau* and *Delphine* they in turn left their mark on *Corinne*, for Staël read Cottin and Krüdener's novels and displayed a similar awareness of music's relationship to society, sensibility, and the soul. Lori Jo Marso calls our attention to the irony that Staël strategically opposed Rousseau's characterization of women by emulating his heroines.[92] Cottin and Krüdener contributed to the first step of this process by embracing Rousseau's depiction of Julie. By taking Rousseau's writings to heart rather than taking exception to them, they ultimately demonstrated greater mastery over the mechanism of sensibility and explored music's connection to the sensitive soul somewhat further than their contemporaries. The significance of their inclusion of the soul in this equation should not be taken lightly. Whereas Charrière stages a confrontation between the morality of her heroine and the negative social connotations that her musical talents imply, Cottin and Krüdener investigate music's power to wrest the soul of the listener away from the realm of madness and the occult. By staging Malvina's favourable response to the contemporary practice of music therapy and Gustave's effort to exorcise the sensual side of his sensibility, Cottin and Krüdener second Rousseau's attempt to extend the power of music beyond the senses and the heart to the soul itself. In so doing they recalled the age-old association between music and spirituality that had gone into recession in the heyday of the Enlightenment.

6 Staël's Sweet Revenge

Quand on sent faiblement [la musique] on exige qu'elle se conforme avec fidélité aux moindres nuances des paroles; mais quand elle émeut jusqu'au fond de l'âme, toute attention donnée à ce qui n'est pas elle ne serait qu'une distraction importune, et pourvu qu'il n'y ait pas d'opposition entre le poème et la musique, on s'abandonne à l'art qui doit toujours l'emporter sur tous les autres.

[When we feel [music] only faintly we demand that it faithfully conform to the slightest nuances of speech, but when it stirs us to the depths of our souls, any attention given to something other than the music would be nothing but an importune distraction, and provided that there is no opposition between the poem and the music, we abandon ourselves to the art that will always take precedence over all others.]

Staël, *De l'Allemagne*

Germaine de Staël was enamoured of Charrière's writing, so much so that Charrière felt obliged to curb Staël's enthusiasm when she made a pilgrimage to Colombiers, giving her much the same reception as Voltaire had given the young Rousseau. The two authors were separated by their age, sensibility, politics, and affections. Charrière was deeply dismayed by the course the Revolution took, regarding the civil bloodbath with horror. Though Staël did not approve the carnage, she was perhaps more sympathetic to the end in view.[1] Nevertheless, she is said to have exclaimed, in tribute to Charrière's work, that 'elle n'aurait jamais pu supporter la Terreur sans la lecture de *Caliste*' (she could never have survived the Terror without reading *Caliste*).[2] Charrière held Staël accountable for having drawn Benjamin Constant into the fray, and their shared affection for the young idealist, along with the unexpected course of the Revolution, rendered the differences between them insurmountable. Roughly a generation older than Staël, Charrière belonged more entirely to the Enlightenment, with its powers of discernment and pervasive irony, whereas Staël cherished the ideals and displayed the spiritual elan that came to characterize literary Romanticism.[3] The two were also diametrically opposed in their reception of Rousseau. Staël launched her literary career with her *Lettres sur les ouvrages et le caractère de J.-J. Rousseau*, published when she was only twenty-two, to which, it will be remembered, both Champcenetz and Charrière responded.[4] At this point, Staël had already read Rousseau's two *Discours*, his *Lettre à d'Alembert*, *Julie*, *Emile*, and his *Contrat social* attentively. Critics have since heralded her letters as signalling the advent of literary criticism in France. At the time, however, Charrière could not pass up the opportunity to reprimand the ebullient Staël for soft-pedalling her critique of Rousseau, a reprimand that Mary Wollstonecraft sternly echoed.[5] That Staël initially glossed over several of Rousseau's objectionable statements is undeniable. In her assessment of Rousseau's *Lettre à d'Alembert*, whose precepts Staël's heroine Corinne would later flagrantly disregard, she states, 'Le seul tort qu'au nom des femmes je reprocherais à Rousseau, c'est d'avoir avancé, dans une note de sa lettre sur les spectacles, qu'elles ne sont jamais capables des ouvrages qu'il faut écrire avec de l'âme ou de la passion' (The only wrong I would reproach Rousseau on behalf of women is to have suggested, in a note to his letter on the theatre, that they are incapable of works that must be written with soul or passion).[6] By thus isolating one of Rousseau's statements about women, Staël implicitly condones the rest. With time, however, Staël's criticism of Rousseau's views became increasingly strident and critics have recently made a concerted effort to restore Staël's credibility as a protofeminist thinker.[7] Though several studies have been dedicated to Staël's depiction of the woman artist, the generic nature of this category has diverted attention from the specifically musical content of her novel *Corinne, ou l'Italie*. Yet Staël stages her opposition to Rousseau's writings most persuasively in her musical tableaux. Like many young women of her time, Staël studied music as a child. She was not, however, a composer in her own right, and therefore had less reason than Charrière to be troubled by the passage in *Emile* that differentiated between girls' and boys' musical education. She was directly affected by the notorious passage in *Emile* in which Rousseau suggested that the talents of the exceptional woman render her unfit for marriage, however. Her novel *Corinne, ou l'Italie* reveals, moreover, that by 1807 she had mastered the terms of the aesthetic quarrels of the eighteenth century. Her reaction to Rousseau's writings on women and music, albeit subtle and delayed, furnished the raw materials from which she forged a series of tableaux that expose the stark contradiction between the merit of women's musical pursuits and the nature of their social condition.

If we take a closer look at Staël's youthful *Lettres sur les ouvrages et le caractère de J.-J. Rousseau*, in which she condoned all but one of Rousseau's statements about women, we notice that she is already far more critical than she lets on. Though Charrière felt obliged to elaborate upon Staël's opposition to Rousseau's ideas on women's education in her *Courte réponse à une longue réplique* for Champcenetz's benefit, the grain of the idea that Charrière sought to amplify was already there. Staël more readily concedes women's natural fragility than does Charrière, yet she expresses reservations about Rousseau's program of separate education, which seems to risk 'fortifiant ... les femmes dans leur faiblesse' (reinforcing ... women's weakness).[8] Charrière and Staël thus both reject Rousseau's inclination to shelter Sophie, Charrière on the grounds that women should be prepared against the potential dangers of the world and Staël because she has greater respect for submission through love than submission through weakness. The obvious solution, according to each, is to grant women the right to strive for the same educational standards as men. In Staël's words, 'Si les femmes, s'élevant au-dessus de leur sort, osaient prétendre à l'éducation des hommes ... quelle noble destinée leur serait réservée!' (If women, raising themselves above their station, dared to aspire to men's education ... what a noble destiny would await them!).[9] Staël ventures another objection to Rousseau's ideas in her *Lettres*, this time in the realm of politics. At this early stage in her writings, before she had lived in a republic herself, Staël was inclined to trust Rousseau's judgment as to whether the separation of spheres in a republic is preferable. She takes issue, however, with such a notion as applied to a monarchy, and goes so far as to praise women's comportment under such a regime above that of men. Since women are already slaves to domesticity under every system of government, she states, they manage to preserve their sense of self under despotic regimes, whereas men, who are accustomed to civil liberty, suffer more from the loss of it:

Je hasarderai de dire que dans une monarchie, les femmes conservent peut-être plus de sentiment d'indépendance et de fierté que les hommes:

la forme des gouvernements ne les atteint point; leur esclavage toujours domestique est égal dans tous les pays: leur nature n'est donc point dégradée, même dans les Etats despotes; mais les hommes, créés pour la liberté civile, quand ils s'en sont ravi l'usage, se sentent avilis et tombent souvent alors au-dessous d'eux-mêmes.

[I would venture to say that in a monarchy women may retain a greater sense of independence and of pride than men. The form of government does not affect them. Their domestic servitude is equal in all countries. Their nature is therefore not degraded, even in despotic nations. But men, when they have robbed themselves of the use of the civil liberty for which they were created, feel debased and are frequently unworthy of themselves.][10]

Such a statement vividly displays the sense of solidarity with her sex and resentment of their chains that Staël is often accused of lacking.

In the course of the next twelve years, Staël's views on women and the conviction with which she was willing to state them developed considerably. In *De la littérature*, published in 1800, Staël devotes a passage exclusively to women in the section entitled 'Femmes qui cultivent les lettres' (Women of Letters). As a concession to the predominant republican ideology that Rousseau had espoused, she opens her discussion with a statement that seems to contradict her earlier characterization of a woman's lot as an 'esclavage domestique': 'Certainement il vaut beaucoup mieux, en général, que les femmes se consacrent uniquement aux vertus domestiques' (Certainly it is preferable, in general, that women consecrate themselves entirely to domestic virtues).[11] Yet the words 'en général' provide a sort of escape clause for those women who do not fit the norm. Such a statement accords perfectly with Staël's beliefs, for she considered domestic virtues to be laudable in women who are not otherwise remarkable. She immediately tempers this apparent concession to domesticity, however, stating unequivocally that she fails to understand why men are more inclined to tolerate a mediocre woman's neglect of her domestic virtues than a superior woman's display of her exceptional talents. In a later passage, Staël again pays lip service to the cultivation of domestic skills with these words: 'Si les Français pouvaient donner à leurs femmes toutes les vertus des Anglaises, leurs moeurs retirées, leur goût pour la solitude, ils feraient très bien de préférer de telles qualités à tous les dons d'un esprit éclatant' (If the French could endow their women with the virtues of English women, their retiring habits, their taste for solitude, they would do well to prefer such qualities to all the advantages of a brilliant mind). Yet her very next words reveal that she is simply repeating a commonplace with which she does not remotely agree, for she goes on to say that were French men to persuade their wives to adopt English virtues, 'ce qu'ils pourraient obtenir de leurs femmes, ce serait de ne rien lire, de ne rien savoir, de n'avoir jamais dans la conversation ... une idée intéressante' (what they could obtain from their wives is to read nothing, to know nothing, and never to embellish their conversation ... with an interesting idea).[12] Uneducated themselves, she notes, such women will be incapable of instructing their children, thus lessening the filial bond that Rousseau considered of such primordial importance to the family unit and to society at large.

By the turn of the century, then, Staël was no longer willing to give Rousseau the last word. In *De la littérature* she resumes her examination of how extraordinary women are viewed in monarchies and republics that she had begun in her *Lettres* twelve years earlier. This time, however, her discussion is fraught with the disillusionment of having lived under both regimes. Whereas she had previously acknowledged Rousseau as the authority on republics, she now expresses her own opinion in fairly intransigent terms:

> Si l'on voulait que le principal mobile de la république française fût l'émulation des lumières et de la philosophie, il serait très raisonnable d'encourager les femmes à cultiver leur esprit ... Néanmoins, depuis la Révolution, les hommes ont pensé qu'il était politiquement et moralement utile de réduire les femmes à la plus absurde médiocrité.

> [If one wanted the main goal of the French Republic to be the emulation of philosophy and enlightenment, it would be quite reasonable to encourage women to cultivate their mind ... Nevertheless, ever since the Revolution men have thought that it was politically and morally useful to reduce women to the most absurd mediocrity.]

Staël claims, moreover, that women were responsible for the ascendancy of public opinion over people's conduct under the Ancien Régime and that they had earned the respect the Republic now denies them.[13] Though her detractors reproached her for using her discussion of women's issues as an occasion to bemoan her personal situation and justify her lifestyle, Staël can hardly, in this instance, be accused of

neglecting the concerns that touched the lives of her female compatriots. Indeed, she reproaches her contemporaries for their own lack of
solidarity, asking, rhetorically: 'Font-elles jamais alliance avec une femme
célèbre pour la soutenir, pour la défendre, pour appuyer ses pas
chancelants?' (Do they ever ally themselves with a famous woman to
support her, to defend her, to guide her stumbling steps?).[14]

In order to ensure that readers of her *Lettres* would benefit from the
fruits of her more mature reflection, Staël added a second preface to the
work in 1814 in which she addressed the 'woman question' that she had
previously eschewed.[15] She reiterates that governments based on the
family unit have nothing to fear from educating their female citizens,
who are not likely to rebel against a happy fate, and that enlightenment
helps convert the impulses of passionate natures and lead them to the
voluntary observation of a moral code. Education is meant to enrich a
life lived according to society's dictates and thereby render it tolerable.
She thus dissociates herself, once and for all, from the notion that a
woman's fulfilment of her domestic duties is preferable to the cultivation of her other talents, attributing such a preference to men alone:

> Beaucoup d'hommes préfèrent les femmes uniquement consacrées aux
> soins de leur ménage; et pour plus de sûreté à cet égard, ils ne seraient pas
> fâchés qu'elles fussent incapables de comprendre autre chose: cela dépend
> des goûts; d'ailleurs, comme le nombre des personnes distinguées est très
> petit, ceux qui n'en veulent pas auront toujours assez d'autres choix à
> faire.

> [Many men prefer women who consecrate themselves entirely to their
> housework and, in order to ensure it, they would not be adverse to their
> being incapable of understanding anything else. To each his own. Besides,
> since the number of extraordinary individuals is quite small, for those
> who have no use for them there will always be plenty of other fish in the
> sea.][16]

Here Staël finally makes it clear that she neither aspires to nor necessarily espouses domestic virtues. Nor does she reinforce the distinction
between 'élévation d'âme' and 'force de tête' that she had originally
made in the body of her *Lettres*, suggesting by this omission that she is
no longer persuaded that the heart rather than the mind is the proper
province of women. In *De l'Allemagne* (1810) Staël warned women not
to compete openly with men but rather to cede them the field.[18] Here,
however, Staël renders her statement more innocuous by stating that

she has greater respect for a woman who does not seek to win personal glory with her talents. Staël had also previously remarked that she had greater respect for a woman who was passionate but chaste. Ultimately, however, she did not erect this statement into a model of conduct for any other than her literary heroines.[18] Staël's views thus became increasingly feminist, in the modern sense of the term, as she matured. While the forty-year-old Charrière was critical of the younger author's apparent adulation of Rousseau, it is plain that by the time Staël had gained the wisdom of Charrière's years she too regarded her erstwhile father figure with a more objective eye.

Staël makes but a passing reference to Rousseau's musical interests in her *Lettres* of 1788, stating simply: 'Rousseau a écrit plusieurs ouvrages sur la musique' (Rousseau has written several works on music).[19] Though she does not allude to Rousseau's controversial remarks during the opera quarrels or to his posthumously published *Traités sur la musique*, she does mention *Le Devin du village*, *Pygmalion*, and several of Rousseau's romances, all of which she had heard. She also articulates a certain number of musical insights which indicate that her understanding of the art was closely in line with that of her predecessor. When describing the romances, Staël assigns somewhat different functions to the words and the music and considers the power of each to be reduced when they are forced to move in tandem. This notion lay behind Rousseau's approach to operatic reform. Staël expressed particular admiration for Rousseau's *Pygmalion*, in which he alternated the words and the music so that each could fulfil its own potential:

Quand les paroles succèdent à la musique, et la musique aux paroles, l'effet des unes et de l'autre est plus grand; elles se servent mieux quand elles ne sont pas forcées d'aller ensemble. La musique exprime les situations, et les paroles les développent. La musique pourrait se charger de peindre les mouvements au-dessus des paroles, et les paroles des sentiments trop nuancés pour la musique.

[When words succeed the music and music succeeds the words the effect of each is enhanced. They serve each other better when they are not obliged to go together. Music expresses situations and words develop them. Music is capable of depicting movement above and beyond words and words can depict sentiments that are too nuanced for music.][20]

Staël makes several remarks in reference to Rousseau's romances, moreover, that she would thematize in her novel *Corinne, ou l'Italie* some twenty years later. She observes that the romances 'me rappelaient cette musique plutôt calme que sombre, qui se prête aux sentiments de celui qui l'écoute, et devient pour lui l'expression de ce qu'il éprouve' (reminded me of that music, more calm than somber, that adapts itself to the sentiment of the listener and becomes for him the expression of what he feels).[21] Her statement implies that music enables a soul in misfortune to shed soothing tears, but may prove uplifting to a soul free of sorrow. Staël would later draw a similar distinction between Oswald's (melancholy) and Corinne's (ecstatic) response to music, as well as between Corinne's differing responses to music before and after Oswald breaks her heart. Staël then exclaims in her *Lettres*: 'Que la musique retrace puissamment les souvenirs!' (How powerfully music retraces memories!), explaining that the tune of a romance once sung by her lover stirs past emotions in a woman's heart and renders a man's memory of his faults intolerable. Herein lies the key to Oswald's regret over his father, to Corinne's regret over Oswald and, ultimately, to Oswald's regret over Corinne.[22] Staël would later thematize these early musical insights in her portrait of a woman who displays the very essence of Rousseauian musical sensibility and yet falls prey to the perceived incompatibility of female talent and domestic happiness that Rousseau's writings helped perpetuate.

Though Staël's initial reference to Rousseau's writings on music appears to refer primarily to his musical compositions, the evidence suggests that by the time she began her novel *Corinne, ou l'Italie* in 1805 she had become thoroughly acquainted with his musical discourse. In Corinne's salon conversation the comte d'Erfeuil claims the true art of tragedy and comedy for France, leaving Italy the somewhat dubious merit of having invented what became the stock characters and scenarios of the Théâtre-Italien.[23] Eager to defend her homeland, Corinne echoes Rousseau's more favourable view of the Italians, describing their language as inherently musical and enumerating the resulting beauties of the Italian poetic line. Because the sound of Italian is pleasing the ear, she explains, Italian poets tend to rely upon the sound of their verses to the detriment of the meaning. They consequently produce poetry that is more lyrical than French though less profound.[24] Corinne reinforces our impression of the musicality of the Italian language by characterizing Italian poetry in terms that the French usually applied to music. She describes, for instance, not the subject of the poems but the mimetic effect of the sound of the poetic line: 'La mesure des vers, les rimes harmonieuses, ces terminaisons rapides, composées de deux syllabes brèves ... imitent quelquefois les pas légers de la danse; quelquefois des tons plus graves rappellent le bruit de l'orage ou l'éclat des armes' (The metre of the lines, the harmonious rhymes, those sudden endings of two short syllables ... sometimes indicate a light dancing step; sometimes more solemn tones recall the sound of the storm or the clash of arms).[25] Her description of the poem's sonority thus recalls the mimetic understanding of music characteristic of mid-eighteenth-century French audiences. Corinne suggests that the words of the poem are, indeed, of secondary importance, asking, 'Pourquoi demander au rossignol ce que signifie son chant?' (Why ask the nightingale the meaning of his song?).[26] Her question is reminiscent of that which Fontenelle once asked of music – 'Sonate, que me veux-tu?' (What do you want of me sonata?) – with the key difference that Corinne considers Fontenelle's question to be moot. By recalling Fontenelle's words, Staël calls the reader's attention to the shift in listeners' expectations that had occurred in the course of the century, for whereas Fontenelle expected music to convey meaning, Corinne argues that poetry need not signify anything beyond its sound.[27]

Corinne's characterization of Italian poetry contrasts strongly with the narrator's description of how most Italians recite: 'La plupart des Italiens ont, en lisant les vers, une sorte de chant monotone, appelé *cantilene*, qui détruit toute émotion. C'est en vain que les paroles sont diverses ... puisque l'accent ... ne change presque point' (Most Italians read verse in a kind of monotonous chant called *cantilena* that destroys all feeling. The impression is the same, however different the words, since the tone, which is even more affecting than the words, almost never varies).[28] The deadening effect of the Italian monotone, which counteracts the language's natural propensities, extends to the music that Corinne and Oswald hear in the streets, the cathedrals, and the canals of Italy. It blends almost imperceptibly with the paintings, the monuments, and nature that are the objects of their contemplation.[29] The verses of the *Miserere* that the couple hears in the Sistine Chapel alternate between the 'céleste' (heavenly) and the 'sourd et presque rauque' (muffled and almost harsh), rapidly countering enthusiasm with discouragement.[30] This same antiphonal chant, when taken up by the Venetian gondoliers, is again likened to a monotone when heard from nearby.[31] Staël appears to have savored this monotone, which she may have observed when travelling through Italy collecting materials for her novel. Yet the backdrop of an Italy devoid of the lyricism that

Corinne attributes to the Italian language serves primarily to cast the exceptional nature of her own declamatory powers into relief.

Corinne's manner of reciting verses provides a striking contrast to that of her compatriots. In her improvisation at the Capitol, she restores variety of tone and accent to the poetic line, giving rise to a description of the Italian language that surges forth from the text in a passage of untempered Rousseauian lyricism:

> Quand ces paroles italiennes, brillantes comme un jour de fête, retentissantes comme des instruments de victoire que l'on a comparés à l'écarlate parmi les couleurs; quand ces paroles, encore toutes empreintes des joies qu'un beau climat répand dans tous les cœurs, sont prononcées par une voix émue, leur éclat adouci, leur force concentrée, fait éprouver un attendrissement aussi vif qu'imprévu.

> [When Italian words, sparkling like a festive day, ringing out like the sound of victorious trumpets, which has been likened to scarlet amongst the colours, when these words, still marked by the happiness spread in all hearts by a beautiful climate, are uttered with feeling, their softened brilliance, their concentrated power, give rise to an emotion as keen as it is unexpected.][32]

Staël's choice of words and images in this passage suggests that she was familiar with Rousseau's description of the affinity between language, music, climate, and colour in his *Essai sur l'origine des langues*.[33] Staël's description of 'ces paroles, encore toutes empreintes des joies qu'un beau climat répand dans tous les cœurs' echoes the section of Rousseau's *Essai* entitled 'Formation des langues méridionales' (Formation of the Southern Languages), in which he states that 'dans les climats doux, dans les terreins fertiles il fallut toute la vivacité des passions agréables pour commencer à faire parler les habitans. Les premières langues [étaient] filles du plaisir et non du besoin' (in mild climates, in fertile terrains, it took all the liveliness of the agreeable passions to begin to make the inhabitants speak. The first languages [were] daughters of pleasure and not of need).[34] As if to confirm the source of Staël's inspiration, the narrator concludes the description of Corinne's improvisation with the following remark: 'L'expression de la peine, au milieu de tant de jouissances, étonne, et touche plus profondément que la douleur chantée dans les langues du nord, qui semblent inspirées par elle' (The expression of grief in the midst of so many delights is more surprising and deeply moving than sorrow expressed in the northern tongues it seems to have inspired).[35] This description is reminiscent of the section of Rousseau's *Essai* entitled 'Formation des langues du nord' (Formation of the Northern Languages), in which he remarks:

Quelle différence entre des inflexions touchantes qui viennent des mouve-ments de l'ame aux cris qu'arrachent les besoins physiques? Dans ces affreux climats où ... la terre ne donne rien qu'à force de travail et où la source de vie semble être plus dans les bras que dans le cœur ... le prémier mot ne fut pas ... *aimez-moi*, mais, *aidez-moi*.

[What a difference there is between the touching inflections which come from the movements of the soul and the cries wrested by physical needs. In these dreadful climates where ... the earth yields nothing but to the force of labor and where the source of life seems to be in the arms more than in the heart ... the first word ... was not 'love me,' but 'help me.'][36]

Staël had developed her own theory of the rapport between the literatures of the northern and southern countries and the climates in which they arose at some length in *De la littérature*. Her analysis is frequently likened to Montesquieu's, however, which differs from Rousseau's in that Montesquieu accorded the positive valence to the northern countries: 'On a ... plus de vigueur dans les climats froids. L'action du cœur et la réaction des extrémités des fibres s'y font mieux ... le sang est plus déterminé vers le cœur, et réciproquement le cœur a plus de puissance' (One is ... more vigorous in cold climates. The action of the heart and the reaction of the nerve endings are better made ... blood is more determined when nearer the heart and, in return, the heart is more powerful).[37] In *De la littérature*, Staël states that 'toutes mes impressions, toutes mes idées me portent vers la littérature du nord' (all of my impressions, all of my ideas predispose me towards the literature of the north), northern literature being not the literature of conquest but the indigenous literature represented by Ossian and the song of the Niebelungen.[38] In *Corinne*, however, Staël accords the posi-tive valence to 'les joies qu'un beau climat répand dans tous les cœurs,' which are contemplated with greater felicity than is 'la douleur chantée dans les langues du nord, qui semblent inspirées par elle.'[39] Thus nei-ther Montesquieu's analysis of the effect of climate on the nations and the arts nor Staël's own theory of its effect on literature but rather Rousseau's theory of the origin of music and language was the model for Corinne's song.[40]

Though the primary evidence that Staël read Rousseau's *Essai* is the affinity of these textual passages, the *Essai*'s peculiar publication history confirms the possibility. While critics have surmised that the work was originally part of Rousseau's *Discours sur l'inégalité* published in 1754, Rousseau excised it from the *Discours* and returned to it during the controversy with Rameau, completing it by 1761. Contrary to his original intent, he did not publish it during his lifetime. It first appeared posthumously in 1781 as part of a collection entitled simply *Traités sur la musique*.[41] Staël may have had this collection in mind, noted but not yet thoroughly perused, when she mentioned in her *Lettres* of 1788 that Rousseau had written 'plusieurs ouvrages sur la musique.'[42] Staël makes no mention of the *Essai* in her correspondence.[43] She must have known of its existence, however, for in Book XI of his *Confessions* Rousseau wrote:

> Outre ... mon *Dictionnaire de musique*..., j'avais quelques autres écrits de moindre importance, tous en état de paraître, et que je me proposais de donner encore, soit séparément, soit avec mon recueil général, si je l'entreprenais jamais. Le principal de ces écrits, dont la plupart sont encore en manuscrit dans les mains de Du Peyrou, était un *Essai sur l'origine des langues*.

> [In addition to ... my *Dictionary of Music* on which I still kept working from time to time, I had some other writings of lesser importance, all in a condition to appear and which I still intended to give, either separately, or with my general collection if I ever undertook it. The principal one of these writings, the majority of which are still in manuscript in Du Peyrou's hands, was an *Essay on the Origin of Languages*.][44]

Staël is thus the only author in my study who may have been familiar with what has come to be Rousseau's most famous work on the origins of music, language, and society. The likelihood that she was acquainted with the work opens up dramatic possibilities for the interpretation of the role she assigns to music in *Corinne*.

Corinne's ability to restore the natural inflections to the Italian language would suggest that her improvisations are inherently musical, yet critical studies have systematically downplayed the musical aspect of her art. A handful of articles have been devoted to Corinne, *musicienne*.[45] Critics often refer to Corinne as a poet, however, to the exclusion of the musical component of her poetry; as an artist or exceptional woman, which eliminates the specificity of her artistic talents; or as a literary woman, a description which is supported by a single passage as opposed to the multiple references to her musical skills.[46] Those who acknowledge music's central importance in the novel have difficulty accounting for the absence of music in the textual transcriptions of Corinne's improvisations. Anne Deneys-Tunney concludes from this anomaly that music is 'by its very essence that which cannot be inscribed in a novel, that which escapes worded descriptions – the supplement that the novel represses, suppresses, expelling it outside of its form.'[47] Simone Balayé explains, however, that Staël did not, at first, intend to make Corinne an 'improvisatrice,' but rather a poet, changing her mind only after witnessing a performance by the Signora Mazzei towards the end of her Italian tour. The fact that Corinne's improvisations are culled from a number of Greek and Latin poets and historians may account for the relative paucity of musical description in passages that are meant to be sung and accompanied on the lyre.[48] Yet music permeates Corinne's improvisations – as it does Italian poetry – at every level. Staël describes Corinne's language of choice as one in which 'la mélodie des sons ajoute un nouveau charme à la vérité de l'accent: c'est une musique continuelle qui se mêle à l'expression des sentiments' (the musical sound adds a new charm to the sincerity of the tone. There is a continual music which blends with the expression of feelings).[49] Corinne enhances this musicality with her declamatory style, which resembles 'des airs différents joués tous par un instrument céleste' (different airs [played] on a celestial instrument).[50] She augments the suggestive power of her words with the sparse but penetrating tones of the lyre, on which she relies, at times, to complete her thought when words fail her.[51] Her improvisations thus hearken back to the Greek art of declamation, in the days before music and poetry were separated, that was idealized by so many eighteenth-century French aestheticians, including Batteux and Rousseau. Music is such an intrinsic part of her art that when the Neapolitans wish her to perform for them, they place her lyre at the designated site of the performance to represent their expectations.[52] François Gérard similarly depicts the instrument in his painting entitled *Corinne au cap Misène* (Corinne at Cape Miseno) as a key to the heroine's identity, and one is inclined to wonder whether Staël herself, who sat for the painting, did not insist upon its inclusion (figure 7).[53] In the painting, Corinne, inspired by a passing thought or a faraway fanfare, raises her eyes above the sightline of the external beholders, the internal beholders absorbed in turn by the spectacle of her absorption, and her lyre at the ready to move them with her lament.

Her lyre becomes, in a sense, a stand-in for the music book that lies open next to Domenichino's *Sybilla Cumana* (Cumaean Sibyl) to whom Corinne is likened, suggesting that music and not a higher power is the source of her inspiration (figure 8).[54] By stipulating that Corinne is named after a Greek lyric poet rather than for the Italian *improvisatrice* Corilla, moreover, Staël enhances our awareness of the musical aspect of her art, for lyric poetry is, by definition, musical.[55]

The fusion of Corinne's poetic and musical skills is complemented, completed in a sense, by her execution of the *tarantelle*: 'Corinne, en dansant, faisait passer dans l'ame des spectateurs ce qu'elle éprouvait, comme si elle avait improvisé, comme si elle avait joué de la lyre ...; tout était langage pour elle' (As she danced, Corinne made the spectators experience her own feelings, as if she had been improvising, or playing the lyre ... Everything was language for her).[56] Her sensitive rendering of the arts of music, poetry, and dance, along with the art of spiritual conversation to which they are compared, suggests that Corinne does not, strictly speaking, embody the historical ideal of the eighteenth century, the age of Greek lyric poetry, so much as Rousseau's ahistorical ideal: 'L'age d'or où parole, musique, danse, poésie étaient confondues' (The golden age in which language, music, dance, and poetry were combined).[57] At this early stage in society, midway between nomadic wandering and civilization, music and language were not yet fully separated, and the rhythm of their verbal expression led people to break naturally into the gesture of the dance. Italian is the modern language that best conserved the musicality of this early stage of linguistic development, and Corinne is one of the few remaining artists capable of restoring its inherent sonority as she sings. The state of exaltation that Corinne experiences while improvising, a state in which she is able to discourse on subjects that transcend the personal to embrace all of humanity, closely resembles Jean Starobinski's description of the dual capacity of a person living in Rousseau's idealized social state: 'Dans la parole chantante, le sujet se communique sans se quitter. Il sort de lui-même pour s'offrir à autrui dans la parole; et il revient à lui-même dans la présence affective constante qui anime la parole' (In sung speech, the subject communicates without leaving himself. He comes out of himself to offer himself to another in language and returns to himself in the constant affective presence that animates language).[58] By investing Corinne's conversation and improvisations with the very essence of Rousseau's musical discourse, Staël exposes the bitter irony of her heroine's fate as the incarnation of Rousseau's musical ideal falls victim to the negative perception of women's musical pursuits that his writings helped perpetuate.

Before we can fully appreciate the significance of Staël's musical tableaux, we must first examine the social status of the musical arts in her text, a status that severely restricts Corinne's liberty to deploy them. Though Staël admittedly had fewer personal reasons than Charrière to single out music in her text, and though her heroine is more multitalented than is Charrière's Caliste, the role Staël accords to the musical arts indicates that the particularly prevalent association between music and immorality in eighteenth-century French society did not escape her attention. The characters in the novel repeatedly call Corinne's morals into question. She is suspect, first and foremost, because she is Italian. Oswald is disturbed when he first hears Corinne speak English with a flawless accent. The change in language seems to naturalize her, rendering her less foreign and, implicitly, more reliable. At that moment the narrator observes: 'Oswald avait beaucoup de préventions contre les Italiennes: il les croyait passionnées, mais mobiles, mais incapables d'éprouver des affections profondes et durables' (Oswald was very prejudiced against Italian women. He thought they were passionate but fickle, incapable of experiencing deep, permanent affection).[59] Passion, then, can be excused in the name of constancy, but Italian women are unfaithful. Corinne confirms this impression when she remarks, innocently enough: 'Il est ... plus aisé en Italie que par-tout ailleurs de séduire avec les paroles sans profondeur dans les pensées' (It is easier in Italy than anywhere else to charm without any deep thoughts or novel images).[60] She little suspects that in showing a predilection for the Italian language she is incurring a moral taint. Oswald interrogates Corinne as to her artistic preferences as well, and his question seems to contain an unspoken judgment: 'Mais vous, madame ... à laquelle de vos poésies donnez-vous la préférence? Est-ce à celles qui sont l'ouvrage de la réflexion ou de l'inspiration instantanée?' (But you, Madam ... which of your poems do you prefer? The works of reflection or the works of sudden inspiration?).[61] Corinne's choice of improvisation over the more reflective arts of writing or composition, suggests a certain inconstancy that meets with disapproval. Though Corinne is not a singer, per se, she nevertheless vocalizes her poetry, interspersed with her lyre, adding an individuality and physical presence to her performance, which is more sensualized than had she relied on her instrument alone. Unlike most performers, however, Corinne does not merely imitate or execute but rather creates, rendering her art deeply personal despite the fact that universal themes are the subjects of her song. While the art of composition had been closely associated with rationality and science ever since Rameau, Corinne's compositions are spontaneous and rely as much on her sensibility, or powers of empathy and discernment, as on her intellect. Her marked preference for the Italian language, the physicality of her performance, and the spontaneity of her improvisations all convene to cast doubt upon her integrity. So long as she remains in Italy, the generosity of public opinion allows her to practise her art with relative impunity; the only prejudicial statements are uttered by those who pass through on their Italian tour. Yet the description of the freedom she enjoys in Italy merely serves to cast the negative public perception of music in England into relief – music, as opposed to poetry, for while the two arts are considered inseparable in Italy, they are subtly differentiated in England, where music is looked at askance.

The daughter of an Italian woman and an Englishman, Corinne was born and raised in Italy, where she remained with her aunt when her mother died and her father returned to England, in order to complete her education. After the death of her aunt, she joins her father in the little town of Northumberland where he has since remarried and had another daughter by his second wife, Lady Edgermond. Corinne's stepmother allows her to share some of the fruits of her Italian education with her half-sister Lucile, with one important exception. Corinne is permitted to instruct Lucile in drawing and, what is more surprising given the English suspicion of all things foreign, the Italian language. Corinne stipulates, however, that 'ma belle-mère ne voulait pas qu'elle sût la musique' (my stepmother did not want her to learn music).[62] Though she offers no further explanation of Lady Edgermond's restriction of Lucile's musical pursuits at the time, it soon becomes clear that Northumberland is characterized by a pervasive bias against the musical arts. The very air of the provincial English town is devoid of the tones that surrounded Corinne in Italy: 'Chaque jour j'errais dans la campagne, où j'avais coutume d'entendre le soir, en Italie, des airs harmonieux chantés avec des voix si justes, et les cris des corbeaux retentissaient seuls dans les nuages' (Every day I would wander in the countryside where, usually, in the evening, in Italy, I would hear harmonious melodies perfectly sung, and where the crows' squawks rang out alone in the clouds).[63] Finding the conversation of the women who call upon Lady Edgermond to be insipid, Corinne attempts to lend a little life and purpose to their gatherings by proposing that they read verses or play music. The suggestion is mild, for Corinne stops short of asking them to create; instead, she simply asks them to execute and savour the arts in question. Yet each member of Lady Edgermond's circle manages to find an excuse not to attend.

Ignoring – or perhaps misreading – these signs, Corinne prepares to meet Oswald's father, who is considering her as a possible match for his son. Rather than restricting herself to speaking Italian or displaying one of her drawings, as Lady Edgermond's restrictions might have suggested, Corinne seizes the opportunity to make her talent for music, dance, and improvisation known. These arts are, unfortunately, all characterized by their musicality, creativity, spontaneity, and performativity, traits which enhance the artist's investment in her work and which imply that she is likely to overstep the bounds of feminine modesty. Sure enough, Corinne reminds Oswald's father of 'une de ces belles Grecques qui enchantaient et subjuguaient le monde' (one of those beautiful Greek women who delighted and conquered the world).[64] He is not, moreover, unaware of the moral implications of such a statement, and hastens to add, in the letter he writes to Corinne's father disapproving the match: 'Ne vous offensez pas de l'idée que cette comparaison peut suggérer. Sans doute votre fille n'a reçu de vous, n'a trouvé dans son cœur que les principes et les sentiments les plus purs' (Do not take offence at the idea which this comparison may suggest. I am sure you have given your daughter, and she has found in her heart, only the purest principles and feelings).[65] His statement recalls the fact that the Greek *hétaïres* were allowed to develop their musical talents because they were free from the moral strictures placed on other members of their sex. In retrospect, Corinne senses that she may have misjudged her audience, and begins to understand that the arts of display, and in particular the musical ones, do not necessarily give rise to untempered admiration. Years later, this insight still haunts her. Whereas Corinne eagerly awaits Oswald's approval before performing in *Romeo and Juliet*, her reaction is not the same when she is urged to accept a part in an *opéra-comique*: 'Corinne, depuis qu'elle aimait Oswald, n'avait jamais voulu lui faire connaître son talent en ce genre' (Since she had come to love Oswald, Corinne had not wanted to acquaint him with her talent in this sphere).[66] Though this disinclination may reflect Corinne's awareness that tragedy better suits Oswald's melancholy temperament than comedy and that his national pride leads him to prefer English to French or Italian works, the fact that Corinne is loathe to reveal her capacity to perform in an *opéra-comique* indicates that she fears the negative connotations that characterize a woman's talent in this genre.

The circumstances under which Corinne chooses to leave the country corroborate the evidence that music poses a social problem in Northumberland. The death of her father leaves her with no further ties to England. Realizing that once she is of age she can return to Italy and resume her artistic pursuits, Corinne threatens to do so during one of her frequent confrontations with her stepmother, who promptly encourages her to leave.[67] Corinne does not follow through with her plan right away, however, lacking the courage to take such an extreme course of action. Instead, she remains in a state of indecision until one day, after seven years of relative silence, the air once again fills with the sound of Italian song. Corinne's emotional response is immediate: 'Je ne puis exprimer l'émotion que je ressentis, un déluge de pleurs couvrit mon visage, tous mes souvenirs se ranimèrent' (I cannot tell you the emotion I felt. A flood of tears covered my face and all my memories revived).[68] Though the music stirs all of Corinne's longing and desire for her country, she stipulates in her letter to Oswald that it was not the music that convinced her to return to Italy. Rather, it was Lady Edgermond's abrupt entry and heartless demand that Corinne stop the singing 'parcequ'il était scandaleux d'entendre de la musique le dimanche' (because it was scandalous for music to be heard on a Sunday).[69] At this confirmation of the musical taboo, Corinne makes up her mind and leaves England the next morning on the same boat as the musicians.

Whereas Caliste had used her musical talents to acquire a position in society, Corinne prefers to abandon her name and rank for her love of music. Interestingly, her social status, though originally higher and more stable than that of Caliste, proves to be equally problematic. Caliste's father refused her his name and her mother effectively eliminated her from the class system by giving her up for money. Corinne, on the other hand, was born with both name and rank, and very enviable ones at that. She thus possesses all the necessary qualities to attract a husband and ensure her personal happiness. Her talents, however, effectively exclude her from the marital system. As M. Edgermond remarks, citing Thomas Walpole, '*Que fait-on de cela à la maison?*' (*What would you do with that at home?*).[70] Even if Corinne were willing to silence her muse and devote herself entirely to household duties, the men she meets tend to agree that it would be a shame. M. Edgermond goes on to observe that 'chez nous, où les hommes ont une carrière active, il faut que les femmes soient dans l'ombre, et ce serait bien dommage d'y mettre Corinne; je la voudrais sur le trône de l'Angleterre, mais non pas sous mon humble toit' (in our country, where men have an active career, women must be in the shade and it would be a pity to put Corinne there. I should want to put her on the English throne and not under my humble roof).[71] Oswald's father had made a similar observation, noting that talents such as Corinne's required either Italy or the stage. A throne, a stage, another country ... anywhere as long as it is as far as possible from English domesticity. Yet, as the comte d'Erfeuil's comment reveals, Corinne's situation in Italy is itself rather anomalous. 'Quel dommage que ce soit une personne riche qui ait un tel talent!' (What a pity that it is a rich person who has such a talent!), he exclaims. 'Car, si elle était pauvre, libre comme elle l'est, elle pourrait monter sur le théâtre; et ce serait la gloire de l'Italie qu'une actrice comme elle' (For, if she were poor, free as she is, she could go on the stage; and an actress like that would be the glory of Italy).[72] Even in Italy, then, a woman of fortune is not meant to degrade herself by going professional. Corinne, moreover, makes quite sure that she will not be confused in the public eye with women from this walk of life. She is highly selective about when and before whom she will display her talents, as Oswald hastens to impress upon M. Edgermond when he mistakenly assumes that Corinne 'existait par ses talents, et saississait volontiers l'occasion de les faire connaître' (supported herself by her talents and would be glad to take the opportunity of making them known).[73] She has, indeed, chosen Italy *instead* of the stage. The Italians are sufficiently discreet, thank heavens, not to ask Corinne her family name, yet it remains highly unusual not to have one. The presiding impression, therefore, is that society – whether English or Italian – is not sure what to make of Corinne, or where to put her. Like Caliste, Corinne has no designated niche, and consequently must forge her own. Once she has tasted a life of independence outside the class system, however, she is loathe to submit to the yoke of social obligation once again, and is inclined to wonder whether marital happiness is not an oxymoron.

In order to dissociate musicality and immorality in the public imaginary, and to afford her heroine a chance to combine love and marriage, Staël designs a series of musical tableaux which, like those of Charrière, are strategic in their use and social in their import, yet which underline the catalytic role of the music in the tableau more than any others we have seen to date. As I demonstrated above, Corinne's improvisations, like Italian poetry, are inherently musical. I would argue, however, that her musical tableaux, and not her improvisations, are the primary locus of music in the novel. In them, Corinne is inclined to pick up her harp rather than her lyre, to sing rather than recite, and to listen rather than perform. The musical tableaux in Staël's novel are informed by Rousseau's vision of the earliest societies, when 'le langage, musical et poétique, n'[était] pas encore un agent de division. Il autoris[ait] la communication expressive du sentiment et la pleine compréhension réciproque' (language, both musical and poetic, was not yet an agent of division. It authorized the expressive communication of sentiment and full, mutual comprehension).[74] This reciprocity of sentiment sets Staël's tableaux apart from those of her contemporaries, for they are instances in which unobstructed communication can take place between two characters, allowing them to penetrate the veil that separates individuals and 'li[re] dans leurs coeurs' (to read in their hearts).[75] They thus approach the ideal of transparency that Starobinski so persuasively traces throughout Rousseau's writings.[76] Musical tableaux arise in the context of Corinne and Oswald's relationship at moments when Staël wishes to bring about a reconciliation between the lovers. The first intimation of the role that music will play can be seen in their first private interview. The encounter can hardly be called an interview, for the couple find themselves unable to exchange any meaningful phrases. Oswald has come to pay his respects, having learned from the comte Erfeuil that Corinne had been deeply moved by the story of Oswald's past prowess, a sure sign of her interest. Upon finding Corinne alone, however, Oswald 'se sentit plus timide que jamais' (felt more nervous than ever). The power of their emotion, their unfamiliarity with each other's natures, their acute consciousness of their own sensibilities, and their concern for social convention combine to render it virtually impossible for them to communicate. Significantly, at this very moment, 'dans sa distraction, cherchant une contenance, [Corinne] posa ses doigts sur la harpe qui était placée à côté d'elle et fit quelques accords sans suite et sans dessein' (in an effort to save face she fingered the harp beside her and struck a few random chords).[77] The effect is instantaneous. The sounds increase Oswald's emotion and therefore his resolve; they bring the look of inspiration to Corinne's eyes that is visible when she feels herself transported beyond the realm of personal concerns and inhibitions. Emboldened by the sounds of the harp, the couple is on the verge of expressing their shared emotion when the arrival of other visitors puts an end to their tête-à-tête. The music's effect is thus preempted, or postponed, yet the couple's intimacy increases from here on with little further impediment.

A similar moment later in the narrative brings Oswald to the verge of proposing. Upon hearing the 'harpes éoliennes que le vent faisait résonner' (the sound caused by the wind in the aeolian harps) which Corinne has placed in her garden at Tivoli, Oswald is suddenly 'inspiré par le sentiment le plus pur' (inspired by the purest feeling) and becomes convinced that his father has sanctioned their union from on high.[78] He declares to Corinne that they need no longer hesitate to join their fates, not anticipating her reply that they should live for the present and let the future take care of itself. Oswald is deeply hurt, for his statement is an implicit request that Corinne reveal to him the secret of her past, and he understands her reply as an implicit refusal.[79] His sense of inspiration curtailed by this series of *non-dits*, Oswald sinks into a sullen silence, which he maintains throughout the tour Corinne gives him of her picture gallery. Up to this point, the lovers' shared musical moments cannot be considered tableaux, as I have defined them, yet they are indicative of the catalytic role that music plays in the narrative. Dismayed at Oswald's change of heart Corinne hopes that the last painting in her gallery will enable him to give vent to his feelings. Oswald stops short before a painting by George Augustus Wallis based upon the poetry of Ossian that depicts a Scottish youth asleep on his father's tomb.[80] While gazing at the painting Oswald starts to identify with his fellow countryman and his eyes fill with tears at the memory of his own father. David Denby calls attention to the tears this tableau occasions in his study of sentimental fiction. Yet the visual impact of the painting alone is insufficient to trigger Oswald's response. Seating herself in front of the painting, in which a bard hurries to join the young man and help him mourn the dead, Corinne starts to sing the Scottish romances the bard was likely to play, accompanying herself on the harp. Corinne thus brings the painting to life, transforming the literal tableau, which calls Oswald's homeland to mind yet does not have the requisite cathartic effect, into a musical tableau capable of producing the desired reaction. At this moment, 'Oswald ne résista point à l'émotion qui l'oppressait, et l'un et l'autre s'abandonnèrent sans contrainte à leurs larmes' (Oswald could not resist the feeling which overwhelmed him, and they both unrestrainedly gave way to their tears).[81] For the first time in the narratives that we have examined, the author distinguishes between the effect of a musical tableau and of a tableau *tout court* by juxtaposing the two. While the sight of Corinne's painting is moving, the sound of Corinne's harp brings on the true catharsis. The moment is revelatory, for Corinne both provokes Oswald's catharsis intentionally, revealing her power to manipulate the

musical tableau's effect on the beholder, and fully shares in his catharsis, suggesting that she herself is unable to escape the music's effect.
This dual capacity to control and to sustain the emotional effect of the
musical tableau is akin to her ability to expound and critique her own
ideas simultaneously, to imbue her improvisation with the subject of
her own meditations while transcending them to embrace the concerns
of humanity. Both susceptible and savvy to the sway music has over the
emotions, Corinne is equally capable of making others suffer and of
suffering herself.

A second musical tableau arises when Corinne takes Oswald to the
first concert he has attended since his father's death. As they enter the
concert hall, Corinne is visibly moved by the audience's prompt applause and cries of 'Vive Corinne!' Her evident pleasure at the public
acclaim arouses Oswald's jealousy, and he resumes his sullen silence,
sequestering himself in the far corner of their box seat. Corinne, in the
meantime, turns her attention to the music. Once again identifying
Italian song as the essence of music and likening it to the climate in
which it is cultivated, the narrator suddenly gives voice to an arresting description: 'De tous les beaux-arts, [la musique] est celui qui agit
le plus immédiatement sur l'ame ... Ce qu'on a dit de la grace divine,
qui tout à coup transforme les cœurs, peut, humainement parlant,
s'appliquer à la puissance de la mélodie' (Of all the arts, [music] is the
one that acts most directly on the soul ... What has been said about
divine grace suddenly transforming hearts can, humanly speaking, be
applied to the power of melody).[82] This description corresponds to the
notion that Starobinski identifies as central to Rousseau's musical
theory. The romance, Starobinski explains, 'se passe ... du truchement
de la sensation, pour atteindre *directement* l'âme de l'auditeur. Car la
mélodie a le pouvoir de toucher le cœur à coup sûr: proposition
capitale dans la théorie musicale de Rousseau' (bypasses the senses to
reach the soul of the listener *directly*, for melody has the power to
touch the heart: a central tenant in Rousseau's musical theory).[83] The
heart, the soul, melody, immediacy, the passions – all the elements are
present. Starobinski supports his statement with a reference to Saint-
Preux's letter to Julie on Italian music, with which Staël was unques-
tionably familiar: 'C'est de la seule mélodie que sort cette puissance
invincible des accents passionnés; c'est d'elle que dérive tout le pouvoir
de la musique sur l'âme' (It is from melody alone that this invincible
power of impassioned accents arises; from it derives the whole power
of music over the soul).[84] Turning her attention from the spectacle of

Oswald's irritation to the concert before her, Corinne finds the music so moving that she becomes absorbed in the emotion it arouses within her: 'son émotion l'absorbait toute entière' (she was completely overcome by emotion). The duet on stage strikes a sympathetic chord in the heart-strings of the listeners. Focusing her attention on the perfect unison of the two voices, evocative of Rousseau's notion of melody at its most pure, Corinne forgets her surroundings and the subject of their misunderstanding. Oswald, in turn, is moved by the music and by the spectacle of Corinne's absorption, which persuades him that she is less affected by the attentions of her admiring public than he feared. While the attention of the lovers is directed towards the union of voices on stage ours is directed towards the union of hearts in the box. As Oswald's chagrin dissipates, he gradually traverses first the physical then the emotional distance that separates him from Corinne:

> Il se rapprocha doucement, et Corinne l'entendit respirer auprès d'elle dans le moment le plus enchanteur de cette musique céleste; c'en était trop, la tragédie la plus pathétique n'aurait pas excité dans son cœur autant de trouble que ce sentiment intime de l'émotion profonde qui les pénétrait tous deux en même temps.

> [Quietly he came near to Corinne and she heard him breathing beside her at the most enchanting moment of this heavenly music. It was too much; the most moving tragedy would not have aroused so much agitation in her heart as the profound feeling of deep emotion that they both experienced simultaneously and that was exalted more and more with each new sound.][85]

In this passage, which refers first to Oswald, then to Corinne, it becomes impossible to tell whose heart is intended by the words 'son cœur.' They have, for all intents and purposes, become one, and the effect of the music upon their hearts is stronger than any tragedy. This statement is far from neutral in view of the fact that the couple had experienced an intense mutual catharsis when Corinne played Juliet before Oswald in the Italian translation of Shakespeare's play. So completely did the couple identify with the lovers that they lost the ability to distinguish between fiction and reality as both performer and beholder became completely absorbed in the sense of emotional affinity produced in the space of this nonmusical tableau.[86] The passage above emphasizes, however, that their sense of communion is enhanced by the music of the concert. The sound of the voices, and not the words they utter, enables their estranged souls to reestablish a common ground: 'Les paroles que l'on chante ne sont pour rien dans cette émotion ... le vague de la musique se prête à tous les mouvements de l'âme, et chacun croit retrouver dans cette mélodie ... l'image de ce qu'il souhaite sur la terre' (The words of the singer are of no importance in such emotion ... the vagueness of the music lends itself to all the emotions of the soul, and everyone thinks that, in the melody ... he finds again the image of what he desires on earth).[87] Corinne thus exercises her greatest ascendency over Oswald not in her moments of poetic triumph but rather when she joins him as a beholder in a musical cathersis and communion of hearts.

The purity of the sentiment with which Oswald is filled when he hears the aeolian harps and the pleasure he experiences at the sight of Corinne's absorption during the concert suggests that the emotion they sustain when listening to music is morally sound. The fanfare that precedes her improvisations and gives Corinne the necessary courage for the creative act is also intrinsically moral: 'La musique double l'idée que nous avons des facultés de notre ame; quand on l'entend, on se sent capable des plus nobles efforts ... elle a l'heureuse impuissance d'exprimer aucun sentiment bas, aucun artifice, aucun mensonge' (Music redoubles our perception of our souls' abilities. On hearing it we feel capable of the noblest efforts ... Fortunately, it is powerless to express any base feeling, any deceit, any lie).[88] This view of music is consistent with Rousseau's notion that the golden age in which poetry, music, and elevation of soul were one preceded the corrosive influence that society exercised on the individual soul and its power to communicate. Staël infuses her musical tableaux with the association Rousseau wished to reinstate between music and pure sentiment. By allowing the lovers to communicate freely in moments of Rousseauian transparency Staël combats any notion in the mind of the reader that Corinne's love of the musical arts or of Oswald is anything but sincere. We are thus disinclined to share the prejudices of English society when Corinne describes the suspicion with which women's musical talents are viewed, or to understand Oswald's affinity for Lucile, with whom he experiences no such communion of hearts. Staël designs her tableaux to combat the negative light in which the secondary characters cast Corinne's talent and sensibility. Placing us in the position of the beholder, she ensures that we are persuaded of the morality of the lovers' musical moments.

Yet Corinne's musical sensibility, which enables her to draw confidence and inspiration from a few felicitous chords, also hastens her untimely demise. To dramatize her heroine's tragic end, Staël draws upon the musical intuitions she expressed in her *Lettres* some twenty years earlier, including the close association between music and memory, and music's ability to enhance the listener's courage or intensify her despair. Oswald had difficulty listening to music after his father's death and was unable to linger in the streets of Italy to listen to the singing: 'Il redoutait ces accords ravissants qui plaisent à la mélancolie, mais font un véritable mal, quand des chagrins réels nous oppressent' (He dreaded the enchanting harmonies which are a pleasure to the melancholy but cause genuine pain when we are burdened by real sorrows).[89] Corinne clearly comprehends music's cathartic effect on the listener, for she induces Oswald to shed tears for his father by touching the strings of her harp. Yet she also proves susceptible to its ability to enhance the listener's sorrow once her own misfortunes multiply. Persuaded that Corinne's exceptional talents are incompatible with domestic happiness, Oswald leaves her for her lovely yet otherwise unremarkable English half-sister Lucile. Thereafter, Corinne must abandon her art, for when she attempts to play, 'la musique ne lui causait qu'un tressaillement douloureux' (music only made her quiver painfully).[90] The pain the music induces comes from the strength of its association with memory. Previously, when Corinne was overcome with nostalgia at the sound of the Italian songsters in the little town of Northumberland, the narrator reminded us that the music occasioned her reaction, for 'rien ne retrace le passé comme la musique' (nothing brings back the past like music).[91] After Oswald abandons her, Corinne's chagrin becomes too oppressive to allow her to listen to music any more. Her harp and lyre are thus silenced, but the music that wafts upon the air of Italy gradually saps her strength and leads her inexorably to the tomb. Corinne's own suffering suggests the means of avenging herself on her lover. Recalling, surely, the success of her previous experiment when she allowed Oswald to mourn his father by adding music to a painting, she designs two final musical tableaux to ensure he will mourn her as well. As acutely aware as Caliste and Gustave of the tableau's strategic potential, Corinne uses it neither to defend her virtue nor to protect that of her lover but rather to wreak vengeance on the man who has done her wrong.

In the first tableau, Corinne takes advantage of her uncanny resemblance to her niece. The little girl born to Oswald and Lucile is the spitting image of Corinne. They have, moreover, named her Juliette for the role Corinne had triumphantly incarnated in Rome. Without her mother's knowledge, Juliette has gone to visit her aunt who teaches her to sing and play. Chancing to see his daughter as she is practising the tunes Corinne taught her to pick out on the lyre, Oswald is struck by the fact that she is the very picture of Corinne *musicienne* in miniature. In Staël's words 'on croyait voir la miniature d'un beau tableau' (it was as if you saw a miniature of a beautiful picture).[92] Oswald recognizes the tune Juliette is singing as the Scottish air that Corinne used quite intentionally to provoke his catharsis while looking at the painting in her gallery. When questioned, the child reveals that Corinne has asked her to play the tune for Oswald each year on the 17th of November, the anniversary of the day he left her.[93] Upon seeing Corinne's likeness, hearing the Scottish tune, and recognizing her motives, Oswald is overcome with remorse, as we may assume he will be at least once a year as the musical miniature grows into a musical tableau. Purposely schooling Juliette in the art that she was forbidden to teach Lucile, Corinne arrogates the art that posed the greatest stumbling block for her in the small town of Northumberland into the instrument of her revenge.

So as to leave no doubt in Oswald's mind as to who is responsible for her untimely demise, Corinne designs a final tableau in which she bids farewell to the public she held so dear, whose attentions Oswald resented. Too far gone to give voice to her thoughts, Corinne sings her song by proxy, writing the words she would have sung had she been able, and having a young girl sing them for her. The performance takes place in a sort of amphitheatre. The sight of the young girl, whose soul is tranquil and full of hope, contrasts strongly to the sight of Corinne, who is altered beyond recognition. No longer able to rely on her harp or lyre, Corinne has made arrangements for a musical prelude: 'Une musique noble et sensible prépara les auditeurs à l'impression qu'ils allaient recevoir' (Noble, sensitive music prepared the listeners for the impression they were about to receive).[94] Oswald is visibly affected by the sight of Corinne, the shadow of her former self, and the sound of the prelude that renders memories more poignant before the song begins. Corinne consecrates her last words not to the man she loved, but to her country, her religion, and to those who loved her for her talent. Her lines are nevertheless riddled with implicit reproaches aimed at Oswald. 'Non,' the child declares in Corinne's name, 'je ne me repens point de cette exaltation généreuse, non, ce n'est point elle qui m'a fait verser des pleurs dont la poussière qui m'attend est arrosée' (No, I do not repent of that noble rapture, of that uplifting passion. No, that is not what made me shed tears, which still water the dust that awaits me).[95] Of her religion, she sings, 'Si j'avais placé ma tête dans le ciel à l'abri des affections orageuses, je ne serais pas brisée avant le temps' (If I had raised my head to heaven when I would be shielded from passionate affections, I would not be prematurely destroyed). To Italy she sings 'Belle Italie! c'est en vain que vous me promettez tous vos charmes, que pourriez-vous pour un cœur délaissé?' (Beautiful Italy, you promise me all your charms in vain. What could you do for a deserted heart?).[96] Her art is not responsible for her sorrow, from which her religion might have protected her yet against which her homeland could do nothing. Oswald, who had asked Corinne to no avail whether or not she blamed him for her misery, now has his answer. The memory of what Corinne was, the spectacle of what she has become, and her swan song, which persuades Oswald that he alone is to blame for her demise, leaves him fainting with remorse.

Though Corinne's musical tableaux serve as an instrument of revenge they are also a vehicle of social reform. Just as Caliste left behind a generation of musically accomplished orphan girls to continue her efforts to combat the notion that music is the source of a woman's social degradation, Corinne ensures that at least one young lady will serve as living proof that musical talent is perfectly compatible with the decency of the domestic interior. In *De la littérature*, Staël suggested that English women would benefit from a more extensive education, which would make their society more agreeable and render them more capable of educating their children in turn. She pointed out, with incontrovertible logic, that a more thorough education would by no means detract from their morals: 'Ou la morale serait une idée fausse, ou il est vrai que plus on s'éclaire, plus on s'y attache' (Either morality is a false concept or it is true that the more enlightened one is the more attached one becomes to it).[97] Her description of the heartless reception superior women could expect to receive in the French Republic, where they will first be slandered then left to their own devices, corresponds closely to the fate Corinne suffers in England and Italy. This resemblance indicates that Staël designed the end of her novel not as a critique of her heroine, as has been suggested, but as a critique of contemporary society.[98] Creating a heroine who incarnates the musical ideal Rousseau evoked in his writings, Staël immolates this ideal to the society whose prejudices his statements tended to reinforce. Staël's tableaux are designed to persuade us (and remind Oswald) of her heroine's intrinsic merit, creating

a disjunction between our perspective and that of the secondary characters in the novel, who are not privy to such musical moments. Though
Corinne precedes Oswald to the tomb, her ability to haunt him from
beyond it suggests that society will ultimately have to contend with the
legions of its female victims.

One of the primary explanations given for the difficulty women have
experienced in making lasting contributions to the musical field is the
very effervescence of the art, for while many women who were musically proficient are remembered, they are no longer remembered as
musicians.[99] Music's tendency to fade from the record, leaving behind
the occasional instrument depicted on a vase or evoked in a text, has
continued to plague the historical record until fairly recently.[100] Sappho
(another of Staël's heroines) and Corinne, both known to their contemporaries for their poetry set to music, have come to be known as poets,
though their victories in poetic competitions were at times attributed to
their superior musical skills.[101] Often improvised instead of notated,
their music simply vanished. Jane Girdham evokes the difficulties historians encounter when attempting to divine the role music played in
theatrical performances. Though music was an intrinsic part of English
theatre, its presence was seldom noted in advertisements or commented
upon in critical reviews. Reconstituting an accurate idea of the musical
interludes in the absence of such commentary is practically impossible,
for while musicians no longer improvised, they relied on their knowledge of harmony to flesh out sparsely notated scores.[102] In those
instances when text and music were composed as an ensemble, the
text occasionally appears to have been preserved as a sort of reductive
stand-in for the whole. Of all nine of Charrière's operas, for instance,
we retain some of the libretti but none of the scores.[103] As a result,
while women were recognized by their contemporaries for the excellence of their performances and compositions, their reputations, unlike those of actresses and painters, swiftly faded, leading Evelyne
Pieiller to ask:

> Tout le monde connaît Madame de Sévigné. Qui connaît Élisabeth Jacquet
> de la Guerre? Tout le monde, ou presque, connaît la Champmeslé. Qui
> connaît la Maupin? Une femme ... de lettres, une comédienne: elles ont
> survécu. Un compositeur, une chanteuse: elles ont disparu. Même siècle,
> même célébrité.

[Everyone knows Madame de Sévigné. Who knows Élisabeth Jacquet de la Guerre? Everyone, or almost everyone, knows la Champmeslé. Who knows la Maupin? A woman ... of letters, an actress; they have survived. A composer, a singer; they have disappeared. Same century, same fame.][104]

If the ephemeral nature of music was one of the reasons women musicians have consistently disappeared from the historical record, the pervasive association between music and immorality was certainly another. Oddly, however, the authors in my study are credited neither for the musicality nor for the morality of their heroines. Ellen Moers's article 'Performing Heroinism' presents a puzzling instance of this critical oversight. The only mention she makes of Corinne's musical talents occurs in a list where she identifies her as a '[p]oet, improvisatrice, dancer, actress, translator, musician, painter, singer, lecturer.' Subsequently, however, Moers consistently refers to Corinne's *literary* genius.[105] She stipulates that '[i]n the novels women wrote after Mme de Staël, the actress did not become the principal descendant of her performing heroine,' intimating that the obstacle to such a legacy was the actress's inherent immorality. She then claims, however, that Corinne's principal descendant was the opera singer, implying that the opera singer was free from such a stigma. '[T]here is no other kind of heroine,' she claims, 'who can so plausibly be made a chaste as well as a mature and desirable woman. George Sand keeps Consuelo a virgin, even a married virgin, for more than a thousand pages.'[106] Yet the notion of a chaste opera singer (which to this day escapes us) would have been completely counterintuitive for Sand's generation were it not for the concerted efforts of Charrière, Cottin, Krüdener, and Staël, who wrote against the French literary tradition that depicted women musicians either as seductresses or as ripe for seduction.

The decision of these authors to record the stories of women musicians is of capital importance, for, as Letzter and Adelson note, without such a tribute to women's musical activities, other women are less likely to brave the presumed social interdiction of their talents. Citing Gilbert and Gubar, they remind us that 'Harold Bloom's paradigm of the "anxiety of influence" works in reverse for women. Because a woman's entry into a creative discipline represents a transgression, "she can begin ... only by actively seeking a female precursor, who ... proves by example that a revolt against patriarchal ... authorship is possible."'[107] Staël's choice of improvisation as Corinne's art form par

excellence calls attention to the ephemeral as well as the morally suspect nature of her art. 'Fait étrange,' Claire Dehon says of Corinne, 'elle
excelle dans l'improvisation et ainsi elle ne laissera aucune œuvre après
sa mort. Un pareil choix étonne lorsqu'on considère que Mme de Staël
rêvait d'atteindre l'immortalité grâce à ses nombreux écrits. Quelle
qu'en soit la raison, l'œuvre éphémère de Corinne souligne sa destinée
tragique' (Strange to say, she excels in improvisation and hence none of
her works will survive her. Such a choice is particularly surprising if we
consider that Mme de Staël dreamt of becoming immortal through her
writing. Whatever the reason, Corinne's ephemeral works enhance her
tragic destiny).[108] Dehon's statement suggests that we cannot conflate
Corinne's improvisations with Staël's writing without overlooking a
fundamental difference in their chosen forms of artistic expression. This
difference was linked, I would argue, to the growing perception in the
eighteenth century that the musical and visual arts provided a means of
escaping linguistic constraints. Though women authors were clearly
concerned about their own social status, they frequently conceived of
heroines who expressed themselves through song rather than living by
their pen. The woman musician is often read as a stand-in for the
woman author. I find this reading to be rather reductive because it
suggests that when writing about women musicians, women authors
were really referring to themselves. I would suggest, to the country, that
they endowed their heroines with a form of self-expression that surpassed what they could ever hope to achieve, because music was thought
to be more expressive than language and was therefore subject to greater
social sanctions. Aware of the notion that music was free from the
limitations of the other arts but hemmed in by the notion that women
should not express themselves so freely, these authors invested their
heroines with this coveted freedom and power of expression. Eighteenth-century women authors looked to music as that alternate form
of expression that women would later seek in alternate forms of writing, escaping linguistic and defying social constraints via their heroines
in the space of the tableau. By downplaying the fact that their heroines
affect their social ascent, combat social prejudice, and avenge themselves
upon society by musical means, we deprive women who aspire to become musicians of the positive role models these authors provided. By
ignoring their attempt to bring the impasse between women, music, and
society to public attention, we detract from the efficacy of their social
critique and the value of their literary contribution.

While these authors did not go as far as their predecessors in experimenting with the form of the musical tableau, they went farther in exploiting its function. Diderot, Cazotte, and Beaumarchais countered Rousseau's critique of the limitations of the French language by creating tableaux through which they convey music while continuing to write in French. The form of their tableaux thus put the lie to Rousseau's assertions. Charrière, Cottin, Krüdener, and Staël created musical tableaux that conform, by and large, to the structure that we have seen before. Yet their characters are so acutely aware of this structure that they, like their authors, place it in the service of their own political ends. While we can only suspect Biondetta of reconstructing her harpsichord in order to tempt Alvare, it is quite clear that Caliste uses the musical tableau to defend her virtue, the doctor to bring Malvina back to the land of the living, Gustave to exorcise his desire, and Corinne to chastise her lover. By delegating the creation of musical tableaux to their characters, who use them to catalyze the reactions and determine the fates of the inscribed beholders, the authors reveal their awareness of the tableau structure as such. Together they created a series of musical tableaux that, in their function rather than their form, collectively served to dissociate musicality and immorality in the minds of their contemporaries and readers, freeing women of subsequent generations from the suspicion that surrounded their musical pursuits.

Afterward

Rira bien qui rira le dernier ...

He laughs best who laughs last ...

Diderot, Le Neveu de Rameau

Rousseau's influential yet controversial statements – which seemed to deny French and Italians, men and women equal access to music's enhanced powers of expression – led his contemporaries and readers to interrogate the relationship between music, meaning, and morality. Since reading the open-ended invitation implicit in Saint-Preux's letter to Julie and the challenge implicit in Rousseau's writings on society, education, and the arts, the authors who took part in, actively followed, or were duly influenced by the contemporary debates about aesthetics and morality collectively transformed the way in which music figured in literary texts. Diderot, Cazotte, and Beaumarchais explored aesthetic solutions to the questions that Rousseau raised about music, language, and nationality, designing musical tableaux that reinforced France's pride in its nation and language and contributing towards the reform of French literature, theatre, and opera. Charrière, Cottin, Krüdener, and Staël addressed the social problem that lay at the heart of Rousseau's discussion of music, morality, and gender, designing musical tableaux that served to dissociate music and immorality in the French imaginary and enabling women to participate in the Romantic cult of the artist. Though obliged to pick their battles, each group of authors remained acutely aware of the other set of concerns. While the men chose to foreground questions of national equality they played upon the moral ambiguity of women's musical activities. While the women chose to foreground questions of sexual equality they spoke to the embattled issue of national music. The difference between them is therefore a matter of emphasis and can largely be viewed as a joint endeavour.

In order to emphasize the reciprocity of their interests I will briefly examine the attention the authors in my study devoted to one another's causes. Though it did not constitute the focus of their musical tableaux, Diderot, Cazotte, and Beaumarchais nevertheless acknowledged the moral problem that music posed for women. In *Le Neveu de Rameau*, for instance, the Philosopher and the Nephew engage in an extended conversation about the education of young girls. Upon learning that the Philosopher's daughter is already eight years old, Rameau's Nephew exclaims with dismay: 'Il y a quatre ans que cela devrait avoir les doigts sur les touches' (She should have been touching the keys for four years).[1] When the Philosopher patiently explains that his daughter is instead taking lessons in grammar, history, geography, morality, fables, and drawing, for he prefers that she learn to reason than to rhyme, the Nephew objects: 'Eh! laissez-là déraisonner tant qu'elle voudra, pourvu, qu'elle soit jolie, amusante et coquette' (Oh! let her be as unreasonable as she likes, so long as she is pretty, entertaining, and coquettish).[2] The lessons that will enable her to develop these qualities, which the Nephew considers necessary to a woman's social advancement, are music, song, and dance. The Nephew later regrets that he himself had a son instead of a daughter, saying that he would better be able to ensure his son's fortune had he been a girl. Yet his plans for the social advancement of young women include expertly inducing an innocent girl to respond to the advances of a nobleman (never to be heard from again) and concluding an agreement with his wife whereby she will actively promote her wares and he will live off the proceeds. We can therefore easily imagine to what end the Nephew would have wanted his hypothetical daughter to devote her musical talents.[3] Despite the suggestive overtones of their discussion, Diderot himself escapes any suspicion that he might have condoned the age-old association of women's musical talent with their seductive wiles, for the Philosopher adamantly disapproves of the Nephew's recipe for social success.

Cazotte, as the reader may recall, likewise plays upon this trope. In the fourth canto of *Ollivier* Fleur-de-Mirte willingly plays musical notes at Zerbin's dictation, engaging in a musical conversation with King Macore without grasping the full significance of the sound. Obediently playing a series of no's that really mean yes, she unwittingly signs her future away to a tyrant she hardly knows.[4] Yet by putting his heroine wise to the situation and providing her with a safe escort off the island,

Cazotte, too, avoids becoming complicit with the association of women, music, and immorality. The fact that Cazotte's other seductive, singing heroine is none other than the devil in disguise has earned him a reputation for misogyny. I would argue, however, that the final line of *Le Diable amoureux* once again places Cazotte above suspicion. After listening to Alvare's narrative, the one we have presumably just read, the doctor summoned to assess his situation suggests that if he were to marry a young woman of his mother's choosing he would not be tempted to 'la prendre pour le diable' (take her for the devil).[5] The doctor thereby intimates that the suspicion surrounding Biondetta's identity is all in Alvare's head, reminding us that Alvare, as the narrator of his own tale, controls our perception of Biondetta. According to this reading, Alvare, not Cazotte, is the misogynist. Cazotte thus once again strikes such a delicate balance that unless we pay close attention to the structure of his text we risk misreading it entirely.

Unlike Cazotte, Beaumarchais had a reputation for defending women's rights. Yet he, too, walks a fine line in his *Figaro* comedies, for song is not only a privileged moment during which feelings are avowed and exchanged, it is also a vehicle for seduction. In *Le Barbier de Séville* Rosine pretends to drop a copy of her song (suggestively entitled 'La Précaution inutile') out the window, arousing Bartholo's suspicions. In the ensuing discussion 'perdre sa chanson' (to lose her song) rapidly becomes a euphemism for losing something far more valuable. The so-called song is, in fact, a note asking the Count, disguised as Lindor, to sing his intentions to the tune that Rosine specifies.[6] Sheet music is thus a stand-in for a love letter and the song the only means by which the lovers can communicate. Beaumarchais enhances the sexual implications of this ruse in *Le Mariage de Figaro*, in which Suzanne fixes the time and place of her rendezvous with the Count, who wishes to capitalize on his 'droit du seigneur' in a note stating simply: 'Chanson nouvelle, sur l'air: ... Qu'il fera beau, ce soir, sous les grands marronniers' (New lyric to the old tune: 'How sweet at eve ... Under the spreading chestnut trees').[7] The duplicity is double, in this case, for the Countess has dictated the (musical) note. Upon learning that the note is from Suzanne and unaware that the note sets a trap for the Count, Figaro flies into a jealous rage and launches into his tirade on female infidelity, reinforcing the association between *chansons*, love letters, and women's wiles.[8] The consequences of this association prove to be still more dire when a woman is not singing but is sung to, for instead of being reviled as a seductress she is condemned for being seduced. Such is the fate of the Countess, who, as we have seen, is visibly moved by Chérubin's song, a song that will prove to be her undoing in the third play in the trilogy when she bears Chérubin's child. Beaumarchais again forestalls the notion that he shares the suspicion surrounding the female performer or beholder, however, when Marceline come to the defence of women who are the innocent victims of seduction in the trial scene.[9] Women, she claims, are first abused then accused and the on-stage audience applauds her insistence that men, not women, ought to take the rap. Diderot, Cazotte, and Beaumarchais were thus aware of the stigma against women's musical sensibility. Though they did not condone such unfavourable characterizations, they felt free to play upon them in their works. While their inclination to make light of the situation can be interpreted as indifference, it can also be interpreted as using comic relief to bring the matter to public attention.

Charrière, Cottin, Krüdener, and Staël were, similarly, attentive to the questions of music and nationality that had plagued their predecessors. In an arresting article, Beatrice Guenther asserts that in Krüdener's and Staël's novels, 'it is not the drama of national identity that holds front stage,' claiming instead that they made their greatest contribution by 'exploring and representing how identity is shaped by gender rather than by nation.' While I agree with her assertion, the implication is nevertheless that the question of national identity provides a rich and varied backdrop to the gender question that these authors chose to foreground. Like their predecessors, Charrière, Cottin, Krüdener, and Staël elected to set their stories in practically every western European nation other than France. This variety may, in part, be attributed to the surprising array of national heritages on which they were able to draw. Charrière was born in Holland and raised in Switzerland, Krüdener was born in Russia but lived primarily in Germany and France, and Staël, whose father was Swiss, spent most of her adult life in exile in Germany and Italy. All four authors travelled outside their nations' borders and read even more extensively. They pay tribute in their works, moreover, to the literary heritage of Homer and Ossian. The couples in their novels, like the settings of their stories, are studies in national contrasts. Charrière's William, an Englishman, writes to Cécile's mother, who is Swiss, of Caliste, ostracized for her Italian musical education. Cottin's Malvina, a Frenchwoman at sea in Scottish society, falls tragically in love with Edmond, an Englishman who shares her affinity for music. Krüdener's Gustave is drawn to Valérie by virtue of their shared Swedish heritage, yet falls victim to his more acute sensitivity to everything Italian. Staël, in a sense, completes the contours of the map sketched by her contemporaries by forging a heroine, half English, half Italian, who loses her Scotsman to the ideal English wife before falling victim in turn to her Italianate sensibility. Though the breadth and diversity of this European landscape may at times seem to be but an elaborate compilation of literary tropes or of international influences and their corresponding stereotypes, they nevertheless both reflect and contribute to the increasingly cosmopolitan notion of the individual that was on the rise towards the end of the century.

Of particular interest, however, is the role that music plays within this shifting landscape. The prevailing concern of authors who participated in the opera quarrels of the 1750s and 1770s had been to reinforce the connection between the French language, music, and nation. This was the compelling connection, albeit negatively phrased, that Rousseau first made in his *Lettre sur la musique française*. The writings of Diderot, Cazotte, and Beaumarchais, who defended the musicality of the French tongue, fed into the theories of music and nationalism that came to the fore in the nineteenth century and contributed to the persistent differentiation of the French operatic tradition from the nationalist movements that arose in Germany and Italy. Charrière, Cottin, Krüdener, and Staël consistently identify music with one side of a national divide, yet render it capable of appealing to a listener on the other side, revealing the underlying affinity that would unite performer and beholder were it not for the intervening social divisions and cultural differences. This pattern, it seems to me, cannot simply be attributed to the growth of a cosmopolitan spirit or a turn-of-the-century notion of 'Europe' but rather reflects the specific role music was thought to play in these developments as part of the century's transition from an ideal of national to one of international music. To explain where I believe these authors' texts were leading, I will briefly return to certain of Staël's statements, for she spoke most directly to the issue of the role of women and music in international relations.

Women's powers of empathy, Staël's novel suggests, render them particularly capable of sensing and giving artistic expression to the timeless, universal joys and sorrows of mankind. The artistic medium most suited to such expression, she confirms in *De l'Allemagne*, is music. Staël opposes Italian to German music, much as Rousseau opposed it to French. The Germans, she argues, write music that is overintellectualized and conforms too closely to their language. 'La musique réveillant en nous le sentiment de l'infini,' she writes 'tout ce qui tend à particulariser l'objet de la mélodie doit en diminuer l'effet' (As music awakens in us the sense of the infinite all that tends to particularize the subject of the melody detracts from its effect).[10] Staël singles out the operas of Gluck as representative of the German national tradition. The reader will remember the following passage in which Gluck, somewhat counterintuitively, claims to share an ideal of international music with Rousseau, who was known for having opposed the French and Italian traditions:

> Avec l'aide du fameux M. Rousseau de Genève, que je me proposois de consulter, nous aurions peut-être ensemble, en cherchant une mélodie noble, sensible & naturelle, avec une déclamation exacte selon la prosodie de chaque Langue & le caractère de chaque peuple, pû fixer le moyen que j'envisage de produire une musique propre à toutes les nations, & de faire disparoître la ridicule distinction des musiques nationales.

> [With the aid of the famous Mr Rousseau of Geneva, whom I intended to consult, we might together, by seeking a noble, sensitive, and natural melody, with a declamation that conforms exactly to the prose of each language and the character of each people, have discovered the means I envision of producing a music suited to all nations, and of eliminating the ridiculous distinction between national musics.][11]

Staël's text sheds light upon Gluck's association with Rousseau, for though one believed in international music and the other helped reify national musical traditions, they both hoped to attain their respective ideals through a notion of linguistic specificity. This becomes Staël's chief complaint. Though Gluck's linguistic versatility enabled him to contribute to the German, French, and Italian national operas, Staël remarks that Gluck's music is constrained by language. Protesting that 'les arts sont au-dessus de la pensée: leur langage ce sont les couleurs ou les formes, ou les sons' (the arts go beyond thought, their language is colours, forms, or sounds), she proposes to attain Gluck's ideal of international music by *escaping* these linguistic constraints.[12] In *Corinne, ou l'Italie* Staël's heroine contrasts the ability of the Italian *commedia dell'arte* to appeal to the sensibilities of the surrounding nations with the relative insularity of the English and French theatrical traditions. In *De l'Allemagne* Staël extends this observation to the domain of the musical arts, remarking that the Italians alone (who she claims are musicians by nature) are content to approximate language and thought and write melodies that speak directly to the soul. Staël's text thus seems to suggest that while language tends to reify national identity, music is capable of transcending it, and that the Italians are more successful than the surrounding nations in writing music of international appeal precisely because they have not yet attained national status. The ability to transcend the particular is Corinne's artistic forte and is the basis of Staël's explanation as to why Italian music, like Italian comedy, successfully infiltrated the artistic traditions of the surrounding nations in the course of the eighteenth century. Staël and her contemporaries thus consciously strove to move beyond Rousseau's strict association of music and language and his strict divisions between the nations and the sexes, investing their heroines with a freedom and power of expression that ultimately surpassed their own.

The musical tableau combined the forces of music, word, and image, which together contributed to the creation of a reading, listening, and viewing public independent of the monarchy and in possession of its own voice. The demagogic potential of this voice, which Rousseau had hoped to restore, was vividly illustrated during the Revolution when opera, theatre, and spectacle were effectively used to manipulate public opinion.[13] In a more pacific arena, the power that the late eighteenth-century musical tableau exercised over the beholder is visible in the works of Stendhal, Hoffman, Hugo, Balzac, Sand, and Nerval. To illustrate the influence of the musical tableau on the Romantics, I will briefly examine the texts of Balzac and Sand.

Though Balzac's knowledge of his French predecessors was, to some extent, filtered through his French and German contemporaries, we can nevertheless trace the heritage of his three musical novellas – *Sarrasine*, *Gambara*, and *Massimila Doni* – to the eighteenth century.[14] Saint-Preux's letter to Julie is the narrator's implicit reference when he describes Sarrasine's first exposure to Italian opera as follows: 'Pour la première fois de sa vie il entendit cette musique dont M. Jean-Jacques Rousseau lui avait si éloquemment vanté les délices, pendant une soirée du baron d'Holbach' (For the first time in his life he heard the music whose beauties Mr Jean-Jacques Rousseau had so eloquently described to him one evening at the Baron d'Holbach's).[15] To his dismay, Sarrasine eventually finds out what Saint-Preux already knows, namely, that the aria that affords him such ineffable pleasure is sung by a castrato, not a woman. What Balzac seems to have gleaned from the tableaux of his predecessors is a sense of the pertinence or pedantry of the aesthetic notions that were central to the musical debates of the preceding century. Throughout the three stories he maintains the opposition of music to the soul (Italy), the mind (Germany), and the senses (France). Though he refers to Gambara as a character worthy of Hoffmann, the composer's harmonic ravings are strikingly reminiscent of Rameau the uncle and, in this sense, may be considered an oblique response to Diderot's *Neveu de Rameau*. Mariane Bury attributes the French/Italian poles in Balzac's novellas to his familiarity with Stendhal's writings. Yet Rousseau and Staël had already firmly established 'les trois principaux axes de l'amour, de la musique et de la patrie' (the three principal axes of love, music, and country) that structure *Massimila Doni*.[16] Massimila herself – who possesses the gift of effortless conversation and whose political and aesthetic insights are the marvel of the Italians – bears an uncanny resemblance to Corinne. Her views on music belong, moreover, by and large to the previous century.

Staël's influence is still more visible in the novels of George Sand. By the mid-1830s Sand had read several of Staël's works and considered her the superior intellect.[17] The similarities between Staël's *Corinne* and Sand's *Consuelo* are numerous. Both are set in Italy, land of expressive freedom for women, and in a land of oppression – England in Staël's case, Bohemia in Sand's – that serves as a stand-in for French social strictures. Both heroines are forced to reconcile their personal life with their artistic calling. More importantly, however, Sand seems to have learned the 'lesson' of Staël's novel, and cures Consuelo of the penchant for public acclaim that Staël repeatedly designates as Corinne's fatal flaw. She adheres to the tradition, started by Charrière and Staël, of closing her novel on a note of hope in a subsequent generation of musicians that is expected to carry on the fight for social recognition.[18] Finally, Consuelo benefits from Caliste and Corinne's struggles to protect their moral integrity from the ravages of public opinion. Whereas Caliste is highly sensitive to the names she is called in private and goes to great lengths to prevent herself from becoming again what she once was, and Corinne feels the need to justify herself in her lover's eyes even though she considers herself to be worthy of his affection, Consuelo is able to lead her life oblivious, or indifferent, to the widespread suspicion of her morals and secure in the knowledge that such suspicion will not ultimately affect her.[19] She need not stoop to the musical 'tacking' that Caliste is obliged to employ, nor to Corinne's acts of musical vengeance. Her musical performances, whether conscious or not, prove to any attentive beholder that her soul is beyond reproach, as Sand demonstrates in some truly striking musical tableaux of which I will give a single example.

In a tableau strongly reminiscent of Cottin and Krüdener's interest in music's relationship to medical science and religion, Consuelo is left unattended in the throes of a raging fever. Not until Albert breaks into her chamber is the negligent family circle alerted to the dire nature of her condition. Consuelo has successfully eluded the grasp of all who seek to calm her in the midst of her delirium and Albert only just manages to prevent her from throwing herself out the window. At this point

> Albert lui prodigua en espagnol les plus doux noms et les plus ferventes prières: elle l'écoutait, les yeux fixes et sans le voir ni lui répondre; mais tout à coup, se relevant et se plaçant a genoux sur son lit, elle se mit à chanter une strophe du *Te Deum* de Haendel qu'elle avait récemment lue et admirée. Jamais sa voix n'avait eu plus d'expression et plus d'eclat. Jamais elle n'avait été aussi belle que dans cette attitude extatique, avec ses cheveux flottants, ses joues, embrasées du feu de la fièvre, et ses yeux qui semblaient lire dans le ciel entr'ouvert pour eux seuls. La chanoinesse en fut émue au point de s'agenouiller elle-même au pied du lit en fondant en larmes; et le chapelain, malgré son peu de sympathie, courba la tête et fut saisi d'un respect religieux. A peine Consuelo eut-elle fini la strophe, qu'elle fit un grand soupir; une joie divine brilla sur son visage.

> [Albert called her the sweetest names and uttered the most fervent prayers in Spanish. She listened to him, her eyes fixated yet without seeing or responding to him. But all of a sudden, she rose and, kneeling on her bed, began to sing a verse of Handel's *Te Deum* that she had recently read and admired. Never did her voice have more vibrancy and expression. Never had she been so beautiful as in this ecstatic attitude, with her hair awry, her cheeks aglow with the fire of the fever, her eyes appearing to read in the heavens that had opened for them alone. The canoness herself was moved to kneel at the foot of the bed, dissolved in tears, and the chaplain, despite his unsympathetic nature, bowed his head and was seized with a religious respect. As soon as Consuelo finished the verse, she gave a great sigh and a divine joy shone on her face.][20]

Consuelo's musical utterance, which, in her state of mental distraction, surges forth from her distraught soul, is enough to inspire catharsis in the unemotional Chanoinesse and belief in the hypocritical chaplain, a stirring testimony to Sand's appreciation of the power of the musical tableau over the (inscribed) beholder.

The contrast between the texts of Balzac and Sand is intriguing, for it indicates that they retained different aspects of the musical tableaux they had read, suggesting that their perspectives were very much in keeping with those of their predecessors. Like Diderot, Cazotte, and Beaumarchais, Balzac proliferates discussions of musical aesthetics in an effort to lend them an air of authenticity but also to make a point about international relations. Sand, on the other hand, gears her musical descriptions – less littered with the debris of past musical debates – towards conveying the essence of her heroine's character to the reader. Like Charrière, Cottin, Krüdener, and Staël, she deemphasizes the aesthetic level of her text to allow her heroine's musical genius to shine through. The central concern of her 'politics of location' is thus not the nation's pride of place in Europe but individual rights and liberties within the nation.[21] Balzac and Sand perpetuate the gender divide that we have seen in French authors' affinities for the aesthetic or social problems music posed and the national or gender politics it catalyzed. When we read their texts we get the sense, however, that by their day the aesthetic issues had been largely explored, the ideological battles won. The Romantics have been credited with some of the most arresting scenes of music in literature, aesthetics of the theatre, theories of music and nationalism, and musical heroines of the nineteenth century. It is not insignificant, however, that despite the wealth of their own musical era – rich in the compositions of intriguing figures such as Mozart, Rossini, Berlioz, Chopin, and Liszt – they frequently chose to set their stories in the contentious musical milieu of eighteenth-century France. Their appreciation of the aesthetic insights and adherence to the political stances that their predecessors sought to promulgate via the musical tableau remain a lasting tribute to its power of persuasion.

Notes

Preface

1 Rousseau, *Lettre sur la musique française*, 292; *Letter on French Music*, trans. Scott, 144.
2 Dubos, *Réflexions critiques*, 1:414.
3 Ibid., 1:482. Cynthia Verba goes so far as to suggest that Dubos considers music to be more powerful than painting (*Music and the French Enlightenment*, 36).
4 See chapter 2, 'Expression as Imitation,' in Johnson, *Listening in Paris*.
5 Batteux, *Les Beaux-Arts*, 285–6.
6 Rousseau, *Essai sur l'origine des langues*, 377; *Essay on the Origin of Languages*, trans. Scott, 291.
7 See the introduction and first two chapters of Wettlaufer, *In the Mind's Eye*.
8 In his recent study of modern musical narratives *Listening In*, Eric Prieto remarks: 'Musical expression, as Rousseau defines it, is a form of representation that passes through the mediating consciousness of an observer' (5). Rousseau's exploration of music's expressive powers is thus closely linked to Diderot's emphasis on the presence (or presumed absence) of the beholder in his art and theatre criticism of the 1760s. For a more ample discussion of Rousseau's perception of the relationship between tableau and beholder, see chapter 3 of Joan Landes, *Women and the Public Sphere*, 66–89.
9 Cited in Mooij, *Caractères principaux*, 22.
10 Rousseau, *Emile*, 768, cited in Gutwirth 'Madame de Staël,' 106, and Cusset, 'Rousseau's Legacy,' 402–4.
11 Thomas and Dill, 'Disciplines, Interdisciplinarity, and Cultural Studies,' 36–9.

Introduction: Tableau Theory

1 Rousseau, *Julie, ou la Nouvelle Héloïse*, 86–7; *Julie, or the New Heloise*, trans. Stewart and Vaché, 109.

2 Rousseau, *Julie, ou la Nouvelle Héloïse*, 85, my emphasis; *Julie, or the New Heloise*, 107–8. Note the similarity in wording between Saint-Preux's remark and Diderot's description of the soul as a 'tableau mouvant d'après lequel nous peignons sans cesse' that I discuss in chapter 1, pp. 41–2.

3 Diderot, *Le Neveu*, 5; *Rameau's Nephew*, trans. Barzun and Bowen, 9–10.

4 For the first subject, see Rousseau's *Lettre sur la musique française, Essai sur l'origine des langues*, and *Lettre à M. Burney et Fragmens d'observations sur l'Alceste de Gluck*, as well as two of his compositions, *Le Devin du village* (an opéra-comique) and *Pygmalion* (a mélodrame). For the second subject, see his first *Discours*, his *Lettre à d'Alembert*, and *Emile*.

5 For the use of the term in the dictionaries of the Académie, the *Encyclopédie* of Diderot and d'Alembert, and the nineteenth-century Littré, see Goodden, '*Une Peinture parlante*,' 397, and Frantz, *L'Esthétique du tableau*, 9–10, 19.

6 Frantz, *L'Esthétique du tableau*, 10.

7 Diderot, *Entretiens*, 88.

8 See also Daniel Brewer's discussion of Diderot and Fried in *The Discourse of Enlightenment*, 132–67.

9 See Thomas, *Aesthetics of Opera in the Ancien Régime*, 204–5.

10 See Frantz, *L'Esthétique du tableau*, chapter 2.

11 Diderot, *Entretiens*, 89–90.

12 Frantz, *L'Esthétique du tableau*, 47.

13 Ibid., 44.

14 See ibid., 61, 62, 67. The notion of maintaining the fiction of the spectator's absence that informs Frantz's work is drawn from Fried, *Absorption and Theatricality*, 96.

15 Frantz emphasizes the reciprocity of Diderot's innovations in theatre and painting in *L'Esthétique du tableau*, 67, 86. Fried has two theories of the relationship between the tableau and the beholder, a dramatic and a pastoral theory (*Absorption and Theatricality*, 131–2). My interest is in the former.

16 Fried, *Absorption and Theatricality*, 104.

17 Ibid., 64.

18 Caplan, *Framed Narratives*, 5.

19 Ibid., 6.

20 Denby, *Sentimental Narrative*, 75.

21 Revaz defines the tableau by its tendency to signify simultaneously rather than sequentially in 'Narration, description, ou tableau?' 124.

22 See also Lopes's introduction to *Foregrounded Description in Prose Fiction*, 6–27. Like other critics I have cited, Lopes thinks of the tableau as a frozen image or as one in a series of pictures in a gallery. The need to qualify the term 'tableau' as 'static,' 'motionless,' or 'descriptive,' nevertheless suggests that the term itself does not necessarily imply stasis. Interestingly, Lopes argues for the internal dynamism or narrative quality of foregrounded description, which remains a more two-dimensional textual feature than the tableaux I discuss.

23 Goodden, '*Une Peinture parlante*,' 410.

24 Ibid., 398.

25 Caplan, *Framed Narratives*, 18, and Williams, 'Description and Tableau,' 469, 481.

26 Frantz contends that the notion of fixity or fetishism is, by and large, antithetical to Diderot's aesthetic thought. He has therefore sought to restore the original energy (specifically emotional dynamism or erotic energy) of Diderot's concept to our current understanding of what transpires within the space of the tableau. See chapters 1 and 5 in *L'Esthétique du tableau*.

27 Diderot, *Entretiens*, 90–1.

28 Fried, *Absorption and Theatricality*, 75.

29 Ibid., 56.

30 Ibid., 85.

31 Ibid., 56.

32 Denby, *Sentimental Narrative*, 76.

33 Delon, 'L'Esthétique du tableau,' 27.

34 For Goodden's definition of hypotyposis, see chapter 1, p. 40. See also Frantz, *L'Esthétique du tableau*, 9–10. The term dates back to Artistotle's *Poetics*.

35 Denby, *Sentimental Narrative*, 76.

36 Gerald Prince would frequently ask this question in his course on twentieth-century French literature at the University of Pennsylvania.

37 Caplan, *Framed Narratives*, 16.

38 Fried characterizes Belisarius's blindness as 'an exemplary mode of obliviousness' (*Absorption and Theatricality*, 149).

39 Fried, *Absorption and Theatricality*, 149, 155.

40 Ibid., 150.

41 Diderot, *Entretiens*, cited in Fried, *Absorption and Theatricality*, 95.

42 This question seems to be on the tip of Denby's pen when he writes: 'I

wish to press the notion of tableau further. In as much as it is the central imaginative and affective core of a story, the tableau operates as a metaphor for the whole, a form of synecdoche. For that reason, it is an easily repeated, reproduced form of the entire narrative sequence, in the way that the print doubles the text ... Here, the visual metaphor is stretched to the limit; the repetition in question may indeed be a narrative repetition, in which a previously narrated story is retold to another listener, himself situated within the narrative' (*Sentimental Narrative*, 77). As Bruce Morrissette observes, many literary critics make implicit reference to the *mise en abyme* without identifying it as such ('La Duplication intérieure,' 140).

43 Dällenbach, *Le Récit spéculaire*, 22–3, 31.

44 Ibid., 30–1, 51.

45 Ibid., 95–9.

46 Ibid., 74.

47 Ibid., 82.

48 Ibid., 87–8, 95.

49 Ibid., 78.

50 The following passage from Denby's analysis gives credence to this interpretation, though he still makes no mention of the *mise en abyme* itself: 'Tableau, memory and narrative repetition all function within a logic of *reception*. Hence the sustained importance in the sentimental text of phrases which serve to introduce the reaction of a subject to fictive reality. Subjects are constantly described as reacting (usually with tears) "au récit de," "au souvenir de" or "au spectacle de" some moving act or segment of narration. This repetition, this process of internal quotation, has no sense outside the reception framework: it is the reaction of an observing subject which gives sense to the narrative' (*Sentimental Narrative*, 77). Denby thus suggests that the *reacting* – as opposed to the active – subject structures the narrative and serves as the focal point for the larger community of sentimental readers that arose in the late eighteenth century.

51 Forestier, *Le Théâtre dans le théâtre*, 11.

52 Ibid., 117–18.

53 Ibid., 12–13.

54 Ibid., 227–8.

55 Ibid., 12, 14.

56 Denby, *Sentimental Narrative*, 76.

57 Frantz intimates that both the energetic (pulsionnelle) and emotional (passionnelle) power of the tableau are inextricably linked to its sensuality (*L'Esthétique du tableau*, 14).

58 Szondi, '*Tableau* and *Coup de théâtre*,' 328–9, 334–5, and Denby, *Sentimental Narrative*, 80.
59 Caplan, *Framed Narratives*, 21. Emphasis in original.
60 Fried, *Absorption and Theatricality*, 78.
61 Ibid., 31.
62 For a further discussion of this phenomenon, see Ubersfeld, *L'Ecole du spectateur*, 59, 111–16.
63 Barthes, 'Diderot, Brecht, Eisenstein,' 70–1.
64 Mulvey, 'Visual Pleasure and Narrative Cinema,' 37.
65 Rousseau, *Lettre à d'Alembert*, 114. See also Starobinski, *La Transparence et l'obstacle*, 116–21.
66 Mulvey, 'Visual Pleasure and Narrative Cinema,' 40. For my discussion of Marshall, see the preface, p. xv.

1. Diderot and Musical Mimesis

1 See Versini's comments in volume 4 of Diderot, *Œuvres*, 131. See also Sacaluga, 'Diderot, Rousseau, et la querelle musicale,' and Lang, 'Diderot as Musician.' Lang states, unequivocally, that 'Diderot was decidedly for Italian opera, as were all the other philosophes' (102).
2 Diderot would eventually modify his opinion as to which of the two composers was the more gifted, but would maintain his view that a composition depends neither on the music nor on the language but rather on the poet's genius. See Bardez, *Diderot et la musique*, chapter 4, 'Musique et paroles.'
3 I refer to Rousseau's *Lettre sur la musique française*, his *Discours sur l'origine et les fondements de l'inégalité parmi les hommes*, and his *Essai sur l'origine des langues* (begun in 1754, completed in 1761, published in 1781).
4 Diderot, *Sourds et muets*, 136–7.
5 Ibid., 164.
6 Ibid., 165.
7 The languages that were suited to literature and the stage included Latin, Greek, Italian, and English, all of which were thought to be languages of imagination and the passions. Rousseau would echo this idea in his *Lettre sur la musique française* and his *Discours sur l'inégalité*.
8 Diderot, *Sourds et muets*, 187.
9 Ibid., 191.
10 Ibid., 165–6. Emphasis in original.
11 Ibid., 170. Emphasis in original.

12 Alain Niderst notes: 'Jean-Jacques Rousseau, malgré *Le Devin du Village*, et le succès alors remporté, estimait que la langue française était impropre au chant. Diderot, au contraire, encouragea et imita les efforts de Duni pour donner au français la même douceur et le même brio qu'à l'italien' (Despite *The Village Soothsayer* and the success with which it met, Jean-Jacques Rousseau considered the French language to be unsuited to song. Diderot, on the contrary, encouraged and emulated Duni's efforts to give French the same sweetness and flexibility as Italian) ('Diderot et la musique,' 141).

13 Diderot, *Sourds et muets*, 168–9.

14 Ibid., 185, 187, 191.

15 Ibid., 168. This remark has been viewed with some scepticism. Lang suggests that Diderot was simply being modest and was actually quite proficient, having studied composition with Rameau, Philidor, and Blainville ('Diderot as Musician,' 97).

16 Johnson, *Listening in Paris*, 35–50.

17 Diderot, 'Lettre à Mlle de la Chaux,' 207.

18 Presuming that Diderot shared his contemporaries' conviction that the aesthetic hierarchy should be stacked in favour of mimesis, Chouillet asserts that Diderot's doubt as to whether music is an imitative art led him to relegate music to the *bottom* of the aesthetic hierarchy (*Idées esthétiques*, 248). This interpretation does not take into account the implications of the latter half of the passage, however. Didier remains more true to Diderot's words and aesthetic principles by interpreting the passage as follows: 'Ainsi s'explique le paradoxe: le plaisir musical sera plus grand précisément *parce que* le sens du hiéroglyphe est moins net' (Hence the paradox: the pleasure we derive from music is enhanced *because* the meaning of the hieroglyph is less clear) ('L'Écoute musicale,' 70. My emphasis).

19 The first quarrel was waged between partisans of Lully, the composer of Italian origin who had established the French operatic tradition at the court of Louis XIV, and partisans of Jean-Philippe Rameau, the most renowned French composer of the eighteenth century. Although the controversy entailed allusions to Italian music, it remained largely within the bounds of a single national tradition and therefore did not compromise national pride to the same degree. For a discussion of the third quarrel see chapter 3.

20 Grimm's letter has also been interpreted as the last hoorah of the *Querelle des Lullistes et des Ramistes*.

21 The performance took place on 1 August 1752. Wokler hypothesizes that the Italian piece simply proved to be a better crowd-pleaser than Lully's

great work. The theme of a seductive servant girl was more captivating than an allegory with mythological figures, and the simplicity of a string quartet and harpsichord demanded less effort on the part of its listeners than Lully's richly textured orchestration ('*La Querelle des Bouffons*,' 95).

22 Johnson describes the layout of the Opéra in *Listening in Paris*, 18.

23 Diderot mistakenly refers to Tarradellas' opera *Sésostris* by the name of the main character, Nitocris (*Œuvres*, 132–3). Johnson refers to the opera as Gouachino Cocchi's *Nitocri* ('The Encyclopedists,' 18). There is, therefore, apparently some confusion as to which opera Diderot had in mind.

24 Diderot, *Au petit prophète*, 423–4.

25 Diderot, *Trois chapitres*, 503–4.

26 Ibid., 499.

27 Ibid., 504.

28 The assumption that Rousseau's opera was a contribution to the French side of the quarrel was quite natural, given that prior to the quarrels he had published his 'Lettre sur l'opéra italien et français,' in which he examined both musical traditions impartially, expressed respect for their separate national traditions, and showed little inclination to rank them, though he ultimately expressed his fundamental preference for French opera. So radical was his subsequent conversion to the Italian side that Neubauer doubts the authenticity of the first letter (*Emancipation of Music*, 94). As we saw in the introduction, however, Rousseau later attributed a similar about-face to Saint-Preux in his letter to Julie about Italian music.

29 Diderot, *Trois chapitres*, 506–7. Didier describes the passage as a musical dialogue ('Opéras imaginaires,' 255).

30 Diderot, *Trois chapitres*, 510.

31 Rousseau, *Lettre sur la musique française*, 292–5.

32 In the 'Avertissement' to his letter, Rousseau writes: 'Cette Lettre, à peu de lignes près, est écrite depuis plus d'un an, et je la laisse aller pour écarter de mon Portefeuille et de mes yeux tout ce qui tient au sujet qu'elle traite, et que je confesse avoir aimé avec trop de passion' (I wrote this letter, with the exception of a few lines, more than a year ago, and I am releasing it in order to rid my briefcase and my sight of everything to do with its subject, which I confess to having loved too passionately) (*Lettre sur la musique française*, 289, my translation). This passage does not appear in *The Collected Writings of Rousseau*.

33 Rousseau, *Confessions*, 384–5, and Sacaluga, 'Diderot, Rousseau, et la querelle musicale,' 158–64.

34 See, respectively, Sacaluga, 'Diderot, Rousseau, et la querelle,' 160;

Johnson, 'The Encyclopedists,' 23–4; and Wokler, *La Querelle des Bouffons,*' 100.

35 Rousseau, *Lettre sur la musique française*, 294; *Letter on French Music*, 145.

36 Caveirac, 'Lettre d'un Visigoth,' in Launay, *La Querelle des Bouffons*, 1060.

37 Caux and Cappeval, 'Apologie du goût françois,' in Launay, *La Querelle des Bouffons*, 1561.

38 De Bonneval, 'Apologie sur la musique françoise,' in Launay, *La Querelle des Bouffons*, 1158–9.

39 The debaters even seized the opportunity to take a couple of potshots at Rousseau's recent opera *Le Devin du village*, suggesting that he must have sought to humiliate himself by writing a treatise accusing the French of having no taste when they had just widely acclaimed his opera (Launay, *La Querelle des Bouffons*, 975), or – better yet – that he had written the opera in order to *prove* that the French had no music (ibid., 1530).

40 Cited in Godechot, 'Nation,' 485.

41 Cited in Auroux, 'Langue,' *Dictionnaire européen*, 641.

42 Launay, *La Querelle des Bouffons*, 1371.

43 Ibid., 1571 and 1059–60.

44 Ibid., 896. Emphasis in original.

45 Godechot contrasts Rousseau's sense of nation with Voltaire's utopian vision of a pan-European unity ('Nation,' 489).

46 Thiesse, *La Création des identités nationales*, 30.

47 Grimm and Rousseau respectively. See Jourdan, 'Seconde lettre du correcteur des Bouffons à l'écolier de Prague,' in Launay, *La Querelle des Bouffons*, 575–6.

48 Castel, in Launay, *La Querelle des Bouffons*, 1369–70. Though he himself was against such an attitude, Jourdan also testifies to the nature of the French national response: 'Les Partisans de la Musique Françoise regardent comme mauvais citoyens ceux qui ne l'aiment pas, & ils traitent le goût pour la Musique Italienne, d'injure à l'honneur de la France' (The partisans of French music consider those who do not like it to be bad citizens and treat the taste for Italian music as an insult to France's honour) (Jourdan ou l'Héritier, 'Lettre critique et historique sur la musique françoise, la musique italienne, et sur les Bouffons,' in Launay, *La Querelle des Bouffons*, 461).

49 Diderot, *Entretiens*, 132.

50 Rousseau, *Lettre sur la musique française*, 316; *Letter on French Music*, 163.

51 Diderot, *Entretiens*, 168.

52 Ibid., 171.

53 Ibid., 161–2.

54 Rousseau, *Essai sur l'origine des langues*, 379. See also my discussion in the preface, p. xv.

55 Chouillet points to Diderot's ideal of simultaneity over sequentiality, saying: 'Le vrai but de sa recherche se situe au point de rencontre des différents modes d'expression. Il s'agit de saisir, au-delà de l'ordre énonciatif, ce point idéal où les représentations successives du discours se fondent en une représentation unique' (The true end of his quest is located at the nexus of different modes of expression. His aim is to capture, beyond the enunciative order, the ideal moment where the successive representation of discourse melts into a single representation) (*Idées esthétiques*, 176).

56 Diderot, *Sourds et muets*, 158.

57 Music, according to the deaf friend, is but 'une façon particulière de communiquer la pensée' (a certain means of communicating thought) (ibid., 146).

58 Ibid., 147.

59 Goodden, '*Une Peinture parlante*,' 397. For a more extensive discussion of Diderot's notion of the hieroglyph, see Arbo, 'Diderot et l'hiéroglyphe musical'; Brewer, *The Discourse of Enlightenment*, 125–7; Thomas, *Music and the Origins of Language*, 167–70; and Christensen, 'Bemetzreider's Dream.'

60 Diderot, *Sourds et muets*, 169.

61 Ibid., 170–1.

62 Ibid., 169, 172, 178.

63 Ibid., 182.

64 Ibid., 185.

65 Ibid., 161–2.

66 See the introduction, pp. 12–14. According to Chouillet, the tableau constitutes the '"modèle idéal," qui formera le pivot de la méditation esthétique de Diderot à partir de 1758' ('ideal model' that will form the crux of Diderot's aesthetic meditation from 1758 on) (*Idées esthétiques*, 255).

67 Diderot, *Entretiens*, 147.

68 Diderot, *De la poésie dramatique*, 278.

69 Frantz has suggested that Diderot was more successful at responding to such questions as 'Comment l'écriture peut-elle noter la voix, l'accent, la pantomime? Mieux, s'en faire l'équivalent? comment noter le geste?' (How can writing denote voice, accent, pantomime, or, even better, equal them? How does one denote gesture?) in his narrative than in his theatrical works, and particularly in those narrative works that combine theatricality and music (*L'Esthétique du tableau*, 149–50).

70 Didier expresses the counterintuitive nature of this notion with her ques-

tion: 'Comment dire la musique ou du moins comment l'inscrire dans un texte littéraire?' (How can music be spoken or at least inscribed in a literary text?) ('Texte de la musique,' 287).

71 Neubauer, *Emancipation of Music*, 117–18.
72 Diderot, *Entretiens*, 139.
73 Fabre, introduction, Diderot, *Le Neveu de Rameau*, xxxix, xl.
74 Diderot, *Le Neveu*, 26, 28; *Rameau's Nephew*, trans. Barzun and Bowen, 25–6.
75 Diderot, *Paradoxe*, 39.
76 Diderot, *Le Neveu*, 78; *Rameau's Nephew*, 63.
77 Ibid. See p. 30.
78 Diderot, *Le Neveu*, 79–80; *Rameau's Nephew*, 63–4.
79 Pappas suggests that Diderot incorporated the positions that it would have been politically unwise to express at the time of the quarrels into *Le Neveu* ('L'Opéra français contre l'italien,' 233).
80 Diderot, *Le Neveu*, 81–2; *Rameau's Nephew*, 66.
81 See Filoche 'Le Neveu de Rameau,' 104–5.
82 Diderot draws the definition of 'chant' and of music's capacity to imitate silence from Rousseau's *Dictionnaire de musique*. Sacaluga relates that Rousseau had his *Dictionnaire* sent to Diderot well after their definitive break, writing to his editor that 'cet ouvrage avait été fait pour lui' (this work was written for him) (Rousseau to Diderot, 14 March 1767, cited in Sacaluga, 'Diderot, Rousseau, et la querelle,' 164). Diderot draws his analysis of the Italian language from Rousseau's *Lettre sur la musique française*.
83 Diderot, *Le Neveu*, 85–6; *Rameau's Nephew*, 69.
84 Fabre, in Diderot, *Le Neveu*, 225, n. 276.
85 Diderot, *Le Neveu*, 86.
86 Diderot, *Le Neveu*, 88–9; *Rameau's Nephew*, 71. See also Pappas, 'L'Opéra français contre l'italien,' 236.
87 In 'Sur la pantomime dramatique,' Diderot indicates that he favours the notion that the French might shed their old musical skins: 'De misérables bouffons paraissent à Paris en 1751; mais ces misérables bouffons nous font entendre de l'excellente musique; et la nôtre, pauvre, monotone et timide, s'affranchit de ses limites étroites; le préjugé que la mélodie de Lully et de Rameau était la seule dont la déclamation et la prosodie de notre langue pouvaient s'accomoder, tombe; et nous avons des opéras-comiques qu'on applaudit sur tous les théâtres de l'Europe' (Some miserable buffoons appear in Paris in 1751, but these miserable buffoons play excellent music for us and ours – poor, monotonous, and timid – frees itself from its tight constraints. The prejudice that the melodies of Lully

and Rameau are the only ones suited to the declamation and prosody
of our language dissipates, and we now have comic operas that are ap-
plauded on all the stages of Europe) (cited in Golub, 'Diderot et l'opéra-
comique,' 262).

88 In his chapter, 'Forgetting Theater,' Marshall provides an exceptional
analysis of the Nephew's gradual loss of identity in the course of the pantomime, linking this development to his revelation as genius and musician
(*The Surprising Effects of Sympathy*, 105–34). I am particularly interested,
however, in the parallels between the mimetic structure of the Nephew's
imitation and of music itself, including the relationship between performer and beholder that Marshall explores to a greater extent in the
context of *Le Paradoxe sur le comédien*. Though Marshall refers to the pantomime as a tableau, I seek to bring greater specificity to our understanding
of the term. For another insightful reading of the 'pantomime de l'homme-
orchestre,' see Christian Roche's dissertation, entitled '"En littérature
comme en musique": De Rameau au *Neveu de Rameau*,' in which he reads
Diderot's text in light of Rousseau's and Rameau's musical theories.
Though separately conceived our analyses concur on several points.

89 Diderot, *Le Neveu*, 83; *Rameau's Nephew*, 67.

90 Diderot, *Le Neveu*, 84; *Rameau's Nephew*, 67. See Diderot's theory of the
'dédoublement du spectateur' (doubling of the spectator) in his discussion
of Vernet's *oeuvre* (*Ruines et paysages, Salon de 1767*, 199).

91 Diderot, *Le Neveu*, 84; *Rameau's Nephew*, 68.

92 Diderot, *Le Neveu*, 84–5; *Rameau's Nephew*, 68.

93 See article 'Imitation' in Rousseau's *Dictionnaire*, 860–1.

94 Chouillet points to the pantomime's reproduction of the structure of mimesis and the Nephew's progressive penetration of the intervening layers of
mediation in the following passage: 'Il n'est pas jusqu'aux pantomimes du
Neveu qui ne vérifient dans une certaine mesure la théorie de la musique-
imitation. Ses gestes imitent les instruments, et les instruments reprodui-
sent une ligne mélodique, la ligne mélodique s'inspire du 'cri animal de la
passion,' jusqu'à un moment idéal, où de proche en proche, le témoin de
la scène est mis en présence de la nature même, tandis que se sont effacés
tous les chaînons intermédiaires' (Even the Nephew's pantomimes corroborate, to a certain extent, the theory of music as imitation. His gestures
imitate the instruments and the instruments reproduce a melodic line.
The melodic line is inspired by the 'cry of animal passion' until the ideal
moment when, ever so gradually, the witness of the scene is confronted by
nature herself, as all the intervening links in the chain are erased) (*Idées
esthétiques*, 548). Though Chouillet's interpretation is inspired, he uses it to

reinforce the prevailing notion of Diderot's critical stance towards French music. He does not, moreover, differentiate significantly between this extended pantomime and those of the harpsichord and the violin that precede it and continues to associate the 'pantomime de l'homme-orchestre' with the hieroglyph or a series of iterative tableaux (549).

95 Rex, 'Le Neveu de Rameau,' 12 as well as the conclusion of Rex's article.
96 See Diderot, 'Lettre à Mlle de la Chaux,' 60, and Paradoxe, 39, as well as my discussion on pp. 30–1.
97 Rush, 'Geste et parole,' 57. Emphasis in original.
98 Diderot, Paradoxe, 42.
99 Didier, 'Texte de la musique,' 309.
100 Diderot, 'Sourds et muets,' 148–9.

2. Cazotte and Reader Re-creation

1 Cazotte went to school with Jean-François Rameau, the nephew of Jean-Philippe Rameau the composer and the model for Diderot's fictional character. Cazotte also immortalized the Nephew in a poem entitled 'Le Ramaïde' and the two wrote the one-act opera entitled 'Les Sabots' together on a dare.
2 Johnson, Listening in Paris, 36.
3 Cazotte, La Guerre de l'opéra, 331, and Johnson, Listening in Paris, 36–7.
4 Cazotte, La Guerre de l'opéra, 333, and Johnson, Listening in Paris, 37.
5 Cazotte, La Guerre de l'opéra, 341.
6 Cazotte, Observations, 852.
7 Cazotte, La Guerre de l'opéra, 341.
8 Ibid., 321.
9 Décote, L'Itinéraire, 73.
10 Ibid., 76–7, 69.
11 Wokler maintains that the question 'Could sentiment act as the ultimate arbiter in aesthetic judgment' was a central subject of debate at the time ('La Querelle des Bouffons,' 115).
12 Décote, L'Itinéraire, 71.
13 Cazotte, Observations, 848.
14 Ibid., 855.
15 Rousseau, Lettre sur la musique française, 328; Letter on French music, 174.
16 Cazotte, Observations, 854–5.
17 Cazotte, Observations, 856–7.
18 Décote, L'Itinéraire, 79.
19 Wokler, 'La Querelle des Bouffons,' 106–13.

20 Décote, *L'Itinéraire*, 79.

21 Castex mentions the fourth canto in his description of Cazotte's whimsical choice of subject, but does not go on to analyse the musical content (*Le Conte fantastique en France*, 28).

22 Cazotte, *Ollivier*, 1.

23 Such utopias can be found in Montesquieu's *Lettres persanes* and Voltaire's *Candide*.

24 Another possible source of this idea is Diderot's *Lettre sur les sourds et muets*, in which he states that upon seeing the 'clavecin oculaire' his deaf-mute suddenly thought he understood what music was: 'Il crut que la musique était une façon particulière de communiquer la pensée, et que les instruments, les vielles, les violons, les trompettes étaient entre nos mains d'autres organes de la parole' (He thought that music was another means of communicating thought and that instruments – violas, violins, and trumpets – were, in our hands, other organs of speech) (146). Though Cazotte may well have read Diderot's letter, it is not the sustained subject of his parody.

25 The term 'Mélologue' is derived from the Greek for 'song' (mélo) and for 'word' (logos).

26 Cazette, *Observations*, 843.

27 Cazotte, *Ollivier*, 87. Zerbin notes that because their society had already advanced well beyond the stage at which gesture would have sufficed as a means of communication, another system of communication was needed. A difference between Cazotte's island and Rousseau's utopia of the *Essai* is therefore apparent. On Cazotte's island, instrumental music contains the dangerous supplement that Derrida describes as the negative effect of civilization.

28 Rousseau, *Letter on French Music*, 145–7.

29 Rousseau, *Lettre sur la musique française*, 293–4; *Letter on French Music*, 145.

30 Rousseau, *Lettre sur la musique française*, 307; *Letter on French Music*, 156.

31 Rousseau, *Lettre sur la musique française*, 326; *Letter on French Music*, 172. Emphasis Rousseau's.

32 Cazotte, *Ollivier*, 88.

33 Rousseau, *Lettre sur la musique française*, 327; *Letter on French Music*, 173.

34 Cazotte, *Ollivier*, 80.

35 Rousseau, *Lettre sur la musique française*, 307–8; *Letter on French Music*, 157.

36 Rousseau, *Lettre sur la musique française*, 305; *Letter on French Music*, 154.

37 Cazotte, *Ollivier*, 84–6.

38 Rousseau, *Lettre sur la musique française*, 318; *Letter on French Music*, 165.

39 Rousseau, *Lettre sur la musique française*, 303; *Letter on French Music*, 153.
40 Cazotte, *Ollivier*, 84.
41 Ibid., 89.
42 Rousseau, *Lettre sur la musique française*, 312; *Letter on French Music*, 161.
43 Rousseau, *Lettre sur la musique française*, 310; *Letter on French Music*, 158. It is quite possible that Diderot's dialogue of the violins in *Les Trois chapitres* served as an additional source of inspiration.
44 Cazotte, *Ollivier*, 89.
45 Ibid., 90.
46 Rousseau, *Lettre sur la musique française*, 303; *Letter on French Music*, 153.
47 Cazotte, *Ollivier*, 91–2.
48 Rousseau, *Lettre sur la musique française*, 328; *Letter on French Music*, 173.
49 Cazotte, *Ollivier*, 87–8.
50 Cited in Décote, *L'Itinéraire*, 215.
51 Efforts to explain Cazotte's invocation of the supernatural have revealed that he was raised on a diet of 'contes de fée' and the 'merveilleux oriental' (Décote, *L'Itinéraire*, 19, 40, and Charles Nodier as cited in Hunting, 'Les Mille et une sources,' 251), that he drew from a well-established literary tradition of pacts with the devil, devils in the guise of women, and love affairs between sylphs and mortals (Hunting, 'Les Mille et une sources,' 246, 270–3, 277, and Milner, *Le Diable*, 82–3), that he was inspired by Villars's *Comte de Gabalis*, Bakker's *Le Monde enchanté*, de Voraigne's *La Légende dorée*, and de Rosset's *Histoires tragiques* (Décote, *L'Itinéraire*, 274, and Hunting, 'Les Mille et une sources,' 248), that he was influenced by his own translation and continuation of *Les Mille et une nuits* (Hunting, ibid., 247), and that as a mystic, he sincerely believed that Enlightenment philosophers, women, and revolutionaries were possessed (Fleurant, 'Mysticism in the Age of Reason,' 71–5). For the status of *Le Diable amoureux* as the forerunner of fantastic fiction, see Castex, *Le Conte fantastique*, and Todorov, *Introduction à la littérature fantastique*.
52 Whereas critics who consider Cazotte's work as source tend to use the term *fantastique*, those who seek his sources are as likely to use the term *merveilleux*. Such a discrepancy reveals the possibility that at the time Cazotte was writing, the term *merveilleux* might have been used interchangeably with or even been preferred to *fantastique* as an apt description of the super- or unnatural elements in his work. The term *merveilleux* is found, for example, in Fréron's review and in the title of the most widely known tale of *Les Mille et une nuits*: 'Aladin et la lampe merveilleuse.' Cazotte uses both terms in his text, appropriately enough since the Littré

defines the *merveilleux* as '[l]'intervention d'êtres surnaturels ... dans les ...
ouvrages d'imagination' (the intervention of supernatural beings ... in
fictional works) and the *fantastique* as '[q]ui n'a que l'apparence d'un être
corporel' (that which but appears to be corporeal), both eminently suitable
to his subject. Furthermore, the Littré associates the *merveilleux* with
poems and the *fantastique* with 'contes de fée' and 'contes des revenants,'
both genres in which Cazotte was well-versed. A key distinction arises in
the associations the Littré draws between the two terms and lengthier
forms of fiction, however. Whereas the Littré cites Voltaire and Huet's
recommendations that the *merveilleux*, whether in novels or at the theatre,
be tempered with a healthy dose of the *vraisemblable*, it avers that the term
fantastique usually refers to the tales popularized by Hoffmann. The Littré's
literary associations with the term *merveilleux* therefore date from eighteenth-century France, whereas those it provides for the term *fantastique*
date from nineteenth-century Germany. I use the term 'marvellous' to
refer to those un-natural elements which, when tempered with a just
measure of the *vraisemblable*, can produce the fantastic.

53 See Décote, *L'Itinéraire*, 302; Blanchard, 'Cazotte,' 34, 37; and Schuerewegen, 'Pragmatique et fantastique,' 63–5, 70.

54 For a list of Cazotte's songs, see Décote, *L'Itinéraire*, 59. The romances he
recast to compose the poem *Ollivier* are entitled 'La Veillée de la bonne
femme ou le réveil d'Enguerrand' and 'Les Prouesses inimitables d'Ollivier,
Marquis d'Edesse' (ibid., 123–4).

55 See the excerpt from Gérard de Nerval in the appendix to Cazotte's *Le
Diable amoureux*, 147.

56 Cazotte, *La Guerre de l'opéra*, 338.

57 Cazotte, *Observations*, 847–8.

58 Décote, *L'Itinéraire*, 73, 77–8.

59 Charles Dill and Downing Thomas corroborate Kintzler's assessment of
the centrality of the marvellous to the early modern conception of opera,
citing treatises by Bossuet, Boileau, Saint-Evremond, and Terrasson to
this effect (Dill, *Monstrous Opera*, 39, and Thomas, *Aesthetics of Opera in the
Ancien Régime*, 104). Thomas identifies, moreover, not the marvellous
alone but the interaction of the natural and the supernatural realms as
intrinsic to operatic productions (ibid., 45; see also pages 75, 89, 98, 103–4,
117, 158–9).

60 Kintzler, *Poétique de l'opéra*, 277. The theorists whom Kintzler cites as
having recorded and contributed to the theory of the *tragédie en musique*
include Corneille, as the first theoretician of the theatrical *merveilleux*

(*Poétique de l'opéra*, 266); Charles Perrault, in his *Critique de l'opéra ou examen de la tragédie intitulée Alceste* (253); La Bruyère, in his 'Des Ouvrages de l'esprit' of *Les Caractères*, which in turn influenced l'abbé de Mably, Cahusac, and Le Brun and became general cultural knowledge (256); and Batteux, in the section *Les Beaux-Arts* of his *Principes de la littérature* (269). In his *Lettres à Madame la marquise de P*** sur l'opéra*, the abbé de Mably does not consider it worthwhile to enumerate the rules that governed French opera at the time, stating: 'Je dois avertir le lecteur qu'il ne doit pas s'attendre à trouver dans cet ouvrage de longs details [sur les règles de l'opéra]. Il serait inutile de lui remettre sous les yeux ce qu'on trouve déjà dans mille autres livres qui sont entre les mains de tout le monde' (I should notify the reader that he should not expect to find elaborate details in this work on [the rules of opera]. It would be useless to remind him of what can be found in a thousand other books that are at everyone's fingertips) (cited in *Poétique de l'opéra*, 260).

61 Kintzler, *Poétique de l'opéra*, chapter 2, 'Théâtre lyrique, théâtre dramatique: Le Parallélisme et la logique du merveilleux.' For an overview of Kintzler's theory, see schéma no. 16 on page 276.

62 Ibid., 270.

63 Ibid., 282.

64 Ibid., 274–5. For a discussion of the causal relationships in Kintzler's theory, see my article '*La Vraisemblance du merveilleux*: Operatic Aesthetics in Cazotte's Fantastic Fiction,' *Studies in Eighteenth-Century Culture* 34 (2005): 173–96.

65 Cazotte, *Le Diable amoureux*, 62, 60; *The Devil in Love*, trans. Sartarelli, 12, 11.

66 Cazotte, *Le Diable*, 74.

67 Ibid., 88–9.

68 In the 1772 version of the story Alvare – driven by sprites in the form of horses – could not stop his headlong course through his mother's village until six leagues beyond it (Cazotte, *Le Diable* 185–6, n. 25).

69 Kintzler, *Poétique de l'opéra*, 281.

70 Ibid., 287, 291–2.

71 Ibid., 292–4.

72 Ibid., 283.

73 Marmontel similarly distinguishes between two degrees of the marvellous, the first being 'le merveilleux naturel,' meaning all the natural catastrophes or coincidences that are hard to believe but the likes of which we sometimes see, and the second being 'le merveilleux surnaturel,' consist-

ing of all that falls outside the laws of nature and yet is commonly thought
to transpire in the realm of gods and demons ('Merveilleux,' 698–700).

74 Kintzler, *Poétique de l'opéra*, 283.
75 Cazotte, *Le Diable*, 56; *The Devil*, 6.
76 Kintzler, *Poétique de l'opéra*, 283.
77 Cazotte did not publish this version, written after his 1772 edition, but
    simply read it aloud to his friends.
78 Kintzler, *Poétique de l'opéra*, 285.
79 Ibid., 285–6.
80 Ibid., 296–7.
81 Cazotte, *Le Diable*, 105, my emphasis; *The Devil*, 59–60.
82 Cazotte, *Le Diable*, 92; *The Devil*, 44.
83 The groom at the wedding they attend is 'vêtu d'un pourpoint de satin
    noir taillé en couleur de feu' (dressed in a black satin doublet slashed with
    fire-red) (Cazotte, *Le Diable*, 108; *The Devil*, 64). There, Alvare consults
    three Egyptian women whom he refers to as 'sorcières' and whose sooth-
    saying powers and physiognomy seem to confirm their identity (Cazotte,
    Le Diable, 112).
84 While Cazotte made bold to satirize such sects in his novella, his corre-
    spondence reveals that he did not harbour mystical convictions himself
    until much later ('Lettre 53,' in *Correspondance*, 132). That he adapted these
    marvellous elements from stage scenarios is therefore a more plausible
    explanation of his references to the necromantic arts than is Kenneth J.
    Fleurant's suggestion that such was Cazotte's perception of reality
    ('Mysticism,' 71–5).
85 Kintzler, *Poétique de l'opéra*, 287.
86 Ibid., 297.
87 We accept that animals and objects speak and that creatures and objects
    possess supernatural powers in a folk tale because it is one, but the world
    of the folk tale is not subjected to the laws of the natural world.
88 Cazotte, *Le Diable*, 60–3; *The Devil*, 13.
89 Cazotte, *Le Diable*, 60.
90 Cazotte, *Le Diable*, 63–4; *The Devil*, 14.
91 Cazotte, *Le Diable*, 63; *The Devil*, 12.
92 Cazotte, *Le Diable*, 69; *The Devil*, 20.
93 Cazotte, *Le Diable*, 69.
94 Cazotte, *Le Diable*, 64; *The Devil*, 14.
95 Cazotte, *La Guerre de l'opéra*, 339.
96 While Hunting alludes to the fact that the camel addresses Alvare in

Italian, she pursues the question of why a camel but not the question of why Italian ('Les Mille et une sources,' 250).

97 For a more extensive analysis of the gender play in *Le Diable amoureux*, see my article entitled 'The Devil in Drag: Moral Injunction or Social Leaven?' *Paroles Gelées* 17, no. 2 (1999): 30–42.

98 Clément-Pierre Marillier (1740–1808) was well known for his illustrations of contemporary fairy tales and novels. The engravings in the 1979 GF-Flammarion edition of Cazotte's text are presumed to be by Jean-Michel Moreau, also known as Moreau le Jeune (1741–1814), based on drawings by Marillier. Cazotte identifies these drawings as the originals, in the 'Avis de l'auteur à propos de l'illustration de la première édition du *Diable amoureux*' (Cazotte, *Le Diable*, 180). The provisional titles of the engravings are mine.

99 Alvare noted Biondetta's preoccupation with this harpsichord earlier in the story, when he mentioned that, happening to pass by Biondetta's room, he saw her 'courbée près d'une fenêtre, fort occupée à rassembler et recoller les débris d'un clavecin' (crouching near a window, very busy reassembling and gluing the various parts of a harpsichord) (Cazotte, *Le Diable*, 76; *The Devil*, 27).

100 Cazotte, *Le Diable*, 180.

101 Rousseau, *Lettre sur la musique française*, 743, 748.

102 Cazotte, *Le Diable*, 88; *The Devil*, 39.

103 Wokler, '*La Querelle des Bouffons*,' 95–6, and Cazotte, *La Guerre de l'opéra*, 339–40.

104 Cazotte, *Observations*, 857.

105 Schuerewegen disagrees with Todorov, who states that the fantastic effect of *Le Diable amoureux* dissipates along with Alvare's uncertainty, leaving the reader out of the equation and relegating Cazotte's novella to the category of the *fantastique-étrange* ('Pragmatique et fantastique,' 61).

106 Todorov, *Introduction*, 28–62.

3. Beaumarchais's Staged Songs

1 See Castries, 'Le Musicien de mesdames de France,' in *Beaumarchais*, 51–61.

2 Beaumarchais, *Théâtre*, 22. Emphasis in original.

3 For a more elaborate exploration of this subject, see my chapter entitled 'From the Comédie-Française to the Opéra: Figaro at the Crossroads,' in *Operatic Migrations: Transforming Works and Crossing Boundaries*, ed. Downing Thomas and Roberta Marvin, forthcoming from Ashgate.

4 Beaumarchais acknowledges that without Diderot's example he might have lacked the temerity to pursue this path, though he stipulates that he had started to develop his own theory of the *drame* long before Diderot circulated his ideas on the subject. For a more extensive comparison of Diderot's and Beaumarchais's theories of the drama, see Didier, *Beaumarchais*; Hayes, 'Rewriting Bourgeois Drama'; and Niklaus, 'Beaumarchais.'

5 Beaumarchais, *Essai*, 122.

6 Ibid.

7 Beaumarchais, *Théâtre*, 225; *The Figaro Trilogy*, trans. Coward, 194.

8 Fleck, *Music, Dance, and Laughter*, 137.

9 For the Italian and French origins of Molière's *comédies-ballets*, see the exhibition catalogue, *Molière en scène*, 10; of the *opéra-comique*, see Rougemont, *Vie théâtrale*, 43–4; of Beaumarchais's comedy, see Niklaus, 'La Genèse,' 1088. Fleck traces the trajectory from low to high art in *Music, Dance, and Laughter*.

10 For the identification of Molière as the source of Beaumarchais's inspiration see Rex, 'The "Storm" Music,' 244.

11 Cooper, 'Opera,' 572–3.

12 M. Robinson, 'Opera,' 558.

13 Biondetta's barcarole in *Le Diable amoureux* thus seems to parody Rousseau's attempt to set French words to music in the Italian style.

14 Heartz, 'Rousseau,' 271. For the evolution of the *opéra-comique* in the latter half of the century, see chapter 7 in Thomas, *Aesthetics of the Opera*.

15 Larthomas, *Beaumarchais*, 16–17, 20–1.

16 Ibid., 19–20.

17 J.-P. Beaumarchais, 'Un Inédit de Beaumarchais,' 976–99.

18 Beaumarchais, *Théâtre*, 39.

19 Ibid.

20 Ibid., 40.

21 Scherer, *Dramaturgie*, 24; *Molière en scène*, 15.

22 Beaumarchais, *Théâtre*, 44; *The Figaro Trilogy*, 6.

23 P. Robinson, 'La Musique des comédies,' 377.

24 Niklaus, 'Beaumarchais,' 496.

25 Frantz states that 'Beaumarchais considère la musique d'entracte non pas comme extérieure au tableau dramatique mais comme un élément dramatique interne' (Beaumarchais considers the intermission music not as external to the dramatic tableau but as an internal dramatic element) (*L'Esthétique du tableau*, 221, n. 3). He argues that Beaumarchais's refusal to relegate incidental music to the intermissions and his insistance that it be

woven into the dramatic fabric, enabled him to escape, or dispel, the deadening effects of language (259).

26 P. Robinson, 'La Musique des comédies,' 376–7, 411.

27 Ibid., 403.

28 Jean-Pierre de Beaumarchais located the reference to this song, absent from the manuscript on which current editions are based, in an 1828 edition of the *Barbier* (P. Robinson, 'La Musique des comédies,' 400–1).

29 P. Robinson identifies the original song lyrics in 'La Musique des comédies,' 403.

30 Beaumarchais, *Théâtre*, 67; *The Figaro Trilogy*, 33.

31 P. Robinson, 'La Musique des comédies,' 468; Beaumarchais, *Théâtre*, 216; *The Figaro Trilogy*, 183.

32 Beaumarchais, *Théâtre*, 39. P. Robinson observes: 'La musique joue dans cette pièce le rôle d'un langage dramatique autonome' ('La Musique des comédies,' 390).

33 Beaumarchais, *Théâtre*, 54; *The Figaro Trilogy*, 18.

34 The *opéra-comique* was composed by Monsigny in 1760. See P. Robinson, 'La Musique des comédies,' 397.

35 Niklaus, 'Beaumarchais,' 497 and Rougemont, 'Beaumarchais dramaturge,' 714.

36 Beaumarchais, *Essai*, 123. This is an echo, or reversal, of Diderot's observation that '[i]l n'y a point de bon drame, dont on ne puisse faire un excellent roman' (there is no good *drame* from which one cannot make an excellent novel) (Niklaus, 'Beaumarchais,' 497).

37 Diderot, *Eloge de Richardson*, cited in Rougemont, 'Beaumarchais dramaturge,' 711.

38 Bérubé, 'La Portée sociale des didascalies,' 1332.

39 Rougemont suggestively states: 'Les indications dites scéniques ... acquièrent dans le drame une fonction seconde qui est de ... commenter l'action de même que fait l'intervention d'auteur dans le roman' (In the *drame*, stage directions ... acquire a secondary function, which is to ... comment upon the action just like the author's interventions in a novel) (*Vie théâtrale*, 31).

40 P. Robinson, 'La Musique des comédies,' 375. Such a measure is unnecessary in an *opéra-comique* since the genre itself leads the audience to expect that the characters will break into song.

41 Ibid., 411, 419. For a detailed analysis of Rosine's romance, see ibid., 386–92.

42 Beaumarchais, *Théâtre*, 80; *The Figaro Trilogy*, 50.

43 P. Robinson, 'La Musique des comédies,' 388, 390, suggests as much.

44 Molière, 'Malade imaginaire,' II. v. 1136–9.

45 Beaumarchais, *Théâtre*, 81; *The Figaro Trilogy*, 52.

46 The comic layers in Bartholo's response are multiple. Not only does he fall asleep but also, when he awakens, he protests that he would rather hear Rosine sing a ditty from his youth. He then proceeds to sing a stanza including the words 'Je ne suis point Tircis ...,' another, more explicit allusion to Molière's *Le Malade imaginaire*, for Tircis is the name Cléonte adopts when singing the duet with Angélique. Bartholo's reaction, as I have noted, bears a striking resemblance to Act I, scene ii of Molière's *Le Bourgeois gentilhomme*.

47 Beaumarchais, *Théâtre*, 82; *The Figaro Trilogy*, 52.

48 Beaumarchais, *Théâtre*, 162; *The Figaro Trilogy*, 115.

49 P. Robinson, 'La Musique des comédies,' 449; Barker, *Greuze*, 32–3.

50 Beaumarchais, *Théâtre*, 162; *The Figaro Trilogy*, 114.

51 P. Robinson, 'La Musique des comédies,' 441.

52 Beaumarchais, *Théâtre*, 163, my translation. David Coward's translation does not lend itself to being excerpted in this manner.

53 P. Robinson provides an intriguing description of the Marlborough fad as well as the subject of the original song ('La Musique des comédies,' 436–8).

54 Beaumarchais, *Théâtre*, 164; *The Figaro Trilogy*, 117.

55 As I noted in my introduction, Forestier includes ballets, *chansons*, *intermèdes*, and *divertissements* in his list of possible 'spectacles intérieures' (internal spectacles) and provides a thorough analysis of the *opéra impromptu* in Moliere's *Malade imaginaire* that was the model for the music lesson in Beaumarchais's *Barbier* (*Le Théâtre dans le théâtre*, 11–12, 156–7, 230–2).

56 Abbate, *Unsung Voices*, 97, 119.

57 The play was accepted by the Comédie-Française in 1781 but was not staged until 1784 (Castries, *Beaumarchais*, 361, 368).

58 Castries, *Beaumarchais*, 375.

59 Beaumarchais thus contributed to the growing awareness that music could be placed at the service of the nation, as the proliferation of songs during the Revolution and the establishment of the first national conservatories attest.

60 Beaumarchais, *Théâtre*, 36.

61 For Beaumarchais, see Scherer, *Dramaturgie*, 33; for Molière, see *Molière en scène*, 15; for Gluck, see Prod'homme, *Christoph-Willibald Gluck*, 179.

62 Croll, 'Gluck,' 458.

63 Croll explains Sedaine's place in the history of the *opéra-comique* ('Gluck,' 574). Brown documents the presence of Rousseau's *Devin du village* in Vienna (*Gluck and the French Theatre*, 403–4).

64 Cited in Brown, *Gluck and the French Theatre*, 437. Many of Gluck's Viennese works involved a blend of music and either pantomime or ballet.

65 Prod'homme, *Christoph-Willibald Gluck*, 98.

66 Hédoin, *Gluck*, 4.

67 Letter from Le Bailli du Roullet to the director of the Opéra in the *Mercure de France*, 1 August 1772, cited in Prod'homme, *Christoph-Willibald Gluck*, 169–70.

68 'Préface à Alceste,' cited in Desnoiresterres, *Musique française*, 65–6.

69 'Lettre de M. le Chevalier Gluck à l'auteur du Mercure de France' in Lesure, *Querelle des Gluckistes et des Piccinnistes*, 10.

70 Marie-Antoinette was Gluck's staunch supporter, for he had been her singing teacher in Vienna. She invited him to Paris, the story goes, because she was discontented with the musical productions. Mme DuBarry, Louis XV's mistress, was told that the best way to counterattack would be to back a rival composer (Hédoin, *Gluck*, 15).

71 Rousseau, 'Lettre à M. Burney,' 445.

72 The term *mélodrame* came to designate various combinations of spoken words and instrumental music and, after the Revolution, of dialogue and pantomime before coming to refer to a primarily spoken genre (Thomasseau, *Le Mélodrame*, 8–11, and Mason, 'The Melodrama,' 24–5, 37). Its ultimate spoken form is thought to have been informed by the theories of the *drame*. The evolution of the *mélodrame*, which arose, on the one hand, from Diderot's and Beaumarchais' theories of the *drame* and, on the other, from Rousseau's and Beaumarchais's experiments with combinations of music and language, is emblematic of the period of generic flux in the realms of the sung and the spoken theatre through which Beaumarchais was obliged to chart his course.

73 Rousseau, 'Lettre à M. Burney,' 448, 'Letter to Mr Burney,' trans. Scott, 497. The italics indicate that Rousseau's editors gleaned the description of *Pygmalion* from other passages in his writings; see 449, n. 1.

74 Beaumarchais, *Théâtre*, 44; *The Figaro Trilogy*, 6.

75 Beaumarchais, *Théâtre*, 39–40.

76 Beaumarchais, 'Aux abonnées de l'opéra,' 497.

77 Ibid., 500.

78 See the 'Préface à Alceste,' cited above, p. 106.

79 Beaumarchais, 'Aux abonnées de l'opéra,' 507.

80 Brown uses the phrase 'economy of language' to describe Calzabigi's libretto of *Orfeo* (*Gluck and the French Theatre*, 364).

81 Arnould, 'Beaumarchais and the Opera,' 78.

82 Beaumarchais, 'Aux abonnées de l'opéra,' 507.

83 Rousseau, *Lettre sur la musique française*, 292.

84 Desnoiresterres, *Musique française*, 113–14.

85 Attributed to Grimm, April 1774, in *Correspondance littéraire*, vol. 10, 416–18, cited in Prod'homme, *Christoph-Willibald Gluck*, 198.

86 Pappas, 'L'Opéra française contre l'italien,' 238.

87 Cazotte, *Observations*, 857. Note the similarity to Diderot's phraseology on p. 38.

88 Diderot, *Le Neveu*, 109; *Rameau's Nephew*, 87.

89 Though the letters in Lesure's collection date from 1774 to 1783, the debate came to a head in the years 1777–9. See Lesure's introduction to *Querelle des Gluckistes et des Piccinnistes*.

90 Forestier refers to this process as 'la dénégation' (denial) (*Le Théâtre dans le théâtre*, 138–9).

91 Johnson, *Listening in Paris*, 111.

92 Ibid., 117.

93 Ibid., 121.

4. Charrière's Exercises in Equivocation

1 Trousson characterizes Charrière's attitude towards Rousseau as that of an 'admiratrice mesurée' (tempered admirer) ('Isabelle de Charrière,' 56). Letzter indicates that Charrière considered the rising author-cult to be dangerous ('Isabelle de Charrière,' 29).

2 These texts include 'De Rousseau' (1788–9), *Court réplique à l'auteur d'une longue réponse* (1789), *Plainte et défense de Thérèse Levasseur* (1789), *Eclaircissements relatifs à la publication des Confessions de Rousseau* (1790), *Eloge de Jean-Jacques Rousseau* (1790), and *A Monsieur Burke* (1791) (Letzter, 'Isabelle de Charrière,' 27). For Charrière's resistance to Rousseau's views on women, marriage, and education, see Letzter, 'Lire ou ne pas lire?' and Bérenguier, 'From Clarens to Hollow Park.'

3 Trousson, 'Deux lecteurs,' 191.

4 Letzter, 'Lire?' 210. See my discussion in the preface.

5 Charrière (*Œuvres*, 10:345), cited in Trousson, 'Isabelle de Charrière,' 12, and Letzter, 'Lire?' 211.

6 Rousseau, *Emile*, my translation. The translation of *Emile* has not yet appeared in the *The Collected Writings of Rousseau*.

7 Champcenetz's text is entitled 'Réponse aux Lettres sur le caractère et les ouvrages de J.-J. Rousseau: Bagatelle que vingt libraires ont refusé de faire imprimer' (Letzter, 'Isabelle de Charrière,' 32, n. 21).

8 Charrière, *Courte réplique*, 163.
9 This was not Charrière's only act of ventriloquism. She had also written in Thérèse Levasseur's defence as though she were Thérèse herself in her *Plainte et défense de Thérèse Levasseur* of 1789.
10 Charrière, *Courte réplique*, 168–9.
11 See also Letzter, 'Lire?' 210.
12 Ibid.
13 See Bérenguier, 'From Clarens to Hollow Park.'
14 Charrière, 'De Rousseau,' 125. Charrière later integrates a similar passage into her *Eloge de Jean-Jacques Rousseau* (integral text reproduced in Trousson, 'Deux lecteurs,' 207). For Rousseau's estimation of his own musical affinity and abilities, see his *Confessions*.
15 Letzter and Adelson, *Women Writing Opera*, 141–3. Letzter and Adelson write that '[Charrière] considered the Italian language to be superior to the French for a musical setting but, like Rousseau, admitted that good French opera was possible, provided that the librettist was finely attuned to the defects of the language' (142). As we have seen, Rousseau's admission of this possibility came around the time of the *Querelle des Gluckistes et des Piccinnistes*, long after his assertion that the French could have no music had catalyzed the opposition of his contemporaries.
16 Charrière to Chambrier d'Oleyres, 19 January 1791, Letter 756, in Charrière's *Correspondance*, 3:268–9. For their discussion of the *Querelle des Gluckistes et des Piccinnistes*, see Chambrier d'Oleyres to Charrière, 11 December 1790, Letter 746, 3:252–3.
17 Wolf-Catz stipulates that Charrière's mother was a musician and responsible for Charrière's early musical education ('Belle van Zuylen,' 19–20).
18 Charrière to Chambrier d'Oleyres, 10 February 1786, Letter 585, in Charrière, *Correspondance*, 2:497.
19 Charrière to her brother Vincent, 9 November 1786, in *Correspondance*, 2:499–500, cited in Letzter and Adelson, *Women Writing Opera*, 155.
20 Scores were not usually printed unless a work was highly successful, whereas none of Charrière's operas ever reached the stage. For a discussion of Charrière's operas, see Letzter and Adelson, *Women Writing Opera*, 174–206.
21 Letzter and Adelson, *Women Writing Opera*, 59–64.
22 On 13 January 1789 Charrière wrote to Chambrier d'Oleyres: 'A Vienne M. Stahl connoit Salieri & croit que les Pheniciennes ne seroient pas mal entre ses mains. Si nous pouvions les y faire tomber j'en serois bien aise. Il y a certainement de beaux morceaux dans Tarare & il sait le francois parfaitement' (M. Stahl knows Salieri in Vienna and thinks that the *Phéniciennes*

would fare well in his hands. If we could ensure that they end up there I would be delighted. There are certainly some beautiful passages in *Tarare* and he speaks French perfectly (Letter 642, in *Correspondance*, 3:127). See also Letzter and Adelson, *Women Writing Opera* 181.

23 Charrière to Chambrier d'Oleyres, 29 September 1792, Letter 854, in *Correspondance*, 3:419.

24 Charrière to Ludwig Ferdinand Huber, 26 January 1792, in *Correspondance*, 6:481, cited in translation in Letzter and Adelson, *Women Writing Opera*, 210.

25 Charrière to her brother Vincent, 7 March 1791, Letter 767, in *Correspondance*, 3:286. Chambrier d'Oleyres specifically recommends that she consult Rousseau's definitions of recitatif *obligé, parlé*, and *accompagné* in Chambrier d'Oleyres to Charrière, 1 September 1792, Letter 849, in *Correspondance*, 3:412.

26 Rousseau, *Emile*, 715. Rousseau adds that girls should, as a rule, have a healthy dose of singing and dancing when young so that they may render their husbands' homes agreable once married and stave off their female tendency to become 'maussades, grondeuses, insupportables dans leurs maisons' (sullen, scolding, unbearable in their homes) (*Emile*, 716, my translation). Music lessons were thus to be used to curb women's tempers and tongues.

27 Rousseau, *Emile*, 404–7, 747.

28 Ibid., 717–18

29 Ibid.

30 Ibid., 790. My emphasis.

31 Roster attests to the intensification of the debate across Europe (*Les Femmes et la création musicale*, 123).

32 See Vilcosqui, 'La Femme dans la musique française,' 21; Bessièreset and Niedzwiecki, *Femmes et musique*, 9–10; and Touliatos, 'The Traditional Role of Greek Women in Music,' 114–16.

33 Cited in Roster, *Les Femmes et la création musicale*, 77.

34 Ibid., 79, and Drinker, *Music and Women*, 235–6.

35 Castile-Blaze, *L'Académie Royale de Musique* (Paris, 1855). Cited in Vilcosqui, 'La Femme dans la musique française,' 38.

36 Vilcosqui, 'La Femme dans la musique française,' 39.

37 Vilcosqui draws this citation from *Statut pour l'Académie Royale de Musique* of 1770, reproduced in Guy Bernard, *L'Art de la musique* (Paris: Saghare, 1961), 40–3.

38 Note that the term 'fille d'opéra' thus carries a connotation that 'comédienne' did not, though Rousseau's diatribe against professional actresses

in his *Lettre à d'Alembert* would suggest that becoming an actress remained a somewhat dubious decision for women who wished to maintain their reputation (69–76). See also Cowart, 'Of Women, Sex, and Folly.'

39 Danielou, *Madame de Maintenon*, 91. The Marquis de Dangeau's journal entry of 18 August 1688 indicates that *Esther* was, in fact, considered an opera with spoken passages rather than a play with incidental music: 'Racine, par ordre de Madame de Maintenon, fait un opéra dont le sujet est Esther et Assuerus. Il sera chanté et récité par les petites filles de Saint-Cyr. Tout ne sera pas en musique. C'est un nommé Moreau qui fera les airs' (At the request of Madame de Maintenon, Racine is writing an opera on the subject of Esther and Ahasuerus. It will be sung and recited by the little girls of Saint-Cyr. Not all will be set to music. Someone named Moreau will compose the songs.) (Vilcosqui, 'La Femme dans la musique française,' 63).

40 Pieiller, *Musique maestra*, 88.

41 Letzter and Adelson paraphrase the statement Candeille makes in her *Essai sur les félicités humaines, ou Dictionnaire du bonheur*, 'Profession,' 2:188–9 (*Women Writing Opera*, 45).

42 Burgan, 'Heroines at the Piano,' 51–2.

43 See, for example, Mrs More's *Strictures on the Modern System of Female Education* of 1799, cited in Loesser, *Men, Women, and Pianos*, 281.

44 Leppert, *Music and Image*, 47–8. Leppert explains that by the eighteenth century in England, women's musical activities had been largely rid of their sexual connotations, which (like the association of women, sexuality, and the theatre) were considered 'old hat' (ibid., 30).

45 Vilcosqui's catalogue extends from page 114 to page 122 of *La Femme dans la musique française*. On page 117 he notes the hidden joke in an anonymous portrait of a nun before her harpsichord:

> Sur le pupitre de son instrument, cette digne religieuse a disposé une chanson du début du XVIIIe siècle intitulée *La Furstemberg*. Si la musique est parfaitement lisible, les paroles, que nous possédons par ailleurs, ne figurent pas:
>
> > L'autre jour dans un boccage
> > J'aperçus la fille à Miché
> > D'un air gai qui baisait de bon courage
> > Le mouton d'un jeune berger.
> > Je sentis naître dans mon âme
> > Les transports d'une amoureuse flamme
> > Alors je la pris et lui dis:
> > 'il faut que je te baise aussi.'

[This worthy nun has placed a song from the beginning of the eighteenth century entitled *La Furstemburg* before her on her instrument.
While the music is perfectly legible, the words, which we have obtained
from another source, do not appear:

> The other day in a grove
> I espied Miché's daughter
> Gaily and courageously kissing
> A young shepherd's sheep.
> I felt arise within my soul
> The transports of an amorous flame
> So I took her and I said
> 'I must kiss/possess you too.'

46 Loesser, *Men, Women, and Pianos*, 197.
47 Though the figure of the seductive music teacher was present in English
caricatures and public discourse, he was often, notably, foreign (Leppert,
Music and Image, 56–66). According to Mary Burgan the figure of the foreign
music teacher does not enter English literature until the end of the nineteenth century ('Heroines at the Piano,' 60). He was already a prominent
figure in French texts at the time Charrière and Staël were writing, however.
48 Loesser, *Men, Women, and Pianos*, 190.
49 Cited in ibid., 281.
50 Wolf-Catz notes that, in general, 'on a beaucoup écrit sur la vie de Belle
van Zuylen mais, en comparaison, très peu sur son œuvre' (much has
been written on the life of Belle van Zuylen but, in comparison, very little
on her works) ('Belle van Zuylen,' 20).
51 Charrière completed part one of *Caliste, ou Lettres écrites de Lausanne* in 1785.
She is thought to have written part two sometime between 1785 and her
departure for Paris. By the time she met Benjamin Constant in 1787 *Caliste*
was already in its third edition (Rossard, *Pudeur et romantisme*, 61–2).
52 Charrière went to France in 1750, and England in 1767. She subsequently
returned to France in the years 1786–7.
53 Charrière, *Caliste*, 42.
54 In view of this initial exposition, I find Coulet's statement that Charrière's
novel 'ne comporte pas d'exposés ni de discussions sur les questions
politiques, philosophiques et pédagogiques' (includes neither expositions
on nor discussions of political, philosophical, and pedagogical questions)
to be somewhat puzzling ('Une Romancière moderne,' 154).
55 Charrière, *Caliste*, 114.
56 Rowe, *The Fair Penitent*, Act V, scene i.
57 *Daily Courant* of 8 June 1703, cited in Harley, *Music in Purcell's London*, 122–3.

58 Girdham, *English Opera*, 41.
59 Ibid., 63.
60 Charrière, *Caliste*, 114.
61 See Fauchery's inclusion of Caliste under the category 'courtesan' in *La Destinée féminine*. See also Bessièreset and Niedzwiecki, *Femmes et musique*, 9, and Touliatos, 'The Traditional Role of Greek Women in Music,' 114.
62 Charrière, *Caliste*, 115.
63 Ibid., 125.
64 Ibid., 175.
65 Danielou recounts that the abbé Hebert expressed his disapproval of the performances, saying: 'Une fille qui a fait un personnage dans une comédie aura beaucoup moins de peine à parler en tête-à-tête à un homme ayant pris sur elle de paraître tête levée devant plusieurs' (A girl who has acted a part in a comedy will have much less difficulty speaking to a man in private, having presumed to appear before many with her head held high). He reiterated his protests until Mme de Maintenon was forced to put an end to the performances (*Madame de Maintenon*, 91).
66 Psalm 104:33–4, in *La Sainte Bible*, 611–13.
67 Charrière, *Caliste*, 124.
68 Ibid., 163.
69 Ibid., 124.
70 Douthwaite indicates that Cécile and her mother face the same problem in the first part of *Caliste*: 'The "foreignness" [of the female correspondents in the novel] comes ... from their uncertain status in class society. Though of noble name, the mother and daughter suffer the social indignity of the impoverished aristocracy, and actively seek solutions to avoid any further "embourgeoisement" of their sort. Their ultimate goal in the novel is to find a *place* in society for eighteen-year-old Cécile, preferably through a profitable marriage' ('Female Voices,' 71).
71 Coulet sees an echo of *La Nouvelle Héloïse* in Caliste's resolution ('Une Romancière moderne,' 162).
72 Douthwaite, 'Female Voices,' 71–3. Moser-Verrey summarizes the views of Godet, Starobinski, and Didier on Charrière's utopia ('Isabelle de Charrière,' 75–6).
73 Charrière, *Caliste*, 32–3.
74 Coulet states that 'Caliste, dont la condition n'est pas celle du peuple ... est plutôt une déclassée' (Caliste, whose social condition is not that of the people ... is nonetheless lower-class) ('Une Romancière moderne,' 154).
75 Charrière, *Caliste*, 166.
76 Ibid., 122.
77 Lest Caliste's behaviour be interpreted as gallingly flirtatious, I would

recall Letzter's observation, in reference to another of Charrière's texts: 'Charrière reveals that she is aware of the discourse of misogyny, which attributes fickleness and unpredictable mutability to women, playfully turning these supposed defects of women into laudable qualities' ('Isabelle de Charrière,' 31).

78 Charrière, *Caliste*, 125.

79 For the choice of the term 'respectability,' see Reynold, 'L'Evolution littéraire,' 253).

80 Charrière, *Caliste*, 147.

81 Ibid., 134.

82 See also Sarah Gore's dissertation entitled 'Sonorous Bodies: Music in the Novels of Diderot and Burney.'

83 Charrière, *Caliste*, 160.

84 Ibid., 163.

85 Ibid., 185. The author thus invests this final scene with her own musical affinities. Charrière displayed a marked preference for Italian music, and considered Pergolesi to be the foremost among Italian composers.

86 The manner of Caliste's death may have been inspired by a couplet in the song sung by Calista in Act V, scene i of Nicholas Rowe's *The Fair Penitent*, which reads: 'Listen, fair one, to thy knell, / This musick is thy passing bell.'

87 Charrière, *Caliste*, 186.

88 Rossard, *Une Clef du romantisme*, 65.

89 Letzter, 'Lire?' 213.

90 Ibid., 215.

91 '[Charrière's] ambiguity and indirectness must ... be seen as the textual tactics of a woman intellectual who wanted to express views diverging from Rousseauist ideology without being silenced' (Letzter, 'Isabelle de Charrière,' 29). Letzter points out that when Charrière was too pointed in her criticism her pamphlets were soon removed from circulation.

92 Letzter, 'Isabelle de Charrière,' 35. Letzter goes on to say that Charrière believed that 'women need "force d'esprit," far more than chastity or modesty, to resist their temptations.' In accordance with this view, Caliste appears to be moral by calculation rather than conviction.

93 Vissière, *Ecrits 1788–1794*, 28.

5. Cottin, Krüdener, and Musical Mesmerism

1 Cottin's novels include *Claire d'Albe* (1798), *Malvina* (1801), *Amélie Mansfield* (1802), *Mathilde* (1805), and *Elisabeth ou les exilés de Sibérie* (1806), all of which were best-sellers (Spencer, 'Sophie Cottin,' 93). Krüdener's include *Geraldine I* (1789–90), *Alexis ou Histoire d'un soldat russe*, *La Cabane des lataniers*, and *Elisa ou l'Education d'une jeune fille* (1796–8), *Les Malheurs*

de l'Helvétie (1798), *Valérie* (1803), *Les Gens du monde* (1805), *Othilde*, and *Le Camp de Vertus* (after 1815); *Valérie* was by far the most successful (Schwartz, 'Juliane von Krüdener,' 254–5).

2 Cazenobe, 'Une Préromantique méconnue,' 182, 189; Ley, 'Le Roman *Valérie* jugé par Goethe,' 312; and Ley, 'Goethe et Mme de Krüdener,' 54.

3 Both Cottin and Krüdener read and were influenced by Staël's *Lettres sur les ouvrages et le caractère de J.-J. Rousseau* (1788) and her *Delphine* (1800) but professed less of an affinity for Charrière's writing. Their appreciation of Rousseau is likewise more comparable to that of the young Staël.

4 Gaulmier, 'Roman et connotations sociales,' 16, and Lacy, 'A Forgotten Best-Seller,' 362.

5 The Romantics who appreciated Cottin's works include Hugo, Stendhal, and Sand (Spencer, 'Reading in Pairs,' 167; Cazenobe, 'Une Préromantique méconnue,' 202; and Gaulmier, 'Sophie et ses malheurs,' 4). Bernardin de Saint-Pierre wrote a favourable review of *Valérie* and Chateaubriand predicted its success (Ley, 'Mme de Krüdener à Paris,' 100, 105–7).

6 See Tomlinson, *Metaphysical Song*, 3–33.

7 Thomas, *Music and the Origins of Language*, 157. See also Austern, 'Musical Treatments for Lovesickness'; Carapetyan, 'Music and Medicine in the Renaissance'; Gouk, 'Music, Melancholy, and Medical Spirits'; and 'Rorke, 'Music Therapy in the Age of Enlightenment.'

8 See Bates, 'The Mystery of Truth.' Both Cazotte and Krüdener harboured mystical leanings.

9 See Hadlock, 'Sonorous Bodies.'

10 The French treatises on music and medicine date from 1751, a decade before Rousseau wrote *Julie* (Thomas, *Music and the Origins of Language*, 154). Riskin makes the connection between Mesmer, Rousseauism, and popular science in *Science in the Age of Sensibility*, 179, 194. Saint-Martin was one of Rousseau's devotees (see Bates, 'The Mystery of Truth').

11 See my introduction, p. 5.

12 See Force, 'Self-Love, Identification, and the Origin of Political Economy,' 53–6, and Thomas, *Music and the Origins of Language*, 155.

13 Rousseau, *Julie, ou la Nouvelle Héloïse*, 85; *Julie, or the New Heloise*, 107–8.

14 Rousseau, *Julie, ou la Nouvelle Héloïse*, 87; *Julie, or the New Heloise*, 109.

15 Kramer, 'Music as Cause and Cure of Illness,' 339.

16 Gaulmier, 'Sophie et ses malheurs,' 10; Gaulmier, 'Roman et connotations sociales,' 16; and Call, *Infertility and the Novels of Sophie Cottin*, 26–7. For Cottin's near-conversion experience when she and her cousin Julie identified with Rousseau's description of Julie and Claire, see Cusset, 'Rousseau's Legacy,' 405, and 'Sophie Cottin,' 27.

17 Call, *Infertility and the Novels of Sophie Cottin*, 27, and Spencer, 'Reading in Pairs,' 166.
18 Rossard, *Pudeur et romantisme*, 15.
19 Sykes suggests as much, citing Cottin herself in support of his point (*Madame Cottin*, 126).
20 This is also the trait that sets her off from other women authors of the time (Rossard, *Pudeur et romantisme*, 16).
21 Cited in Gaulmier, 'Sophie et ses malheurs,' 6.
22 Cazenobe, 'Une Préromantique méconnue,' 199.
23 Cusset, 'Rousseau's Legacy,' 416.
24 See Call, *Infertility and the Novels of Sophie Cottin*, 18–19, 28.
25 Cusset, 'Sophie Cottin,' 27, and Call, *Infertility and the Novels of Sophie Cottin*, 73.
26 See Gaulmier, 'Roman et connotations sociales,' 13, and Call's third chapter entitled 'Back in Step with Jean-Jacques: *Malvina*,' in *Infertility and the Novels of Sophie Cottin*, 75 and 80.
27 The discussion of women authors can be found in the first edition of Cottin's *Malvina*, 2:81–90.
28 Ibid. Clare's excuse for having violated this sacred code of female conduct is that she needed the money for a charitable cause, namely, to support her sister whom Edmond had left with child. Cottin, too, had sold her first novel to help a friend.
29 Ibid. Rousseau's words were 'Les femmes, en général, n'aiment aucun art, ne se connaissent à aucun, et n'ont aucun Génie' (Women, in general, do not like any art, know nothing about any, and have no Genius) (*Lettre à d'Alembert*, 94–5n; *Letter to d'Alembert*, trans. Bloom, 327n).
30 Ibid.
31 Ibid. Staël was irked by this tirade against women authors, especially since it was evidently she whom Cottin had in mind when she alluded to Sappho and the notoriety women acquired from their ill-fated affairs. Cottin's friends persuaded her to suppress her tirade in subsequent versions of the novel.
32 My references from here on in will be to the 1824 edition of Cottin's novel (unless stated otherwise), which is more readily accessible to the reader and reflects the author's final revisions.
33 For Malvina's defence of fallen women, see Cottin, *Malvina*, 1:250.
34 Ibid., 2:25.
35 See note 27.
36 Ibid., 3:98. Emphasis in original.
37 Ibid., 4:109 (1st edition).

38 Spencer, 'Reading in Pairs,' 94–5.

39 Sykes, *Madame Cottin*, 230–1.

40 'Before they are overcome by pain and destroyed by life, these women fight long and arduous battles, cross entire continents, challenge authority, and defy the social order in their attempt to change the world' (Spencer, 'Reading in Pairs,' 96).

41 Cottin, *Malvina*, 4:73, 109 (1st edition).

42 See Sykes, *Madame Cottin*, 4.

43 Rossard, *Pudeur et romantisme*, 20, and Cazenobe, 'Une Préromantique méconnue,' 194.

44 Cottin, *Malvina*, 1:31.

45 Ibid., 1:96.

46 Ibid., 1:96–7.

47 Ibid., 1:168.

48 Ibid., 1:180.

49 Ibid., 1:213. Such lessons were often musical, although in this particular instance M. Prior is teaching Malvina the Erse language so that she may better appreciate the poems of Ossian, from which her name is derived.

50 Cottin was quite familiar with contemporary English novels, and though she alludes most openly to Richardson's work it is not impossible that she would have been aware of Austen's as well. *Pride and Prejudice*, in which Austen contrasts Mary's pedantic technical expertise to Elisabeth's less studied yet more tasteful execution, was published in England in 1798. Cottin's decision to render a salon performance that bespeaks the English rather than the French literary tradition may have been an effort to give an air of authenticity to the Scottish setting of an evening passed between three characters of French and three of English extraction.

51 'Miss Melmor essaya; mais elle était exécutrice et non pas musicienne; elle jouait comme un maître, et déchiffrait comme une écolière; de sorte qu'il lui fut impossible de faire ce qu'on lui demandait' (Miss Melmor tried, but she was a technician and not a musician. She played like a master and sight-read like a student, so that it was impossible for her to do what was asked of her) (Cottin, *Malvina*, 1:115–16).

52 'Mistriss Birton ... voulait qu'on crût qu'elle aimait passionnément la musique; mais une heure d'harmonie était tout ce qu'elle pouvait supporter' (Mistress Birton wanted others to think that she was passionately fond of music, but an hour of harmony was more than she could bear) (ibid., 1:117).

53 'A l'aide d'une main légère, et d'une oreille délicate, Malvina rendit les partitions les plus compliquées avec goût et facilité: on pouvait avoir une

exécution plus rapide, mais non pas un jeu plus agréable' (With the help of a light hand and a delicate ear, Malvina performed the most difficult pieces with taste and ease. One might have played them more rapidly but not more agreeably) (ibid., 1:116–17).

54 Ibid., 1:114–15.

55 Gluck wrote *Armide* in 1776 and converted *Alceste* into French in 1777. The performances of these operas touched off the *Querelle des Gluckistes et des Piccinnistes* in Paris. Though Italian, Sacchini, who wrote *Oedipe* in 1787, was associated with the Gluckistes during the debate.

56 Rousseau, *Julie, ou la Nouvelle Héloïse*, 86; *Julie, or the New Heloise*, 108.

57 Letzter and Adelson, *Women Writing Opera*, 4.

58 Cottin, *Malvina*, 2:23–35 (1st edition).

59 For the entirety of this scene, see Cottin, *Malvina*, 1:223–31.

60 Ibid., 2:237.

61 Ibid., 3:205.

62 Unlike previous scenes, the music chosen is a romance, not an aria. One wonders whether Cottin might not have had in mind Rousseau's stipulation that French music 'est plus propre aux chansons qu'aux Opera' (is better suited to songs than to Operas) and that a song is consequently more likely than an aria to touch the listener's heart (Rousseau, *Julie, ou la Nouvelle Héloïse*, 133; *Julie, or the New Heloise*, 108).

63 Cottin, *Malvina*, 3:212.

64 Ibid., 3:218–19.

65 Guenther, 'Letters Exchanged across Borders,' 79, and Schwartz, 'Juliane von Krüdener,' 254–5.

66 Ley, 'Le Roman *Valérie*,' 313–14.

67 Kohler, '*Valérie* ou Maîtres et imitateurs,' 5; Lacy, 'A Forgotten Best-Seller,' 362–3; and Ley, 'Le Roman *Valérie*,' 313–15.

68 Lacy, 'A Forgotten Best-Seller,' 364–7, and Kohler, '*Valérie* ou Maîtres et imitateurs,' 3.

69 Lacy claims that *Valérie* 'affirms the preëminence of virtuous passion or passionate virtue as a moral ideal' ('A Forgotten Best-Seller,' 364–7).

70 Ley, *Saint-Pierre, Staël, Chateaubriand, Constant, et Krüdener*, 131, 116. Krüdener refers to herself in the third person.

71 Or rather, Staël vied with her. Krüdener was ultimately far more complimentary of *Delphine* than Staël was of *Valérie*, though Krüdener hastened to point out that she was, to a certain extent, the model for Staël's heroine. Staël, on the other hand, awaited the publication of *Valérie* with trepidation, writing her father 'Tu as deviné que j'étais occupée de *Valérie*; je te prie de la lire bien vite et de m'écrire si cela me détrône' (You suspected that I was preoccupied with *Valérie*. I beg you to read it quickly and to let

me know whether it dethrones me (Ley, *Saint-Pierre, Staël, Chateaubriand, Constant, et Krüdener*, 133).

72 Krüdener, *Valérie*, 145.

73 Ibid., 184. Krüdener's letters and personal journal corroborate the belief expressed in this citation.

74 See Ley, *Mme Krüdener et son temps*.

75 Staël immortalized Krüdener's performance in *Delphine* before Krüdener incorporated in into her own novel. The *tarantelle* was a dance that imitated the movements of those attempting to rid themselves of the effects of the tarantula's poison, in keeping with the Tarantism movement in Italy, which was closely related to the rise of music therapy in France. For a thorough discussion of Tarantism, see part 4 of *Music as Medicine*, edited by Peregrine Horden.

76 Guenther, 'Letters Exchanged across Borders,' 87.

77 Krüdener, *Valérie*, 32, 43.

78 Ibid., 58.

79 Krüdener, *Valérie*, 64–7.

80 Rousseau, *Julie, ou la Nouvelle Héloïse*, 87; *Julie, or the New Héloïse*, 109.

81 Krüdener, *Valérie*, 72–4.

82 Ibid.

83 Ibid., 85–6.

84 Ibid.

85 Ibid., 128.

86 Ibid., 129. One wonders whether Krüdener's stipulation that Valérie was not a trained musician was inspired by the contrast Saint-Preux draws between the machinations of the trained singer and the natural tones of one who sings effortlessly. He describes Julie's voice as 'naturellement si légère et si douce' (so naturally light and sweet) (Rousseau, *Julie, ou la Nouvelle Héloïse*, 88; *Julie, or the New Heloise*, 110).

87 Krüdener, *Valérie*, 123.

88 Ibid., 121–2.

89 Ibid., 125–6.

90 Ibid.

91 Rousseau, *Julie, ou la Nouvelle Héloïse*, 87; *Julie, or the New Heloise*, 109. See the introduction, p. 4.

92 See Marso, *(Un)Manly Citizens*.

6. Staël's Sweet Revenge

1 Staël had been prepared for the notion of a republic by her father, Jacques

Necker who, like Rousseau, hailed from the Protestant republic of Geneva. See Tenenbaum, 'Liberal Heroines.'

2 Rossard, *Une Clef du romantisme*, 64.

3 Though Staël was a reader of Kant and Goethe, a member of the *Groupe de Coppet*, and wrote her novels at the beginning of the nineteenth century, she was raised on the writings of Rousseau in the salons of the Ancien Régime, and set her novels during the Revolution. Because her aesthetic heritage remains, by and large, that of the French Enlightenment, I wish to reclaim her, for the purposes of this study, for the long eighteenth century.

4 Staël started her *Lettres* in 1786 and published them in 1788.

5 See Trouille, 'A Bold New Vision of Woman.'

6 Staël, *Lettres*, 47. See Rousseau, *Lettre à d'Alembert*, 94–5n excerpted in chapter 5 n. 29 above.

7 See especially Gutwirth, 'Madame de Staël'; Trouille, 'A Bold New Vision of Woman'; and Marso *(Un)Manly Citizens*.

8 Staël, *Lettres*, 69.

9 Ibid., 63. Staël later reinforces the call for equal education in *De la littérature* in what Gutwirth has called her 'most ringingly egalitarian statement' ('Madame de Staël,' 104): 'Eclairer, instruire, perfectionner les femmes comme les hommes ... c'est encore le meilleur secret ... pour toutes les relations sociales et politiques auxquelles on veut assurer un fondement durable' (To enlighten, to instruct, to perfect women like men ... is still the secret ... to all social and political relations to which one wants to give a sound basis) (Staël, *De la littérature*, 338).

10 Staël, *Lettres*, 46–7.

11 Staël, *De la littérature*, 332.

12 Ibid., 336.

13 Ibid., 335–6.

14 Ibid., 341.

15 Gutwirth reveals the feminist bent of Staël's second preface in her article 'Madame de Staël, Rousseau and the Woman Question.'

16 Staël, *Lettres*, 39.

17 Staël, *De l'Allemagne*, 218. See also Gutwirth 'Madame de Staël,' 104.

18 Many critics have found fault with Staël for praising qualities in women that she did not display in her own life. We might note, however, that the ability to admire qualities one does not posses or actions one cannot emulate was also one of Rousseau's most salient characteristics.

19 Staël, *Lettres*, 79.

20 Ibid., 79.

21 Ibid., 80.

22 Ibid. As Starobinski points out, Rousseau identifies music as a 'signe
mémoratif' in his *Dictionnaire de musique* (*La Transparence et l'obstacle*, 113).
According to Roussel, 'Mme de Staël a vu combien chez Rousseau bonheur,
mémoire, et musique sont liés entre eux, et elle a fait, semble-t-il, l'ex-
périence de cette association' (Madame de Staël saw the extent to which
happiness, memory, and music are interrelated in Rousseau's writing and,
it would seem, experienced this association directly) (*Jean-Jacques
Rousseau*, 349–50).

23 Staël, *Corinne, ou l'Italie*, 180. The comte d'Erfeuil does not, of course,
acknowledge that French comedy and the *opéra-comique* were indebted to
their Italian origins. While Corinne accepts his characterization of Italian
theatre, she sees in the stock characters of the *commedia dell'arte* the very
essence of comedy, which suits in turn all nations at all times (181).

24 Ibid., 83.

25 Ibid., 174; *Corinne, or Italy*, trans. Raphael, 110.

26 Staël, *Corinne, ou l'Italie*, 174; *Corinne, or Italy*, 109.

27 Staël, *Corinne, ou l'Italie*, 67. Staël savoured in vocal music what Corinne
savoured in poetry, namely, the sound of the words rather than their
meaning. Staël thus considered the voice to be the most perfect of instruments. For the century's trajectory, see Neubauer, *The Emancipation of
Music from Language*, and Johnson, *Listening in Paris*.

28 Staël, *Corinne, ou l'Italie*, 67; *Corinne, or Italy*, 33.

29 Staël, *Corinne, ou l'Italie*, 225, 356, 408.

30 Staël, *Corinne, ou l'Italie*, 266–7; *Corinne, or Italy*, 175.

31 Staël, *Corinne, ou l'Italie*, 430; *Corinne, or Italy*, 292.

32 Staël, *Corinne, ou l'Italie*, 67; *Corinne, or Italy*, 33.

33 Though the analogy between language, climate, and the passions constitutes the clearest affinity to Rousseau's text, the analogy Staël draws
between the ring of the Italian words, the clarion call of victory instruments, and the colour scarlet is also reminiscent of the parallel Rousseau
establishes between melody and drawing, on the one hand, and harmony
and colour, on the other, in the section of his *Essai* called 'De la mélodie'
(Rousseau, *Essai*, 118–19). Staël later has Corinne observe: 'Vous sentez que
c'est ... sous un beau ciel que s'est formé ce langage mélodieux et coloré'
(You can feel that this melodious, highly coloured language was formed ...
beneath a beautiful sky) (Staël, *Corinne, ou l'Italie*, 83, *Corinne, or Italy*, 44–5).
She has clearly retained the broad analogy between music and painting in
Rousseau's *Essai* rather than the more specific one between melody and line.

34 Rousseau, *Essai*, 407; *Essay*, 315.

35 Staël, *Corinne, ou l'Italie*, 67; *Corinne, or Italy*, 33.

36 Rousseau, *Essai*, 407–8; *Essay*, 315–16.

37 Montesquieu, *De l'esprit des lois*, 246.

38 Staël, *De la littérature*, 205.

39 Staël, *Corinne, ou l'Italie*, 67.

40 For a more detailed analysis of the above see my article 'Revoicing Rousseau: Corinne and the Song of the South' in *Phrase and Subject: Studies in Music and Literature*, ed. Delia da Sousa Correa, forthcoming from Oxford: Legenda.

41 Porset, 'Avertissement,' 7–8, 14–15.

42 Staël, *Lettres*, 79.

43 See Staël's *Correspondance*.

44 Rousseau, *Les Confessions*, cited in Porset, 'Avertissement,' 8–9; *The Confessions*, trans. Kelly, 469.

45 Including those of Bailbe, Balayé, Deneys-Tunney, Didier, and Naudin.

46 The allusion to literary talents can be found in the praise bestowed upon Corinne during her crowning at the Capitol, which Staël characterizes as somewhat inappropriate because too general: 'Tous l'exaltaient jusques aux cieux; mais ils lui donnaient des louanges qui ne la caractérisaient pas plus qu'une autre femme d'un génie supérieur. C'était une agréable réunion d'images et d'allusions à la mythologie, qu'on aurait pu, depuis Sapho jusqu'à nos jours, adresser de siècle en siècle à toutes les femmes que leurs talents littéraires ont illustrées' (All of them lauded her to the skies, but the praise they gave her made no distinction between her and any other woman of genius. Their verses were a pleasant combination of imagery and mythological allusions which, from Sappho's day to our own, might have been addressed throughout the centuries to all women renowned for their literary talents) (Staël, *Corinne, ou l'Italie*, 54; *Corinne, or Italy*, 24). Though DeJean notes that the Greek Corinne and Sappho 'both perform their poetry to musical accompaniment' ('Portrait of the Artist as Sappho,' 127), she refers to Corinne as a 'literary woman,' stating at one point that Corinne 'announced her intention of embarking on a literary career' (130). Corinne's description of her intent, however, is as follows: 'Il me vint dans l'idée ... de retourner en Italie pour y mener une vie indépendante, tout entière consacré aux arts' (I once had the idea that ... I could return to Italy to lead an independent life entirely devoted to the arts) (Staël, *Corinne, ou l'Italie*, 379; *Corinne, or Italy*, 255). At best then, Corinne can be described as intending to embark on a career in belles-lettres or the beaux-arts, under which opera and music were subsumed.

47 Deneys-Tunney, '*Corinne*', 61–2.
48 'Les improvisations de Corinne sortent de Virgile, d'Horace, de Tibulle, de Properce et des grands historiens, de Tacite et Tite-Live. Mme de Staël regarde, elle écrit sous leur indéfinissable influence, celle aussi de Dante, de l'Arioste et du Tasse' (Corinne's improvisations are taken from Virgil, Horace, Tibula, Propertius, and from the great historians, Tacitus and Livy. Madame de Staël looks and writes under their indefinable influence as well as that of Dante, Ariosto, and Tasso) (Balayé, 'Carnets de voyage,' 113–14).
49 Staël, *Corinne, ou l'Italie*, 191; *Corinne, or Italy*, 121.
50 Staël, *Corinne, ou l'Italie*, 67; *Corinne, or Italy*, 33.
51 Staël, *Corinne, ou l'Italie*, 85.
52 Ibid., 348.
53 DeJean, 'Portrait of the Artist as Sappho,' 122, 129.
54 Spear, *Dominichino*, 41, and Roulin, 'Bonstetten et Mme de Staël,' 183, n. 18. Spear and Roulin identify the *Sibylle du Dominiquin* to which Oswald and Lucile compare Corinne and that Staël, in all likelihood, saw in the course of her travels as the one dating from 1622–5 that was in the Ratta collection at the time, in which the sibyl has a book featuring a musical score under her left wrist. The painting is currently located in a private collection in Brechin, Angus.
55 See Staël, *Corinne, ou l'Italie*, 592, n. 29.
56 Ibid., 148; *Corinne, or Italy*, 91.
57 Starobinski, 'Rousseau et l'origine des langues,' 375. For the analogy between Corinne's art of conversation and improvisation, see Staël, *Corinne, ou l'Italie*, 84, 183.
58 Ibid.
59 Staël, *Corinne, ou l'Italie*, 69; *Corinne, or Italy*, 35.
60 Staël, *Corinne, ou l'Italie*, 83; *Corinne, or Italy*, 45.
61 Staël, *Corinne, ou l'Italie*, 84; *Corinne, or Italy*, 45.
62 Staël, *Corinne, ou l'Italie*, 372; *Corinne, or Italy*, 251.
63 Staël, *Corinne, ou l'Italie*, 378; *Corinne, or Italy*, 255.
64 Staël, *Corinne, ou l'Italie*, 466; *Corinne, or Italy*, 317.
65 Ibid.
66 Staël, *Corinne, ou l'Italie*, 433; *Corinne, or Italy*, 294.
67 Staël, *Corinne, ou l'Italie*, 382.
68 Staël, *Corinne, ou l'Italie*, 384; *Corinne, or Italy*, 259.
69 Staël, *Corinne, ou l'Italie*, 385; *Corinne, or Italy*, 260.
70 Staël, *Corinne, ou l'Italie*, 204; *Corinne, or Italy*, 131.
71 Ibid.

72 Staël, *Corinne, ou l'Italie*, 202; *Corinne, or Italy*, 130.
73 Staël, *Corinne, ou l'Italie*, 169; *Corinne, or Italy*, 105.
74 Starobinski, 'Rousseau et l'origine des langues,' 374.
75 Starobinski, *La Transparance et l'obstacle*, 19–20, 23.
76 This interpretation was suggested by the title of Bowman's article, 'Communication and Power in Germaine de Staël: Transparency and Obstacle,'
77 Staël, *Corinne, ou l'Italie*, 81; *Corinne, or Italy*, 43.
78 Staël, *Corinne, ou l'Italie*, 231; *Corinne, or Italy*, 149.
79 Ibid.
80 Though Staël refers to the story as that of Caïrbar, Balayé explains that the painting is, in fact, of Duthcaron's son Connal. See Staël, *Corinne, ou l'Italie*, 629, note o; *Corinne, or Italy*, 418, n. 154. A possible study for this painting, or one very much like it, can be found in Wild, *George Augustus Wallis*, 467. It differs from the painting Staël describes in that the man seated on the tomb holds his harp in his hand.
81 Staël, *Corinne, ou l'Italie*, 238; *Corinne, or Italy*, 154.
82 Staël, *Corinne, ou l'Italie*, 247; *Corinne, or Italy*, 161–2.
83 Starobinski, *La Transparance et l'obstacle*, 111. Emphasis Starobinski's.
84 Rousseau, *Julie, ou la Nouvelle Héloïse*, Lettre XLVIII, cited in Starobinski, *La Transparance et l'obstacle*, 112; *Julie, or the New Heloise*, 108. Staël's awareness of Rousseau's predilections may shed some light on why she chose to render certain passages of her text more musical than others. While Saint-Preux's praise of Italian music is eloquent, his critique of French opera is scathing. Could this be why Corinne's performance of an *opéra-comique* is singularly devoid of music? The *opéra-comique* in which Corinne plays a role does not, notably, function as a tableau. It is almost an anti-tableau in that Oswald's presiding emotion, one of despair, does not remotely correspond to the gaity the genre would warrant and is caused not by Corinne's sublime performance but rather by the news that he must leave her that evening. Her performance, which alternates between buffa arias and improvised dialogue, is strangely lacking in either musical content or emotional effect (Staël, *Corinne, ou l'Italie*, 434–6). Madelyn Gutwirth provides a compelling analysis of this scene as the turning point between Corinne's voice and silence in the novel in 'Du silence de Corinne et de sa parole.'
85 Staël, *Corinne, ou l'Italie*, 249–50; *Corinne, or Italy*, 163.
86 For Corinne's performance in *Romeo and Juliet*, see Staël, *Corinne, ou l'Italie*, 195–200.
87 Staël, *Corinne, ou l'Italie*, 250; *Corinne, or Italy*, 163.
88 Staël, *Corinne, ou l'Italie*, 248; *Corinne, or Italy*, 162.

89 Staël, *Corinne, ou l'Italie*, 246; *Corinne, or Italy*, 160.

90 Staël, *Corinne, ou l'Italie*, 474; *Corinne, or Italy*, 323.

91 Staël, *Corinne, ou l'Italie*, 384; *Corinne, or Italy*, 259.

92 Staël, *Corinne, ou l'Italie*, 575; *Corinne, or Italy*, 396.

93 DeJean refers to the 17th of November as the anniversary of the day Corinne originally sang the Scottish romances for Oswald at Tivoli ('Portrait of the Artist as Sappho,' 134). It was shortly before Easter, however, when the couple visited Tivoli. 17 November was the date on which Corinne performed in an *opéra-comique* only to have Oswald announce that he was leaving her as the curtain fell (Staël, *Corinne, ou l'Italie*, 434). Oswald is therefore overcome with guilt and not nostalgia.

94 Staël, *Corinne, ou l'Italie*, 581; *Corinne, or Italy*, 400.

95 Staël, *Corinne, ou l'Italie*, 582; *Corinne, or Italy*, 401.

96 Staël, *Corinne, ou l'Italie*, 583; *Corinne, or Italy*, 401.

97 Staël, *De la littérature*, 336.

98 Balayé claims that 'Mme de Staël punit ses héros pour leur lâcheté sociale, comme elle tue ses héroïnes pour leur faiblesse et pour montrer que la société ne peut progresser par les femmes' (Madame de Staël punishes her heroes for their social cowardice, just as she kills her heroines for their weakness and to show that women cannot contribute to social progress) ('Préromantisme,' 159).

99 See Touliatos's description of Telesilla, a skilled musician remembered for her valour ('The Traditional Role of Greek Women in Music,' 112).

100 The following phrase is used to characterize Laïs: 'Citée comme musicienne, mais, de musique, aucune trace' (Remembered as a musician but no trace of her music) (Bessièreset and Niedzwiecki, *Femmes et musique*, 5).

101 Bessièreset and Niedzwiecki, *Femmes et musique*, 5, 8–9

102 Girdham, *English Opera*, 41, 71–2.

103 Letzter and Adelson, *Women Writing Opera*, 174.

104 Pieiller, *Musique maestra*, 12.

105 Moers, 'Performing Heroism,' 334.

106 Ibid., 339–41.

107 Cited in Letzter and Adelson, *Women Writing Opera*, 2.

108 Dehon, 'Corinne,' 3.

Afterward

1 Diderot, *Le Neveu*, 66; *Rameau's Nephew*, 27.

2 Diderot, *Le Neveu*, 67; my translation.

3 Diderot, *Le Neveu*, 60–1, 128–9.

4 Cazotte, *Ollivier*, 89–90.
5 Cazotte, *Le Diable*, 125; *The Devil*, 84.
6 Beaumarchais, *Théâtre*, 48–9.
7 Beaumarchais, *Théâtre*, 210; *The Figaro Trilogy*, 175.
8 Beaumarchais, *Théâtre*, 224.
9 Ibid., 202.
10 Staël, *De l'Allemagne*, 2:84.
11 'Lettre de M. le Chevalier Gluck à l'auteur du Mercure de France' in Lesure, *Querelle des Gluckistes et des Piccinnistes*, 10. See chapter 3, p. 107.
12 Staël, *De l'Allemagne*, 2:84. This progression reflects a general fin-de-siècle movement that Neubauer has documented in *The Emancipation of Music from Language*.
13 See Chartier's definition of the public sphere, following Habermas, in his chapter 'Espace public et opinion publique' (*Les Origines culturelles de la Révolution française*, 32–52). See also Johnson's chapters entitled 'Musical Experience of the Terror' and 'Musical Expression and Jacobin Ideology' (*Listening in Paris*, 116–54).
14 Gendzier's careful documentation of Balzac's references to Diderot's works indicates that Balzac had probably read *Le Neveu* before writing his three musical short stories, *Sarrasine*, *Gambara*, and *Massimila Doni* (Gendzier, 'Balzac's Changing Attitudes towards Diderot,' 125, 131–2). In his preface to the recent edition of these three stories, Brunel identifies E.T.A. Hoffmann as Balzac's most likely source of inspiration. Yet Hoffmann acknowledged having been inspired by Cazotte. See also Wasselin, 'Le Paradoxe sur le musicien, ou la métamorphose du Neveu de Rameau en musicien fou d'E.T.A. Hoffmann,' and Winkler, 'Cazotte lu par E.T.A. Hoffmann: Du *Diable amoureux* à *Der Elementargeist*.'
15 Balzac, *Sarrasine, Gambara, Massimila Doni*, 57.
16 Bury, 'Les Français en Italie dans *Massimila Doni*,' 211.
17 Sourian, 'L'Influence de Mme de Staël sur les premiers œuvres de George Sand,' 37.
18 Gutwirth mentions that *Consuelo* ends with 'the birth of a new generation of artists of revolt in her son Zdenko' ('Corinne and Consuelo,' 23), the male counterpart of Charrière's *orphelines* and Staël's Juliette.
19 I differ here in my understanding of Corinne from the reading Gutwirth provides in her article 'Corinne and Consuelo as Fantasies of Immanence.' I would agree with her statement that 'chastity is not essential to Corinne's own notion of integrity,' for Corinne is able to envision living with Oswald without being married. Corinne protests, however, when Oswald

is tempted to take advantage of their solitude to possess her, casting doubt on Gutwirth's assertion that 'her utopia is one of sensual pleasure' (25). Sensory pleasure, perhaps, but not sensual. The contrast Oswald draws between Corinne as an 'experienced' and Lucile as an 'innocent' woman is based on the fact that whereas Corinne had received the attentions of two suitors prior to Oswald's arrival, Lucile, at her tender age, has hardly even seen another man. Corinne's 'experience' is affective, not physical. The subtle distinction between Corinne and Lucile is thus a far cry from that which separates Corilla, who lives with Ansoleto in complete abandon, and Consuelo, who lives with him in fraternal love in Sand's novel. Gutwirth's suggestion that Corilla is a Corinne surrogate (23) downplays the important fact that the suspicion of Corinne's morality is largely unfounded and arises from the public suspicion that surrounds a woman who chooses to lead the independent life of an artist. Were Corinne, like Corilla, truly corrupt, Staël's novel would have had little power as a social critique.

20 Sand, *Consuelo*, 367.
21 A phrase borrowed from Giusti's title, 'The Politics of Location: Italian Narratives of Mme de Staël and George Sand.'

Works Cited

Primary Sources

Balzac, Honoré de. *Sarrasine* (1830), *Gambara* (1837), *Massimila Doni* (1839). Ed. Pierre Brunel. Paris: Gallimard, 1995.

Batteux, Charles. *Les Beaux-Arts réduits à un même principe*. Paris: Durand, 1747.

Beaumarchais, Pierre-Augustin de. 'Aux abonnés de l'Opéra qui voudraient aimer l'opéra (1787).' In *Œuvres*, ed. Pierre Larthomas. Bibliothèque de la Pléiade. Paris: Gallimard, 1988.

– *Essai sur le genre dramatique serieux* (1767). In *Œuvres*, ed. Pierre Larthomas. Bibliothèque de la Pléiade. Paris: Gallimard, 1988.

– *Lettre modérée sur la chute et la critique du Barbier de Seville* (1775). In *Théâtre de Beaumarchais*, ed. René Pomeau. Paris: GF-Flammarion, 1965.

– *Théâtre de Beaumarchais: Le Barbier de Séville* (1773), *Le Mariage de Figaro* (1781), *La Mère coupable*. Ed. René Pomeau. Paris: GF-Flammarion, 1965.

Cazotte, Jacques. *Correspondance de Jacques Cazotte*. Ed. Georges Décote. Paris: Klincksieck, 1982.

– *Le Diable amoureux* (1776). Paris: GF-Flammarion, 1979.

– *La Guerre de l'opéra: Lettre à une dame de Province* (1753). In Launay, *La Querelle des Bouffons, texte des pamphlets*, 1:319–42.

– *Observations sur la lettre de J.-J. Rousseau sur la musique française* (1753). In Launay, *La Querelle des Bouffons, texte des pamphlets*, 2:839–59.

– *Ollivier* (1763). In *Œuvres badines et morales, historiques et philosophiques*, ed. Jean-François Bastien. Vol. 1. New York: Georg Olms Verlag, 1976.

Charrière, Isabelle de. *Caliste, ou Lettres écrites de Lausanne* (1787). Paris: Editions des femmes, 1979.

– *Correspondance.* In *Œuvres complètes,* ed. Candaux. Vols 2, 3, 6.

– *Courte réplique à l'auteur d'une longue réponse* (1789). In *Œuvres complètes,* ed. Candaux. Vol. 10.

– 'De Rousseau (1788–9).' In *Œuvres complètes,* ed. Candaux. Vol. 10.

– 'Eclaircissements relatifs a la publication des *Confessions* de Rousseau (1790).' In *Œuvres complètes,* ed. Candaux. Vol. 10.

– *Eloge de Jean-Jacques Rousseau* (1790). In *Œuvres complètes,* ed. Candaux. Vol. 10.

– *Lettres de Mistress Henley publiées par son amie,* ed. Joan Hinde Stewart and Philip Stewart. New York: Modern Language Association, 1993.

– *Œuvres complètes,* ed. Jean-Daniel Candaux. 10 vols. Geneva: Slatkine, 1979–84.

Cottin, Sophie. *Malvina.* 4 vols. Paris: Maradan, 1800.

– *Malvina.* 3 vols. Vols 2–4 of *Œuvres complètes.* Paris: Ménard et Desenne, Fils, 1824.

Diderot, Denis. *Au petit prophète de Boehmischbroda* (1753). In Launay, *La Querelle des Bouffons, texte des pamphlets.* 1:413–27.

– *De la poésie dramatique* (1758). In *Œuvres esthétiques,* ed. Paul Vernière. Paris: Bordos, 1988.

– *Entretiens sur le Fils naturel* (1758). In *Œuvres esthétiques,* ed. Paul Vernière. Paris: Bordas, 1988.

– *Jacques le fataliste et son maître* (1765–84). In *Œuvres,* ed. André Billy. Bibliothèque de la Pléiade. Paris: Gallimard, 1951.

– *Lettre à Mlle de la Chaux.* In *Œuvres complètes,* ed. Jacques Chouillet. Vol. 4. Paris: Hermann, 1978.

– *Lettre sur les sourds et muets* (1751). In *Œuvres complètes,* ed. Jacques Chouillet. Vol. 4. Paris: Hermann, 1978.

– *Le Neveu de Rameau* (1765–72). Ed. Jean Fabre. Geneva: Droz, 1977.

– *Œuvres,* ed. Laurent Versini. Vol. 4. Paris: Robert Laffont, 1996.

– *Paradoxe sur le comédien* (1773). Paris: Gallimard, 1994.

– *Ruines et Paysages, Salon de 1767.* Paris: Hermann, 1995.

– *Les Trois chapitres* (1753). In Launay, *La Querelle des Bouffons, texte des pamphlets,* 1:491–511.

Dubos, Jean-Baptiste. *Réflexions critiques sur la poësie et sur la peinture* (1719). Geneva: Slatkine Reprints, 1967.

Krüdener, Barbara Juliana von. *Valérie* (1803). Paris: Klincksieck, 1974.

Launay, Denise, ed. *La Querelle des Bouffons, texte des pamphlets.* Geneva: Minkoff Reprints, 1973.

Lesure, François. *Querelle des Gluckistes et des Piccinnistes: texte des pamphlets.* Geneva: Minkoff Reprints, 1984.

Marmontel, Jean-François. *Eléments de littérature*, vol. 4 of *Œuvres complètes*, ed. Mathieu Villenave. Geneva: Slatkine Reprints, 1968.

Molière, J.-B. P. de. *Le Bourgeois gentilhomme*. In *Œuvres complètes*, ed. Georges Couton. Vol. 2. Bibliothèque de la Pléiade. Paris: Gallimard 1971.

– *Le Malade imaginaire*. In *Œuvres complètes*, ed. Georges Couton. Vol. 2. Bibliothèque de la Pléiade. Paris: Gallimard 1971.

Montesquieu, Charles. *De l'esprit des lois*. Vol. 1. Paris: Garnier, 1973.

Rousseau, Jean-Jacques. *Les Confessions*. In *Les Confessions, autres textes autobiographiques*, vol. 1 of *Œuvres complètes*, ed. Gagnebin and Raymond.

– *Dictionnaire de musique* (1749–64). In *Ecrits sur la musique, la langue et le théâtre*, vol. 5 of *Œuvres complètes*, ed. Gagnebin and Raymond.

– *Discours sur l'origine et les fondemens de l'inégalité parmi les hommes* (1754). In *Du contrat social, écrits politiques*, vol. 3 of *Œuvres complètes*, ed. Gagnebin and Raymond.

– *Emile* (1762). In *Emile, Education, Morale, Botanique*, vol. 4 of *Œuvres complètes*, ed. Gagnebin and Raymond.

– *Essai sur l'origine des langues* (1761). In *Ecrits sur la musique, la langue et le théâtre*, vol. 5 of *Œuvres complètes*, ed. Gagnebin and Raymond.

– *Julie, ou la Nouvelle Héloïse* (1761). Paris: GF-Flammarion, 1967.

– *Lettre à d'Alembert* (1758). In *Ecrits sur la musique, la langue et le théâtre*, vol. 5 of *Œuvres complètes*, ed. Gagnebin and Raymond.

– 'Lettre à M. Burney et Fragmens d'observations sur l'Alceste de Gluck (1777).' In *Ecrits sur la musique, la langue et le théâtre*, vol. 5 of *Œuvres complètes*, ed. Gagnebin and Raymond.

– *Lettre sur la musique française* (1753). In *Ecrits sur la musique, la langue et le théâtre*, vol. 5 of *Œuvres complètes*, ed. Gagnebin and Raymond.

– *Œuvres complètes*, ed. Bernard Gagnebin and Marcel Raymond. 5 vols. Bibliothèque de la Pléiade. Paris: Gallimard, 1959–95.

Rowe, Nicholas. *The Fair Penitent*. In *New English Theatre*, ed. Thomas Lowndes, Thomas Caslon, and William Nicoll. Vol. 2. London, 1776.

Sainte Bible, La. Trans. Louis Segond. Paris: Alliance biblique universelle, 1993.

Sand, Georges. *Consuelo* (1842). Paris: Phébus, 1999.

Staël, Germaine de. *Corinne, ou l'Italie* (1807). Ed. Simone Balayé. Paris: Gallimard Folio, 1985.

– *Correspondance*. Ed. Béatrice W. Jasinski. Paris: Pauvert, 1972.

– *De la littérature* (1800). Paris: GF-Flammarion, 1991.

– *De l'Allemagne* (1810). 2 vols. Paris: GF-Flammarion, 1968.

– *Lettres sur les ouvrages et le caractère de J.-J. Rousseau* (1788). In *Œuvres de jeunesse*, ed. Simone Balayé and John Claiborne Isbell. Paris: Desjonquères, 1997.

Translations

Beaumarchais, Pierre-Augustin de. *The Figaro Trilogy*. Trans. David Coward. New York: Oxford University Press, 2003.

Cazotte, Jacques. *The Devil in Love*. Trans. Stephen Sartarelli. New York: Marsilio, 1993.

Diderot, Denis. *Rameau's Nephew and Other Works*. Trans. Jacques Barzun and Ralph H. Bowen. Indianapolis: Hackett, 1956, repr. 2001.

Rousseau, Jean-Jacques. *The Confessions*. Vol. 5 of *The Collected Writings of Rousseau*, ed. Roger D. Masters, Christopher Kelly, and Peter G. Stillman. Trans. Christopher Kelly. Hanover, NH: University Press of New England, 1995.

– *Essay on the Origin of Languages*, in *Essay on the Origin of Languages and Writings Related to Music*. Vol. 7 of *The Collected Writings of Rousseau*, ed. Roger D. Masters and Christopher Kelly. Trans. John T. Scott. Hanover, NH: University Press of New England, 1998.

– *Julie, or the New Heloise*. Vol. 6 of *The Collected Writings of Rousseau*, ed. Roger D. Masters and Christopher Kelly. Trans. Philip Stewart and Jean Vaché. Hanover, NH: University Press of New England, 1997.

– *Letter on French Music*, in *Essay on the Origin of Languages and Writing Related to Music*. Vol. 7 of *The Collected Writings of Rousseau*, ed. Roger D. Masters and Christopher Kelly. Trans. John T. Scott. Hanover, NH: University Press of New England, 1995.

– *Letter to d'Alembert and Writings for the Theater*. Vol 10 of *The Collected Writings of Rousseau*, ed. Roger D. Masters and Christopher Kelly, trans. Allan Bloom. Hanover, NH: University Press of New England, 2004.

Staël, Germaine de. *Corinne, or Italy*. Trans. Sylvia Raphael. New York: Oxford University Press, 1998.

Secondary Sources

Abbate, Carolyn. *Unsung Voices: Opera and Musical Narrative in the Nineteenth Century*. Princeton: Princeton University Press, 1991.

Arbo, Alessandro. 'Diderot et l'hiéroglyphe musical.' *Recherches sur Diderot et l'Encyclopédie* 30 (2001): 65–80.

Arnould, E.J. 'Beaumarchais and the Opera.' *Hermathena* 79 (1952): 75–88.

Auroux, Sylvain. 'Langue.' In *Dictionnaire européen des Lumières*, ed. Michel Delon. Paris: Presses universitaires de France, 1997.

Austern, Linda Phyllis. 'Musical Treatments for Lovesickness: The Early Modern Heritage.' In *Music as Medicine: The History of Music Therapy since*

Antiquity, ed. Peregrine Horden, 213–45. Aldershot and Burlington, VT: Ashgate, 2000.

Bailbe, Joseph-Marc. 'De Madame de Staël au Romantisme: L'Enthousiasme musical.' In *Actes du colloque Vie musicale et courants de pensée, 1780–1830*, ed. Michelle Biget, 71–82. Mont Saint-Aignan: Etudes musicologiques de la Révolution française, 1988.

Balayé, Simone. 'A propos du "préromantisme": Continuité ou rupture chez Madame de Staël.' In *Le Préromantisme: hypothèque ou hypothèse?* ed. Paul Viallaneix, 153–68. Paris: Klincksieck, 1975.

– *Les Carnets de voyage de Madame de Staël*. Geneva: Droz, 1971.

– 'L'Improvisation de Corinne au capitole: Les Strophes sur les poètes italiens. Manuscrits inédits de Madame de Staël.' In *Resonant Themes: Literature, History and the Arts in Nineteenth and Twentieth-Century Europe*, ed. Stirling Haig, 17–32. Chapel Hill: University of North Carolina Press, 1999.

Bardez, Jean-Michel. *Diderot et la musique: Valeur de la contribution d'un mélomane*. Paris: Honoré-Champion, 1975.

Barker, Emma. *Greuze and the Painting of Sentiment*. Cambridge: Cambridge University Press, 2005.

Barthes, Roland. 'Diderot, Brecht, Eisenstein.' In *Image, Music, Text*, ed. and trans. Stephen Heath. New York: Noonday Press, 1977.

Bates, David. 'The Mystery of Truth: Louis-Claude de Saint-Martin's Enlightened Mysticism.' *Journal of the History of Ideas* 61, no. 4 (2000): 635–56.

Beaumarchais, Jean-Pierre de. 'Un Inédit de Beaumarchais: Le Sacristain.' *Revue d'histoire littéraire de la France* 74 (1974): 976–99.

Becq, Annie. *Genèse de l'esthétique française moderne 1680–1814*. Paris: Albin-Michel, 1984.

Bérenguier, Nadine. 'From Clarens to Hollow Park, Isabelle de Charrière's Quiet Revolution.' *Studies in Eighteenth-Century Culture* 21 (1991): 219–43.

Bérubé, Georges-L. 'La Portée sociale des didascalies dans *Le Mariage de Figaro* de Beaumarchais.' *Studies on Voltaire and the Eighteenth Century* 265 (1989): 1330–3.

Bessièreset, Yves, and Patricia Niedzwiecki. *Femmes et musique*. Brussels: Commission des communautés européennes, 1985.

Blanchard, J.M. 'Cazotte: Du nouveau dans la nouvelle.' *Romanic Review* 65, no. 1 (1974): 31–44.

Boon, Tili. 'The Devil in Drag: Moral Injunction or Social Leaven?' *Le Corps et l'Esprit in French Cultural Production* 17, no. 2 (1999): 30–42.

– 'Women Performing Music: Staging a Social Protest.' *Women in French Studies* 8 (2000): 40–54.

Bowman, Frank. 'Communication and Power in Germaine de Staël: Transparency and Obstacle.' In *Germaine de Staël: Crossing the Borders*, ed. Madelyn Gutwirth, Avriel Goldberger, and Karyna Szmurlo, 55–68. New Brunswick, NJ: Rutgers University Press, 1991.

Brewer, Daniel. *The Discourse of Enlightenment in Eighteenth-Century France: Diderot and the Art of Philosophizing*. Cambridge: Cambridge University Press, 1993.

Brown, Bruce Alan. *Gluck and the French Theatre in Vienna*. Oxford: Clarendon Press, 1991.

– 'Lo specchio francese: Viennese Opera Buffa and the Legacy of French Theatre.' In *Opera Buffa in Mozart's Vienna*, ed. Mary Hunter and James Webster, 50–81. New York: Cambridge University Press, 1997.

Burgan, Mary. 'Heroines at the Piano: Women and Music in Nineteenth-Century Fiction.' In *The Lost Chord: Essays on Victorian Music*, ed. Nicholas Temperley, 42–67. Bloomington: Indiana University Press, 1989.

Bury, Mariane. 'Les Français en Italie dans *Massimila Doni*.' *L'Année Balzacienne* 13 (1992): 207–20.

Call, Michael J. *Infertility and the Novels of Sophie Cottin*. Newark: University of Delaware Press, 2002.

Caplan, Jay. *Framed Narratives: Diderot's Genealogy of the Beholder*. Minneapolis: University of Minnesota Press, 1985.

Carapetyan, Armen. 'Music and Medicine in the Renaissance and in the 17th and 18th Centuries.' In *Music and Medicine*, ed. Dorothy M. Schullian and Max Schoen, 117–57. New York: Henry Schuman, 1948.

Castex, Pierre-Georges. *Le Conte fantastique en France de Nodier à Maupassant*. Paris: Librairie José Corti, 1951.

Castries, Duc de. *Beaumarchais*. Paris: Éditions de Tallandier, 1985.

Cazenobe, Colette. 'Une Préromantique méconnue, Madame Cottin.' *Travaux de littérature* 1 (1988): 175–202.

Chartier, Roger. *Les Origines culturelles de la révolution française*. Paris: Seuil, 1991.

Chouillet, Jacques. *La Formation des idées esthétiques de Diderot 1745–1763*. Paris: Armand Colin, 1973.

Christensen, Thomas. 'Bemetzreider's Dream: Diderot and the Pathology of Tonal Sensibility in the *Leçons de clavecin*.' In *Music, Sensation, and Sensuality*, ed. Linda Phyllis Austern, 39–56. New York: Routledge, 2002.

– *Rameau and Musical Thought in the Enlightenment*. Cambridge: Cambridge University Press, 1993.

Conroy, Peter V., Jr. 'Songs and Sonnets: Patterns of Characterization.' In *Molière and the Commonwealth of Letters: Patrimony and Posterity*, ed. Roger Johnson Jr, Editha S. Neumann, and Guy T. Trail, 532–41. Jackson: University Press of Mississippi, 1975.

Cooper, Martin. 'Opera: France, *opéra-comique*.' In *The New Grove Dictionary of Music and Musicians*, ed. Stanley John Sadie and John Tyrrell. Vol. 13. London: Macmillan, 1980.

Cossy, Valérie. '"Pour qui écrire désormais?" Esthétique et révolution dans les œuvres d'Isabelle de Charrière et Germaine de Staël.' In *Progrès et violence au XVIIIe siècle*, ed. Valérie Cossy and Deidre Dawson, 233–55. Paris: Honoré-Champion, 2001.

Coulet, Henri. 'Une Romancière moderne: Isabelle de Charrière: L'Exemple des premiers romans.' *Quaderni di lingue e letterature* 19 (1994): 153–62.

Cowart, Georgia. 'Of Women, Sex, and Folly: Opera under the Old Regime.' *Cambridge Opera Journal* 6, no. 3 (1994): 205–20.

– *The Origins of Modern Musical Criticism: French and Italian Music, 1600–1750.* Ann Arbor, MI: Uuniversity of Michigan Research Press, 1981.

Croll, Gerhard. 'Gluck, Christoph Willibald.' In *The New Grove Dictionary of Music and Musicians*, ed. Stanley John Sadie and John Tyrrell. Vol. 7. London: Macmillan, 1980.

Cuillé, Tili Boon. '*La Vraisemblance de merveilleux*: Operatic Aesthetics in Cazotte's Fantastic Fiction.' *Studies in Eighteenth-Century Culture* 34 (2005): 173–96.

Cusset, Catherine. 'Rousseau's Legacy: Glory and Femininity at the End of the Eighteenth Century: Sophie Cottin and Elisabeth Vigée-Lebrun.' In *Femmes savantes et femmes d'esprit: Women Intellectuals of the French Eighteenth Century*, Roland Bonnel and Catherine Rubinger, 401–18. New York: Peter Lang, 1994.

– 'Sophie Cottin ou l'écriture du déni.' *Romantisme* 3, no. 77 (1992): 25–31.

Danielou, Madeleine. *Madame de Maintenon éducatrice*. Paris: Éditions Bloud et Gay, 1946.

Dällenbach, Lucien. *Le Récit spéculaire*. Paris: Seuil, 1977.

Décote, Georges. *L'Itinéraire de Jacques Cazotte (1719–1792): De la fiction littéraire au mysticisme politique*. Geneva: Droz, 1984.

Dehon, Claire L. 'Corinne: Une Artiste heroine de roman.' *Nineteenth-Century French Studies* 9 (1980–1): 1–9.

DeJean, Joan. *Ancients against Moderns: Culture Wars and the Making of a Fin de Siècle*. Chicago: University of Chicago Press, 1997.

– Portrait of the Artist as Sappho.' In *Germaine de Staël: Crossing the Borders*, ed. Madelyn Gutwirth, Avriel Goldberger, and Karyna Szmurlo, 122–40. New Brunswick, NJ: Rutgers University Press, 1991.

Delon, Michel. 'De Hugo à Beaumarchais: La Mémoire d'une chanson.' *La Revue des lettres modernes: Histoire des idées et des littératures* 840–4 (1988): 59–75.

– 'L'Esthétique du tableau et la crise de la représentation classique à la fin du

XVIIIe siècle.' In *La lettre et la figure: La littérature et les arts visuels à l'époque moderne*, ed. Wolfgang Drost, Géraldi Leroy, and Reinhard Lüthje, 11–29. Heidelberg: Carl Winter Universitätsverlag, 1989.

Denby, David. *Sentimental Narrative and the Social Order in France, 1760–1820*. Cambridge: Cambridge University Press, 1994.

Deneys-Tunney, Anne. '*Corinne* by Madame de Staël: The Utopia of Feminine Voice as Music within the Novel.' *Dalhousie French Studies* 28 (1944): 55–63.

Desnoiresterres, Gustave. *La Musique française au XVIIIe siècle: Gluck et Piccinni, 1774–1800*. Geneva: Slatkine Reprints, 1971.

Didier, Beatrice. *Beaumarchais ou la passion du drame*. Paris: Presses universitaires de France, 1994.

– 'L'Écoute musicale chez Diderot.' *Diderot Studies* 23 (1988): 55–73.

– *La Musique des lumières*. Paris: Presses universitaires de France, 1985.

– 'L'Opéra fou des Bijoux.' *Europe; revue littéraire mensuelle* 661 (1984): 142–50.

– 'Les Opéras imaginaires de Diderot.' In *Diderot, les beaux-arts et la musique*, ed. Henri Coulet, 241–60. Aix-en-Provence: Université de Provence, 1986.

– 'Le Texte de la musique.' In *Interpréter Diderot aujourd'hui*, ed. E. de Fontenay and J. Proust, 287–317, Paris: Le Sycamore, 1984.

Dill, Charles. *Monstrous Opera: Rameau and the Tragic Tradition*. Princeton: Princeton University Press, 1998.

Doody, Margaret Anne. 'Missing *Les Muses*: Madame de Staël and Frances Burney.' *Colloquium Helveticum* 25 (1997): 81–117.

Douthwaite, Julia. 'Female Voices and Critical Strategies: Montesquieu, Graffigny, and Madame de Charrière.' *French Literature Series* 16 (1989): 64–77.

Drinker, Sophie. *Music and Women: The Story of Women in their Relation to Music*. Washington: Zinger, 1948.

Fabre, Jean. Introduction to *Le Neveu de Rameau*, by Denis Diderot. Geneva: Droz, 1963.

Fauchery, Pierre. *La Destinée féminine dans le roman européen du XVIIIe siècle*. Paris: Colin, 1972.

Filoche, Jean-Luc. '*Le Neveu de Rameau* et la Querelle des Bouffons: un son de cloche inédit.' *Diderot Studies* 21 (1983): 95–109.

Fleck, Stephen H. *Music, Dance, and Laughter: Comic Creation in Molière's Comedy-Ballets*. Paris: Papers on French Seventeenth Century Literature, 1995.

Fleurant, Kenneth J. 'Mysticism in the Age of Reason: Jacques Cazotte and the Demons.' *French Review* 49, no. 1 (1975): 68–75.

Force, Pierre. 'Self-Love, Identification, and the Origin of Political Economy.' *Yale French Studies* 92 (1997): 46–64.

Forestier, Georges. *Le Théâtre dans le théâtre sur la scène française du XVIIe siècle*. Geneva: Droz, 1996.

Frantz, Pierre. *L'Esthétique du tableau dans le théâtre du XVIIIe siècle*. Paris: PUF, 1998.

Fried, Michael. *Absorption and Theatricality: Painting and Beholder in the Age of Diderot*. Chicago: University of Chicago Press, 1980.

Gaulmier, Jean. 'Roman et connotations sociales: Mathilde de Madame Cottin.' *Roman et société*, 7–17. Colloque 6 novembre, 1971. Paris: Colin, 1973.

– 'Sophie et ses malheurs ou le Romantisme du pathétique.' *Romantisme* 3 (1972): 3–16.

Gendzier, S.J. 'Balzac's Changing Attitudes towards Diderot.' *French Studies* 19 (1965): 125–43.

Girdham, Jane. *English Opera in Late Eighteenth-Century London: Stephen Storace at Drury Lane*. Oxford: Clarendon Press, 1997.

Giusti, Ada. 'The Politics of Location: Italian Narratives of Mme de Staël and George Sand.' *Neohelicon* 22, no. 2 (1995): 205–19.

Godechot, Jacques. 'Nation, patrie, nationalisme et patriotisme en France au XVIIIe siècle.' *Annales historiques de la Révolution française* 206 (1971): 481–501.

Golub, Maria Majno. 'Diderot et l'opéra-comique: Absolution du burlesque, réussite du pathétique.' In *Diderot, les beaux-arts et la musique*, ed. Henri Coulet, 261–75. Aix-en-Provence: Université de Provence, 1986.

Goodden, Angelica. '*Une Peinture parlante*: The Tableau and the Drama.' *French Studies* 38 (1984): 397–413.

Gore, Sarah. 'Sonorous Bodies: Music in the Novels of Diderot and Burney.' PhD diss., Harvard University, 1994.

Gouk, Penelope. 'Music, Melancholy, and Medical Spirits in Early Modern Thought.' In *Music as Medicine: The History of Music Therapy since Antiquity*, ed. Peregrine Horden, 173–94. Aldershot and Burlington, VT: Ashgate, 2000.

Guenther, Beatrice. 'Letters Exchanged across Borders: Mme de Staël's *Delphine* and the Epistolary Novels of Juliane von Krüdener and Sophie Mereau.' *Comparatist* 22 (1998): 78–90.

Guerlac, Suzanne. 'The Tableau and Authority in Diderot's Aesthetics.' *Studies on Voltaire and the Eighteenth Century* 219 (1983): 183–94.

Gutwirth, Madelyn. 'Corinne and Consuelo as Fantasies of Immanence.' *George Sand Studies* 8, nos 1–2 (1986–7): 21–7.

– 'Du silence de Corinne et de sa parole.' In *Benjamin Constant, Madame de Staël et le Groupe de Coppet*, ed. Etienne Hofmann, 427–34. Oxford: Voltaire Foundation, 1982.

– 'Madame de Staël, Rousseau, and the Woman Question.' *PMLA* 86 (1971): 100–9.

Hadlock, Heather. 'Sonorous Bodies: Women and the Glass Harmonica.' *Journal of the American Musicological Society* 53 (2000): 507–42.

Harley, John. *Music in Purcell's London: The Social Background*. London: Dennis Dobson, 1968.

Hayes, Julie C. 'Rewriting Bourgeois Drama: Beaumarchais's Double Plan.' In *L'Age du théâtre en France / The Age of Theater in France*, ed. David Trott and Nicole Boursier, 41–56. Edmonton, AB: Academic Printing and Publishing, 1988.

Heartz, Daniel. 'The Beginnings of Operatic Romance: Rousseau, Sedaine and Monsigny.' *Eighteenth-Century Studies* 15, no. 2 (1981–2): 149–78.

– 'Goldoni, Opera Buffa, and Mozart's Advent in Vienna.' In *Opera Buffa in Mozart's Vienna*, ed. Mary Hunter and James Webster, 25–49. New York: Cambridge University Press, 1997.

– *Mozart's Operas*. Berkeley and Los Angeles: University of California Press, 1990.

– 'Rousseau, Jean-Jacques.' In *The New Grove Dictionary of Music and Musicians*, ed. Stanley John Sadie and John Tyrrell. Vol. 16. London: Macmillan, 1980.

Hédoin, P. *Gluck: son arrivée en France, la révolution qu'il a opérée sur notre première scène lyrique, difficultés qu'on lui a suscitées, la guerre des Gluckistes et des Piccinnistes, détails anecdotiques en partie inédits, conclusion*. Paris: Charles de Mourgues Frères, 1859.

Horden, Peregrine, ed. *Music as Medicine: The History of Music Therapy since Antiquity*. Aldershot and Burlington, VT: Ashgate, 2000.

Howarth, William D. *Beaumarchais and the Theatre*. London: Routledge, 1995.

– 'Beaumarchais homme de théâtre et la Révolution française.' In *Beaumarchais: Homme de lettres, homme de société*, ed. Philip Robinson. New York: Peter Lang, 2000.

Hunting, Claudine. 'Les Mille et une sources du *Diable amoureux* de Cazotte.' *Studies on Voltaire and the Eighteenth Century* 230 (1985): 247–71.

Jackson, Susan K. 'The Novels of Isabelle de Charrière, or, A Woman's Work is Never Done.' *Studies in Eighteenth-Century Culture* 14 (1985): 299–306.

Johnson, James H. 'The Encyclopedists and the *Querelle des Bouffons*: Reason and the Enlightenment of Sentiment.' *Eighteenth-Century Life* 10, no. 2 (1986): 12–27.

– *Listening in Paris: A Cultural History*. Berkeley and Los Angeles: University of California Press, 1995.

Kintzler, Catherine. *Poétique de l'opéra français de Corneille à Rousseau*. Paris: Minerve, 1991.

Kohler, Pierre. '*Valérie* ou Maîtres et imitateurs de Mme de Krüdener.' *Bulletin de l'Institut National Genevois* 45, no. 1 (August 1992): 1–30.

Kramer, Cheryce. 'Music as Cause and Cure of Illness in Nineteenth-Century Europe.' In *Music as Medicine: The History of Music Therapy Since Antiquity*, ed. Peregrine Horden, 338–52. Aldershot and Burlington, VT: Ashgate, 2000.

Lacy, K. Wesley. Jr. 'A Forgotten Best-Seller: Mme de Krüdener's *Valérie.*' *Romance Notes* 18 (1978): 362–7.

Landes, Joan B. *Women and the Public Sphere in the Age of the French Revolution.* Ithaca, NY: Cornell University Press, 1988.

Lang, Paul Henry. 'Diderot as Musician.' *Diderot Studies* 10 (1968): 95–107.

Larthomas, Pierre. *Beaumarchais: Parades, édition critique.* Paris: Société d'édition d'enseignement supérieur, 1977.

Leppert, Richard. *Music and Image: Domesticity, Ideology and Socio-Cultural Formation in Eighteenth-Century England.* Cambridge: Cambridge University Press, 1988.

Letzter, Jacqueline. 'Isabelle de Charrière Versus Germaine de Staël: Textual Tactics in the Debate about Rousseau.' *Studies on Voltaire and the Eighteenth Century* 362 (1998): 27–40.

– 'Lire ou ne pas lire? La Question de l'éducation dans *Sainte Anne* d'Isabelle de Charrière.' In *Une Européenne: Isabelle de Charrière en son siècle. Colloque de Neuchâtel, 11–13 november 1993*, ed. Doris Jakubec, Jean-Daniel Candaux, and Anne-Lise Delacrétaz, 209–16. Neuchâtel: Editions Gilles Attinger, 1994.

Letzter, Jacqueline, and Robert Adelson. 'Un Drame d'ambitions déçues: Les Opéras d'Isabelle de Charrière.' *Revue d'histoire du théâtre* 3 (1997): 235–54.

– *Women Writing Opera: Creativity and Controversy in the Age of the French Revolution.* Berkeley and Los Angeles: University of California Press, 2001.

Ley, Francis. *Bernardin de Saint-Pierre, Madame de Staël, Chateaubriand, Benjamin Constant, et Madame de Krüdener.* Paris: Editions Montaigne, 1967.

– 'Goethe and Mme de Krüdener.' *Etudes germaniques* 23 (1968): 54–7.

– 'Mme de Krüdener à Paris 1802–4.' *Revue d'histoire littéraire de la France* 99, no. 1 (1999): 99–108.

– *Mme de Krüdener et son temps, 1764–1824.* Paris: Plon, 1962.

– 'Le Roman *Valérie* jugé par Goethe, Jean-Paul, et Sophie LaRoche.' *Revue d'histoire littéraire de la France* 96, no. 2 (1996): 313–16.

Loesser, Arthur. *Men, Women and Pianos: A Social History.* New York: Simon and Schuster, 1954.

Lopes, Jose-Manuel. *Foregrounded Description in Prose Fiction: Five Cross-Literary Studies.* Toronto: University of Toronto Press, 1995.

Marshall, David. *The Surprising Effects of Sympathy: Marivaux, Diderot, Rousseau, and Mary Shelley.* Chicago: University of Chicago Press, 1988.

Marso, Lori Jo. *(Un)Manly Citizens: Jean-Jacques Rousseau's and Germaine de Staël's Subversive Women.* Baltimore, MD: Johns Hopkins University Press, 2002.

Mason, James Frederick. 'The Melodrama in France from the Revolution to the Beginning of Romantic Drama, 1791–1830.' PhD diss., Johns Hopkins University, 1912.

Milner, Max. *Le Diable dans la littérature française de Cazotte à Baudelaire 1772–1861*. Paris: Librairie José Corti, 1960.

– Introduction to *Le Diable amoureux*, by Jaques Cazotte. Paris: Garnier-Flammarion, 1979.

Moers, Ellen. 'Performing Heroinism: The Myth of Corinne.' In *The Worlds of Victorian Fiction*, ed. Jerome H. Buckley, 319–50. Harvard English Studies 6. Cambridge, MA: Harvard University Press, 1975.

Molière en scène. Catalogue for Exhibition shown at the Musée Lambinet, Versailles, 3 May – 14 August 1996.

Mooij, A.L.A. *Caractères principaux et tendances des romans psychologiques chez quelques femmes-auteurs, de Mme Riccoboni à Mme de Souza (1757–1826)*. Groningen: Drukkerij de Waal, 1949.

Morrissette, Bruce. 'Un Héritage d'André Gide: La Duplication intérieure.' *Comparative Literature Studies* 8, no. 2 (1971): 125–42.

Moser-Verrey, Monique. 'Isabelle de Charrière en quête d'une meilleure entente.' *Stanford French Review* 11 (1987): 63–76.

– 'Les Jeux de l'amour et de la prudence selon Isabelle de Charrière: Portraits, tableaux et scènes.' *Tangence* 60 (1999): 134–55.

Mulvey, Laura. 'Visual Pleasure and Narrative Cinema.' In *Feminism and Film*, ed. E. Ann Kaplan, 34–47. Oxford: Oxford University Press, 2000.

Naudin, Marie. 'Mme de Staël précurseur de l'esthétique musicale romantique.' *Revue des sciences humaines* 35, no. 139 (1970): 391–400.

Nerval, Gérard de. Appendix to *Le Diable amoureux*, by Jacques Cazotte. Paris: GF-Flammarion, 1979.

Neubauer, John. *The Emancipation of Music from Language: Departure from Mimesis in Eighteenth-Century Aesthetics*. New Haven, CT: Yale University Press, 1986.

Niderst, Alain. 'Diderot et la musique.' In *Diderot, les beaux-arts et la musique*, ed. Henri Coulet, 135–46. Aix-en-Provence: Université de Provence, 1986.

Niklaus, Robert. 'Beaumarchais et le drame.' In *Missions et démarches de la critique: mélanges offerts au Professeur J.A. Vier*, ed. René Marache and Henri Le Moal, 491–9. Paris: Klincksieck, 1973.

– 'La Genèse du Barbier de Séville.' *Studies on Voltaire and the Eighteenth Century* 57 (1967): 1081–91.

O'Reilly, Robert F. 'Cazotte's *Le Diable amoureux* and the Structure of Romance.' *Symposium* 31, no. 3 (1977): 231–42.

Pappas, Jean. 'L'Opéra français contre l'italien: La Solution de Diderot dans le

Neveu de Rameau.' In *Diderot, les beaux-arts et la musique*, ed. Henri Coulet, 233–40. Aix-en-Provence: Université de Provence, 1986.

Pieiller, Evelyne. *Musique maestra: Le Surprenant mais néanmoins véridique récit de l'histoire des femmes dans la musique du XVIIe au XIXe siècle.* Paris: Editions Plume, 1992.

Pomeau, René. *'Le Barbier de Séville*: De l'"intermède" à la comédie.' *Revue d'histoire littéraire de la France* 74 (1974): 963–75.

– 'Le Cas de Rameau le neveu: Ethique et esthétique.' In *Langue, littérature du XVIIe et du XVIIIe siècle*, ed. by Roger Lathuillère, 527–34. Paris: Sedes, 1990.

Porset, Charles. Avertissement for *Essai sur l'origine des langues, où il est parlé de la mélodie et de l'imitation musicale*, by Jean-Jacques Rousseau. Paris: Nizet, 1970.

Prieto, Eric. *Listening In: Music, Mind, and the Modernist Narrative.* Lincoln: University of Nebraska Press, 2002.

Prod'homme, Jacques-Gabriel. *Christoph-Willibald Gluck.* Paris: Librairie Arthème Fayard, 1985.

Rebejkow, Jean-Christophe. 'Diderot et la pantomime: Vers un nouveau "genre" musical.' *Francofonia* 10, no. 19 (1990): 61–73.

– 'Sur *Le Devin du village* de Jean-Jacques Rousseau et ses relectures par Diderot.' *Francofonia* 20 (1991): 61–74.

Revaz, Françoise. 'Narration, description ou tableau? Approche linguistinque d'une classification rhétorique.' *Etudes de lettres* 3 (1991): 113–33.

Rex, Walter E. *'Le Neveu de Rameau*: Musique et structure.' *Recherches sur Diderot et sur l'Encyclopédie* 27 (1999): 7–23.

– 'The Rustic Operas of Diderot's *Neveu de Rameau*.' In *Diderot, Digression and Dispersion*, ed. Jack Undank and Herbert Josephs, 205–18. Lexington, KY: French Forum, 1984.

– 'The "Storm" Music of Beaumarchais' *Barbier de Séville*.' In *Opera and the Enlightenment*, ed. Thomas Bauman and Marita Petzoldt McClymonds, 243–59. Cambridge: Cambridge University Press, 1995.

Reynold, G. de. 'L'Evolution littéraire de la suisse romande.' *Revue de Fribourg* 38 (1907): 241–54.

Rice, John A. *Antonio Salieri and Viennese Opera.* Chicago: University of Chicago Press, 1998.

Riskin, Jessica. *Science in the Age of Sensibility: The Sentimental Empiricists of the French Enlightenment.* Chicago: University of Chicago Press, 2002.

Robinson, Michael F. *'Opera buffa* into *opéra comique*, 1771–90.' In *Music and the French Revolution*, ed. Malcolm Boyd, 37–56. New York: Cambridge University Press, 1992.

– 'Opera: Italy, *opéra buffa.*' In *The New Grove Dictionary of Music and Musicians*, ed. Stanley John Sadie and John Tyrrell. Vol. 13. London: Macmillan, 1980.

Robinson, Philip. 'La Musique des comédies de Figaro: Eléments de dramaturgie.' *Studies on Voltaire and the Eighteenth Century* 275 (1990): 359–499.

– 'La Théâtralité de Figaro.' *Revue de littératures française et comparée* 2 (1993): 81–7.

Roche, Christian. '"En littérature comme en musique": De Rameau au *Neveu de Rameau.*' PhD diss., University of Colorado, 2003.

Rorke, Margaret Ann. 'Music Therapy in the Age of Enlightenment.' *Journal of Music Therapy* 28, no. 1 (2001): 66–73.

Rossard, J. *Une Clef du romantisme: La Pudeur.* Paris: A.G. Nizet, 1975.

– *Pudeur et romantisme.* Paris: Nizet, 1982.

Roster, Danielle. *Les Femmes et la création musicale: Les Compositrices européennes du Moyen Age au milieu du XXe siècle.* Trans. Denise Modigliani. Paris: L'Harmattan, 1998.

Rougemont, Martine de. 'Beaumarchais dramaturge: Le Substrat romanesque du drame.' *Revue d'histoire littéraire de la France* 84, no. 5 (1984): 710–21.

– *La Vie théâtrale en France au XVIIIe siècle.* Paris: Champion-Slatkine, 1988.

Roulin, Jean-Marie. 'Bonstetten et Mme de Staël, ou comment lire Virgile après Ossian?' In *Resonanze classiche nell'Europa romantica*, ed. Annarosa I. Poli and Emanuale Kanceff, 175–87. Montcalieri, Italy: Centro Interuniversitario di Ricerche sul'Viaggio in Italia, 1998.

– 'Le Grand siècle au futur: Voltaire, de la prophétie épique à l'écriture de l'histoire.' *Revue d'histoire littéraire de la France* 5 (1996): 918–33.

Roussel, Jean. *Jean-Jacques Rousseau en France après la Révolution, 1795–1830.* Paris: Armand-Colin, 1972.

– 'La Musique "à la coupelle de la raison": de Rousseau à Diderot.' In *Diderot, les beaux-arts et la musique: Actes du colloque international tenu à Aix-en-Provence les 14, 15, et 16 Décembre, 1984*, ed. Henri Coulet, 221–31. Aix-en-Provence: Université de Provence, 1986.

Rush, Jane. 'Geste et parole dans *Le Neveu de Rameau.*' *Francofonia* 13, no. 25 (1993): 51–63.

Sacaluga, Servando. 'Diderot, Rousseau, et la querelle musicale de 1752: Nouvelle mise au point.' *Diderot Studies* 10 (1968): 133–73.

Scherer, Jacques. *La Dramaturgie de Beaumarchais.* Paris: Librairie Nizet, 1994.

Schuerewegen, Franc. 'Pragmatique et fantastique dans "Le Diable amoureux" de Cazotte.' *Littérature* 60 (1985): 56–72.

Schwartz, Lucy M. 'Juliane von Krüdener (1764–1824).' In *French Women Writers: A Bio-Bibliographical Source Book*, ed. Eva Martin Sartori and Dorothy Wynne Zimmerman, 253–61. New York: Greenwood Press, 1991.

Sourian, Eve. 'L'Influence de Mme de Staël sur les premières œuvres de George Sand.' *George Sand Studies* 7, nos 1–2 (1984–5): 37–45.

Spear, Richard E. *Domenichino, 1581–1641*. Milan: Electa, 1996. – Exhibition shown at the Palazzo Venezia, Rome, 10 October 1996–14 June 1997.

Spencer, Samia I. 'Reading in Pairs: *La Nouvelle Héloïse* and *Claire d'Albe*.' *Romance Languages Annual* 7 (1995): 166–72.

– 'Sophie Cottin (1770–1807).' In *French Women Writers: A Bio-Bibliographical Source Book*, ed. Eva Martin Sartori and Dorothy Wynne Zimmerman, 90–8. New York: Greenwood Press, 1991.

Starobinski, Jean. 'Critique et principe d'autorité (Madame de Staël et Rousseau).' In *Le Préromantisme: Hypothèque ou hypothèse?*, ed. Paul Viallaneix, 326–43. Paris: Klincksieck, 1975.

– *Jean-Jacques Rousseau: La Transparence et l'obstacle suivi de sept essais sur Rousseau*. Paris: Gallimard, 1971.

– 'Rousseau et l'origine des langues.' In Starobinski, *Jean-Jacques Rousseau*, 356–79.

Sykes, L.C. *Madame Cottin*. Oxford: Blackwell, 1949.

Szmurlo, Karyna. 'Le Jeu et le discours feminin: La Danse de l'héroïne staëlienne.' *Nineteenth-Century French Studies* 15, nos 1–2 (1986–7): 1–13.

Szondi, Peter. '*Tableau* and *Coup de Théâtre*: On the Social Psychology of Diderot's Bourgeois Tragedy.' *New Literary History* 11, no. 2 (1980): 323–43.

Tenenbaum, Susan. 'Liberal Heroines: Mme de Staël on the "Woman Question" and the Modern State.' *Annales Benjamin Constant* 5 (1985): 37–52.

Thiesse, Anne-Marie. *La Création des identités nationales: Europe XVIIIe-XXe siècle*. Paris: Seuil, 1999.

Thomas, Downing A. *Aesthetics of Opera in the Ancien Régime, 1647–1785*. Cambridge: Cambridge University Press, 2002.

– *Music and the Origins of Language: Theories from the French Enlightenment*. Cambridge: Cambridge University Press, 1995.

– 'Notes on Performativity and Mood in *Le Mariage de Figaro* and *Le nozze di Figaro*.' *Ars Lyrica* 11 (2000): 115–31.

Thomas, Downing A., and Charles Dill. 'Disciplines, Interdisciplinarity, and Cultural Studies: A Dialogue on Music's Place.' *Rethinking Cultural Studies* 1 (2000): 32–40.

Thomas, Ruth P. 'Theatre as Metaphor in Mme de Charrière's *Caliste*.' *Women in French Studies* 9 (2001): 152–64.

Thomasseau, Jean-Marie. *Le Mélodrame*. Paris: Presses Universitaires de France, Collection *Que sais-je?* 1984.

Todorov, Tzvetan. *Introduction à la littérature fantastique*. Paris: Seuil, 1970.

Tomlinson, Gary. *Metaphysical Song: An Essay on Opera*. Princeton: Princeton University Press, 1999.

Touliatos, Diane. 'The Traditional Role of Greek Women in Music from Antiquity to the End of the Byzantine Empire.' In *Rediscovering the Muses*, ed. Kimberly Marshall, 111–23. Boston, MA: Northeastern University Press, 1993.

Trouille, Mary Seidman. 'A Bold New Vision of Woman: Staël and Wollstonecraft Respond to Rousseau.' *Studies on Voltaire and the Eighteenth Century* 292 (1991): 293–336.

– *Sexual Politics in the Enlightenment: Women Writers Read Rousseau*. Albany: State University of New York Press, 1997.

Trousson, Raymond. 'Deux lecteurs de Rousseau au XVIIIe siècle: Madame de Charrière et Elie Luzac,' *Lias* 2 (1978): 191–255.

– 'Isabelle de Charrière et Jean-Jacques Rousseau.' *Bulletin de l'Académie royale de langue et de la littérature française* 43, no. 1 (1985): 5–57.

Ubersfeld, Anne. *L'Ecole du spectateur*. Paris: Editions sociales, 1981.

Verba, Cynthia. *Music and the French Enlightenment: Reconstruction of a Dialogue 1750–1764*. Oxford: Clarendon Press, 1993.

Versini, Laurent. Introduction to *Œuvres*, by Denis Diderot. Paris: Robert Laffont, 1996.

Vilcosqui, Marcel. 'La Femme dans la musique française 1643–1774.' Diplôme de musicologie, Conservatoire National Supérieure de Musique, Paris, 1973.

Vissière, Isabelle, ed. *Isabelle de Charrière, une aristocrate révolutionnaire: Ecrits 1788–1794*. Paris: Edition des femmes, 1988.

Wasselin, Christian. 'Le Paradoxe sur le musicien, ou la métamorphose du Neveu de Rameau en musicien fou d'E.T.A. Hoffmann.' *Corps écrit* 26 (1988): 117–21.

Wettlaufer, Alexandra K. *In the Mind's Eye: The Visual Impulse in Diderot, Baudelaire and Ruskin*. New York: Rodopi, 2003.

Wild, Monika von. *George Augustus Wallis (1761–1847). Englischer Landschaftsmaker Monographie und Œuvre Katalog*. New York: Peter Lang, 1996.

Williams, Anne Patricia. 'Description and Tableau in the Eighteenth-Century British Sentimental Novel.' *Eighteenth-Century Fiction* 8, no. 4 (1996): 465–84.

Winkler, Markus. 'Cazotte lu par E.T.A. Hoffmann: Du *Diable amoureux* à *Der Elementargeist*.' *Arcadia: Zeitschrift für Vergleichende Liiteraturwissenschaft* 23, no. 2 (1988): 113–32.

Wokler, Robert. '*La Querelle des Bouffons* and the Italian Liberation of France: A Study of Revolutionary Foreplay.' *Eighteenth-Century Life* 11, no. 1 (1987): 94–116.

Wolf-Catz Helma. 'Belle van Zuylen / Madame de Charrière, écrivain néerlandais de renommée européenne.' *Septentrion* 5, no. 1 (1976): 19–29.

Index